A COMPANION TO WORLD MYTHOLOGY

A COMPANION TO WORLD

Mythology

RICHARD BARBER

Illustrated by Pauline Baynes

Delacorte Press/New York

Published by
Delacorte Press
1 Dag Hammarskjold Plaza
New York, N.Y. 10017

This work was first published in Great Britain by
Kestrel Books (Penguin Books Ltd.).

Manufactured in Italy

First U.S. printing

79-16843

ISBN: 0-440-00750-X

Printed in Italy

J
291, 211
B

CONTENTS

PREFACE

MYTHS are stories about gods or godlike beings. They are to be found everywhere; the bushmen of Australia, backward though they may seem in many ways, have their own very distinctive myths, while even the most complex civilizations retain a large heritage of myths. Whether we are looking at paintings, reading books, listening to music, or studying the art and stories of other continents, myths recur again and again. No one can hope to know all the myths he or she is likely to come across; and one purpose of this book is to help to identify the gods who figure in different myths.

Myths are also stories, some of the world's greatest stories. So this is not merely a reference book; it is also a collection of tales. The same themes, as scholars well know, recur in myths from the opposite ends of the earth, and the variations on particular themes can be traced from one civilization to another.

But the world of myths is an enormous one: it leads on the one hand into the mysteries of religion and philosophy, and on the other to the larger-than-life – but far from sacred – world of folktale. I have tried to concentrate on the central core of mythical stories, and so the heroes of folktale and the gods of the 'great' religions – Christ, Mohammed, Jahweh, Buddha, Confucius – are not included here. Nor are the literary heroes to be found among the entries, such as King Arthur, Charlemagne and Alexander from medieval European literature. These are relatively easy lines to draw: the most difficult areas have been the uncharted waters of African and North American Indian myths. Here folktale and myth intermingle. The materials are vast but have hardly been sorted out by scholars yet, and there are no clear and general stories such as those to be found where traditions have been fixed by being written down. So of the hundreds of North American Indian gods there can only be a selection here. Cottie Burland, who came in at a late stage to advise on the American material, was extremely helpful in checking the material which I had written. In Africa, where (in Dr Innes' words) 'there are several hundred languages, there must be hundreds of names for the supreme god; it would be pointless to list them all.'

I have concentrated on figures who have a substantial or coherent story; this obviously means that some relatively minor figures get a full entry. Also, there has had to be some degree of personal choice, and I have obviously preferred figures which I found most interesting. So what follows does not lay any claims to completeness; but I hope it will hold the reader's interest and lure him on to read beyond the entry which he has actually looked up.

As far as possible entries have been made under the name of the god or character in the original language. In other words, the names have not been translated unless they are generally used. *Quetzalcoatl* means 'Feathered Serpent', but he is usually referred to by the first name; while the American Indian hero 'Child of the Water' has a number of different names in different tribes, and his English name is therefore used.

These, then, are the general principles on which I have worked. I am most grateful to the advisory editors, who have been unfailingly helpful and have preserved me from many of the pitfalls which await the unwary explorer in these fields. Any errors and omissions which remain are my own responsibility.

RICHARD BARBER

Advisory Editors:

HILDA ELLIS DAVIDSON (Norse)

A. J. HAY (Chinese and Japanese)

GORDON INNES (African)

WENDY O'FLAHERTY (Indian)

COTTIE BURLAND (American)

JOHN SHARWOOD-SMITH (Classical)

About the pictures

IT seemed right to try to depict the gods and mythological characters of this book as they had been imagined by the people of the countries concerned over the years rather than to draw upon my own ideas. So, where possible, I have used the earliest references available and when, with my limited time and resources, no pictorial references could be found, I have used the earliest art-style of that particular country. I hope this has made for pictures that are not merely decorative, but also interesting and informative. Sometimes, of course, no picture reference of any kind was available, and in that case I had to fall back on imagination.

Where there are several well-known depictions of a god, I have tended to superimpose them in order to convey a general impression of how he was imagined. Some gods came to be represented by objects, as Thor by his hammer, and I have included examples of this. Finally, I have tried to resist the temptation of making all gods look like weird monsters with huge eyes and long teeth: to the people who worshipped them they were in the main perfectly ordinary-looking people, not bigger in stature or odder in appearance but with strange attributes and gifts and with overwhelming magical powers.

PAULINE BAYNES

Aah: Egyptian god of the moon.

Aapep: The great serpent-god of Egyptian myth, who inhabited the underworld and challenged the sun-god *Auf* on his journey through the region each night.

Abore: Among the Warrau Indians of Guyana it was believed that Abore had taught men all kinds of skills, which he had learned from the evil frog-woman Wowta, who had made him her slave while he was still a boy. He escaped from her by luring her into a tree full of wild honey; the tree was hollow, and she stuck fast inside it.

Absyrtus: Brother of *Medea* and brother-in-law of the Greek hero *Jason*; Jason killed him as he and Medea escaped from Colchis, and the *Furies* pursued him for this. The *Argo* was driven far across the seas to Italy, until its crew eventually reached Aeaea, the island of *Circe*. Although Circe was Absyrtus' aunt, she performed the ritual which purged Jason of his guilt without knowing that her nephew was his victim.

Abyrga: In Central Asian belief, Abyrga was a giant snake which lay wound three times round the world mountain *Sumur*, its head resting on the mountain-top and its tail in the ocean at the foot of the mountain.

Acca Larentia: A Roman goddess of the underworld, thought to be the wife of Faustulus, the herdsman who brought up *Romulus and Remus*.

Achates: In Roman myth, the faithful companion of *Aeneas* on his travels, particularly at Carthage.

Achelous: A Greek river-god, father of *Deianeira*. *Heracles* had to wrestle with him to win Deianeira for his bride. The god was able to change his shape as he pleased, and he became first a serpent, then a bull. But Heracles was too strong for him, and broke off one of his horns. So Heracles won Deianeira; and the *Naiads* took the broken horn and filled it with fruit and flowers as a horn of plenty or cornucopia.

Acheron: One of the five rivers surrounding *Hades* in Greek belief. It lay somewhere on the edge of the world, beyond the stream of *Ocean*.

Achilles: Achilles is the central figure of the

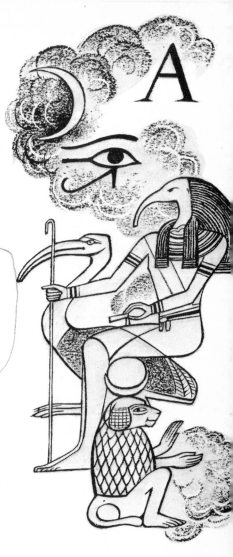

Iliad by Homer, the great epic which tells of the legendary war between the Greeks and the Trojans. He was the son of *Thetis*, the immortal sea-nymph, and *Peleus*, king of Iolcus. Thetis tried to make him invulnerable when he was born, by dipping him in the river *Styx*. There was a spot on his heel where she had held him which was not touched by the liquid, and he could be wounded there. She was told that Achilles would either live a long and unexciting life, or he would go to Troy with the Greek army and win undying fame. Thetis preferred the idea of long life, and so Achilles was sent to the island of Skyros, where he was brought up dressed as a girl, so that the Greeks would not find him. But *Odysseus* and *Diomedes*, knowing that Troy could not be taken without him, tracked him down and identified him in spite of his disguise. They managed this by leaving armour in the girls' quarters and hiding themselves to see which of the girls looked at it with interest and picked it up to try it. When Thetis heard that he was going to Troy after all, she had a superb set of armour made for him by *Hephaestus*, the god of fire. For Achilles' adventures at Troy, see the *Trojan War*.

Achinoin and Couroumon: In the myths of the Carib Indians of the West Indies, two stars controlled rain, winds and tides. Achinoin produced rain and strong winds, while Couroumon controlled the tides, and caused large waves.

Actaeon: Actaeon, son of *Aristaeus*, came across the Greek goddess *Artemis* as she was bathing naked. As Artemis was the most modest of the goddesses, she was very angry, and turned Actaeon into a stag. In this shape, his own hounds hunted and killed him.

Adaheli: The sun-god in Surinam Indian myth.

Adapa: A very wise Sumerian priest of *Ea*. One day, as he was fishing on the River Euphrates, his boat was capsized by a gust from the south wind; he cursed the wind, and thus broke its wing. The gods, alarmed by his power, summoned him and offered him the bread and water of immortality, but Ea had told him beforehand that he would be given the bread and water of death, so he refused, and was sent back to earth.

Aditi: In Hindu myth, mother of the gods, pro-

2

tector of mankind, and the goddess who nourished cattle and children. She was mother of the *Adityas*, mother of *Vishnu*, and also the mother of *Indra*.

Adityas: In Hindu myth, the Adityas were the eight sons of *Aditi*. She rejected one of them, Marttanda, who became the sun; the other seven, including *Varuna*, became gods. Later stories increased the number of Adityas to twelve, one for each month of the year. They were gods of light in its various forms: their names were *Mitra, Aryaman, Bhaga, Varuna*, Ansa, *Indra* and Dhatri. The original group of Adityas consisted of only three gods, Mitra, Varuna and Aryaman, who are also found in Iranian myths.

Adlet: In Eskimo myths from Canada and Greenland, there was a terrible race of monsters which lived on the blood of men, called Adlet or Erqigdlit. They were descended from an Eskimo woman who married a red dog and had ten children. Five of these were monsters; the other five were dogs like their father. The dogs were set adrift in a boat and voyaged across the ocean; when they landed, on the other side, they settled there, and white men were descended from them. The five monsters produced even worse monsters, and these were the Adlet.

Adlivun and Adliparmiut: *Sedna*, the Eskimo goddess, rules over an underworld called Adlivun, whose entrance is guarded by a great dog. Everyone who disobeys Sedna while they are alive must go there for one year after they die: according to the Greenland Eskimos, all except murderers can eventually reach Adliparmiut, which is darker and further away, but is less dreadful than Adlivun, despite the great storms which rage there. Hunting is allowed in Adliparmiut. Some Eskimo tribes believe that the spirits from Adlivun return to their villages, dressed in worn-out clothes, bringing disease and death.

Adonis: *Myrrha*, daughter of the king of Cyprus, refused to honour the Greek goddess *Aphrodite*, and for this she was made to fall in love with her own father. To save her from his wrath, and to prevent him from committing the crime of killing her, the gods turned her into a tree. From this tree Adonis was born. Aphrodite gave the child to *Persephone* to look after, then Persephone refused to give him back to her. Finally *Zeus* had to intervene, ordering that he should spend four

months in each year with Persephone, and the rest with Aphrodite. Another story tells how Aphrodite met him out hunting for the first time, and fell in love with him because he was the most handsome of all men. Despite her warnings, he was killed by a boar. From his blood sprang roses, from Aphrodite's tears for him, anemones. He was made immortal, and was a god of the returning seasons and the new crops. His worshippers used to mourn for him, and the river at Byblos in Syria was said to run red with his blood. Little gardens were planted in his honour, in shallow soil; the plants sprang up quickly, and withered away almost at once.

Adrastus: King of Argos in Greece who sheltered *Tydeus* and *Polyneices* during their exile and made up the quarrel between them. They married his daughters, and he promised to restore their kingdoms to them. He gathered a great army, and began the expedition known as the *Seven Against Thebes.* The attempt was doomed from the start, as the seer *Amphiaraus* knew, and all the chieftains except Adrastus were killed. Adrastus escaped because of the swiftness of his horse *Arion*, born of *Poseidon* and *Demeter*, and in some versions of the story went to Athens. Here he gained *Theseus'* aid, and returned to Thebes, where he defeated the Thebans, and arranged for the funeral of the dead warriors.

Aeacus: Son of the Greek god *Zeus* and Aegina; father of *Peleus* and grandfather of *Achilles*.

Aeetes: Father of *Medea*, and king of Colchis in Asia Minor. He owned the *Golden Fleece*, which had been given to him by *Phrixus* in exchange for one of his daughters in marriage. He tried to prevent *Jason* from carrying it off by giving him a series of impossible tasks.

Aegeus: Father of *Theseus*, possibly the Greek god *Poseidon* under another name. The Aegean Sea was named after him.

Aegir: A giant who lived under the sea and was its ruler. Because the Norsemen were great seafarers, Aegir was important to them, though he was usually hostile: if a ship was lost at sea, it was said to have been 'swallowed up by the jaws of Aegir'. He was married to *Ran*, and their daughters were sea-giantesses, just as *Poseidon* in Greek myth was father of the *Nereids* or sea-nymphs; but the Norsemen, faced with the stormy North Sea, regarded

Aegir's daughters as fierce, unfriendly beings, very different from the enchanting Nereids of the Mediterranean. Aegir had a great hall under the sea, where the gods used to come and feast, and he was called the 'ale-brewer of the gods'. Once he refused to supply them with ale until they produced a large enough vessel to brew it in, which led to *Thor's* adventures with *Hymir*. At his feasts, the hall was lit with heaps of shining gold instead of with torches. In early Saxon days, one out of every ten prisoners was sacrificed to their sea-god in order to ensure that the raiders would return home safely from abroad.

Aegisthus: The son of *Thyestes* by his own daughter, the Greek king Aegisthus carried on the feud between Thyestes and his brother *Atreus*. He succeeded in seducing *Clytemnestra*, the wife of Atreus' son *Agamemnon*, while Agamemnon was away at the *Trojan War*, and the two of them killed Agamemnon on his return. Aegisthus was killed by Agamemnon's son *Orestes* in revenge.

Aello: One of the *Harpies*, whose name means Stormwind in Greek.

Aeneas: The legendary founder of the Roman people, Aeneas was the cousin and son-in-law of King *Priam* of Troy, son of *Anchises* and the goddess *Aphrodite* or *Venus*. At the fall of Troy, he escaped with his aged father, carrying him on his shoulders, and with his young son Ascanius; but his wife Creusa was killed. On his wanderings, he travelled to Delos, Crete and the Strophades, where the *Harpies* attacked him and his men; he continued to Sicily where his father died, and then to Carthage in North Africa, where he met and fell in love with *Dido*, the queen of Carthage. Despite their love, he obeyed the gods' command to continue on his way to Italy, the land for which he was destined by fate. Dido pleaded with him to stay, and killed herself as his ships departed. When he reached Italy, he consulted the *Sibyl* at Cumae, who used her prophetic powers to advise him, and guided him to the underworld, telling him to pluck the Golden Bough at Avernus in order to gain entrance to *Hades*. Here he met his father's ghost, who showed him a vision of the future kings of Rome, and urged him to journey onwards to his appointed destiny there. Aeneas returned with the Sibyl to the upper world. He made his way northwards, to the Kingdom of Latium, near the future site of Rome, where he met King *Latinus*

5

and his daughter Lavinia. Aeneas fell in love with Lavinia, but events led to war between him and Latinus. Aeneas gained an ally *Evander*, the Arcadian king who ruled the land where Rome was later to be built. In the fighting, Turnus, his rival for the hand of Latinus' daughter, was killed by Aeneas, and Latinus was defeated. Aeneas made a generous peace with Latinus, promising him that the people over whom he ruled should keep their name and language, which was Latin, and should be united with his own followers. Aeneas then founded the city of Lavinium, named after Lavinia, whom he married and here he ruled for the rest of his life.

This story, which was first told about 600 BC, was the basis for the greatest of the epic poems in Latin, Vergil's *Aeneid*, which was very important to the Romans. In it, Vergil provided a past history which suited Rome's new ambitious outlook as conqueror of the Mediterranean lands.

Aeolus: The Greek god of the winds, whom *Odysseus* visited on his wanderings. Aeolus received him kindly, and as he left, tied up all the winds in a bag except for the one which would blow him back to Ithaca. Just as he and his men were in sight of the island, the crew, who thought that the bag was full of treasure, took advantage of Odysseus' falling asleep to undo it. The other winds rushed out of the bag and blew them back to Aeolus' island, where the god refused to help them any further.

Aerope: The wife of *Atreus*, who was seduced by her brother-in-law *Thyestes* as part of the sequence of crimes and murders which arose from the curse on the house of Atreus in Greek myth.

Aesir: There were two separate races of gods in Norse myth, perhaps originally the gods of two different peoples. One was the Aesir, whose chief was *Odin* and to which *Thor* and most of the other gods belonged; the other was the *Vanir* to which *Njord, Frey* and *Freyja* belonged. Long ago, and for reasons which were almost forgotten, there had been a war between the Aesir and the Vanir. It may have started because Freyja had worked magic on the Aesir and they had attacked her; and the Vanir fought with magic rather than real weapons. Eventually a truce was agreed upon, and two hostages were sent from each side. The Vanir sent their leaders, Njord and his son Frey, while the Aesir sent *Hoenir* to rule in Vanaheim in the place of Njord, and *Mimir* to

6

advise him. The other Vanir found that Hoenir, although handsome and strong, was not very skilful in giving counsel, and usually relied on Mimir; they felt that they had been cheated, and so they cut off Mimir's head in revenge and sent it to Odin. However, Njord and Frey continued to live with the Aesir in *Asgard*, and the peace was not broken.

It was when peace was first made between the Aesir and Vanir that the wise dwarf *Kvasir* was created; all the gods spat into a great vessel, and from this the dwarf was made. He was able to answer all questions, but was soon killed by two other dwarfs. From his blood they made mead; and anyone who drank this became either a prophet or a poet.

Agamemnon: The most important of the descendants of *Atreus*. He was the leader of the Greeks in the *Trojan War*, since he was overlord of much of Greece. Before the expedition began, he killed a deer sacred to *Artemis*, who sent a plague on the Greek camp at Aulis, and a contrary wind which prevented them from sailing. The priests advised Agamemnon that the goddess would only cease to be angry if he sacrificed his daughter *Iphigeneia* to her, which he did with great reluctance. *Clytemnestra*, Iphigeneia's mother, never forgave him for this. At Troy, he caused the quarrel with *Achilles* when he took a slave-girl who had been allotted to Achilles as his share of the spoils, because he had been forced to return *Chryseis*, the girl he had captured. On his return from the Trojan War, he brought *Priam*'s daughter *Cassandra* with him; but they were both murdered by Clytemnestra and *Aegisthus*, because of the curse on the house of Atreus inflicted by the gods.

Agastya: A Hindu sage and poet, son of both *Mitra* and *Varuna*. His powers were as great as those of the gods themselves; he made mountain ranges bow to him, and he once drank up the ocean because the *Daityas*, enemies of the gods, and hidden themselves in it. He found a wife as a result of a dream in which he saw his ancestors hanging head first by their heels in a pit; they told him that he could release them if he became the father of a son. So he made a girl out of the most beautiful parts of various animals, such as the eyes of the deer. She was brought up by one of the Indian kings, and Agastya later married her. He had great power over evil spirits or *Rakshasas*. His greatest feat was the overthrow of

7

Nahusha, when Nahusha tried to take *Indra's* place in heaven, though one version of the story ascribes the feat to *Bhrigu*, who hid in Agastya's hair.

Agave: Sister of *Semele* in Greek myth. She denied that *Zeus* was father of Semele's son *Dionysus*, and was condemned by the god to become the leader of the *maenads*, or followers of Dionysus. The maenads tore her own son *Pentheus* to pieces when he spied on their ritual dances disguised as a woman.

Agenor: Son of the Greek god *Poseidon*, father of *Cadmus* of Thebes and of *Europa*. When Europa was carried off by *Zeus* in the shape of a bull, Agenor sent his sons out in search of her. Each of them, after long wanderings, settled in a different place and founded a nation.

Agni: The Hindu god of fire, one of the most important gods in their early myths. He ruled over the earth, and was the equal of *Indra*, king of the gods and of *Surya*, the sun. He is represented with seven tongues, because one form of Hindu sacrifice consisted of burning butter in a fire, and Agni was said to lick up the butter with his seven tongues. Another description shows him clothed in black, carrying a banner made of smoke and a fiery spear. His chariot had the winds as its wheels, and was drawn by chestnut horses, while he rode at other times on a ram. Later pictures showed him as a hideous destroyer of demons, with two iron tusks, because fire had ceased to be worshipped in its own right, and Agni's character had been changed accordingly.

Ahalya: In Hindu myth, Ahalya was the wife of a devout sage, and *Indra* once made love to her. In revenge, her husband made her invisible, but *Rama* lifted the spell and persuaded her husband to forgive her.

Ahayuta Achi: In Zuñi Indian myth, the Ahayuta Achi are the twin gods of war. They were the sons of the sun and a woman named Dripping Water, but they lived with their grandmother, Spiderwoman. The many stories about them usually speak of them as small boys, but even when young they made the great journey to heaven to find their father, the sun, and they slew many monsters. They also provided mankind with implements, and taught men to hunt. As gods, they live inside the mountains, and guard the Zuñi villages; they destroy monsters and evil-doers, but encourage gamblers and mischief-makers. The Zuñi and Hopi Indians regard twins as the children of two fathers – one natural father and the sun. So the Ahayuta Achi belonged to different clans. The Pueblo Indians also speak of them, and tell how on their journey to seek the sun, they were laughed at and abused by other boys and men; but they triumphed in the end over their persecutors.

Ahpuch: God of death in Maya myth.

Ahsonnutli: The creator-god of the Navaho Indians, who is both man and woman at once. He-she made heaven and earth, and placed men at the twelve points of the compass to hold up the sky. Known also as the 'Turquoise Man-Woman', he-she seems to be the same as the 'Turquoise Woman' of other Navaho stories.

Ahura Mazda: In Iranian myth, the creator of all good beings. His enemy was *Angra Mainyu*, the god of evil, and the battle between them went on unceasingly, with equally matched forces. At the end of the world Ahura Mazda will at last be the victor, and evil will be washed away by a flood of molten metal.

From the very beginning battle was waged between Ahura Mazda and Angra Mainyu. Ahura Mazda created purely spiritual beings, but Angra Mainyu made evil beings with bodies, and Ahura Mazda had to counteract this by creating the world. He began with the heavens, but as fast as he created something Angra Mainyu created its opposite, until Ahura Mazda set a great wall round the sky to keep his enemy out. Then he created the waters and the spring *Anahita*, source of all life and strength, which was worshipped as a goddess. Nonetheless Angra Mainyu managed to spoil many things made by Ahura Mazda. He gave fire its smoke, where it had once been pure and bright; and put thorns on trees, and gave them poisonous fruits.

Aiapayec: The supreme god of the Mochica people of the coast of Peru. Originally a cat-god, he is shown as a man with huge fangs, wrinkled face and cat's whiskers. Even though he ruled everything in the world, he lived among ordinary people, and could appear either as man or as god. He was master of all kinds of skills, and Mochica pottery shows him as farmer, fisherman, doctor, hunter and musician. As protector of mankind, he fought and defeated all kinds of demons,

9

vampires, and serpents. His court consisted of birds of different kinds; his constant friend was the dog, and the lizard was his servant.

Ailill: King of Connaught and husband of *Medhbh* in Irish myth. He owned the white bull of Connaught which she coveted; to have its equal she obtained the Brown Bull of *Cuailgne*.

Airavata: When the Indian gods 'churned the ocean' (see *amrita*), one of the things they produced was the elephant Airavata, which *Indra* took as his steed.

Aizen-Myoo: In Japanese Buddhist belief, the god who can control men's evil tempers and desires; he appears as a fierce six-armed man with three eyes, but is kindly in his actions.

Ajax: 1. Leader of the men from Salamis in the *Trojan War*. He was one of the best of the Greek warriors when it came to fighting, but he was not very distinguished off the battlefield. When *Achilles* died, his armour was claimed by both *Odysseus* and Ajax, and the argument was settled by *Athene*. She called on a number of Trojan prisoners to say who had done more damage to Troy, and Odysseus won because of his cunning and wise counsel. At this Ajax went mad, and killed a number of sheep, because he thought they were Odysseus, Agamemnon and the other Greeks. When he came to his senses, he killed himself out of shame.

2. 'Ajax the lesser', one of the Greek warriors in the *Trojan War*. Violent and ruthless, he led the men from Locris; on his way home he was shipwrecked, and *Poseidon* saved him. But as he stood on a rock at the water's edge, he boasted that he had escaped despite the gods. At this Poseidon struck the rock and drowned him.

Aker: Double-headed lion god of the ancient Egyptians, who represented the earth: later replaced by *Geb*.

Akongo: The creator-god of the Nkombe tribe of the Congo; he created men as a potter shapes clay.

Ala: Goddess of the earth (also called Ani) in the myths of the Igbo people of Nigeria, shown as a mother with a child on her knees. She ruled all men, dead or alive.

Alberich: A dwarf king in Scandinavian myth.

He plays an important part in Richard Wagner's cycle of operas *The Ring of the Nibelungs*, in which he is the first owner of the famous ring.

Alcathous: The son of *Pelops* and *Hippodameia*, he slew the lion which ravaged the flocks on Mount Cithaoron, and became king of Megara as a result. Other versions of this Greek myth say that it was *Heracles* who slew the lion.

Alcestis: Wife of *Admetus* in Greek myth; when the gods decreed his death, she died in his place, but was rescued by *Heracles*, who wrestled with death for her.

Alci: Twin gods worshipped in eastern Germany in the first century AD; they were said to be the same as *Castor and Pollux*. Their chief priest dressed himself in woman's clothes, and no images of them were allowed to be made.

Alcmaeon: Son of *Amphiaraus* and Eriphyle in Greek myth. Because his mother had been bribed to persuade his father to join in the war of the *Seven Against Thebes*, although he knew that it would mean his death, Alcmaeon obeyed his father's parting wish and killed her. Like *Orestes*, he was pursued by the *Furies* for this, but he went to Arcadia, where King Phegeus performed the rites of making him pure again, and thus freed him from the Furies. He married Phegeus' daughter Arsinoe, but the curse on him was still working, and his presence brought a famine in the country. So he went on to the mouth of the river Achelous, where he married Callirhoe. Callirhoe longed to possess the necklace of *Harmonia*, which had been the bride that caused the deaths of Alcmaeon's father and mother. Alcmaeon had given it to Phegeus, but he now obtained it back by a trick. Phegeus' sons killed him for this; but *Zeus*, who was in love with Callirhoe, granted her wish that her two small sons should grow up at once, and they killed Phegeus and his sons in turn. The fatal necklace was presented to *Apollo's* temple at Delphi.

Alcmena: Mother of *Heracles*, she was married to *Amphitryon* in Greek myth. *Zeus* disguised himself as her husband, and made love to her; she had twin sons, Heracles by Zeus and *Iphicles* by Amphitryon.

Alcyone: Wife of *Ceyx* in Greek myth. When he died, she mourned her dead husband so pitifully that the gods had mercy on her and turned her into a sea-bird, the halcyon.

Alecto: One of the *Furies* in Greek myth; her name means 'the relentless one'.

Alfar: Alfar means elves, and the word has come down to us from the Anglo-Saxons, who, like other German and Norse nations, believed in elves in pagan days. They were usually thought of as good spirits, though the dwarfs *(dvergar)* were sometimes called dark elves or black elves. They dwelt in Alfheim, where *Frey* ruled over them, and were the spirits or guardians of nature. After Christianity came to the north, they were regarded as evil, as is shown by an Anglo-Saxon charm against 'the little arrows of the elves', evidently a disease like rheumatism.

Alfrodull: The sun in Norse myth; the name means 'Glory of elves', and there were other names for it as well. The sun was thought to be a girl who drove a chariot across the sky each day, drawn by the horses Arvak and Alsvid. She drove very fast, because she was pursued by the wolf Skoll, offspring of the wolf *Fenrir*. At the end of the world, the wolf will catch her and devour her, but by then she will have had a daughter, who will take her place. The sun gives heat but not light; light comes from the mane of the horse which Day rides, called *Skinfaxi* or 'shining mane'.

Aloadai: Two giants in Greek myth, called Otos and Ephialtes, the sons of *Poseidon* and Iphimedeia. They grew to an immense size very quickly, nine fathoms (fifty-four feet) tall in nine years. They tried to climb to heaven by piling two mountains, Pelion and Ossa, on top of each other, but were prevented by the gods. At another time they seized the war-god *Ares* and shut him in a bronze vessel, where he lay for thirteen months until *Hermes* released him. They were killed by *Zeus* and condemned to punishment in *Tartarus*.

Alpheus: A Greek river-god who loved and pursued the nymph Arethusa. *Artemis* changed the nymph into a stream, and made her flow underground to Sicily; Alpheus followed her, and the two were joined as one river in Sicily.

Althaea: Mother of *Meleager*.

Althaea: Mother of *Meleager*. When the *Fates* decreed he would live as long as a certain piece of wood remained unburnt, Althaea kept a guard on it. But later Meleager killed her brothers and in fury she plunged the wood into fire, killing Meleager.

12

Aluberi: The highest god of all among the Arawak Indians of South America, who had no concern with affairs on earth.

Aluluei: God of seafaring in the myths of the Caroline Islands in the Pacific. Aluluei had two elder brothers who were jealous of him and drowned him; but their father brought him back to life and set eyes like stars in his head to protect him. Then he tricked the two elder brothers into giving Aluluei a canoe. He sailed off with a crew of forty rats, and made himself an island out of sand. His youngest brother Faravai was wrecked there once, and Aluluei would only let him go when he had picked the lice out of his hair. Faravai was frightened by all the eyes in Aluluei's head, but Aluluei taught him that they were the stars in the sky, and how to navigate by them.

Alviss: A dwarf to whom the Norse gods promised *Thor*'s daughter Thrud as his bride, in return for some service he had done them. But Thor was not there when the promise was made, and when Alviss came to claim Thrud, Thor refused to give him to her. Alviss pleaded with him, and Thor agreed that if he could answer all the questions which he asked him, he should have Thrud. Alviss, whose name meant 'All-wise', knew all the answers, but Thor had questioned him for so long that the sun had risen and was shining into the hall. Now the sun is fatal to dwarfs; if they are not back in their underground haunts before dawn, they are turned to stone. So Thor declared in triumph 'The day has caught you, dwarf; the sun, deceiver of your kind, shines in the hall', and Thrud was saved by her father's trick.

Am: A god in the myths of the Portangoro Indians of South America. A rather vague figure, he lived in heaven with the sun and moon, and (according to some) the god Chusman as well. A great flood once swept over the earth, drowning everyone except one man to whom he gave a stick wrapped in a mat, a hollow bamboo and a kind of jug. When the flood vanished, he made a hut with the stick and mat; the next morning, the bamboo turned into a woman and went to fetch water in the jug. After Christian missionaries came to this part of the Americas, the story of the Temptation from the Old Testament was added to this legend.

Ama-terasu: The Japanese sun-goddess, ruler

of the heavens. Her great enemy was her brother, the storm-god *Susa-no-wo*, who destroyed her rice fields and wrecked her palace because he was jealous of her and wanted to rule in her place. At these insults, she retired into a cave, and the world went dark without the sun. All the gods assembled outside the cave, and used every kind of magic to lure her out, including a mirror hung outside the cave. The goddess *Uzume* began to dance, and was so carried away that she took off all her clothes; the gods laughed and clapped, and Ama-terasu asked from her cave what was happening. Uzume said that they had found a better goddess than the sun, at which Ama-terasu looked out and saw her own reflection in the mirror. One of the gods seized her and dragged her out, the sun reappeared, and the evil spirits which had flourished in her absence disappeared.

Ama-terasu then wanted to see that the earth was properly governed, because she was ruler of heaven only, and the earth had no lord. The first god she tried to send, her son Ama-no-Oshiho-mini, watched the gods who lived on earth fighting among themselves and refused to go; the second went, but failed to come back; while the third, Ame-waka-hiko, married the daughter of *Ō-kuni-nushi* and forgot why he had been sent. When the pheasant Na-naki-me was sent to remind him, he tried to kill it; but the arrow went straight through it to heaven, where the gods recognised it, and hurled it back, killing Ame-waka-hiko. Finally the god of thunder and the god of fire were sent, and persuaded Ō-kuni-nushi and his sons to accept Ama-terasu's lordship over the earth. Ō-kuni-nushi withdrew to rule the underworld, and *Ninigi*, Ama-terasu's grandson, became the first ruler of Japan.

Ama-Tsu-Mikaboshi: The Japanese god of evil: his name means 'against star of heaven'.

Amazons: A race of warrior women, led by a queen, whom the Greeks believed to live somewhere to the north. Various heroes fought against them, including *Heracles* and *Theseus*. One of Heracles' twelve labours was to win the girdle of *Hippolyta*, their queen, whom Theseus later married. Another queen, *Penthesilea*, led them against the Greeks at Troy, but was killed by *Achilles*. They were said to be the daughters of *Ares* and *Aphrodite*.

Ambrosia: The magical drink of the Greek gods, which renewed their youth

14

Amenhetep: In Egyptian myth, the god of building. He was architect to King Amenhetep III, and was made a god after his death. (Another Amenhetep, King Amenhetep I, was also made a god, and guarded the graves at Thebes, but the two gods are quite different.)

Amen(-Ra): The god of Thebes in the south of Egypt, who came to be one of the chief gods of Egyptian mythology when a noble family from Thebes became the pharaohs. He was originally a god of air and wind, but later became a fertility god and finally was identified with the sun-god *Ra* himself as Amen-Ra. He was believed to be the actual father of the pharaoh's heir: taking on the appearance of the ruling pharaoh, he visited the queen in this form and she bore his son.

Under the Theban dynasty, the Egyptians became warlike and began to build an empire: so Amen became the god of victory in war, whose power enabled the pharaohs to overcome their enemies. His wife was *Mut*, and *Khensu* was their son. His greatest temple was that at Karnak, much of which still survives today, and he was often addressed as 'Lord of Karnak'.

Ameretat: The Iranian goddess of plants; on a moral level she represented immortality, and was one of the *Amesha Spentas*.

Amesha Spentas: The greater gods of Iranian myths, the 'immortal holy ones'. They were less powerful than *Ahura Mazda* himself, but were the guardians of the world.

They were: Asha, the fire-god (righteousness), *Vohu Manah* ('good mind') the god of lame animals, *Khshathra Vairya* ('desirable kingdom') god of metals, *Spenta Armaiti* (devotion) the earth-god, *Haurvatat* (happiness) the water-goddess and *Ameretat* (immortality) the goddess of plants. Their moral functions were not directly related to their duties as guardian gods, and other spirits also acted as gods of fire and water, for example *Atar* and *Anahita*. Their counterparts under *Angra Mainyu's* leadership were the *devas*.

Amhairghin: In Irish myth, Amhairghin was the leader of the Sons of Mil, who drove the *Tuatha De Danann* into the fairy fortress where they later lived. He was a poet and had magical powers. The Sons of Mil were the forebears of the people who now live in Ireland.

Amida: The Japanese name for *Amitabha*, who ruled the paradise called *Gokuraku-Jōdo*; he was worshipped as a god, and his followers believe that salvation can only be reached through him, rather than through spiritual discipline.

Amida in his terrible form as conqueror of *Emma-o* and of dragons is called Dai Itoku-Myoo.

Amitabha: One of the five *Dhyanibuddhas* or Buddhas of meditation, ruler of the paradise called Sukhavati.

Ammut: The Egyptian goddess who devoured dead souls who were found guilty of wickedness during their lifetimes: she had a crocodile's head, a lion's body and a hippopotamus' hindquarters.

Amphiaraus: Greek seer, who was persuaded to join the *Seven Against Thebes* by his wife Eriphyle although he knew it would lead to his death. *Polyneices* bribed her to do this by giving her the necklace that had belonged to the goddess *Harmonia*. As Amphiaraus left to go to war, he asked his sons to avenge his death; *Alcmaeon* fulfilled this request by killing his mother Eriphyle. Amphiaraus was not actually killed in battle, but his chariot was swallowed up by the earth. The place where he disappeared became a temple famous for its oracles.

Amphion: One of the two sons of Antiope who built the Greek city of Thebes. He was a great musician, and moved the stones for the walls of the city by playing to them and charming them into place.

Amphitrite: The wife of the Greek god *Poseidon*, she was a rather unimportant goddess, and usually appeared simply as the chief of the Nereids.

Amphitryon: Prince of Mycenae in Greece; he was exiled to Thebes. He won his bride *Alcmena* by catching an uncatchable fox and by killing King Pterelaos, who was immortal. He was helped in hunting the fox by *Cephalus*, who had a hound which caught whatever it pursued. Because the fox was fated never to be caught, and the hound to catch its prey every time, *Zeus* had to solve the problem by turning both to stone. King Pterelaos was the ruler of Amphitryon's enemies the Teleboans; and as long as a certain golden hair grew on his head, he was unconquerable. But Pterelaos' daughter fell in love with Amphitryon, and without any encouragement from him plucked out her father's golden hair as a love gift for him. Amphitryon, shocked at such treachery, put her to death when the Teleboans were conquered.

Amrita: The magic juice or water which kept the Hindu gods young, and renewed their strength; also called *soma*. When the gods were defeated by the demons on one occasion, they went to *Vishnu* and asked him to grant them increased power and immortal life. He told them that the amrita which would give them this, besides other precious things, had been lost in the ocean. If they could persuade the demons to help them to churn the ocean, spinning it round and round like milk when butter is made, they would find these treasures. Using a great snake and a mountain, resting on the back of Vishnu in his tortoise *avatar*, to turn the waters, the gods saw, first, the sacred cow Surabhi appear, followed by Varuni, goddess of wine, the Parijata or paradise tree, and the *Apsarases* or nymphs. Then came the moon, and after it a violent poison, which *Shiva* swallowed. *Shri*, the goddess of beauty, appeared, sitting on a lotus, and lastly *Dhanvantari*, who became the god's physician, came out of the waves, clasping a cup full of the precious amrita. Vishnu now drove away the demons, and the gods gained possession of the amrita. See also *Garuda*.

Anahita: One of the *Yazatas* in Iranian myth, Anahita was the spirit of water.

Anatiwa: The Karaya Indians of Brazil tell how a great flood in the days of their ancestors was caused by an evil god called Anatiwa. Their ancestors took refuge on a hill-top, and Anatiwa sent a fish to rub all the earth away. But the water-hen brought more earth as quickly as the fish removed it, and they were saved.

Anaye: The 'alien gods' in the myths of the Navaho Indians, enemies of man, who were always at war with men and the gods who protected them. Most of them were killed long ago, but a few still survived: these were Old Age, Cold, Hunger and Poverty, because if they were not there, men would not pray to the gods for life, warmth and food.

Anchises: Father of *Aeneas*; cousin of *Priam* of Troy.

Andhaka: One of the demons of Hindu myth;

17

he had a thousand arms and heads and two thousand eyes and feet, and he was blind. He once tried to carry off the paradise tree, Parijata, but *Shiva* prevented him and killed him.

Andraste: When the British Queen Boudicca or Boadicea rebelled against the Roman rulers of Britain in the first century A D, she is said to have sacrificed her prisoners in sacred woods to a goddess of victory called Andraste.

Andromache: Wife of the Trojan hero *Hector*, who was taken from Troy, after it fell, by *Neoptolemus*, *Achilles'* son. She later married another of *Priam's* sons, *Helenus*, who founded the city of Epirus in imitation of Troy. Neoptolemus had abandoned her in favour of Hermione, with whom *Orestes* was in love, and was killed by Orestes.

Andromeda: Daughter of Cepheus and Cassiopeia, the king and queen of the Ethiopians. Cassiopeia boasted that she was more beautiful than any of the sea-goddesses, at which a monster appeared from the waves and ravaged the land. An oracle said that the monster would only be appeased if Andromeda was left, chained naked to a rock, for it to devour. *Perseus*, the Greek hero, saw her as he returned from slaying the *Gorgon*, and rescued her by turning the monster to stone with the Gorgon's head; he later married her.

Andvari: Dwarf who possessed a marvellous treasure, which the Norse gods *Odin* and *Loki* extracted from him in order to pay the ransom demanded by *Ottar's* father. When Loki first tried to get the gold from him, Andvari refused, and disguised himself as a fish; but Loki caught him and threatened to kill him if he did not surrender the treasure, even down to the gold ring which he was wearing. Andvari was reluctant, because without it he would not be able to become rich again; and swore that if Loki took it, it would bring disaster to anyone who owned it. Loki insisted, and when the ransom came to be paid, the ring was needed to complete it.

Angiras: The father of *Agni*, the Hindu god of fire. He was regarded as one of the seven great sages (*maharishis*) and was a giver of laws. His descendants, the Angirases, were gods of light and fire, though Agni was by far the most important.

Angra Mainyu: The evil god in Iranian myth, creator of everything wicked, who waged continual war against *Ahura Mazda*.

Anguta: In Central Eskimo belief, Anguta was the supreme being, creator of the earth, sea and heavens. He was father of *Sedna*, in whose story he plays an important part.

Anhert: Egyptian god of the sky, often regarded as the same as *Shu*.

Annwn: The Welsh equivalent of *Hades*, an otherworld inhabited by spirits; ruled by Arawn, who once changed shape with *Pwyll*. A strange poem tells how Arthur (the King Arthur of later romances) once raided it, and how of three ship-loads only seven men returned. There was a magic cauldron of inspiration there, which would not boil the food of a coward, and other mysteries and marvels.

Anta: The Egyptian name of the goddess *Anat*; she was regarded as a war-goddess, and was said to be *Ra*'s daughter.

Antaeus: Son of Earth (*Gaia*) and *Poseidon* in Greek myth. He was a champion wrestler, who could never be conquered because his strength was renewed each time he touched the ground, which was his mother Earth. *Heracles* defeated him in the end by holding him in the air and crushing him to death with his hands.

Antigone: One of the most famous of Greek heroines. She was the sister of *Polyneices* of Thebes, who was killed in the war of the *Seven Against Thebes* fighting against the city and against his brother *Eteocles*. Her uncle *Creon*, the king of Thebes, ordered that no-one should bury Poly-neices' body, because he had died as a rebel. But Antigone set her duty to her brother above the king's orders, and secretly went out and per-formed the burial rites. Creon ordered her to be buried alive, even though she was engaged to his own son Haimon; he changed his mind after the tomb had been sealed, but she had already hanged herself, and Haimon killed himself when her body was found.

Anu: The supreme god of the Sumerians, ruler of the sky and controller of the universe. He was respected by the other gods as peacemaker, and they accepted his authority. In the third and highest heaven where he lived, he was little con-cerned with human beings, but ruled the uni-verse as a whole. He kept the bread and water of eternal life (see *Adapa*).

19

Anubis: The Egyptian god who guarded the body of a dead man while it was being embalmed and after it had been placed in the tomb. He played an important part in the judgement of the dead in the hall of *Osiris*. He was shown as a man with a jackal's head.

Anyiewo: The great snake in the belief of the Ewe people of West Africa, whose reflection is the rainbow. He only appeared after rain, when he came out to graze, and then returned to the ant-hill where he lived.

Aphrodite: The Greek goddess of love, called *Venus* by the Romans. Many pictures show her rising from the sea-foam from which she was born, as in Botticelli's masterpiece 'The Birth of Venus', and she was the goddess of sailors as well. Cyprus was her birthplace, and she was particularly honoured there; she was also the patroness of beauty and sometimes of marriage, while in Sparta she was thought of as a war-goddess. Among mortals whom she loved were *Adonis* and *Anchises*; her husband was the lame fire-god *Hephaestus*, but her best-known affair was with *Ares*, the god of war. *Helios*, the sun-god, told Hephaestus what was going on; so he forged a very strong invisible net in which he trapped Ares and Aphrodite together one day and showed them to the rest of the gods.

Because *Paris* had awarded her the apple of beauty in his famous judgement, she supported the Trojans in the *Trojan War*; when she went into the battle to rescue Paris on one occasion, she was wounded by the Greek hero *Diomedes*. Aphrodite was sometimes said to be the mother of *Eros*.

Apis: The sacred bull which was kept at Memphis in Egypt. It was regarded originally as the god Ptah, but later became *Osiris* in animal shape, and in the days of the Greek rulers of Egypt before the Roman invasion was worshipped as *Serapis* (Osiris-Apis), a kind of state god.

Apocatequil: God of lightning in the myths of the Inca people of Peru, statues of whom were placed on mountain-tops throughout the Inca empire. He and his twin brother released the ancestors of the Incas (see *Paccari-Tambo*) from the underworld, by turning the soil with a golden tool.

Apollo: The Greek god of light, worshipped

under the same name by the Romans. He was often identified with the sun itself, and was also the god of music and archery. He and *Artemis* were twins; their mother was the Titaness *Leto*, their father *Zeus*.

The great temple of Apollo was at Delphi, where his prophetess uttered the famous oracles, foretelling the future. No one except the priests heard her replies, which they wrote down and gave to the person who had questioned her. Apollo also had a temple at Delos, where he and Artemis were born. Because he was god of music, *Orpheus* was closely connected to him, and he was also father of the god of medicine and healing, *Asclepius*. The *Sibyl* at Cumae in southern Italy was another of his prophetesses.

See also *Daphne, Helios, Marsyas, Orestes.*

Apples of Youth: The Norse goddess *Idunn* was the keeper of the magic apples which she and the other gods ate in order to stay perpetually young. One day *Odin, Loki* and *Hoenir* were trying to roast an ox for dinner, but the meat would not cook. A giant eagle offered to help them, if he could have a share in return. The gods accepted, but the eagle helped himself to most of the ox. Loki was furious and attacked him with a pole, which stuck in the eagle's back. Before he could let go, the eagle flew off, and resumed his ordinary shape as the giant ·Thiazi, and took Loki prisoner. He would only release him in return for the goddess Idunn and her apples of youth. This Loki contrived to do, but the theft was quickly discovered because the gods became grey-haired and old. Loki was forced to get the goddess back again. He borrowed *Freyja*'s falcon-shape, and flew to the giant's home. Thiazi was out fishing, and Loki was able to seize Idunn and change her into a nut. He flew off with this, but Thiazi saw him and changed into an eagle again. He chased Loki to *Asgard*, but the gods had seen them coming, and had piled up a huge fire·inside the walls. As soon as Loki was inside, the bonfire was lit, and Thiazi, who was flying so fast he could not stop, scorched his wings in it and fell to the ground inside Asgard, where the gods killed him.

Apsarases: Beautiful girls who lived in Svarga, the heaven of the Hindu god *Indra*. They emerged at the churning of the waters (see *Amrita*). They were beloved of gods, men and demons alike, and had magical powers: they could give good fortune to men, but on the other hand, they could also

produce madness, and charms had to be used against them. See *Amrita, Gandharvas, Pururavas.* but they were wild and disordered creatures. From them Lakhmu and Lakhamu, giant serpents, were born, and then Anshar and Kishar,

Apsu and Tiamat: The first beings in Babylonian myth: Apsu, 'sweet water', was the father, Tiamat, 'salt water', the mother, of everything; parents of the gods. Apsu was tamed by *Ea*, and the younger gods took their place; but Apsu and Tiamat rebelled and sent a swarm of monsters under the command of Kingu to overthrow *Anu, Ea, Marduk* and their allies. Neither Anu nor Ea were brave enough to attack Tiamat, so Marduk was chosen as the leader of the younger gods; he and Tiamat fought in single combat; he overcame her by making the evil wind blow when she opened her mouth to swallow him, so that she could not shut her mouth, and then killing her with an arrow. He then used her body to create the world: half of her became the sky, the other half the earth. The eleven dragons who fought on Tiamat's side were caught in a net and hurled down into the underworld, where they became its gods. The blood of Kingu was used to make man and the work of creation ended with the building of a huge temple to Marduk.

Arachne: A Greek girl who was very skilled at weaving and challenged *Athene*, goddess of spinning and weaving, to a contest although Athene warned her that she could not hope to win. Athene's subject for her piece was the fate of those who challenged the gods to such contests, while Arachne started to weave scandalous stories about the gods in pictures. Athene was so angry at this that she beat her with her weaver's shuttle, and Arachne hanged herself in shame. Athene took pity on her and turned her into a spider, which still weaves most beautifully.

Ares: The Greek god of war, called by the Romans *Mars.* He was the son of *Zeus* and *Hera.* Although he was an important god, there are few stories about him, the best known being that of his love for *Aphrodite.* He was also involved in a quarrel with the *Aloadai*; but all that is known about this is his imprisonment by them in a brass jar, where he stayed for thirteen months until *Hermes* rescued him. He may have been originally a foreign god, worshipped by the Thracians who lived to the north of Greece itself. As Mars, he was the father of *Romulus* and *Remus*.

Argo: In Greek myth, the ship built for *Jason* on his search for the *Golden Fleece*. Argos, son of Arestor was the shipwright, with *Athene*'s help, and the crew were the heroes known afterwards as the Argonauts, including *Heracles, Peleus. Zetes* and *Calais, Meleager, Orpheus*, the pilot *Tiphys* and the look-out Lynceus. The prow of the Argo contained a piece from the sacred oak of Zeus at Dodona, which was able to speak, and advised the Argonauts during the journey.

Argos: 1. Son of Arestor. See *Argo*.
    2. The faithful hound of *Odysseus*, which lived just long enough to recognize his master after his long wanderings.
    3. The hundred-eyed herdsman whom *Hera* set to watch over *Io*, because she was jealous of *Zeus*' love for her and turned her into a heifer. *Hermes* put Argos to sleep by enchanting each of his hundred eyes in turn, and then slew him.

Ariadne: Daughter of King *Minos* of Crete, she fell in love with *Theseus*. She helped him to kill the *Minotaur* by giving him a sword and a ball of thread with which to find his way out of the labyrinth in which the monster lived. She escaped with Theseus when he left Crete, but was abandoned by him at the island of Naxos. Here *Dionysus* found her, wandering disconsolate by the shore. Although she made three attempts to escape from him, she at last yielded to him, and he set the crown she wore at their marriage in the sky, as a constellation of stars.

Arikute and Tamendonar: In the myths of the Tupi Indians of Brazil, a quarrel between the brothers Arikute and Tamendonar resulted in a great flood which covered the earth. They themselves, together with their wives, climbed trees on the highest mountains, and were the only ones to survive. After the flood, their descendants repopulated the earth; but they were divided into two tribes who continually fought each other. Arikute and Tamendonar became the god of night and the god of day, and they renew their quarrel every day.

Arion: The 'very swift' horse of *Adrastus* in Greek myth; he was born of *Poseidon* and

Demeter in the shape of a mare.

Aristaeus: The Greek poet Vergil tells how Aristaeus the shepherd-god caused *Eurydice*'s death; as he pursued her along a river-bank, Eurydice was bitten by a deadly snake on which she trod. For this his bees were destroyed by Eurydice's companions the wood-nymphs, until he sacrificed to them.

Arjuna: A son of *Indra*, one of the five princes called *Pandavas* in Indian myth. His deeds are told in the great epic, the *Mahabharata*, and he was the foremost of the five brothers. He was taught how to fight by two famous warriors, *Drona* and *Parashurama*, and was given weapons by the gods themselves. His father Indra sent him to conquer the *Daityas* living in the sea, which he achieved successfully, and for this exploit he was given a conch-shell trumpet which made a noise like thunder. His greatest campaign was against the enemies of his family, the Kauravas. In this he was helped by *Krishna* himself, who acted as his charioteer. The battle raged for seventeen days, and ended in a duel between Arjuna and Karna, like the duel of *Achilles* and *Hector* in the *Iliad*. Arjuna was almost killed, and only slew Karna when his enemy's chariot became stuck fast in a bog. After this triumph, his brother *Yudhishthira* wanted to offer the greatest of sacrifices, that of a sacred horse which was set loose for a year. An army followed it, and only if all the lands through which the horse passed were conquered, could the sacrifice be made. Arjuna led the army which followed the horse, and fought his way successfully through the lands it crossed. After this triumph, he and his brothers retired to the Himalayas as hermits. See also *Draupadi*.

Artemis: The Greek goddess of hunting, called by the Romans Diana. She was also the goddess of childbirth, and was often identified with the moon, just as her twin brother *Apollo* was identified with the sun: she was worshipped with him at Delos. In particular she was the 'lady of wild things', the protector of the animals in hills and forests. No man or god ever won her love, and she was accompanied by a group of nymphs who likewise avoided love. She was a powerful and majestic goddess quick to anger; she had *Actaeon* torn in pieces when he came across her as she bathed naked, and she killed *Orion* when he tried to compete with her in throwing the discus. But in the *Trojan War*, where she fought on the Trojan side, she met her match in *Hera*, who, meeting

24

her on the battlefield, whipped her with her own bow, and sent her off in tears. For other stories about her, see *Iphigeneia*, *Callisto* and *Britomartis*.

As Diana, she was worshipped at Aricia in central Italy. Here the ritual of the Golden Bough took place. If a runaway slave arrived there and broke off a certain bough, he could challenge the priest to fight him. If he won, he became priest in turn, until slain by a newcomer.

Asase Ya: The earth-goddess of the Ashanti people of West Africa.

Asclepius: The Greek god of healing, son of the nymph *Coronis* and of *Apollo*. He was a mortal, and was brought up by the *centaur Chiron*, because Apollo killed his mother when she was unfaithful to him. He learnt his skill in medicine from Chiron, and was killed by *Zeus* for reviving *Hippolytus*, at *Artemis'* request, for a huge fee. But his merits and good works earned him a place among the gods, like *Heracles*.

Asgard: The stronghold of the *Aesir*, where the Norse gods lived, except for a few of the *Vanir* who lived in Vanaheim. In it were the gods' great halls, such as *Valhalla* and *Valaskjalf* which belonged to *Odin*.

It was fortified by a giant, who offered to build a wall round it during the course of a single winter. He made a bargain with the gods, by which he was to have the goddess *Freyja* as his wife if he finished in time; if he failed, he would be killed. With three days to go before the spring, the work was almost complete, because the giant had a magic horse called *Svadilfari* to help him. But *Loki* changed himself into a mare, and lured Svadilfari away. The giant could not finish the work by himself, so *Thor* killed him with his hammer. *Heimdall* was the watchman at the entrance to Asgard, which could only be reached over *Bifrost Bridge*. At the end of the world or *Ragnarok*, Asgard is to be destroyed; but in its place a new Asgard will be built.

Asgaya Gigagei: The Red Man or Woman of the Cherokee Indians, who is called on in various of their spells to cure illness. The god is either male or female, according to the sex of the patient to be treated. He-she appears to have originally been a thunder-god.

Ashvins: In Hindu myth, divine horse-men, the twin sons of the sun and a mare; they ride across the sky in their golden chariot to prepare

the way for the dawn. They were widely worshipped as gods of youth and handsomeness, who could also cure disease and grant benefits to their devotees. They were originally mortals, and were only made gods through the help of the sage *Cyavana*, whom they had restored to youth.

Ask and Embla: In the beginning the Norse gods *Odin, Hoenir* and *Loki* found two trees on the shore, an ash and an elm. These they gave the gift of life, and Odin added spirit, Hoenir understanding, Loki their senses and outward form, so that they became the first man and woman.

Astarte: 1. In Egyptian myth, Astarte was only thought of as goddess of war, while in Phoenicia she was goddess of both love and war. The Egyptians called her daughter of *Ra*.
    2. The fertility-goddess of Canaan, the same as *Ishtar*. She was goddess of the evening star (Venus), replacing the earlier god Athtar.

Asura: An Indian word which at first meant divine spirit or god, but which later came to mean spirit, particularly evil spirit; so the Asuras were the enemies of the gods. They were born from the breath of *Brahma*: among them were the *Daityas*, though the *Rakshasas*, who also fought the gods, were not included among them.

Ataensic: In the myths of the Huron Indians, who lived north of the Great Lakes in Canada, Ataensic appears as the first woman, mother of all mankind.
    Earth was created by the idea of the ruler of a great island in space, on which a huge apple tree grew. Under this tree, the people used to gather in council. One day the ruler spoke to his people and said: 'We will make a new place where another people may live. Under our council tree is a great sea of clouds which calls for our help, because it is lonely, restless and dark. We will talk to it; the roots of the council tree point to it and will show us the way.' So the great tree was uprooted, and the ruler looked into the hole. He called for Ataensic, who was expecting a child, and sent her down in a great ray of light. The animals and birds who lived in the sea of clouds were alarmed by this light, and decided that only the earth, which lay at the bottom of the waters, could hold the creature who was coming down in the ray of light. Each in turn tried to dive through the waters and bring up some earth, but failed. At last the muskrat succeeded, and the earth was placed on the

turtle's back so that he could support it. As Ataensic fell to earth, the water birds caught her and deposited her on the turtle's back. To this day, earth still rests on the turtle's back: it is he who causes great waves and earthquakes when he becomes restless. Just before Ataensic gave birth to her child, she heard two voices inside her, and she had twins: *Hahgwehdiyu*, the good and gentle spirit, and *Hahgwedaetgah*, the evil spirit and destroyer. Other versions of this myth are told by neighbouring tribes.

Atalanta: A Greek princess who as a baby was left on the mountainside to die because her father wanted a son. A she-bear found her and brought her up. When she found her parents again, she became a great huntress and refused to marry. At last she agreed with her father that she would marry a man who could defeat her in a race. If a challenger lost, he was put to death. She was won in the end by Hippomenes, whom *Aphrodite* favoured. The goddess gave him three golden apples belonging to the *Hesperides*, which he dropped in Atalanta's path as she ran. They were so beautiful that each time she stopped to pick them up, and Hippomenes finished first.

Atalanta took part in the great hunt for the Calydonian boar, which *Artemis* sent to ravage Calydon when its king forgot to sacrifice to her, and it was she who first wounded it. The leader of the hunt, *Meleager*, though he had actually killed it, awarded her the spoils.

Atar: One of the *Yazatas* of Iranian myth, the spirit of fire, which plays an important part in the Zoroastrian religion.

Aten: During the reign of the Egyptian pharaoh Amenhetep III, a new god, called Aten, appeared alongside the earlier sun-gods, *Ra*, *Amen*, *Horus* and *Khepra*. Under his son, Amenhetep IV, the god Aten was not only proclaimed chief god, but all the other gods were abolished, so that Aten was the one and only god. All traces of the old gods were removed, and the king changed his own name to Akhenaten, meaning 'It is well with Aten'. He moved the capital to a new site, where he built new temples to his god. He wrote hymns to Aten, and explained the new teaching, that everything comes from the sun and is controlled by it.

Athene: The Greek goddess of wisdom, called *Minerva* by the Romans. She was a warlike goddess, and protected cities in particular; but

she was also skilled in the more peaceful ways of handicrafts. She was the most strictly chaste of the Greek gods and goddesses.

She was the child of *Metis* and *Zeus*. *Hera* was so jealous of Metis that she threatened to kill her, and Zeus swallowed her to protect her unborn child from Hera's wrath. Athene was born fully armed and shouting her dreaded war cry from the top of Zeus' head, which *Hephaestus* split open with an axe. She was always Zeus' favourite, who called her 'Athene Bright-Eyes'.

She supported the Greeks in the *Trojan War*, and often appeared among their army, carrying the *Gorgon*'s head on her shield. She was *Odysseus'* special patron, and helped him on his return to Ithaca; likewise, she helped *Jason* and the Argonauts. Her hatred of the Trojans sprang from *Paris'* famous judgement, in which she competed with Hera and *Aphrodite* for the apple of beauty.

She was the patron goddess of Athens, which she won in a contest with *Poseidon*. Poseidon produced as evidence of his power a salt spring on the rocky hill of the Acropolis there, which arose when he struck the rock with his trident. But Athene magically produced a fully-grown olive tree, and was declared the victor by the other gods. As goddess of handicrafts, it was she who punished *Arachne* for boasting of her skill in weaving.

Atira: In Pawnee Indian myth, the earth was called h'Atira, mother of all things, and was regarded as sacred. The Pawnee lived by hunting, and when in the late nineteenth century they were urged to settle down and farm instead, their priest answered: 'You ask me to plough the ground! Shall I take a knife and tear my mother's bosom? Then when I die she will not take me to her bosom to rest. You ask me to dig for stone! Shall I dig under her skin for her bones? Then when I die I cannot enter her body to be born again. You ask me to cut grass and make hay and sell it, and be rich like white men! But how dare I cut off my mother's hair? It is a bad law and my people cannot obey it.'

Atlas: Son of *Iapetus,* the brother of *Cronos,* and of Clymene, daughter of *Ocean,* in Greek myth. He was one of the *Titans* who fought against *Zeus,* and he was punished by being made to support the sky. When *Heracles* came to fetch the golden apples of the *Hesperides,* whose garden was in North Africa, not far from where Atlas stood, he relieved Atlas of his burden for a time so that

Atlas could fetch the apples for him.

Atonatiuh: The 'water-sun' in Aztec myth, an age which ended in a great flood in which almost everyone was drowned.

Atreus: King of Mycenae in Greece, he was the son of *Pelops* and *Hippodameia*. Because his father was guilty of a treacherous murder, his sons were accursed. Atreus' brother Thyestes seduced Atreus' wife *Aerope*, and stole the golden ram which was the symbol of the king's power over Mycenae. In revenge, Atreus killed Thyestes' children and served them to .him in a dish. For this, Thyestes invoked a terrible curse on Atreus and his descendants; and the feud continued between *Aegisthus*, Thyestes' son, and Atreus' son *Agamemnon*.

Atropos: One of the Three *Fates* of Greek myth. She either spun the thread of the past, or cut off the thread of each individual's fate.

Atse Hastin and Atse Estsan: In Navaho Indian myth, Atse Hastin and Atse Estsan were the first man and woman, created from ears of maize in the world below the earth by the four winds. They led the human race up into the light. Their children were five pairs of twins, who married the mirage people who lived on earth before men, and the underworld people: their descendants populated the earth.

Atum: The Egyptian sun-god in his human form, shown as lord of all Egypt. He wears both the 'red crown' of Lower Egypt and the pharaoh's crown of Upper Egypt.

Audhumla: In Norse myth, the first living being was a cow which lived in the wilderness called *Ginnungagap* which lay between the world of fire, *Muspell*, in the south, and the world of ice in the north. It was she who fed the giant *Ymir*, and she shaped the father of the gods, *Buri*, from the ice, by licking it away. She probably represents earth's natural fertility and the way in which things grow after the end of winter.

Auf: The Egyptian sun-god in his journey each night through the underworld was called not *Ra*, his daytime name, but Auf. He travelled through the twelve regions of the underworld in a different boat, with serpents at either end, and manned by a different crew of gods. He had to overcome all

kinds of serpents and demons on his way, though some of these evil creatures were friendly in that they lived by devouring the enemies of Ra and *Osiris*.

Augeas: King of Elis, in southern Greece. He owned huge herds of cattle, whose stables were never cleaned until *Heracles* did so as one of his twelve labours.

Aurva: A Hindu *rishi* or sage, who practised great deeds of prayer and fasting. He hated the Kshatriya race because they had slaughtered his kinsmen the Bhrigus, and the various stories about him portray him as burning with rage. There are several versions of the birth of his son, and of how Aurva was responsible for the 'fire in the ocean'. According to one of these stories, his friends said that he should have children, but he replied by producing a devouring flame from his thigh which cried 'Let me eat up the world, for I am hungry'. The world was only saved by *Brahma*, who made a home for the fire at the 'mouth of the ocean'; at the end of each age, this fire helps Brahma to devour the world, and at the end of time will, with Brahma, destroy everything, gods and demons included.

Aurvandill: In Norse myth, husband of the seeress Groa, who charmed *Hrungnir*'s whetstone until it almost came out of *Thor*'s head; Thor was so pleased at her success that he told her stories about her husband, and how he had made his toe into a star. She was delighted by these, and stopped working her charms, so that the whetstone remained in Thor's head. Aurvandill is perhaps the same as the Anglo-Saxon 'earendel' or dawn, and Aurvandill's toe may be the morning star.

Ausaas: Wife of the Egyptian sun-god Herakhty (*Horus*).

Autolycus: A famous trickster in Greek myth, son of the god *Hermes*. He was the grandfather of *Odysseus*, who inherited his cunning. Autolycus' father granted him the power of changing the appearance of anything he stole, and of always escaping without being caught. He stole the cattle of *Sisyphus*, but was for once outwitted, because Sisyphus marked them under their hooves, and traced them to Autolycus' stables.

Avalokiteshvara: The most important of the *Bodhisattvas* in Buddhist myth. He is said to have

30

vowed to deliver all mankind from evil before becoming a Buddha and is the protector of anyone in danger, such as people who have been shipwrecked or attacked by robbers. In Tibetan Buddhism, the Dalai Lama is an incarnation of Avalokiteshvara. In Chinese myth, Avalokiteshvara is a woman, the goddess *Kuan Yin*.

Avya: The Cuboe Indians of Colombia in South America believe that sun and moon are the same, the light made by a man who walks across the sky all the time. He makes less light at night, so that people can sleep. When there is an eclipse, they believe that Avya is ill, because of the spells of an evil magician.

Awonawilona: In the myths of the Zuni Indians of Mexico, Awonawilona was the creator of the world, becoming the sun and making the 'mother-earth' and 'father-sky', from whom all living creatures came, born in four caves deep in the earth. The first man, Poshaiyankya, led the creatures up into the light.

Azazel: In Moslem myth, the lord of evil. When God commanded the angels to bow to Adam, Azazel refused to bow to a being made only of clay. God condemned him to death, but reprieved him until the Day of Judgement. He now lives in deserts, ruins and tombs and is known as Iblis, the ruler of djinns and evil spirits. He lives on sacrifices made to false gods and idols, and tempts men to evil by means of drink and luxurious living.

Azhi Dahaka: The three-jawed, three-headed and six-eyed dragon of evil in ancient Iranian belief, fought by various gods and eventually captured and hidden in a cave. He escaped and overcame King *Yima* who had sinned and lost the favour of the gods.

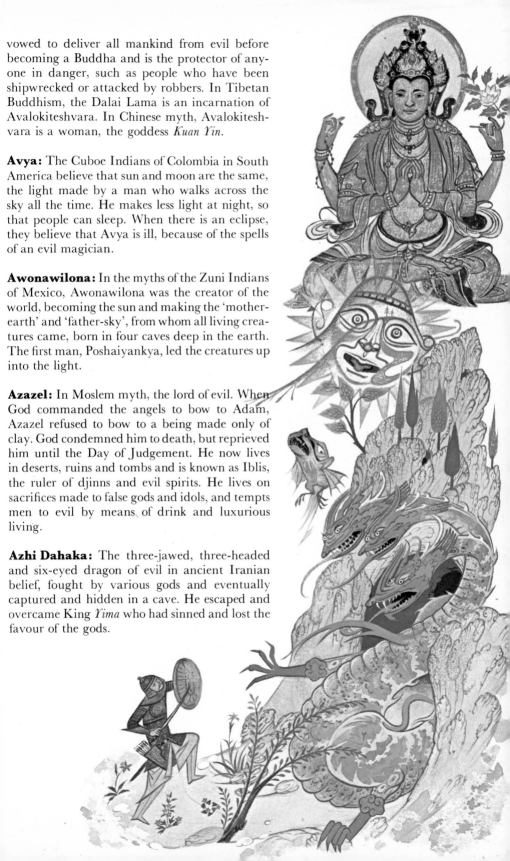

Baal: The thunder-god of the Canaanites, but he was the god who carried out the will of *El*, the supreme ruler of heaven. He was called 'son of *Dagon*', the corn-god, and he appears as a god who dies in the autumn and comes to life again in the spring.

His struggle against the sea-god, *Yamm*, began when Yamm terrified all the other gods into paying him tribute and demanded Baal as his slave, and Baal was only prevented from attacking Yamm by the goddesses *Anat* and Athtarat; but when Yamm sent his messengers to him, he beat them. The god of craftsmen and magic, who is called 'the Skilful and Far-Seeing One', encouraged Baal to fight Yamm, and made him a great club with which to drive off the sea. He killed Yamm and distributed the wild and dangerous waters so that they were under control and useful. Baal was then enthroned as king and the god of craftsmen built a great house for him. Baal now challenged the god of death and the underworld, *Mot*. But Mot said that even though Baal had destroyed monsters like *Lotan*, the seven-headed serpent from the beginning of time, he, Mot, would swallow up Baal. Mot did indeed defeat him, and Baal had to go down to the underworld, to the city of ruin where Mot ruled. The other gods mourned Baal, particularly his sister Anat who, after a long period of mourning, pleaded with Mot to release Baal; when he refused, she grew angry and cut him in two with a knife. Then she burnt him and ground his ashes to scatter on the fields. Baal emerged from the underworld, and renewed the fertility of the fields.

Bacab: In Maya mythology, the four Bacabs were the gods of the four points of the compass. They held up the sky and the earth, and were lords of the seasons.

Bachué: The goddess of farming of the Chibcha Indians of Colombia. She appeared from a lake, with her three-year-old son; when he grew up, he married her. She had four or more children at the time. When there were enough people, she commanded them all to live in peace, and vanished with her husband into the lake.

Badb (Bodb): Irish goddess of battle: she often appeared as a crow, and was one of the three great goddesses of *Tuatha De Danann*.

Baidrama: A twin-god of the Caribbean In-

32

dians; in war-time his statue, in the form of twin men, was burnt until it was a stump. Later it was washed with the juice of a herb and his arms grew again, his body filled out, and his eyes reappeared

Balam: In the myths of the Quiché Indians of Central America, Balam was the jaguar-god, and jaguars were feared as supernatural lords of magic. The four mythical ancestors of the Quiché race, created by *Gucumatz, Tepeu* and *Hurakan* out of maize, were the four balams, gods of north, south, east and west, named Balam-Quitze (Smiling Tiger), Balam-Agab (Night Tiger), Iqi-Balam (Moon Tiger) and Mahucatah (Famous Name). The last was not given his proper name, because he was probably regarded as powerful and dangerous, and to name his true name would arouse his anger. The four balams were able to see things at a great distance, and nothing was hidden from them; but their creators grew jealous of them, and blew a mist over their eyes, so that they had only ordinary human sight.

Bala Rama: The elder brother of *Krishna*, the Hindu god. Krishna was a god in his own right as well as being a form of *Vishnu*, but Bala Rama was the seventh *avatar* or incarnation of Vishnu. Vishnu created them both; Bala Rama, who was fair, was made from a white hair, while the dark Krishna came from a black hair. As a boy, Bala Rama killed demons, including the *asura* called Dhenuka. This demon took the form of an ass to attack Bala Rama, but he seized it by the legs and whirled it round until it was dead. His great weapon was a ploughshare, which he used to direct the river Yamuna when it would not obey him, and to undermine the walls of the city of Hotinapur when its king imprisoned his nephew Samba, Krishna's son, there. His other weapon was the club, and he taught *Bhima* how to use this. Unlike Krishna, he took no sides in the war between the *Pandavas* and the Kauravas. His two great faults were drunkenness and a quick temper; when he was drunk, he once commanded the river Yamuna to come and bathe him.

Balder: The favourite of the Norse gods, son of *Odin*. He was fairskinned and fairheaded, and was popular with everyone, because he was wise and merciful. Two different versions of his death have come down to us. The first story is told by the great Icelandic writer, Snorri Sturluson.

Balder had frightening dreams, in which he thought that his life was in danger, and he told the other gods. They decided that the only remedy was to protect Balder from any possible danger. So the goddess *Frigg*, made everything, all the living creatures, plants, stones, rocks, fire and water, swear that they would never harm Balder. To make sure that the oath worked, they tested it, and when all the gods were sure that Balder could not be hurt, they used sometimes to amuse themselves by throwing things at Balder, who was always unharmed. But *Loki* was jealous of Balder's popularity, and decided to question Frigg to see if she really had taken an oath from every single thing. He disguised himself as a woman, and discovered that Frigg had omitted to take an oath from the mistletoe, because it was too young. So he fashioned a sharp dart from mistletoe wood, and the next time that the gods sported with Balder, he gave it to the blind god *Hoder* to throw, and guided his hand. Balder fell dead, but because the place was holy, the gods could not take vengeance on Loki there and then.

The gods were dumb with grief; but at last Frigg spoke, and offered all her love and favour to anyone who would ride down to *Hel*, the goddess of death, and try to ransom Balder from her. *Hermod*, another of Odin's sons, offered to do this; he was given Odin's magic eight-legged horse *Sleipnir* and set off. Meanwhile the gods prepared Balder's funeral, placing his body on a huge funeral pyre in his own ship Ringhorn. The ship was too heavy to launch and a giantess had to be summoned from *Jötunheim* to push it into the sea. When the giantess arrived, *Thor* was furious at the sight of her, because she was an old enemy of his. But she was there under the gods' protection, and he had to retrain himself. So Thor raised his hammer to bless the ship as it blazed, and as he did so, a dwarf ran under his feet. Still furious, he kicked the dwarf into the fire. Nanna, Balder's wife, had died of grief at losing him, and her body was placed on the pyre as well; and Odin offered the great gold armband *Draupnir*, from which eight other gold bands of the same size came every ninth night.

Meanwhile Hermod had reached Hel's hall in *Niflheim*, and the goddess had agreed to release him provided that everything on earth would weep for him until he was freed. So the gods sent messengers far and wide, and everything wept because Balder was much loved. But as the messengers returned home, they came to a cave where an old giantess sat, called Thokk. They

34

asked her to weep for Balder, but she answered
'The old fellow's son was no use to me alive or
dead: let Hel hold what she has.'
The giantess was Loki in disguise; but because
of her refusal, Balder had to remain in Hel. But
the gods took revenge on Loki in the end.

The other version of the story is told in a book
about the early history of Denmark, written by
Saxo. Saxo regarded the gods as men who,
because they were very clever, had persuaded
the rest of the people to worship them; so he tells
the story in a very different way: Snorri makes
it magical and romantic. Saxo mysterious and
foreboding. But it is also a very different story.
Balder, son of Odin and Hother, son of Helgi,
were rivals for the hand of Nanna, and she
favoured Hother. Balder, driven mad by her
beauty, decided to kill Hother, but before he
could carry out his plan, Hother went hunting,
and losing his way, reached the home of some
mysterious forest maidens. They told him that it
was they who ruled the fortunes of war, and
decided who should be victorious; and they also
warned him to beware of Balder. Then they
vanished. Hother told Nanna's father Gewar of
this, and he said that, although he would prefer
Hother as his daughter's husband, he was afraid
of Balder, who was the son of a god and a mortal
woman, and could only be slain by one particular
sword. This sword belonged to *Miming*, a forest
spirit who lived in cold and impassable country.
Hother set out to gain it, and succeeded in cap-
turing Miming, who gave him the sword in exchange for his freedom. Balder had meanwhile
asked Gewar if he could marry Nanna; and
Gewar had said that he must ask Nanna herself.
Nanna said that she could not marry a god,
because men and gods were too different, and
gods grew weary of mortal wives. Hother now
found an excuse to fight Balder, and in a great
battle at sea, Balder nearly defeated him, because
the gods fought on his side. But Hother cut Thor's
club in half, and the gods fled in dismay. (At this
point Saxo adds: 'If old traditions did not tell us
this, no-one would ordinarily believe that the
gods could be defeated by men', to reassure his
readers that he is not inventing the story). Hother
married Nanna, but soon afterwards was defeated
by Balder, and was forced to flee in turn. The
victory proved a hollow one for Balder, who was
now haunted by visions of Nanna, and became
so ill that he had to be carried round in a chariot.

The kingdom of Denmark was without a
leader, and Hother and Balder fought each other

for the kingship, with varying success. Hother, weary of the struggle, retreated to the forest, where he met the maidens who had first told him about Balder. They encouraged him, and told him that if he could obtain some of the magic food by which Balder kept up his strength he would be victorious. Hother returned to the attack, and on the night before another battle with Balder was to take place, he kept watch, and saw three girls take the magic food to his tent. He followed them to their home, and charmed them with his skill in music, until they were almost ready to give him some of the food. In the end, they refused, saying that they could not cheat Balder in this way, but gave him instead a magic belt which would ensure victory. In the battle, Hother mortally wounded Balder, who lingered on for three days, during which Hel visited him and promised that he should soon feel her embrace. When he died, Odin was furious, and plotted revenge on Hother. This was eventually achieved by his son Boe, who killed Hother in battle but was himself mortally wounded. In the poem *Voluspa*, we learn that Balder will come to rule again after *Ragnarok*; there is no suggestion of this in Saxo, where all the virtues are on the side of Hother, and Balder is painted in the blackest light. It is possible, though difficult to prove, that the *Voluspa* version was affected by the idea of the dying and resurrected Christ. Balder was the father of *Forseti*, the god of justice.

Balor: In Irish myth, Balor was the king of the *Fomorians*, enemies of the *Tuatha De Danann*. He had a huge evil eye which bewitched everyone he looked at; four men were needed to raise the eyelid which covered it. The eye was destroyed by *Lugh* at the second battle of Moytura, and twenty-seven Fomorians were killed by the same sling-shot.

Bastet: An Egyptian goddess, worshipped in the form of a cat, who represented the warmth and light of the sun.

Bat: In Australian aborigine myth, the bat played an important part in the 'dreamtime' or beginning of the world: he was the brother of *Darramulun* and created woman, while in other myths he was the elder brother of Gidja, the moon. Bats appear as ghostly or evil spirits in some American Indian myths: the most important of the bat-gods is *Camazotz*. The Apapocuva Indians of Central America believe that at the end of the world the Eternal Bat and the Blue Jaguar will destroy mankind, while the earth itself is devoured by flames.

Batara Guru: According to a myth from Sumatra, Batara Guru, the sky-god, and his wife had no children. They decided to try doing penance by living very simply to see if this would lead to them being given children, but when they retired to a hut by the seashore, the garden they planted there was destroyed by a serpent. Batara Guru went to chase it away, but it insisted that he should put food in its mouth. He did so, first propping the snake's mouth open in case it bit his hand off; and when he withdrew his hand there was a magic ring on it. With the aid of this he and his wife obtained children. One of their sons created the earth, which was hung on cords from the sky. But the god of the underworld was angry, because the light from the sky no longer reached him, and he destroyed the earth. Only when it was made for the eighth time, with the help of Batara Guru himself, and set on iron pillars, was it safe; but even so the god of the underworld still shakes it angrily from time to time, causing earthquakes.

Baucis and Philemon: The Greek gods *Zeus* and *Hermes* visited Phrygia (in Asia Minor), but found no hospitality except in the cottage of the old couple Philemon and Baucis. In return for their kindness to their guests, and to punish their inhospitable neighbours, the two gods turned the countryside into a lake, in the midst of which Philemon and Baucis' cottage stood, transformed into a temple. The couple wished that they might be the guardians of the temple, and that they might die at the same time. The gods granted their wish, and many years later, as they stood talking outside the shrine, they were both transformed into trees.

Beetle: The Lengua Indians of South America believe that a giant beetle created the world. When he had made the earth, he made evil spirits come out from underneath it; but afterwards he created a man and woman from the grains of earth he had thrown away. They were joined together at first, but Beetle separated them. Among the Sia Indians, there is a myth which tells how Utset gave Beetle a sack of stars and told him to carry them from the underworld to the world above. She forbad him to open it, but he found the sack very heavy, and when he managed to struggle up into the

world above, he bit a tiny hole in one corner to see what was in it. All the stars scattered across the sky, and Utset made the beetle blind because he had disobeyed her. A few stars were left in the sack, and these Utset used to make a few patterns in the sky, the stars we call the Great Bear, Pleiades and Orion's Belt.

Bel: A title meaning 'lord', given to the Babylonian god *Marduk*; it is under this name that he appears in Hebrew stories.

Belenus: A Gaulish god about whom little is known; in Roman times he was identified with *Apollo*.

Bellerophon: Son of Glaucus, king of Corinth in Greece. He was brought up at the court of Argos, where the king's wife Anteia fell in love with him. He did not return her love, and she falsely accused him of trying to seduce her. Her husband sent him to King Iobates, with a sealed letter which asked that Iobates should put him to death. Iobates, unwilling to do this himself, sent him first to kill the *Chimera*, which he did with the help of the winged horse *Pegasus*. He was then sent to fight the *Amazons*, and when he defeated them, an ambush was laid for him on his way back but he killed all his attackers. Iobates realized that the gods must favour him, and gave him his daughter as his bride. But Bellerophon offended the gods by trying to fly to heaven on Pegasus; his children were killed, and he died a wanderer.

Bellona: A minor Roman war-goddess.

Bendigeidfran: Perhaps the same as *Bran* in Irish myth. Bendigeidfran was king of Britain. His brother was *Manawydan*, his half-brothers *Nisien and Efnisien*. He gave his sister Branwen to King Matholwch of Ireland; but Efnisien insulted Matholwch and made Matholwch quarrel with Bran. The quarrel was patched up, but when Matholwch returned to Ireland his subjects mocked him, and he took his revenge by humiliating Branwen. Word of this reached Bendigeidfran, who raised an army and crossed to Ireland; he himself waded across, because the sea was not as deep as it is now. Frightened by Bendigeidfran's army, the Irish made a truce, and offered to make a house for him, since no house had ever been large enough for him before. But when they had built it, they put two hundred bags on the pillars, one on each pillar, with a warrior in each: because they planned to kill Bendigeidfran. Efnisien saw through the trick and killed them all by squeezing them to death. But he went back to his old ways, and threw Bendigeidfran's nephew, whom Matholwch had made king of Ireland under the terms of the truce, into the fire. A great battle followed, in which the Irish were winning at first because they had a magic cauldron which revived dead men if they were thrown into it; then Efnisien got into the cauldron and burst it apart, but died as he did so. Only seven men, all of them British, were left at the end of the battle.

Bendigeidfran was wounded by a poisoned spear, and ordered the others to cut off his head, saying that they were to take it to London and bury it under the White Tower. On the way they would spend seven years at Harlech, where *Rhiannon*'s magic birds would make music to them, and his head would entertain them; and eighty years would pass at Gwales, and they would be carefree and happy, and the head would still entertain them until they opened a door that looked towards Cornwall. All this came to pass as he had foretold; and when they opened the door towards Cornwall, they remembered all their sorrows, and took the head to London. As long as it was buried there no plague ever came across the sea to Britain.

The burial of Bendigeidfran's head is an interesting reminder that the Celts in pagan times particularly worshipped heads; they would decorate their huts with the heads of enemies they had killed, and used to put stone heads in their temples and shrines. Many of these haunting sculptures have survived.

Benten: Daughter of the dragon-king in Japanese myth, goddess of music and eloquence, who appeared from the waves to favour men, and was one of the seven gods and goddesses of good fortune. Her favourite instrument was the *biwa*, a kind of small guitar. Her most famous temples are at Itsuku-shima, where the temple stands on the beach, and at Chikubu-shima, where the temple is on an island in the lake.

Bergelmir: In the Norse story of the beginning of the world, Bergelmir was the only one of the frost-giants to survive when the giant *Ymir* was killed. All the rest were swept away and drowned in the torrent of his blood, which became the sea, but Bergelmir escaped in some kind of vessel, and was the father of a new race of giants.

Berserks: Originally Norse warriors inspired by the war god *Odin* to fight in a kind of frenzy or trance; they used no armour and yet were supposed to be proof against any weapons. Our modern phrase 'going berserk' comes from the way these warriors behaved in battle.

Bes: God of the ancient Egyptians, popular with ordinary men and women. He was shown as a dwarf wearing a lionskin, and he was patron of feasts and dancing and other pleasures. He also guarded men against snakes.

Bestla: In Norse myth, the wife of *Bor* and mother of the god *Odin*.

Bhaga: A minor Hindu god who grants wealth; he is also the god of marriage. He is one of the *Adityas*.

Bhagiratha: Bhagiratha was a Hindu sage whose ancestors, the sons of *Sagara*, had been burnt to ashes by their enemy Kapila. In order to purify their ashes, he persuaded *Shiva* to allow the sacred river *Ganges* to flow down to earth. Bhagiratha led it across the land to the place where the ashes lay, and then to the sea, and it has flowed there ever since.

Bharata: 1. An Indian king who worshipped *Vishnu*, and became a hermit in order to worship him. He rescued a fawn from drowning, but became so fond of it that he forgot Vishnu. When he died, he was born again as a deer, and by his merit was reborn once more as a Brahman, a member of the highest rank of Indian society. But he was physically handicapped, and could only serve as a bearer in religious processions. However, he meditated on Vishnu, and was able to gain exemption from being born again.

2. The hero after whom the princes of the *Pandavas* were named; their wars, the wars of the sons of Bharata, are recounted in the great Indian epic called *Mahabharata*.

3. Half-brother to *Rama*, the central figure of the Indian epic *Ramayana*. His mother, jealous of her stepson, had Rama sent into exile so that Bharata could rule in his place; but Bharata sought out Rama in exile and tried to persuade him to return and take the throne. Rama insisted on completing his exile, so Bharata returned and ruled as regent; as a symbol of Rama's rule, he placed a pair of Rama's shoes

on the empty throne. At the end of Rama's exile and wanderings, and of his war with *Ravana*, Bharata handed the kingdom back to him. Ⓒ

Bhima: Brother of *Arjuna*, son of the wind, and one of the five *Pandava* princes whose adventures form the Indian epic called *Mahabharata*. He was immensely strong, and had a huge appetite: he used to eat as much as his four brothers together. His weapon was a club, and his skill with it made his cousin *Duryodhana* jealous. Duryodhana poisoned him, and threw his body in the river Ganges; but the *Nagas* brought Bhima back to life. From then on the two were deadly enemies; and when the five brothers were in exile Duryodhana tried unsuccessfully to burn them alive in their house. Bhima defended *Draupadi* during the exile, and was the chief champion of the Pandavas in the battle against the Kauravas. Among those he killed were Duhshasana, who had once insulted Draupadi: Bhima took his revenge by drinking his blood, and on the last day of the battle also achieved his revenge on Duryodhana. Duryodhana had made Draupadi sit on his thigh, so Bhima now smashed his thigh with a blow from his club, although this was an unfair blow; and then he killed him. Duryodhana's father tried to revenge his son by crushing Bhima to death in his arms, but the god *Krishna* put an iron stake in Bhima's place, which was shattered.

He was a great enemy of the *Asuras*, and attacked them so fiercely that they promised not to war against men any longer, but only to fight with the gods.

Bhishma: In the Hindu epic, the *Mahabharata*, the son of the goddess of the Ganges and King Santanu. When his father was very old, he decided to marry again, and Bhishma found him a bride. But her parents would only agree to the match if Bhishma agreed never to claim the throne after his father's death, and never to get married himself, so that their daughter's sons would be kings. Bhishma agreed, and acted as regent when his father died. The eldest of his two half-brothers was killed in battle because he ignored Bhishma's advice, and the younger died without children. Their relations, Pandu and Dhritarashtra, succeeded to the throne, and Bhishma acted as regent once more. He also brought up their children, the *Pandavas* and Kauravas, who later quarrelled. Although Bhishma tried to make up the quarrel, he finally took the side of the Kauravas, and was made their commander-in-

chief. In the great batt'^ he refused to fight
against *Arjuna*, until *Duryodhana* taunted him
with being a coward. Arjuna mortally wounded
him with a shower of arrows, and he died fifty-
eight days later.

Bhrigu: A Hindu sage or *maharishi*. He was
once sent by the Brahmans, the priest-class in
Indian society, to discover which gods were
worthy of their honour and sacrifices. He first
visited *Shiva*, who was making love to his wife
and paid no attention to Bhrigu, who cursed him
to be worshipped only in an unmentionable
shape by people who were neither pious nor
respectful. He then went to *Brahma*, who was
surrounded by his sages, and barely noticed
Bhrigu who dismissed him as useless; but when
he went to *Vishnu* he found him asleep. To wake
him up, he stamped on his chest; Vishnu, instead
of being angry, said that he was honoured to
have been touched by a Brahman's foot. So
Bhrigu reported to the Brahmans that Vishnu
was the only god worthy of their respect and
devotion. See also *Agastya*.

Bifrost Bridge: This bridge led from *Asgard*,
home of the Norse gods, to the Well of *Urd*, where
they met each day. It was a fiery rainbow, which
only the gods could cross, and which kept mortals
and giants out of Asgard. It was guarded by the
ever-watchful *Heimdall*. Before the great last
battle of the gods, at *Ragnarok*, this bridge will be
shattered.

Blue Jay: The Indians of the Pacific coast of
North America regard Blue Jay as the creator: in
particular, he decreed how each bird and animal
should live, where each was to make its home
and what it was to eat. He also appears as a
protector of mankind, in a story in which he
captures two people who had murdered children,
and makes them promise not to do it again. His
exploits are similar to those of *Raven*.

Bochica: In the myths of the Chibcha Indians
of Colombia, Bochica was an elderly bearded
man who came from the east and taught them
all kinds of skills, such as how to weave cotton,
grow fruit and build houses. He also taught them
to worship the gods, and then went on his way.
After he had gone, a woman appeared, who tried
to make the people forget his teaching by making
them do nothing but dance and feast; but
Bochica came back and turned her into an owl.

He also defended the Chibcha from the wrath of *Chibchachum*. Like *Tonapa*, the early Spanish settlers thought that Bochica was the apostle St Thomas, who was supposed to have travelled throughout the world teaching the Gospel.

Bodhidharma: A Buddhist monk worshipped as a god by the Chinese; patron of the Zen Buddhist sect.

Bodhisattva: In Buddhist myth, the 'Buddha-to-be', who will come to earth when his help is needed. Any man can become a Bodhisattva if he performs sufficient good works in his earlier lives; the Bodhisattvas live in the heaven of the gods while awaiting their appointed time for rebirth. The next Bodhisattva is *Maitreya*, though there are many others, including *Avalokiteshvara* and *Manjushri*.

Bolthorn: Norse giant whose daughter *Bestla* was the mother of *Odin*, leader of the gods.

Bolverk: One of the many names adopted by the Norse god *Odin* on his adventures; this was his disguise when he visited Baugi and *Suttung*.

Bona Dea: A Roman goddess, whose name means the 'good goddess'; she was said to have been a mortal, who drank too much, and whose husband beat her to death with a myrtle rod. But this was probably only an attempt to explain why neither wine nor myrtle could be used in her rites, unless the wine was called milk. She was a very ancient goddess, and her true story was forgotten before such things were written down.

Bor: Son of the first man, *Buri*, in Norse myth, and father of the Norse gods *Odin* and his brothers *Vili* and *Ve*.

Boreas: The spirit of the north wind in Greek myth. His sons were the Argonauts *Zetes and Calais*.

Bragi: The Norse god of poetry and eloquence, husband of the goddess *Idunn*. He was a minor god, whose job was to prepare *Valhalla* for new-comers; and *Loki* taunted him by hiding among the benches in the hall and avoiding battle. Since 'bragi' meant leader, and *Odin* is also the god of poetry, this may have once been a name for Odin himself rather than a separate god.

43

Brahma: The creator in Hindu myth, he is the first god of the three chief gods, Brahma, *Vishnu* and *Shiva*. He was born from the world-egg at the beginning of time, and created the world, which will remain for two thousand million years. At the end of this time, which is one day to Brahma himself, the world will be burnt, though the gods survive, and Brahma will recreate the world after he has slept. This will happen for a hundred years in Brahma's time, after which everything will go back to its original state. Although he is a very important god, he is no longer worshipped; in early writings he appears as *Prajapati* and there are many different accounts of how he set about the work of creation. Some even deny that he was a separate god, and say that he was *Vishnu* in another form, and the *Mahabharata* describes how he was born from a lotus which sprang from Vishnu's navel. He was red in colour and had four heads; originally there were five, but one was destroyed by Shiva when Brahma mocked him. In later poems, Brahma is said to favour the enemies of the gods such as the *Rakshasas* and *Bali*, and he even appears as the charioteer and son of the god *Rudra*. Unlike the great creator-gods of western myth, he is not very much respected.

Bran: King Bran of Ireland once heard strange and lovely music as he walked outside his palace. He fell asleep, and when he awoke he found a magic branch lying beside him. When he went back into the palace, he met the woman who had made the music and brought the branch; who told him that she came from an island where evil was unknown, and where such music was always heard. Its inhabitants lived at ease, drinking and laughing. She told Bran to set out for this island, which was called the Island of Women.

On the way Bran met his brother the sea-god *Manannan*, who told him in a song that what Bran saw as the sea was for him an immortal wood, peopled by men and women who never died; the salmon were calves and lambs, and its rivers flowed with honey. Bran and his companions came to the land of joy, and sent a man ashore, but he refused to leave again. Then they went on to the Island of Women, where they were welcomed by the queen. They stayed for a year, but grew homesick; the queen let them go but warned them not to set foot in Ireland. When Bran approached the shore, he hailed the people on land and told them his name; and they said 'We do not know Bran, but his setting out is in our ancient tales'. One of the crew leapt ashore, but became a heap of dust when his foot touched the earth. Bran then told of his adventures and set out again for the Island of Women.

See also *Bendigeidfran*; Bendigeidfran may be a corruption of the Welsh for Bran the Blessed, and both he and Bran have many points in common.

Breathmaker: In Seminole Indian stories, Breathmaker taught men how to fish and to dig wells. He also made the Milky Way by blowing at the sky, and Seminole Indians go along it when they die to a 'city in the western sky', unless they have been wicked, in which case their spirits stay in the ground where they are buried. Animals also went to the 'city in the western sky', and an Indian's animals used to be killed when he died, so that they could go with him.

Breidablik: The hall of the god *Balder* in Norse myth, where nothing impure can be found.

Bres: Bres was king of the *Fomorians* when they ruled all Ireland: he was overthrown because he was mean and exacted great tribute. His feasts were such that his guests' 'knives were not greased by them, nor did their breath smell of ale'. *Dagda* had to build a fort for him, while *Ogma* was forced to fetch his firewood. His fall was brought about by a satire of Coirbre, the poet of the *Tuatha De Danann*, the first such satire to be made in Ireland. After this satire was always regarded with awe by the Irish, who thought that it had magical powers.

After his capture in battle, he offered to ensure that Irish cattle should always give milk, and there would be four harvests a year; but this was not enough for his captors, and he had to offer to give advice on ploughing and sowing as well before he was spared.

Brhaspati: The 'Lord of Devotion' in Hindu myth, also called Brahmanaspati, and sometimes regarded as the same as *Agni*. He was magnificent in his appearance, and was the bringer of light to the world; he gave victory and long life to his worshippers.

Briareus: One of the three *Hecatoncheires*.

Brigit: Although little is known about her as a pagan goddess, Brigit seems to have been worshipped under various names by all the Celtic peoples, Gauls, Irish and British. She was said by the Irish to have been the daughter of the *Dagda*,

and was the patron of poets. Many of the stories about the saint called Brigit come from pagan myths: for instance, St Brigit was said to have been born at sunrise, neither in a house nor out of it. She could hang her cloak to dry on a ray of the sun, while any house in which she stayed seemed to have a halo of fire around it. She and nineteen nuns guarded a sacred fire which never went out. All these details belong to pagan rather than Christian belief.

Briseis: The captive girl over whom *Achilles* and *Agamemnon* quarrelled during the *Trojan War*.

Brisingamen: The necklace of the Norse goddess *Freyja*, one of the great treasures of the gods. It was made for her by four dwarfs in return for her embraces. *Loki* once stole it, but *Heimdall* retrieved it from him.

Britomartis: A goddess from Crete, very similar to the Greek *Artemis*, and later thought of as one of Artemis' nymphs. *Minos* loved her, but she escaped from him when he pursued her by leaping over a cliff into the sea, where she was saved by fishermen who caught her in their nets.

Brynhild: One of the *Valkyries*, whom the Norse hero *Sigurd* the Volsung won by breaking through a ring of fire on a mountain-top where she lay in a magic sleep. *Odin* had placed this spell on her because she had given victory to the wrong man in a battle. She and Sigurd never married, but she had a second funeral pyre built and died with him as though she were his wife.

Buchis: A sacred bull kept by the Egyptian priests and regarded as *Ra* and *Osiris* in animal form, though it had originally been sacred to *Menthu*.

Buku: Sky-god of several West African peoples, sometimes worshipped as a goddess and creator of everything, including the other gods.

Bumba: The creator-god in the myths of the Bushongo tribe of southern Africa. One day Bumba had a bad stomach-ache; he was sick, and the sun, moon and stars came out of him: these were followed by eight living creatures, from which all other animals are descended.

Buri: In Norse myth, the first of the race of men and gods. He is described as a man whom the cow *Audhumla* licked from the ice-blocks of *Ginnungagap*, but his descendants were the gods *Odin*, *Vili* and *Ve*.

Burkhan: The creator in Buriat myths from Central Asia. In the beginning there was only water, but Burkhan persuaded a duck to dive down and bring up soil, from which he created the earth: at first it was flat, but the devil had also obtained some earth and used it to create mountains. Burkhan created man as well; and at first men were covered with hair. He went on a journey, leaving a dog to guard them. Now dogs at that time had no fur; and the devil bribed the dog with the promise of hair like man's. So the devil robbed men of their hair, and made them subject to sickness and death.

Byggvir and Beyla: Minor Norse god and goddess, possibly, since their names are connected with barley from which ale is brewed, the spirits of ale and mead.

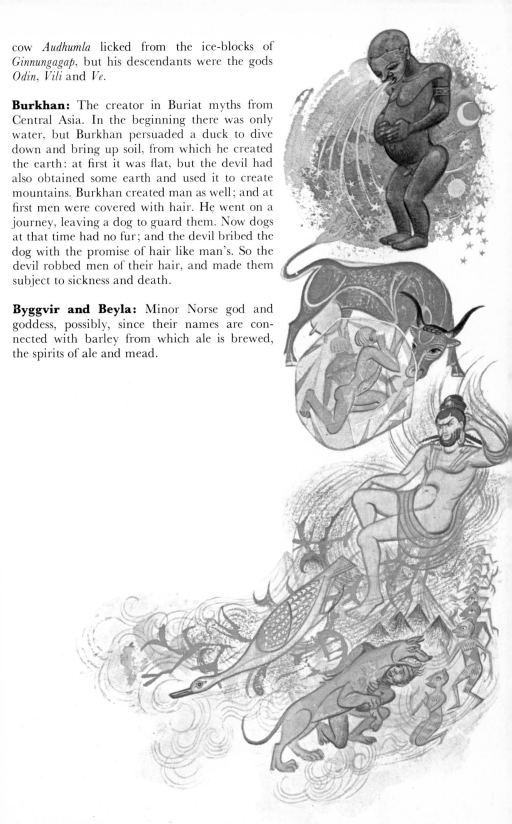

Cabiroi: Gods of fertility worshipped in northern Greece and in Asia Minor. Their cult was mysterious, and little is known about it. They seem to have been protectors of seamen, and there were four of them in all. One of them was sometimes said to be the same as *Hermes*.

Cacus: A Roman god, probably taken over from the Etruscan people. In Etruscan myth, he seems to have been a very handsome youth who was a marvellous singer; but in later Roman stories he was a monster who stole the cattle of *Geryon* from *Heracles*, as Heracles travelled through Italy on his way home. In both stories Heracles killed him.

Cadmus: Sent by *Agenor* in Greek myth to search for his sister *Europa*. *Apollo* told him to stop searching and to build a city instead; he was to follow a certain cow, and was to found the new city where she lay down. He did so, sacrificed the cow to *Athene*, and began Cadmeia or Thebes. The only spring nearby was guarded by a dragon sacred to *Ares*, which Cadmus slew in order to get water. Athene told him to draw its teeth and to sew them; a crop of armed men sprang up, but Cadmus tricked them into attacking each other instead of him. He had to do a year's penance in exile for slaying the dragon. At the end of the year, he had regained the gods' favour, who gave him the daughter of Ares and *Aphrodite*, *Harmonia*, as his wife. In his later years he journeyed to Illyria (Yugoslavia) and was changed, like Harmonia, into an immortal, harmless serpent.

Caeneus: A Greek girl loved by *Poseidon*, who overcame her by force. At her own request, she was turned into a man and made invulnerable. He was one of the *Lapiths* who fell at the battle with the *centaurs*. Because he could not be wounded, he was killed by being trampled deep into the earth under the centaurs' hooves.

Cagn: A supernatural being associated with the *Mantis* among the Bushmen of South Africa. Cagn is said to have created everything, and at first to have been kind to men 'but he got spoilt through fighting so many things'.

Calchas: The prophet of the Greeks in the *Trojan War*. It was he who demanded the sacrifice of *Iphigeneia* and the return of *Chryseis* to her father.

48

Calliope: The Greek *muse* of epic poetry, and mother of *Orpheus*.

Callisto: One of the Greek nymphs who attended *Artemis*. *Zeus* loved her, and she yielded to him, for which Artemis banished her. After her son Arcas was born, *Hera* turned her into a she-bear out of jealousy. Arcas found the bear in a shrine of Zeus, where no animals were allowed, and was about to shoot it when Zeus transformed him and his mother into the Great Bear and Little Bear constellations in the heavens.

Calypso: An immortal nymph who detained *Odysseus* on the Greek island of Ogygia for seven years, as he tried to make his way home after the *Trojan War*.

Camaxtli: War-god of the Mexican tribe called Tlascaltecs, rivals of the Aztecs, later adopted by the Aztecs themselves, and identified with *Xipe Totec*.

Camazotz: The bat-god of Maya myth, one of the demons of the underworld. See *Hunapu*.

Caoilte: The last survivor of the followers of the Irish hero *Fionn*, who was said to have lived so long that he met St Patrick when he first brought Christianity to Ireland. He told St Patrick the stories of Fionn and his men, and the saint gave him his blessing. Although St Patrick was afraid that such tales would keep men from their prayers, angels commanded him to write them down.

Capaneus: One of the *Seven Against Thebes*. He was struck down by a thunderbolt when he scaled the wall of Thebes and was about to enter the city, because he boasted that not even *Zeus* could now keep him out of the town.

Caragabi: According to the Choco Indians of western Colombia, the creator and teacher of mankind was Caragabi, born from the saliva of the high god Tatzitzebe. It was he who placed the sun, moon and stars in the sky, and he caused the tree which contained the spirit of life to be filled. He organized some men into families, but others he turned into the different kinds of animals. He showed men how to gather food plants. When his work was done, he retired to the sky; but his rival Tutruica continually tries to undo his work. Caragabi will return after the

world has been destroyed by fire.

Carancho: In Toba Indian myth, Carancho (Hawk) was a hero who taught man how to use tools, how to practise medicine and how to hunt. But at the same time he made game animals swift and difficult to kill because otherwise men would have wiped them all out. He was a great slayer of evil men and creatures: each night he beat his magician's drum as he waited to hear of the next monster. He was ready to take on impossible tasks, but always triumphed by his cunning and magic. Among the fearful creatures he killed were a man who had a sharp leg which he used to kill people, a man-eating bird, and a monster who caught men in a trap. When women first appeared, they had come down from the sky on a rope to steal food from men: but a bird cut the rope, and they had to stay on earth. They were wild and fierce, and men could not make love to them until Carancho had tamed them.

Carmenta: Perhaps a Roman goddess of fate or birth; her priestesses cast the fortunes of children when they were born.

Cassandra: Daughter of King *Priam* of Troy, she was loved by the Greek god *Apollo*. Although he granted her the gift of prophecy, she refused to yield to him. Because he could not take away the gift, he decreed that although she would always prophesy truly, she would never be believed. When Troy fell, she was taken as a slave by *Agamemnon*, and was killed with him by *Aegisthus* and *Clytemnestra*.

Cassiopeia: Mother of *Andromeda*.

Castor and Pollux: Castor and Pollux (or Polydeuces, as the Greeks called him) were the twin sons of *Leda*; Pollux was the son of *Zeus* and was immortal, while Castor, being the son of Tyndareus, a mere mortal, was subject to death. They took part in the expedition of the *Argo* under *Jason*. Later Castor was killed in battle; but Pollux prayed that he could share his immortality with his twin brother, and Zeus allowed them to spend alternate days in *Olympus* and in *Hades*. They were worshipped in Rome from very early days, and appeared in the city in 499 BC to announce the great victory at Lake Regilius which freed the Romans from the tyranny of the Tarquins. A temple was built on the place where they watered their horses.

Ccoa: The Kauri Indians of southern Peru believe that their lives are controlled by a cat-spirit called Ccoa, who lives on a nearby mountain. He is described as a large cat, standing about eighteen inches high, with phosphorescent eyes. It is he who brings lightning and hail, which is his method of stealing the crops near harvest time. He is the patron of the sorcerers, who grow rich in his service and prosper, as long as they remember to provide the right offerings at the right time, as Ccoa's favours have to be bought. Ordinary people can appease his anger by the right offerings. Children who die before they are baptised become evil spirits serving Ccoa. Ccoa himself is a servant of the aukis or mountain spirits.

Cecrops: A kind of dim ancestor figure to the Greeks, he was said to be half-man and half-snake. Many noble families claimed descent from his daughters.

Centaurs: The children of the Greek hero *Ixion* and the goddess *Nephele* who were half-horse half-man. With the exceptions of *Chiron* and Pholus they were violent and quickly excited, and had little respect for the gods. Their main vice was getting drunk; *Heracles* had a famous battle with them after he had made one of them open a wine-jar for him. The other centaurs swarmed up, attracted by the smell of the wine, and Heracles had to fight them off. At the wedding of *Pirithous* and *Hippodameia*, the *Lapith* chieftain, they got drunk and tried to carry off the women, including the bride. The Lapiths, with *Theseus'* help, fought them off. See also *Chiron* and *Deianeira*.

They may have been a rugged hill-people from Thrace who were great horsemen, transformed into a myth by the more civilized Greeks.

Centzonuitznaua: The four hundred brothers of the Aztec god *Huitzilopochtli*, who tried to kill him when he was born, but were killed by him. They were worshipped as the gods of the southern stars, while Centzon Mimixcoa were the four hundred gods of the northern stars.

Cephalus: Greek hero from Athens, who owned the magic hound from which no beast could escape. It was turned to stone when *Amphitryon* borrowed it to capture an uncatchable fox. He also had a spear which could not miss, and was a great hunter. His wife Procris was jealous of his

constant hunting, thinking he must be having a love-affair. She spied on him, and when he called on the breeze (Aura) to cool him at the end of the day, she started, thinking that this must be the name of her rival. Cephalus threw the spear at the bushes in which she was hidden, mistaking her movement for that of a deer, and killed her.

Cepheus: Father of *Andromeda*.

Cerberus: Three-headed hound which guarded the Greek underworld, *Hades*. He admitted anyone who wanted to enter, but devoured those who tried to get out. *Heracles* overpowered him as one of his twelve labours, and took him to King *Eurystheus* before returning him.

Ceres: The Roman goddess of vegetation, identified with the Greek *Demeter* when the worship of Demeter was introduced to Rome on the instructions written in the Sibylline Books.

Cernobog: The pagan Slav tribes of eastern Europe worshipped a god of good and a god of evil; the latter was called Cernobog, the 'black god', but little is known about him. Christians said that he was the same as the Devil.

Cernunnos: Although a 'horned god', shown as a man with horns or antlers, was widely worshipped by Celtic peoples, only one carving giving a name for this god has come down to us, an altar from Gaul on which he is called Cernunnos.

Ceyx: Husband of *Alcyone*.

Chac, Chacs: Chac (lightning) was the rain-god of the Mayas; his other titles were 'the cutter', the 'opener of the pouch' or 'lord of the nine generations'. He was one of the four great lords, lord of the east. Drawings and sculptures show him as a red man with a long nose. Farmers in particular worshipped him, because they depended on the rain. In Aztec myth he was known as *Tlaloc*. In later myths, the chacs were minor gods rather than one great god; at first they were four in number, one for each direction of the compass, and they worshipped together with the *bacabs*. The hearts of wild animals were sacrificed to the chacs at the spring festival. Modern versions of the myth, under the influence of Christianity, make the chacs little bearded men who live in the sixth heaven and take their orders from 'Jesucristo'. There are different kinds of chacs: some make steady rain, others heavy downpours, but they both work by riding through the air on horses and sprinkling rain from their gourds. They are very fond of smoking, and throw down their cigarette ends from heaven, which become shooting stars.

Chalchiuhtlicue: The Aztec goddess of water, wife or sister of *Tlaloc*, the rain-god, with whom she ruled over the waters. She could be both a goddess who made things clean and pure, and a destroyer who drowned men. See *Five Suns*.

Changing Woman: In the stories of the Navaho Indians and other Apache Indians, Changing Woman was the mother of two great heroes Killer of Enemies and *Child of the Water*. She could change her age as she wanted to, and could become a girl or an old woman: she was the moon, while Killer of Enemies was the sun. For another version of their story, see *Nagenatzani*.

Ch'ang-O: The moon-goddess in Chinese myth, represented as a very lovely girl. She was the wife of *Shên I*.

Charon: The ancient boatman who ferried souls after death to the Greek underworld, plying across the river *Styx*. He had to be paid for his passage, so the dead were buried with a coin in their mouth. *Heracles* forced him to take him over to the underworld even though he was still alive, and for this Charon was punished by being put in chains for a year.

Charybdis: The whirlpool opposite the home of the monster *Scylla*; the Greek heroes *Odysseus* and *Jason* both narrowly escaped from it.

Ch'eng Huang: The Chinese gods of the city, literally 'the gods of walls and moats', responsible for local affairs. Each place had its own god, usually a distinguished local person who was appointed after his death.

Chen Jen: 'The Perfect' in Chinese Taoist myth, those who are perfect in the knowledge of Tao, the Way. They have no physical bodies and can travel between the spiritual and physical worlds.

Cherruve: Spirits of shooting stars in the myths of the Araucanian Indians of South America, drawn as man-headed serpents.

53

Chibchachum: Local god of the Indians near Bogota in South America, who was rejected by them. He sent a flood to punish them, but they appealed to *Bochica*, who saved them and punished Chibchachum by sending him to hold up the earth. Earthquakes were supposed to have been caused by Chibchachum shifting his burden on his shoulders when he grew tired.

Chicomecoatl: The Aztec goddess of crops, particularly of maize.

Chiconamictlan: The home of the dead in Mexican myth. The dead man was given a water-jar and magical spells for his journey there; with the various spells he was able to pass the 'clashing mountains', roads guarded by monsters, eight deserts and eight hills. After he had appeared before *Mictlantecuhtli*, lord of the dead, he travelled on to the stream surrounding Chiconamictlan, carried by the red dog which had been sacrificed to go with him as his companion.

Chih Nü: Daughter of the Chinese Jade Emperor, *Yu Huang*. One day she went down to earth to bathe, and a cowherd took away her clothes on the advice of his ox (who was also his guardian spirit). Without them she was unable to return to heaven, and so married the cowherd. They had two children, but at the end of seven years she found out where he had put her clothes and went back to heaven. The cowherd, in despair, asked his ox what he should do. 'Put each of your children in a basket, tie the baskets to the ends of a pole, and put it on your shoulders. Then hold my tail, and we will go to heaven'. He did this, and found himself before Yu Huang. He demanded to see his wife, and Yu Huang sent for her. When she admitted that he was her husband, Yu Huang made the cowherd immortal. But he separated them: as Chih Nü was goddess of a star east of the Heavenly River, he gave the cowherd a star to the west. They were only able to meet on the seventh day of the seventh month of each year, when all the magpies in the world took up a twig, and made a bridge for them across the river.

Chih Sung-Tzu: The Chinese lord of the rain, who lived on the slopes of the *Kᵛun-Lun* Mountain. His bird was the one-legged shang yang, whose appearance on earth foretold rain.

Child of the Water: In Navaho and Apache

Indian stories from the south-western United States, Child of the Water was the son of *Changing Woman* and the rain or a waterfall. He and his brother Killer of Enemies had many adventures together, mostly concerned with the killing of monsters, such as a giant whose body was made of four coats of rock: Child of the Water shot off the three outer coats, so that he could see the giant's heart beating under the inner coat. Then he shot the giant through the heart and killed him. Child of the Water also created animals by cutting up an antelope he had killed and naming each piece of meat as a different animal. Their characters vary from tribe to tribe: in many cases Killer of Enemies is the powerful leader, in others it is Child of the Water. For another version of their story see *Nagenatzani*.

Chimera: A monster with a lion's head, goat's body and snake's tail, slain by the Greek hero *Bellerophon*.

Chiminagagua: In the myths of the Chibcha Indians of Colombia, Chiminagagua was the creator of the world, who sent out great black birds to carry the sun's rays throughout the world. He sent *Bochica* to teach mankind how to live.

Chingichnich: The Californian Indians say that Chingichnich was the creator, who made the first man and woman out of clay. He was also the god who set out the sacred rites of the initiation ceremony, which all boys had to undergo before they were accepted as men. He set out the rules for everyday life, and taught the first secrets of medicine. See *Wiyot*.

Chiron: The gentlest and wisest of the *centaurs*. He was skilled in medicine, archery and other arts, and was the tutor of such Greek heroes as *Achilles* and *Jason*. *Heracles* accidentally wounded him in his battle with the other centaurs. Because the wound was made with an arrow dipped in the *Hydra*'s blood, it was agonizing and incurable. In the end, Chiron exchanged himself for *Prometheus* so that he could find relief from the pain by dying, as he would otherwise have been immortal and condemned to unending torment. See also *Hippolytus* for another story of his death.

Chryseis: Daughter of Chryses, the priest of *Apollo* at Chryse. The Greek leader *Agamemnon* took her as a slave when Chryse was plundered

during the *Trojan War*. She was returned to her father after Apollo had sent a plague on the Greek camp. Agamemnon took *Briseis* from *Achilles* instead, thus starting their famous quarrel.

Chuchaviva: The rainbow, worshipped as a god by the Chibcha Indians of Colombia; it first appeared at *Bochica*'s command after the great flood; but *Chibchachum* put a curse on it, saying that people would die when it appeared. Chuchaviva helped people who were attacked by fevers.

Chu Jung: Chinese god of fire, who also punished those who broke heaven's laws. He was originally an emperor, called the Red Emperor, who taught the people how to use fire and who reigned for two hundred years.

Chung K'uei: Chung K'uei was a Chinese doctor who was cheated of a first-class degree in the great public examinations on which a man's career depended. He committed suicide on the palace steps; and when the emperor of the time discovered the reason, he awarded him a burial equal to the rank of a member of the imperial family. In gratitude, Chung K'uei protected the emperors from attacks by demons.

Chuvalete: The Morning Star, worshipped as the protector of mankind from the sun's fierce heat by the Cora Indians of Central America.

Cimmerians: A people visited by *Odysseus* on his voyage to *Hades*; the Greeks believed that they lived in a land of mist and darkness on the edge of the stream of *Ocean*.

Cinteotl: Aztec god of maize.

Cipactli: The sea-monster from which the Aztec gods *Tonacatecuhtli* and *Tonacacihuatl* formed the earth.

Cipactonal: see *Oxomoco*.

Circe: The daughter of *Helios*, the Greek sun-god, and Clymene, she was a great worker of magic who lived on the island of Aeaea. *Odysseus* and his men arrived there in their wanderings; she turned half his crew into pigs by giving them a magic drink. Odysseus, armed with the counter-charm, the herb moly, which *Hermes* gave him,

56

frightened Circe into breaking the spell and promising never to harm him or his men. After living with her for a year, he demanded that she should show him the way home, and on her instructions he went to *Hades* to question the seer *Tiresias*.

Cit-Bolon-Tum: Medicine-god of the Mayas.

Citlallatonac and Citlalicue: Names for the Aztec *Tonacatecuhtli* and *Tonacacihuatl*, meaning 'Lord and lady of the Starry Zones'.

Ciuacoatl: Goddess of the earth in Aztec myth; her voice was sometimes heard in the night, and its roaring meant that war was at hand.

Ciuateoteo: In Aztec myth, spirits of the underworld who lived under the protection of *Ciuacoatl*. They carried the sun down from its highest point in the sky to its home in the underworld. They sometimes left the underworld in the shape of eagles, bringing illness to children. They were either the souls of women who had died giving birth to children or who had become warriors.

Clio: The *muse* of history.

Cliodna: An Irish goddess of the otherworld. who had three birds with brilliant plumage whose song could lull the sick to sleep; they were fed on magic apples.

Clotho: One of the Three *Fates*; she spun the thread of fate, and was portrayed by the Greeks as holding a distaff. Alternatively, she was supposed to sing the happenings of the present.

Clytemnestra: Wife of the Greek leader *Agamemnon*, seduced by his cousin *Aegisthus* in revenge for the treatment of his father by Agamemnon's father (see *Atreus*). She helped Aegisthus to murder Agamemnon on his return from the *Trojan War*, because she hated Agamemnon for having sacrificed her daughter *Iphigeneia*. *Orestes* avenged his father's death by murdering his mother and Aegisthus.

Clytie: A nymph who was loved by the Greek sun-god *Helios*; when he deserted her, she gazed so long at him that she was turned into a heliotrope.

Coatlicue: 'The lady of the serpent skirt', an

Aztec goddess of the earth and springtime. Her appearance was awesome: she wore a necklace of severed hearts and hands, from which hung a skull, and had claws instead of hands and feet. She fed on human corpses. She was wife of *Mixcoatl* and mother of *Huitzilopochthli* and *Quetzalcoatl*.

Coeus: One of the old gods or *Titans* in Greek myth, son of *Uranus* and *Gaia*. He was father of the witch-goddess *Hecate*.

Con or Coniraya: A god of the Indians of the coast of Peru, who was sometimes thought of as the same as *Viracocha*. He was the son of the sun, a being who lived in the air, and moved rapidly across the earth, transforming its features as he went by levelling hills and making the plains into mountains. He created men and women and gave them plants for food. But the race of men offended him, and he sent a great drought. *Pachacamac*, another son of the sun, turned these first people into wild cats, and created new men and women.

Conall Cernach: One of the rivals of *Cuchulainn* in Irish myth for the title of champion of Ulster. In the story of *Mac Datho's Boar*, he devoured a giant boar on which the chief of Connaught and his men were about to feast; and a day never passed without him killing one of the men of Connaught. He was unable to prevail against Cuchulainn, but he remained his friend, and it was he who avenged Cuchulainn's death by killing Lugaid.

Conchobar: Conchobar was king of Ulster in *Cuchulainn*'s lifetime, according to Irish myths.

Coqui-Xee: The creator, or god of the beginning of things, in Mixtec myth.

Core: Another name for *Persephone*, daughter of *Demeter* and *Zeus*.

Cormac: On the morning of the feast of Beltane (May Day), the Irish King Cormac met an armed man carrying a branch with three golden apples on it, as he walked on the ramparts of Tara. The branch made marvellous music when shaken, and its sounds healed the sick and wounded by making them sleep. Cormac asked the warrior where he had come from: 'From a land where there is no old age, decay, sorrow,

envy, jealousy, hatred or arrogance', he replied.
Cormac was given the branch in exchange for
three wishes. But a year later the warrior reappeared, wished for Cormac's wife, son and
daughter as his three wishes, and took them
away. Cormac pursued him; a mist came down,
and Cormac found himself alone when it cleared,
before a citadel with bronze ramparts. He
entered the citadel and found himself at the
Spring of Knowledge (*Segais*). He was welcomed
by an armed man and a lovely girl, who gave
him a feast, after which Cormac told how he was
searching for his family. The man lulled him to
sleep with a magic song, and when he awoke his
family were there. A magic gold cup which had
broken in pieces because three lies had been told
over it, was brought, and was mended when
Cormac was told three truths; neither his wife
nor daughter had seen a man, nor his son a
woman, since they were taken from him. The
man revealed that he was *Manannan Mac Lir*, and
that Cormac was now in the Land of Promise.
Cormac awoke next morning with his family at
Tara, and found the golden cup at his side as
proof of his adventure.

Coronis: The Greek god *Apollo* loved the nymph
Coronis, and *Asclepius* was their son. But Coronis
preferred a mortal lover, and the god's messenger,
the crow, told him about this. Apollo shot Coronis
in a fury, but regretted it as soon as he had done
it. The crow, which was white before this, was
changed into a black bird, while the centaur
Chiron saved *Asclepius* and looked after him.

Corybantes: The attendants of the Near
Eastern goddess *Cybele*; they were dancers, skilled
in magic and the cure of illness.

Covetina: A British water-goddess, who had a
shrine near a spring at Carranburgh on Hadrian's
Wall. She is shown in sculptures lying on a leaf
floating on the water, with a goblet in one hand.

Coyolxauhqui: Half-sister of *Huitzilopochtli*, the
Aztec war-god; she urged her four hundred
brothers to kill Huitzilopochtli, but he overcame
them and killed her with a flaming serpent,
keeping her head which became the moon.

Coyote: In North American Indian myths and
folktales, Coyote plays a very prominent part.
He is spoken of as the creator or as the teacher of
men, but he also appears in stories in which he is

a trickster, cunning and taking pleasure in other people's misfortune. His two characters often appear in the same story; but the Navaho Indians use different names for Coyote the creator and Coyote the trickster. The Navaho creation story tells how the first man and woman originally lived in the first world; but this was too small for them, and they moved upwards to the second world. For various reasons they also left this, and reached the third world. This was wide and pleasant, but it was inhabited by a water-monster, Tieholtsodi. Coyote stole the water-monster's children, and in revenge the monster used his magic to flood the world. Coyote and the first man and woman went on up to the fourth world; but Tieholtsodi pursued them, even when they reached the fifth world, until Coyote returned his children. The fifth world is the one in which men now live. Only after death do they go down to the fourth world again. Coyote made the stars, and taught men how to hunt and farm. In the myths of the Pomo Indians, Coyote is the younger brother of the high god Madumda, and it was he who created human beings and stole the sun to keep them warm; Madumda is an inactive, distant god.

In Chemchuevi Indian stories, Puma and Coyote existed at the beginning of the world, when it was still covered in water. When land was formed, Coyote populated it and taught men to eat game. Puma was killed by mysterious enemies, who also brought on the first night by this deed. The night went on and on until Coyote restored the day by shooting a bird, the yellow-hammer. The Crow Indians told how Coyote and his younger brother Cirape made the earth, and created everything on it, but quarrelled over a magic pouch and a magic arrow, and Cirape got the better of the argument. One of the Indian tribes of California say that after a great flood it was Coyote who created more men by planting birds' feathers in the ground so that they became human beings.

For the Zuni Indians, Coyote was a hero who made rules for men to live in peace. He divided the land between the different clans, and in the strips that marked the boundary between each village's land he buried a beetle and a poisonous spider, so that anyone who tried to dig up the land would go blind like a beetle or would die of poison.

Cozaana and Huichaana: The two gods who made living creatures in Mixtec myth: Cozaana

60

made animals, while Huichaana made men and fishes.

Creon: Brother of Queen *Jocasta* of Thebes, he became first regent and then king of Thebes after her tragic marriage to *Oedipus*. It was he who forbade the burial of *Polyneices*, Oedipus' son, after his death in the war of the *Seven Against Thebes*, and who gave orders for *Antigone* to be buried alive for trying to bury him. After a long reign, he was eventually dethroned and killed by a certain Lykos.

Crius: One of the old gods or *Titans* in Greek myth, son of *Uranus* and *Gaia*.

Cronus: The chief of the old gods or *Titans* in Greek myth, son of *Uranus* and *Gaia*. By his wife *Rhea*, he was father of *Poseidon*, *Hades* and *Zeus*; but because he had been told by his parents that he would be overthrown by one of his own sons, he swallowed each child as soon as it was born, until Rhea gave him a stone wrapped in infant's clothes instead of Zeus. Zeus was brought up in a cave on Crete, and when he was old enough raised a revolt against his father. Rhea had deceived Cronus into vomiting up the other children, and they and Zeus, with other allies, fought Cronus for ten years. He was at last defeated, and imprisoned in *Tartarus*. Other stories, however, tell of his reign as a *Golden Age*, when war was unknown and the earth provided everything man needed without cultivation or harvesting, when there were no laws and no need for property. The Romans identified Cronus with *Saturn*.

Crow: In Tlingit myths from the north-west Pacific coast of America, the crow appears as the creator-bird instead of *Raven* or the *Thunderbird*, producing dry land by beating his wings. He also appears as the bringer of light or fire.

Cuailgne, Brown Bull of: The Irish tales tell how Queen *Medhbh* of Connaught invaded Ulster and seized the magic brown bull of Cuailgne or Cooley, while the Ulstermen were sick because of a curse laid on them. However, *Cuchulainn* resisted the army of Connaught until his fellow Ulstermen had recovered and Medhbh and her troops were defeated in a great battle. She retreated, taking the bull with her, but it attacked and killed the magic white bull of Connaught, and then died of exhaustion.

61

Cuchulainn: See also *Curoi*. Hero of Ulster in Irish legend. As a youth, he defeated all the young warriors at *Conchobar's* court single-handed. Later he killed the hound of the smith Culann when it attacked him, and made amends by acting as Culann's hound, 'Cu Chulainn', in its place. He was made invincible by the witch Scathach, and in his 'battle-frenzy' he was terrible to see, hair on end, mouth gaping, with one eye like a needlepoint and the other huge and wide, and a halo of light about his head.

When Queen *Medhbh* of Connaught tried to carry off the magical brown bull of Cooley (*Cuailgne*) the heroes of Ulster were wasting away because of a mysterious sickness, brought on them by a curse. The only one not affected was Cuchulainn, and he defended the province for nine years until the curse was ended, by challenging the men of Connaught to single combats.

At the feast of Bricriu, to which all the Ulstermen were invited, there was a great quarrel over 'the champion's portion', the special piece of the roasted pig which was always given to the greatest hero. Bricriu intended this to happen, and three heroes competed for the portion: Loeghaire, *Conall Cernach* and Cuchulainn. Cuchulainn was the winner in the ordeal set for them, but the other two disputed his title, and they went to King *Curoi Mac Daire* for another trial of strength. Cuchulainn again won, and the verdict was not accepted by the other two. Finally a giant of ugly appearance came to the hall where they were feasting and proposed a challenge: any of the heroes could cut off his head, provided he was allowed to do the same to them the next night. Loeghaire took up his sword and struck off the stranger's head; but the giant picked it up and walked out. When he returned, Loeghaire was not there to fulfil the bargain. The same happened with Conall Cernach and only Cuchulainn was brave enough to appear on the night after he had beheaded the giant. The giant gave him a gentle blow with the back of the axe, declared that Cuchulainn was the champion of Ireland, and revealed that he was Curoi in disguise.

Cuchulainn's death came about as follows. The Irish heroes were bound by certain prohibitions, things that they must not do, called *gessa*. Cuchulainn was forced to break his *gessa*, and so lost his heroic power. This came about through Medhbh, who raised six monstrous children and taught them magic in order to bring about Cuchulainn's death; and they invaded Ulster

62

while the Ulstermen were under a curse. Cuchulainn was warned not to attack them, but they made a magic army out of puffballs and leaves, and nothing could dissuade him from fighting. *The Morigan* broke his chariot to try to stop him; and when he still had his horse harnessed to it the horse spoke to him and warned him not to go. On the way he passed three old women cooking dog's flesh at their hearth. Although a magic taboo prevented him from going near a cooking hearth, they taunted him when he refused to go and join them until he broke his *gessa*. When he ate the flesh his left hand and leg lost their strength, and in the fight that followed he was killed when his own spear was seized by his enemy Lugaid and used against him. See also *Fand, Fraoch*.

Cupara: Among the Jivaro Indians of the Andes, Cupara and his wife were the parents of the sun, and creators of the moon, which they made from mud and which became the sun's wife. The children of the sun and moon were various animals and the food plant manioc. Among the animals was the sloth, which became the ancestor of the Jivaro tribe.

Cupid: The Roman name for *Eros*.

Curoi: Magician, wanderer and king in Irish myth. He appears in the adventures of *Cuchulainn*. He travelled so widely that he was never in Ireland long enough to fight or to eat after he was seven years old: and his castle in Kerry was controlled by a magic spell which made it spin round like a top each evening, so that its entrance could not be found after sunset. In another adventure, he helped Cuchulainn to take a fort in Scotland in return for first choice of the spoils. Cuchulainn broke his part of the bargain so Curoi took all the booty, including the girl Blathnad, and when Cuchulainn tried to stop him, Curoi thrust him into the ground until only his head and shoulders were showing. But Cuchulainn had his revenge by getting Blathnad to betray Curoi. Curoi's poet Fercherdne avenged his master's death by seizing her and throwing himself over a cliff with her so that they were both killed.

Curupira: Guardian spirit of the forests in the myths of Brazilian Indians. He appeared as a bald one-eyed dwarf with huge ears, riding a deer or pig. He helped hunters who killed their

prey outright, and punished those who only wounded animals.

Cyavana: The son of the Hindu sage *Bhrigu*, and himself a sage. He once became so absorbed in a penance he was carrying out that white ants built nests around him until only his eyes could be seen. The princess Sukanya poked at these with a stick, and Cyavana's rage was only calmed when Sukanya was made his wife. But he was old and ugly, and the *Ashvins*, coming to his home one day, tried to lure Sukanya away. She replied by taunting them with not being proper gods because they did not share in the *soma* drinking of the gods, and refused to go with them. In the end they agreed to make Cyavana young again if he could get them the *soma*. They performed their part of the bargain, and restored Cyavana's youth. Cyavana said that they would have to share in sacrifices made to the gods if they were to have the *soma*, and started to sacrifice to them. At this *Indra* tried to attack Cyavana, but he conjured up an enormous demon whose mouth covered earth and sky, and who was about to swallow the gods 'as a sea-monster swallows fishes'. Terrified, Indra relented, and the Ashvins were allowed to share the *soma*.

Cybele: Originally a goddess from what is now Turkey, similar to *Ishtar*. Cybele's image was brought to Rome on the instructions contained in the Sibylline Books (see *Sibyl*) in 205 B C, because, so the prophecy ran, 'Hannibal would leave the country if the Great Mother were brought to Rome'. Her image was a black meteorite, though

she was later shown as a goddess in the Roman manner, distinguished by her crown of towers and her accompanying lions. Her festival, at the beginning of spring, was marked by wild orgies: and to the Romans it was she who was *Adonis'* partner rather than *Aphrodite*.

Cyclops: 1. Sons of *Uranus* and *Gaia*, they were called Brontes, Steropes and Arges. The Greek poet Hesiod tells how they helped *Zeus* in his battle with his father *Cronus* by arming him with thunder, lightning and thunderbolt; in return, he released them from the prison into which Cronus had put them. They were killed by *Apollo* in revenge for the death of *Asclepius*, because it was with the thunderbolt which they had made that Zeus killed him. In later legend, they were shown as the workmen of *Hephaestus*.

2. Another Greek story, that of *Odysseus*, portrays them as one-eyed giants, sons of *Poseidon*. One of them, *Polyphemus*, was blinded by Odysseus.

D

Dadhyanc: A Hindu *rishi* or sage, who was taught secret knowledge by *Indra*, who said that he would cut off his head if he repeated it to anyone else. The *Ashvins* persuaded him to tell them the secret, and in return took off his head and replaced it with that of a horse. Indra cut off this horse's head, and the Ashvins then put back Dadhyanc's proper head. While he was alive, his power was such that the *Asuras* were kept at bay by his presence on earth; after he died, they terrorized everyone, and Indra had to use Dadhyanc's bones in order to kill them.

Daedalus: A Greek master craftsman, who was exiled from Athens for throwing one of his apprentices in the sea because the apprentice had shown himself as clever as his master by inventing the saw. He went to Crete, where his skills were employed by *Minos* to build the labyrinth in which the *Minotaur* was kept. When he had finished, Minos would not let him go, so he made wings of feathers joined by wax for himself and his son *Icarus*. With these the two of them flew towards Sicily; but Icarus went too close to the sun, the wax melted, and he fell into the sea and was drowned. Daedalus reached Sicily safely.

Dagda: In Irish myth, one of the chief gods of the *Tuatha De Danann*. He was known as the 'Lord of Great Knowledge' and as the 'Good god', not because he was morally good, but because he was good at everything. He was married to Boann, the goddess of the river Boyne.

He possessed a magic harp, which the *Fomorians* once stole. He and *Lugh* and *Ogma* set out for the hall of the Fomorians to get it back; when they got there the harp came down off the wall of its own accord. Then the Dagda played three famous melodies: one for weeping, and all the women wept; one for laughing, and all the woman and children laughed; and one for sleeping, and the whole host of the Fomorians slept. The three melodies were traditional music for the harpists of Ireland.

Although the Dagda owned this harp, and a magic club so heavy it had to be carried on wheels and which killed nine men at once, he was a faintly comic figure. He went around in a tunic so short that it hardly covered his bottom, and he had 'a great weakness for porridge' which he used to make in his magic cauldron: anyone who ate from it always went away satisfied.

Before the second battle of Moytura, the Fomorians tried to handicap the Dagda by

66

making him eat a great porridge which they made in a hole in the ground. They put in eighty measures of milk, eighty of meal, eighty of fat and goat's meat, pork and mutton as well. The Dagda took a huge ladle, big enough for two people to sleep in, and ate it all, scraping the sides of the hole with his fingers.

Dagon: The Assyrian god who judged the dead; he was also a god of the earth causing plants to grow. He was particularly worshipped by the Philistines, who prayed to him in their wars against the Hebrews, and offered their spoils in his temple.

Dahhak: An evil spirit in Iranian myth, enemy of *Yima*. Before the end of the world, Dahhak will cause all kinds of evil to happen until *Keresaspa* kills him.

Daityas: In Hindu myth, evil demons who were the enemies of the gods, and tried to seize sacrifices made to them. They had varying success in their wars, but were far from being always defeated.

See *Diti* for a different version of their fate; also *Kartikeya, Rahu.*

Dajoji: In the myths of the Iroquois Indians Dajoji, or the panther, was god of the west wind, summoned by Ga-oh into the sky to make war against storms. He is strong enough to lay whole forests low, to stir the sea into a fury and to control the tempest. The sun himself hides in fear when he hears Dajoji's cry in the night-time.

Daksha: A Hindu sage, son of *Brahma* and *Aditi*, who was a *Prajapati.*

Daksha once made a sacrifice to *Vishnu*, which all the other gods attended, except *Shiva*, whom they had banned from receiving sacrifices. But Shiva's wife *Uma*, who was Daksha's daughter, noticed what was happening and urged Shiva to claim his share. Shiva created a terrible monster which shook the whole earth, and sent an army of lesser gods to break up the ceremony. The other gods were beaten up, and Daksha, in terror, offered a sacrifice to Shiva and worshipped him. But there are other versions of the story as well: one says that Daksha himself was executed, and his head burnt. Shiva then restored him to life by giving him a ram's head instead. Another says that Shiva was forced to stop his attack by Vishnu, and to acknowledge Vishnu as his lord.

67

Danae: A Greek princess, daughter of Acrisius, the ruler of Argos, of whom it was prophesied that her son would kill her father. So Acrisius imprisoned her in a tower; but *Zeus* visited her there, in the form of a shower of gold. When her son *Perseus* was born, he and his mother were set afloat in a chest, which was washed up on the island of Seriphos. Here Polydectes, king of the island, fell in love with Danae, but she resisted him. Perseus protected her from him until he was sent to fetch the *Gorgon*'s head; his mother then took sanctuary in a temple until he returned and rescued her by turning her pursuer into stone with the Gorgon's head.

Danaids: Danaus and Aigyptus were brothers; each had fifty children, all Danaus' children being daughters, all Aigyptus' children sons. The two brothers quarrelled, but as was Greek custom, the sons of Aigyptus wanted to marry their cousins, Danaus' daughters. Danaus could not forbid this, but instead made his daughters murder their husbands on their wedding night. For this they were condemned to stand forever in Tartarus trying to fill a broken water-jar with broken pitchers.

Danann: Obscure Irish goddess, who was mother of *Tuatha De Danann*: their name means Tribes of the Goddess Danann.

Daphne: A Greek nymph and follower of *Artemis* whom *Apollo* loved. Her mortal lover Leucippus disguised himself as a girl to be with her, but was found out and slain by Artemis' companions. Apollo then pursued Daphne, and as she fled, she prayed to the earth to rescue her. As she uttered the prayer, she was rooted to the earth and transformed into the laurel which bears her name.

Daphnis: Half-brother of the Greek god *Pan*, he was blinded by a nymph of the Sicilian countryside where he lived because he refused to love her. He spent the rest of his brief life composing songs about his own sad fate, which is why shepherds loved to sing similar mournful tunes. According to another story *Aphrodite* punished his rejection of love by making him fall hopelessly in love and die of unrequited passion.

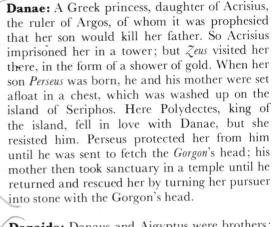

Darana: Among the Australian aborigines called the Dieri, who live in the desert, there is a story that tells how in the 'dreamtime' or beginning of the world Darana (one of the *muramura* or first

68

beings) made rain by 'singing' it magically. This produced flowers and witchetty grubs (one of the aborigines' chief foods); so Darana gathered these and hung them up in bags, and went off on a journey. Two youths broke the bags with boomerangs, producing a great sandstorm. They were killed, and became two sacred stones: if these were scratched there would be a great famine while if they were destroyed the world would be overwhelmed by dust.

Darramulun: Great hero from the sky in Australian aborigine myths: also called Ngurunderi, or Bunjil. He created men and taught them how to use tools and weapons.

Deianeira: Bride of the Greek hero *Heracles*, who won her by wrestling with her father *Achelous*. As he crossed a river with her soon after their marriage, the *centaur* Nessus helped Deianeira across, but while Heracles was still in mid-stream, he tried to attack her. Heracles killed him with an arrow; but as he died he told Deianeira that if she took some of his blood and kept it, she would be able to win back Heracles' love if he ever abandoned her. If this happened, she was to smear the blood on a piece of clothing and send it to him to wear. Years later, Heracles went off with *Iole*; so Deianeira followed Nessus' instructions and sent a robe dipped in the blood. But Nessus had his revenge: for the blood was a deadly poison which killed Heracles, instead of winning him back for Deianeira.

Dei Consentes: The Romans thought of the gods as holding councils on important matters; these were attended by twelve gods, *Jupiter* being the one who actually made the decisions. The twelve were: Jupiter, *Neptune, Mars, Apollo, Vulcan, Mercury, Juno, Minerva, Diana, Venus, Vesta* and *Ceres.*

Deidameia: The bride of *Achilles* and mother of *Neoptolemus* in Greek myth.

Deino: One of the *Graeae* in Greek myth.

Deirdre: When Deirdre was born, the Irish prophet Cathbhach foretold that she would be 'by far the most beautiful girl who had ever been in Ireland', but that she would cause great sorrows to Ulster. The king of Ulster, *Conchobar*, had her brought up to be his wife, despite the prophecy. But she fell in love with Naoise, and

although he was one of Conchobar's warriors and was reluctant to take her from the king, she had her way, and they went into exile with Naoise's two brothers. Eventually Conchobar was persuaded to bring Naoise and his brothers back to Ulster, and Fergus Mac Roich, one of Ulster's heroes, was sent as a guarantee of their safety. But when the three brothers arrived at Conchobar's court he killed them. Fergus, furious at the stain on his honour, went over to the court of Connaught, while Deirdre, after a year with Conchobar when she did nothing but weep for Naoise, threw herself from a chariot and was killed.

Dekanawida: A half-mythical, half-historical hero of the Iroquois Indians of the north-eastern United States. In reality, he seems to have been a fifteenth-century leader who, with *Hiawatha*, brought about an alliance of the five Iroquois tribes. The stories about his birth are pure myth. He had no father, and his mother dreamt before he was born that he would bring disaster to his people, the Hurons, who were the enemies of the Iroquois. So his mother tried to drown him by pushing him through the ice of a nearby river; but each time she woke up next morning to find him safe in her arms. When he grew up, he travelled south and became an Iroquois by adoption; and he did indeed bring great sorrow to the Hurons as leader of the united Iroquois tribes.

Demeter: The Greek goddess of fertility and of the earth's harvests. She was the daughter of *Cronus* and *Rhea*; beloved of *Zeus*, she bore him a daughter, *Persephone*, while to the mortal Iasion she bore Plutus, the god of wealth. When Persephone was carried off by *Hades* to his underworld kingdom to become his queen, Demeter was left to search for her, as no one had seen her disappear. Mourning her loss, she wandered for ten days, until the sun-god *Helios* told her who had carried off her daughter. Out of anger with Zeus, who had allowed this to happen, she abandoned her duties as a goddess and went to live among men. She finally settled as a nurse in the house of Celeus, king of Eleusis, calling herself Doso the Cretan. Here she tried to make the king's son Demophoon immortal by holding him each night in a magic fire. But she was seen by the boy's mother, Metaneira, who cried out and thus broke the spell. Demeter revealed herself, and ordered that a shrine should be built for her at

Eleusis. When it was ready, she went to live there. During all this time, while she was on earth, there was no harvest and the land was barren. All the gods tried to persuade her to return, but it was only when Hades agreed to release Persephone that she consented. Even now, she mourns for the four months of the year that Persephone spent in Hades; and it is this time of Demeter's mourning that we call winter. Because similar stories were told about *Isis*, the Greeks often identified the two goddesses, while the Romans called her *Ceres*. Her great temple was at Eleusis, where the rites called the *Eleusinian Mysteries* were celebrated in her honour.

Deohako: According to the Seneca Indians (one of the Iroquois tribes from the Canadian border) the Deohako were the spirits of maize, beans and gourds, who originally lived together on one hill. But the maize spirit, *Onatha*, wandered away in search of dew and was caught by *Hahgwehdaetgah*, the evil spirit who carried her off underground. She was only rescued when the sun went in search of her; and ever afterwards she stayed among the maize in the fields until it was ripe, in spite of drought or rain.

Deucalion: The Greek equivalent of Noah; he was saved by *Zeus* because he and Pyrrha were the most reverent of mankind when Zeus flooded the earth. After the flood, when Deucalion consulted the oracle of *Themis* to see if the human race could be restored more quickly than by waiting for his descendants he was told that he and Pyrrha must throw behind them as they left the temple 'the bones of their great mother'. He was puzzled by this at first; but 'stones are earth's bones', so they threw stones over their shoulders. Those thrown by Deucalion became men, those by Pyrrha women.

Devas: The evil gods in Iranian myths: they were Aeshma (wrath), Aka Manah (evil intent), Bushyashta (idleness), Apaosha (drought) and Nasu (corpse). Their opponents were the *Amesha Spentas*.

Devi: The wife of the Hindu god *Shiva*; her name means simply 'goddess', and she is also called by a number of other titles – Parvati, Mahadevi, 'the great goddess', Uma. But she has also, like Shiva, a dark and terrible side to her nature, which earns her the names *Durga*, 'inaccessible', or *Kali*, 'black'. As Kali she appears in hideous

form, black-skinned with a horrible face and surrounded by snakes and skulls. The book called *Devi Mahatmya* celebrates her victories over numerous *Asuras*: her greatest victory was that over the demon Durga, whose name she took after she had conquered him in an immense battle; she is also famed for killing the buffalo demon, Mahisha.

Dhanvantari: The physician of the Hindu gods, guardian of the *amrita*.

Dharmapala: 'Protectors of religion' in Buddhist myth, giants of horrible appearance with huge teeth, hair standing on end and tongues sticking out. *Vajrapani (Indra)* was one of them.

Dhyanibodhisattvas: *Bodhisattvas* of meditation, corresponding to *Dhyanibuddhas* in the same way that Buddhas and Bodhisattvas are connected.

Dhyanibuddhas: Buddhas of meditation, five in number, who correspond to the five Buddhas of the present age. They are most important in Tibet, where the Buddhas, particularly Gautama, are less highly thought of.

Dian Cecht: God of healing of *Tuatha De Danann* in Irish myth – he healed the wounded by plunging them in a magic bath. He fashioned *Nuadu*'s silver hand. When a man lost an eye he could replace it with a cat's eye though 'there was advantage and disadvantage to him in that, for by day it was always asleep when it should have been on the alert; and at night it would be starting at every rustle of the reeds and every squeak of a mouse'.

Diarmaid and Grainne: When the Irish hero *Fionn* was an old man, he planned to marry Grainne against her wishes. On their wedding night, she contrived to force Diarmaid, one of Fionn's young warriors, to escape with her. They wandered through Ireland, pursued by Fionn, until *Oengus Mac Oc*, Diarmaid's foster father made peace between Fionn and Diarmaid. Diarmaid went hunting one day against a boar which, so the prophecy ran, would bring about his death: although he slew it, he was wounded, and only Fionn could heal him by giving him a drink of water. But each time he went to fetch it, he thought of Diarmaid's treachery over Grainne, and let the water run through his fingers: and when he came back for the third time, Diarmaid was dead.

Dido: The Queen of Carthage, in Roman myth, who killed herself out of love for *Aeneas*, who abandoned her to fulfil his destined task of founding the Roman race. She may have been the same as an earlier Tyrian goddess, Elissa, since she was said to have come to Carthage from Tyre.

Dilmun: The garden of paradise in Sumerian myth, where *Gilgamesh* visited *Utnapishtim*. It was originally the home of *Ea* (Enki) and his wife; and Ea's son by the goddess *Ninhursag*, Tagtug, became the gardener there, but he ate of the one plant which was forbidden, and so lost the right to immortal life.

Diomedes: 1. Son of the Greek *Tydeus* of Calydon, one of the *Seven Against Thebes*. In the *Trojan War*, he was *Odysseus'* constant companion, and was one of *Athene's* favourites. Athene encouraged him to attack *Ares* and *Aphrodite* when they joined in the battle, and he succeeded in wounding them both. Aphrodite took her revenge by making his wife unfaithful when he returned from the war. For some reason, he became a wanderer, like Odysseus. His tomb was on an island off the south of Italy, where it was guarded by comrades transformed into birds. They sprinkled the tomb with water each day.
2. Lord of Thrace, who owned a herd of man-eating horses. *Heracles* overcame him, and fed him to his own horses, which then became tame.

Dione: An ancient Greek earth-goddess, who may have been the original wife of *Zeus*, before *Hera* was given that title.

Dionysus: The Greek god of divine ecstasy and of wine. He was the son of *Zeus* and *Semele*, who was a mortal. *Hera*, jealous of Semele, appeared to her as an old woman, and suggested to Semele that to make sure that her lover really was Zeus, she should ask him to appear to her in his divine form. Semele persuaded Zeus to do this, but he could not prevent his lightning from consuming her. He rescued her unborn child, which was later born from his thigh and was called Dionysus. In Roman myth he was known as Bacchus.

The worship of Dionysus, which was probably imported to Greece from the East, was not always welcomed, because his devotees performed wild dances and were generally uncontrollable. But those who opposed him were usually punished in some drastic way. *Pentheus* of Thebes was torn to pieces by his own mother, the daughters of

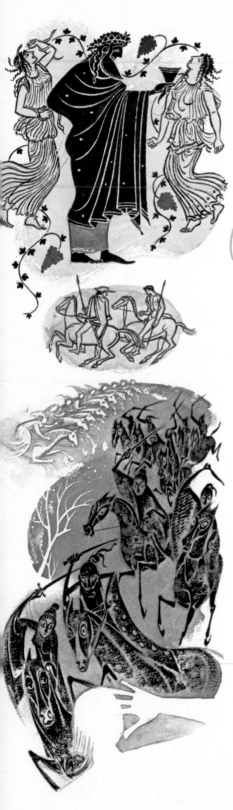

Proteus went mad and killed their own children, and *Lycurgus* was blinded. On others who refused to worship him, Dionysus used his magical powers: when the three daughters of Minyas stayed at home spinning instead of going to his festival, he filled the place where they were working with shadowy wild beasts, turned their thread into vines, and made voices echo round the room from invisible worshippers.

He was accompanied by *satyrs*, *maenäds* and *nymphs* and by *Silenus*, who had once looked after him; they joined in his wild rites, which were designed to purge men of their irrational, emotional desires. See also *Ariadne*.

Dioskouroi: Another name for the twins *Castor and Pollux*, in Greek mythology.

Disir: A whole group of female spirits and minor goddesses in Norse myth are called *disir*; it seems to mean guardian spirits in general, whether of places, harvests or even war – the *Valkyries* are among the *disir*. The sacrifices at harvest and in midwinter were called *disablot* after them. They could also be good and bad spirits with a special interest in one person, as in the story of Thidrandi. In the days when Christianity was first brought to Iceland, one of the old pagan prophets, Thorhall, was staying with his Christian friend Hall. At the winter feast, he sensed some doom threatening, and he warned the guests not to answer any knock at the door during the night. But when the banquet was over, Hall's son Thidrandi, who was still a pagan, heard a knock and opened the door. There was nobody there, but in the distance he saw a group of nine women in black, with drawn swords, galloping towards him from the north, while from the south nine women in white approached. He turned to go back in, but the black spirits caught up with him and gave him a mortal wound. He died the next day; and Thorhall explained that these were not women, but the *disir* of the old religion, who had sensed that a change of religion was coming to the land, and had seized Thidrandi as their share from Hall's family. The white *disir*, because Thidrandi was a pagan, were unable to help him. But the new religion would be a better one.

Diti: A Hindu goddess, daughter of *Daksha*, whose children, the *Daityas*, were all destroyed by *Indra*. She prayed to *Kasyapa*, her husband, for a son who would destroy Indra. But just before the child was born, Indra struck it with a thunderbolt, and the seven pieces became the *Maruts*.

Djanggawul: Two sisters and a brother were the ancestors of the people of northern Australia, according to their myths. They were called Djanggawul, and they made many of the people. At first the two sisters were in charge of the sacred rituals, but one day the brother and the other men stole the sacred objects and from then on the men alone were able to perform the rites and women were excluded.

Dn'il: The central figure of an epic poem from Canaan, Dn'il was a king of that land who had no son. He prayed to the gods for an heir, and the Prince Aqht was born. When Aqht was a boy, the craftsman-god came to Dn'il's palace on his travels, and in return for Dn'il's hospitality gave him a bow such as he made for the gods. Dn'il gave it to Aqht, but warned him to sacrifice to a god the first thing he killed with it. This he presumably failed to do (the text is missing); and the goddess *Anat* tried to get the bow from him. She offered great riches for it, then immortality; but Aqht refused and scorned her offer. Anat seemed amused, but was really furious, and vowed to avenge herself on Aqht. She changed a warrior, Ytpn, into a falcon, and set out to wound Aqht; but Ytpn killed him, and the bow was lost in the sea. At first Aqht was thought to have disappeared; but the appearance of vultures and the wilting of plants where his blood had flowed revealed the murder. Even so, Dn'il did not know that it was Aqht who had been killed. Only after his prayers for the yearly rains had failed, and a great drought followed, did he learn of Aqht's death. He set out to recover his son's body from the vultures, and to bury it. The drought lastèd for seven years; meanwhile, Aqht's sister avenged his death. She disguised herself as the goddess Anat and went to Ytpn's camp, armed with a dagger, where she learnt that it was indeed he who had killed her brother. She made him drunk and killed him. The spell was broken, and Dn'il's prayers brought rain again.

Dohitt: Among the Quechua-speaking Indians of Bolivia, Dohitt was the creator of the world, which was in the form of a raft. He also made men, and then retired to heaven. After a while he returned to earth and transformed some of mankind into the different kinds of animals and birds. It was he who taught men how to farm.

Donar: Early German god of thunder, a fore-runner of the Norse god *Thor*. Donar had a mighty

axe, like Thor's hammer. Thursday in Germany is Donnerstag, Donar's day, just as it is Thor's day with us and Jove's day (jeudi, giovedi) in Latin countries. As with Jove, oak trees were sacred to Donar.

Doris: A Greek sea-goddess, wife of *Nereus*, mother of the *Nereids*.

Drag-Gshhed: The eight terrible gods in Tibetan myth, similar to the Indian Buddhist *Dharmapalas*. Some of the Hindu gods are among them including *Shiva*, *Devi* and *Yama*.

Dragon: In Norse belief, the mounds in which the dead were buried were often guarded by dragons, who defended against marauders the treasure which was placed in the tombs. The dragon may once have been the spirit of death the destroyer, like the 'corpse-tearer' *Nidhogg*, and his fiery breath may have been the great funeral pyre on which heroes were burned. In the Old English poem *Beowulf* the king dies fighting a dragon which has come out of its mound because a slave has stolen a cup from its rich treasure-hoard. *Fafnir*, slain by *Sigurd* the Volsung, is also guardian of gold, but in this case it is his own hoard and not that of a dead man. On carved memorial stones, the serpent-dragon often appears as a symbol for the world of the dead.

Draupadi: An Indian princess, and the central heroine of the epic called *Mahabharata*. She was won by *Arjuna* at a Svayam-vara held by her father; this was a contest where all the princes who were rivals for her hand competed in athletics and feats of arms. When Arjuna and his brothers returned home they told their mother that they acquired something very valuable, and she told them to share it between them. But they meant that they had brought Draupadi with them; as their mother's words were sacred, they had to obey, and the problem was only solved when a sage declared that Draupadi was fated to be the wife of all five brothers, and to spend two days with each at a time. She became a slave when the eldest brother, *Yudhishthira*, lost all his possessions to the Kauravas. She was mistreated by the Kaurava princes, *Duryodhana* and *Duhshasana*, and it was then that *Bhima* vowed to drink the blood of one and to smash the other's thigh, while Draupadi swore to wear her hair loose until Bhima should tie it up with his hands wet with Duhshasana's blood. The five princes and

76

Draupadi spent thirteen years in exile, and during the last year Draupadi was carried off by King Jayadratha, but Bhima and Arjuna brought her back safely and humbled Jayadratha. For the last year of their exile, they had to live in disguise, and all of them went to serve King Virata without revealing that they were related. Draupadi became a servant-girl, but to protect herself from unwelcome attention because of her beauty, said that five *Gandharvas* guarded her and would kill anyone who insulted or attacked her. However, the queen's brother fell in love with her, and forced his attentions on her. She appealed to Bhima, who killed the queen's brother and beat his body until it was a ball of flesh. His death was thought to be due to Draupadi's Gandharvas, and she was condemned to be burnt. But Bhima rescued her by pulling his hair over his face, and seizing a tree as a club. Her enemies thought he was one of the Gandharvas, and fled.

At the end of the great battle between Kauravas and *Pandavas* her five sons were killed. Then she set out with her husbands to retire from the world in the Himalayas, and she died not long after.

Draupnir: The great gold ring of the Norse god *Odin*, given to him by the goddess *Hel*. It was an armband cunningly wrought by dwarfs, and was one of the three treasures of the gods – the others were *Gullinbursti* and *Mjollnir*. Every ninth night, there fell from it eight other rings of equal size.

Drona: In the Indian epic *Mahabharata*, Drona taught both the Kaurava and *Pandava* princes the arts of war. However, he supported the Kaurava princes in the great battle between the two sides, because his oldest enemy, *Drupada*, father of *Draupadi*, was fighting for the Pandavas. Drona killed Drupada on the fourth day of the battle, but soon afterwards he was told that his son had been killed. He was so shocked that he dropped his weapons, and Drupada's son seized the opportunity of avenging his father by cutting off Drona's head.

Drupada: An Indian king who was father of *Draupadi* and enemy of *Drona*.

Dryads: Greek tree-nymphs, spirits of the trees. They died when their trees were cut down.

Dudugera: In New Guinea myth, Dudugera was the son of a woman and a great fish. As a

child, he quarrelled with his playmates, who teased him about his father; so Dudugera's mother decided to send him back to the great fish. Before he left, Dudugera warned her to shelter under a great rock, because he was going to climb a tree and get up into the sky, where he would become the sun. His heat would burn everything up. This happened, and everyone except his mother and her relations were killed; but his mother climbed a hill and threw lime in his face, making him shut his eyes. There was less heat, and they were able to leave the shelter and live as before.

Durga: One of the names of *Devi*, wife of the Indian god *Shiva*. She was given it after she had overcome a demon of that name in a terrible battle.

Durvasas: A Hindu sage, son of the god *Shiva*. He was ill-tempered and used his power of cursing frequently: the most famous incident was when he presented a garland to *Indra*, who failed to receive it with due respect. Durvasas said that his power over the 'three worlds' should decrease, and as a result the *Asuras* managed to defeat the gods. *Indra* and the other gods went to *Vishnu* for help, who told them to seek the *amrita* from the ocean. With this magical drink, their power was restored. On another occasion, *Krishna* entertained Durvasas, but failed to remove some crumbs of food which fell on Durvasas' foot, for which the sage told him how he would be killed. See also *Mugdala*.

Duryodhana: In the Indian epic *Mahabharata*, Duryodhana was the leader of the Kaurava princes against the *Pandavas*. He was especially jealous of the Pandava prince *Bhima*, whom he had once tried to kill because of his skill with the war-club, which was Duryodhana's special weapon. He was responsible for getting the Pandava princes sent into exile, and tried to trap them in a house and burn them alive during the time of their exile. When they returned to the court at Hastinapur, it was Duryodhana who arranged the great gambling match with *Yudhishthira* at which the latter lost all the Pandava possessions, including their wife *Draupadi*, whom Duryodhana and Duhshasana then insulted. For this Bhima vowed to smash Duryodhana's thigh with his club. At the great battle between the Kauravas and Pandavas, Duryodhana was one of the last Kaurava survivors, and hid himself in a lake. It took a great deal of taunting by Bhima to make him come out and fight, but when he did so, the struggle was evenly matched. Bhima remembered his vow, and struck him on the thigh, which was a foul blow; but by this means he was able to give the crippled Duryodhana a deadly blow. In revenge for his death, *Drona*'s son Ashvatthaman killed the five sons of the Pandava princes.

Dusares: God of the vine and of fertility in the kingdom based on the city of Petra, now in Jordan. The festival of his birth was on 25 December, and his mother, Chaabu, was said to be a virgin when he was born.

Dvaraka: The sacred city of the Hindu god-hero *Krishna*: after his death it was swallowed up by the sea.

Dvergar: In Norse myth, the dvergar (dwarfs) were creatures like men, but of small size, who were born from the earth and lived underground. They were great metalworkers and makers of magical treasures such as *Draupnir*, *Gullinbursti* and *Mjollnir*; it was they who made the fetter *Gleipnir* which bound the *Fenris-wolf*, as well as the necklace *Brisingamen*. They were often mischievous or evil; evil dwarfs killed the all-knowing dwarf *Kvasir*; but they were also, like Kvasir, often skilled in mysterious knowledge. *Alviss* was one of the wise dwarfs, and Regin, *Ottar*'s brother and foster father to *Sigurd*, was one of the dwarfs skilled in metalwork; it was he who forged the magic sword Gram. Dwarfs could not appear in daylight; if they were still above ground when the sun rose, they were turned to stone. Echoes were said to be the speech of dwarfs, dvergamal. See also *Andvari*.

Dyai: Dyai is the central character in the myths of the Tucuna Indians of the upper Amazon river. He was the son of Nutapa, and was born from his right knee; Epi, his wicked brother, was born from his left knee. Nutapa was killed by a jaguar, but the brothers brought him back to life. Dyai procured useful things like daylight, sleep and fire, and rescued his ungrateful brother from the difficulties he was always getting into. Before they went their separate ways, Dyai to the east, Epi to the west, they created men from a fish which they had caught on a hook.

Dyaus: The sky-god in early Hindu myths; the name is similar to that of *Zeus*, but Dyaus, or Dyauspitri, remained a vague god who was little worshipped. See also *Prithivi*.

Dzelarhons: In the tales of the North Pacific Coast Indians of America, Dzelarhons appears in a story which records the movement of a tribe to America from Alaska. She arrived on the coast of America with six canoe-loads of the tribe which her uncle Githawn ruled. They landed in the territory of the Grizzly Bear tribe, and the chief's nephew wanted to marry her. But he insulted her by sleeping for the first four nights after their marriage and ignoring her, so Githawn and his people made war on the Grizzly Bear tribe in retaliation. Dzelarhons disappeared, and when Githawn sought her, he found only a granite statue of her far away. She became a supernatural creature, a mountain spirit called the Volcano Woman.

Ea: God of the sea in Babylonian myth, and also of wisdom, represented as a man with a fish's tail instead of legs. *Oannes* may be the same god in another form, and he is also called Enki. He was the creator of many of the things that help men on earth, and taught men crafts and skills. As Enki, he was husband of *Ninhursag*. They had a number of beautiful daughters, whom Enki made love to; and this so annoyed Ninhursag that she cursed him to live underground. The other gods objected, and she lifted part of the curse to allow him to appear occasionally on the land.

It was Enki who overcame the first god, *Apsu*, and controlled him, but Apsu and Tiamat later rebelled and fought against *Anu*, Enki, *Marduk* and the other gods: it was Enki's son Marduk who destroyed Tiamat. See also *Apsu and Tiamat*.

Echidna: In Greek myth, the sister of *Geryon*, and like him a monster. She was half-woman and half-serpent, and lived below ground with her husband *Typhon*; their children were a weird collection of even stranger monsters.

Echo: A nymph loved by the Greek god *Pan*; she refused to yield to him, so he drove the local shepherds mad. They tore her in pieces, and only her voice lingered on.

Another version of the story says that she had roused *Hera*'s jealousy, and the goddess laid a curse on her, which meant that she could never speak first, but could not stay silent when others spoke. She fell in love with *Narcissus*, but he would not talk to her, so she was unable to say anything to him; she wasted away for grief until only her voice was left, repeating the last words of his sentences.

Eileithyia: The Greek goddess of childbirth, closely connected with *Hera*.

Einherjar: The special champions in the host of fallen warriors whom the Norse god *Odin* had summoned to *Valhalla*, so that they could fight for the gods at the great day of *Ragnarok*: 'the host of the Einherjar will not be too great in the day of the gods' need'.

Eir: A minor Norse goddess of healing.

Eithinoha: The Iroquois Indian name for the earth-goddess, meaning simply 'our mother'.

Ek Chuah: Lord of travellers and merchants in

Maya myths; he was associated with the war-god.

Ekeko: The god of good luck among the Aymara Indians of Bolivia. His festival, on 24 January, is still popular; little images of him, a fat little man covered with miniature pots and pans, are kept in houses as good luck and fertility charms.

El: The supreme god of Canaan, who played a part in their myths similar to that of *Zeus* in Greek myth, though he took little part in human affairs. He was the creator, and ruler of heaven; but he did not move from his throne 'at the out-flowing of streams'. He corresponds to *Anu* in Sumerian myth, just as *Baal* is the active god in Canaan, corresponding to *Enlil* or *Marduk*.

Electra: Daughter of the Greek leader *Agamemnon*; she urged her brother *Orestes* to avenge their father's death by killing their mother *Clytemnestra* and her lover *Aegisthus*. She eventually married Orestes' friend Pylades.

Eleusinian Mysteries: Derived from the story of *Demeter*'s stay at Eleusis, these Greek secret ceremonies were jealously guarded, and very little is known of them as a result.

El-lal: Creator-hero of the Patagonian Indians of South America; his father Nosjthej tried to eat him when he was born, but a rat carried him into its hole, which his father could not enter. Despite his father's behaviour, El-lal taught him to use the bow and how to hunt; but once again he tried to kill his son. He followed him across the Andes and almost caught up with him; just in time a huge forest grew up between them, and El-lal escaped. He wooed the sun's daughter, but she refused to marry him, and he decided to leave the world, having taught men how to hunt. He shot arrows into the sea, and a green island rose up, to which a swan carried him; there he rested from his work.

Elysian Plain: Part of the underworld where the blessed spirits dwelt in Greek myth; it was ruled by *Rhadamanthus*, and, in the words of the poet Homer, lay 'at the world's end . . . the land where living is made easiest for mankind, where no snow falls, no strong winds blow and there is never any rain, but day after day the west wind's tuneful breeze comes in from the *Ocean* to refresh its folk.' Life there was like life on earth, but without any kind of care or trouble.

Emakong: Emakong was the man who discovered fire, according to a myth from New Guinea. One day he dropped one of his ornaments in a stream and dived after it. At the bottom, he found himself in the yard of a house belonging to a man also called Emakong. In the house there was a fire, and food cooking on it, which the first Emakong had never seen before, as fire was unknown to men. The men who lived below the stream turned into snakes each night, but were very friendly, and sent Emakong back to the world with some fire and night done up in a parcel.

Emma-o: Japanese god of the underworld, judge of the dead, who assigned souls to their place of punishment. When the soul arrived before him, it was shown its past in a huge mirror. According to one legend, the god himself was tortured once a day by being put on a bed of red-hot iron and having molten brass poured into his mouth. He is the same as the Hindu *Yama*.

Endymion: The most handsome of Greek youths, whom the moon-goddess *Selene* loved. *Zeus* granted him eternal sleep instead of death. The long poem by Keats on Endymion and his love for Selene (or Cynthia) adds many invented details to the original myths.

Enlil: The Babylonian storm-god, who controlled the floods of the great rivers of Sumeria, the Tigris and the Euphrates. He was the right-hand man of *Anu*, and carried out his wishes: but these were not always favourable, and included the dust storms of the desert as well as the rain-bringing winds. He was also god of justice. His special animal was the bull.

Enore: Among the Paressí Indians of the Matto Grosso of Brazil, one version of the creation story tells how Enore, the supreme being, carved the first humans from wood. Enore divided all the good things of the world between their four children; but one of them, Zaluie, refused to take guns, because they were too heavy, and did not want cattle and horses because they would clutter up the village square. So his brother Kamaikore took all these and became ancestor of the powerful and prosperous white men, while the Indians, Zaluie's descendants, have only bows and arrows.

Eos: The Greek goddess of the dawn, whom the

Romans called Aurora. Like the sun-god, she drives a chariot, but it only has two horses instead of four. She loved a mortal called Tithonus, and asked *Zeus* to make him immortal, which he did. But she forgot to ask for him to be eternally young as well; as he grew older and older he shrivelled away and became a grasshopper. Tithonus and Eos had a son, Memnon, who was killed by *Achilles*. In memory of him Eos wept each morning, and her tears became the dew.

Epigoni, War of the: After the defeat of the *Seven Against Thebes*, their sons took up the quarrel and successfully avenged themselves on the city, razing its walls to the ground. This war was called the War of the Epigoni, or Younger Sons; *Diomedes*, the Greek hero in the *Trojan War*, was among them.

Epona: Epona, the Celtic goddess of horses, was the only Celtic god or goddess to be worshipped at Rome. Altars sacred to her show her sitting on a mare.

Epunamun: God of evil among the Araucanian Indians of South America.

Erato: *Muse* of the lyre.

Erebus: The Greek spirit of darkness, which at the very beginning of things sprang from Chaos. The name was sometimes used for the kingdom of *Hades*.

Erechtheus: The first ruler of Athens; Athens was attacked by the men of Eleusis under their king, Eumolpus, a son of *Poseidon*. Erechtheus asked the oracle at Delphi what he should do in order to win the war, and was told to sacrifice one of his daughters. This he did, and the Athenians were victorious, Erechtheus killing Eumolpus himself. Poseidon avenged his son by killing Erechtheus and his whole family.

Ereshkigal: Babylonian goddess of the underworld, who was overcome by the god of war, *Nergal*. He invaded her realm, and overthrew Ereshkigal, but in the end married her.

Erh Lang: Nephew of the supreme Chinese god *Yu Huang*, Erh Lang was also worshipped as a god; he used to drive away evil spirits by setting the dog of heaven, T'ien Kou, to chase them. He was said to know seventy-two ways of changing

84

his shape, and he possessed a mirror which made devils visible.

Erichthonius: Son of the Greek fire-god *Hephaestus* and of *Gaia* or Earth. When he was born, *Athena* put him in a chest and gave him to the three daughters of *Cecrops* to look after, telling them not to look inside. Two of the girls looked in the chest and saw he had serpent's tails instead of feet; they went mad and threw themselves off the rock of the Acropolis at Athens.

Erlik: The devil in central Asian myth: see *Ulgen*.

Eros: The Greek god of love; one of the oldest gods, he was held to have sprung from Chaos itself at the beginning of things. Later, as romantic love in particular rather than love in its widest sense, he was shown as *Cupid*, the love-god with bow and arrows. He himself fell in love with *Psyche*. There is a famous statue of him at Piccadilly Circus in London.

Erymanthian Boar: see *Heracles*.

Eshu: 'Trickster' god of the Yoruba people of West Africa. He confused men and made them go mad, and he could change his shape and appearance, or appear both very small and very large at the same time. But he also knew all the different languages of men, and acted as go-between for men and gods.

Esus: A Gaulish god 'whose savage shrine makes men shudder', according to a Roman poet; human victims were offered to him by being hanged and run through with a sword. Carvings of him show him as a woodcutter, though no stories have survived to explain this.

Etana: In Sumerian myth, Etana was the first king on earth, chosen by the gods. He had no heir, and asked *Shamash* how he could find the herb that would make sure he had a son. Shamash told him to go to a certain mountain and ask an eagle for it. Now this eagle had been punished by the gods for eating the young of a serpent which shared the mountain with him, and his wings had been cut off by the serpent. Etana brought him food until his feathers grew again. At the end of eight months, the eagle was strong again, and offered to take Etana up to heaven, presumably to get the herb. They

reached without difficulty the gates of the heaven where *Anu* lived, but the eagle wanted to go on to heaven itself, which was even higher. On the second part of the journey, Etana grew dizzy from the height, and begged the eagle to turn back, but it refused. Etana fell, dragging the eagle with him, and both were killed.

Eteocles: A Greek prince, son of *Oedipus* of Thebes. He and his brother *Polyneices* agreed that they would rule in Thebes for alternate years. At the end of the first year, when Eteocles was king and Polyneices had gone into exile, Eteocles refused to hand over the town, and it was from this that the war of the *Seven Against Thebes* arose. Eteocles and Polyneices killed each other in the battle.

Eumaeus: The swineherd of the Greek hero *Odysseus*, who welcomed him on his return home and helped him to overcome the suitors of his wife *Penelope*.

Eumenides: Another name for the Greek *Furies*, meaning the 'Kindly Ones'; by giving them a pleasant name, their anger was less likely to be aroused.

Europa: Daughter of King *Agenor* of Tyre. In Greek myth she was carried off by *Zeus* in the form of a white bull which appeared as she was walking in the fields outside the city. It seemed so gentle that she climbed on its back, and the bull swam away with her to Crete. Her two sons by Zeus were *Minos*, later king of Crete, and *Rhadamanthus*.

Eurus: The Greek spirit of the east wind.

Euryale: One of the *Gorgons*.

Eurydice: The wife of the Greek poet and singer *Orpheus*, she was bitten by a deadly snake as *Aristaeus* pursued her along a river-bank. Orpheus obtained leave to take her back from *Hades* provided he did not look back at her, but just as he came up into the daylight he turned, forgetting his promise, before she had reached the world of the living again. So she was lost to him forever, the Roman poet Vergil tells us. Others say that Orpheus was successful, or that he found that he had only rescued her ghost.

Eurynomus: The Greek traveller and writer

Pausanias tells of a famous picture at Delphi depicting the terrors of *Hades*, among which was a monster called Eurynomus, shown with grinning teeth and a body the colour of a fly, which devoured the flesh of the dead, leaving only their bones.

Eurystheus: Lord of Tiryns in Greece, he benefited from *Hera*'s jealousy of *Heracles*; when *Zeus* was tricked into swearing that any child of his blood born that day would rule over mankind, Hera delayed Heracles' birth and hastened that of Eurystheus. So Heracles had to serve Eurystheus, and performed the famous twelve labours in order to gain immortality. Eurystheus is usually shown as a weak and rather frightened man, who is terrified when Heracles successfully brings back the extraordinary monsters he is sent to fetch. After Heracles had succeeded in bringing back the *Nemaean Lion*, he forbade him to enter the city again, and had a large bronze jar made in which he could hide whenever Heracles returned to show his latest prize outside the city walls.

Euterpe: The *muse* of flute-playing or of tragedy in Greek myth.

Evadne: Wife of *Capaneus*, one of the *Seven Against Thebes*; when he died, a huge funeral pyre was built for him, as was the Greek custom. Evadne hurled herself onto this out of grief for his death, and so died with him.

Evaki: Goddess of night in the myths of the Bakairi Indians of South America. She shut the sun in a pot every night and moved it back to its starting place in the sky for the next day. She stole sleep from the eyes of the lizards and shared it among all other living things.

Evander: A minor Roman god, whom Vergil portrays in the *Aeneid* as father of one of *Aeneas'* allies. He greeted Aeneas on the site where Rome was later built, and built a small village there himself.

F

Fafnir: In the Norse story of *Ottar*, which leads into the saga of *Sigurd* the Volsung, Fafnir was the brother of Ottar. He and his brother *Regin* killed their father Hreidmar and seized the ransom paid to him by the gods, which was gold which had once belonged to the dwarf *Andvari*. Andvari had laid a curse on it when it was taken from him, and Fafnir turned himself into a dragon and guarded the gold from everyone, including his brother. Regin persuaded Sigurd to kill Fafnir, planning to kill Sigurd himself once his task was done; but Sigurd then discovered this, and killed Regin instead.

Fand: Wife of the Irish god, *Manannan*; when he abandoned her she went to live with her sister Liban, wife of *Labraid*. Labraid needed the help of the hero *Cuchulainn* to overcome his enemies, and Liban sent a message to him saying that if he came and helped Labraid for a day, Fand would be his. Cuchulainn, thinking it beneath him to come at a woman's command, sent his charioteer Loeg to see if what Liban said about the garden of Fand, where they lived, was true. Loeg went, and returned saying that he had seen all the marvels Liban had described: a house that could hold a hundred and fifty men, purple trees with beautiful songbirds, trees that gave food enough to supply three hundred men, and a barrel of ale which never ran out. Fand herself was as magical and beautiful as anyone could imagine. So Cuchulainn went, and defeated Labraid's enemies: he stayed with Fand for a month, and then returned to Ireland. Here he arranged to see Fand again, but his wife Emer came to him to prevent their meeting, and pleaded with Cuchulainn, who fell in love with her again. Fand nobly sacrificed her claim to Cuchulainn, and her husband Manannan, 'horseman of the crested waves of the sea', came to reclaim her. Cuchulainn mourned Fand's going for a time, but he was given a magic drink which made him forget her, and the same drink made Emer forget that she had been jealous.

Fates (Moirai or Parcae): In Greek myth, the Three Fates are very old women who control the destiny of the world; even *Zeus* himself is bound by what they decide. They are the daughters of Night, and are called *Atropos*, *Clotho* and Lachesis. Atropos spins the past, Clotho the present, and Lachesis the future; another version says that Atropos cuts off the threads, Clotho holds the distaff onto which the thread is wound, and Lachesis actually spins the thread. What they spin is the destiny of each individual; when the thread breaks, a life is ended.

Faunus: A local Roman deity, who was regarded as the foster-father of *Romulus*. He was a kind of lesser version of *Pan*; sometimes there are a number of 'fauns', half-animal, half-human creatures who attend Pan.

Febris: The Roman goddess of fever, after whom the month of February is named.

Feinn: The Feinn or Fianna were the 'troops' or followers of the Irish hero *Fionn*, whose exploits are recorded in a large number of stories; some of these may be historical, while others are folk-tales.

Feng Po: The Chinese god of the winds who carried the winds in a goat-skin bottle. By un-corking the bottle and pointing it in a certain direction, he made the wind blow from that quarter.

Fenja and Menja: Two Norse giantesses who worked the magic mill Grotti for King *Frodi*. Frodi made them grind out gold from it day and night, never allowing them to rest. So they cast a spell on the mill, and made it produce a host of armed men to attack Frodi. With the aid of the magic warriors, Frodi's enemy Mysing overcame and slew him. He carried off Fenja and Menja in one of his ships, and told them to grind salt during the voyage. But they produced so much that the ship sank, and forever after the sea was salty as a result.

Fenrir, Fenris-wolf: The Norse god *Loki* was the father of various monsters and evil creatures, among them the Fenris-wolf, the *Midgard-serpent* and the goddess of the dead, *Hel*. The Fenris-wolf was brought up in *Asgard*, home of the gods, but grew so huge and fearsome that in the end only the god *Tyr* dared to feed him. The gods decided that he would have to be bound, but every attempt failed; the Fenris-wolf shook off the strongest fetters they could forge. *Odin* at last had to enlist the help of the dwarfs, and they made him a chain of invisible things which had never existed, 'the roots of a mountain, the noise of a moving cat, the breath of a fish, the beard of a woman, the sinews of a bear and the spittle of a bird', which

was called the fetter Gleipnir. It was like a silk ribbon, but nothing could break it. The wolf was suspicious, and insisted that one of the gods put his hand in his mouth while he was being bound, as a hostage. Only Tyr was willing to do this; the wolf found himself held fast by Gleipnir, and bit off Tyr's hand in revenge. At the end of the world, at *Ragnarok*, the Fenris-wolf will break his bonds, and hurl himself at Odin. In the fight he will swallow Odin; but Odin's son *Vidar* will seize his jaws and tear him in two.

Finuweigh: A tale from the Philippines relates that the gods first tried to make men of wax, but they melted. So Mehu and Finuweigh, two of the gods, made a man out of dirt. But when they had nearly finished, Finuweigh put the nose on upside down. Mehu told him that men would drown if he left it like that, because the rain would run into their nostrils. Finuweigh refused to change it, so Mehu had to do it quickly while he was not looking, and left his fingermarks on each side of men's noses.

Fionn: Fionn was an Irish hero whose father was killed before he was born. He was brought up in secret by women in the depths of the woods, who taught him the arts of war. When he was eight, he encountered a magician who destroyed the royal court of Tara each Samhain eve (1 November). When the magician appeared and started to lull the defenders to sleep with his music, Fionn managed to remain awake and kill him. This feat won him the leadership of the *Fianna*, hunters and warriors who defended Ireland against her enemies. The stories about him are not unlike those told about the god *Lugh*.

Fir Bolg: The early gods and inhabitants of Ireland, defeated by *Tuatha De Danann*.

Five Suns: In Aztec myth, the world was said to go through five ages, each with its own sun. Four had already passed, and the fifth was the present age. The first age was the age when *Tezcatlipoca* was sun; at first there had only been a half-sun, but this was not bright enough, and the gods made a second half-sun, giving both to Tezcatlipoca to carry across the sky. In those days there were both giants and men; but after 676 years, Tezcatlipoca was thrown down from his place by *Quetzalcoatl*. He became the Jaguar constellation (which we call the Great Bear) and devoured the giants. Quetzalcoatl was also sun for 676 years; at the end of his reign, there was a great wind (Quetzalcoatl was wind-god) which either blew away the people living on earth or turned them into monkeys. *Tlaloc* became sun-god, and occupied this position for 364 years; then Tlaloc's wife *Chalchiuhtlicue* was made sun by Quetzalcoatl. After another 364 years, there was a great deluge (Tlaloc and his wife were rain-gods) and all the men and women were turned into fishes. The heavens had to be created again, which Quetzalcoatl and Tezcatlipoca did; and men were also created afresh. Tezcatlipoca taught the art of making fire to men. A new sun, *Tonatiuh*, was made by Quetzalcoatl, who threw his son by Chalchiuhtlicue into a fire; while Tlaloc's son, also thrown into a fire, became the moon. Both sun and moon had to be fed with human sacrifices, so the gods invented war in order to provide victims.

Other versions list the ages as follows: *Atonatiuh*, which ended with a flood; Ocelotonatiuh, the age of giants; Quiyanhtonatiuh, when it rained fire; Ecatonatiuh, when there were great winds; and the present age, which will end in complete destruction.

Flora: The Roman goddess of flowering or blossoming plants, shown with a wreath of flowers in her hair.

Fomorians: The legendary allies in Ireland of *Tuatha De Danann*, the Fomorians were a monstrous people with one hand, one leg and three rows of teeth. Their leader in war was *Balor*; their king, *Bres*, ruled all Ireland until the Tuatha De Danann drove him out because he was so mean, ending the old friendship between the two peoples.

Fornjöt: In Norse myth, the father of the elements: Kari, wind, *Logi*, fire and *Aegir*, the sea.

Forseti: The son of *Balder*, he was the Norse god of justice, dwelling in the hall Glitnir, built of gold and silver, where he 'stills all strife'. An early saga tells how the Frisians were asked by Charlemagne to tell him what their laws were, and how they were unable to do so until a stranger with a golden axe appeared to them and taught them laws. The stranger was Forseti, and he was particularly worshipped by the Frisians.

Fortuna: The Roman goddess of chance, whose statue at Rome was kept veiled, because the

goddess was said to be ashamed of her favours to mortal men.

Fraoch: Irish hero whose mother was a goddess. He wooed the daughter of *Ailill* and *Medhbh*: her parents tried to get rid of him by sending him to fetch a branch from a magic rowan-tree guarded by a 'peist' or monster. Although badly wounded, he succeeded; and fairy women came and carried him away to their mound to cure his wounds. *Cuchulainn* later killed him.

Fravashis: In Iranian myth, guardian spirits who watched over men and gods alike.

Freki: The wolf of the Norse god *Odin*; the name means glutton, and the wolf is a symbol of the way in which huge numbers of warriors are devoured by wars caused by Odin.

Frey and Freyja: The Norse gods Frey and Freyja were the children of *Njord*, and were the leaders of the group of gods called the *Vanir*. Both were gods of fertility.

Frey was the giver of sunshine and rain, and the gifts of peace and plenty. The stories of the reign of the early Danish king *Frodi* and of Frey's own reign in Sweden are similar, and correspond to the 'Golden Age' of classical mythology. Because his rule produced wealth and prosperity, he was particularly worshipped in Sweden, where his priests used to take his image round the country in autumn and winter to bless the land. He was called 'the god of the world', that is, of the human world or *Midgard*. It was he who owned the golden boar, *Gullinbursti*, and the magic ship *Skidbladnir*.

He was also associated with death and burial: *Odin*'s worshippers were cremated, but Frey's devotees were buried unburnt. In the mythical history of Sweden which tells of his reign as though he were an ordinary king, he is said to have lain in his barrow-grave for three years before the people were told of his death, while gifts were laid in front of it by the priests.

He was, on the whole, a peaceful god, and in his temple at Vatnsdale in Iceland there was a ban on all kinds of weapons. However, his boar symbol protected the wearer in battle, and Frey's boar is often found on Anglo-Saxon jewellery and armour.

One day Frey sat on Odin's seat *Hlidskjalf* when Odin was away, and looking out across the worlds he saw a girl called *Gerd*, who lived in the underworld. Her arms were so white that they lit up sea and sky, and Frey fell so deeply in love that he could not sleep or eat. His servant *Skirnir* was sent to win her for him, and Frey gave him his sword and his horse for the journey. By a mixture of bribes and threats Skirnir won over Gerd, who agreed to meet Frey in the sacred wood where no wind ever blew, in nine nights' time.

At *Ragnarok*, Frey will be slain by *Surt*, because he has no sword to defend himself, having given his own to Skirnir.

Freyja is the goddess of love, the Norse equivalent of *Venus*, but with other, more disturbing powers. She is also the goddess of magic, and she has some powers over the dead. As love-goddess she was accused of being shameless in her love affairs by *Loki*, and she is said to have married her brother Frey. She also has a mysterious husband *Od*, for whom she weeps tears of red gold.

She was the owner of the necklace *Brisingamen*, which Loki once stole from her. As no one could enter her hall without her consent, he turned himself into a fly and crept in through a crack. He found Frejya asleep, and lying on the clasp of the necklace; so he became a flea, and bit her. She turned over, so Loki regained his real shape, unclasped the necklace and took it to *Odin*.

Freyja, too, could change her shape, her special disguise being that of a falcon which Loki sometimes borrowed. This bird-disguise reflects her part as patron of the women seers called 'volva', who worked spells and practised the art of reading the future. The 'volva' wore an elaborate costume, and when she prophesied, she went into a trance, in which her spirit was said to leave her body and travel over vast distances in bird shape, just as Freyja herself did. Like Frey, Freyja had a magic boar, called *Hildisvin*; she drove in a chariot drawn by cats. The popular idea of a witch and her cat may be a dim memory of Freyja.

The giant who built *Asgard*, and *Thrym* who stole *Thor's* hammer, both demanded Freyja as their wife, but on both occasions she escaped having to marry them.

Frigg: The wife of the chief of the Norse gods, *Odin*. She is a rather shadowy mother-figure, with no particular myths of her own. She was goddess of marriage, and her day, Friday, was a lucky day for weddings. She shared Odin's magical powers, and was said to know the future

93

of both men and gods, though she never revealed it. It was she who extracted the oath from all living things that they would not hurt *Balder*. In Germany she was called Frija, and it is not quite clear whether she and *Freyja* were once regarded as the same and only later became two distinct goddesses.

Frodi: Frodi, 'the fruitful one', was an early king of Denmark whose reign was marked by peace and plenty, according to Saxo, a historian writing in the twelfth century A D; the stories about him, which include a description of how his body was carried round the land in a wagon after his death to persuade people that he was still alive, are very much like those about *Frey*, and he may well be the same god, worshipped by the Danes as Frey was by the Swedes.

Frost-Giants: At the beginning of the world, in Norse myth, the first giant was born from *Ymir*'s feet. When the giant Ymir was slain by the gods, all the frost-giants except *Bergelmir* were drowned in his blood, which became the sea. Bergelmir escaped in some kind of boat, and all the later frost-giants were his children. They lived in *Jötunheim*, and were perpetually at war with the gods, of whom they were jealous; they often tried to steal their treasures or to get the gods themselves into their power. *Thor* was their particular enemy. At the day of *Ragnarok* they will fight beside *Surt* against the gods.

Fu Hsi: The Heavenly Emperor in Chinese myth, one of the Three Emperors, half man, half serpent. He discovered the 'eight diagrams', which were the symbols of the teaching of the Taoist religion, from the inscriptions on a tablet given to him by a huge water-horse. He also discovered iron and drove wild animals out of China, as well as making rules for marriage and for writing. He was the Chinese god of hunting and fishing.

Fujin: Japanese god of the winds; shown as an *oni* carrying a bag on his back, in which the winds are contained. Compare *Aeolus*.

Fulla: Servant of the Norse goddess *Freyja*, who carries her coffer; she represents the abundance locked in the earth which Freyja, as goddess of fertility, releases in the form of crops.

Furies: In Greek myth the Furies or Erinyes

punished anyone who offended against the divine laws, in particular anyone who killed their mother or father. They were born from the drops of *Uranus'* blood when he was attacked by *Cronus* and belonged to the old gods. When they pursued *Orestes* to Athens, *Apollo* defended Orestes against their claims at a court presided over by *Athene*. Orestes was acquitted, and Athene appeased the Furies by giving them a temple in Athens, where they were worshipped as the *Eumenides* or 'Kindly Ones'.

Fu Shen: The Chinese 'God of Happiness', often shown with *Shou Hsing* and *Lu Hsing*.

Fylgja: In Norse belief, everyone had a fylgja, who was a guardian spirit which accompanied him in human or animal form, like the Scottish 'fetch' but was not normally visible; indeed, if anyone saw his own fylgja, it was a token of certain death.

G

Gahe, Ga'n: The Chiricahua Apache Indians of the south-western United States believed that the gahe were supernatural creatures who lived inside mountains, like the *hactcin* or *kachinas* of other tribes. The gahe could be heard dancing and beating drums, and they painted their faces for these occasions. In the Chiricahua ritual dances, masked dancers represent the gahe with a different colour for each point of the compass. The exception is the Grey One, who appears as a clown, but is really the most powerful of all. Masks can only be made by someone who has seen the gahe. The gahe are worshipped for their healing powers and their ability to drive away disease. The White Mountain Apache called them ga'n, and believed that they had once lived on earth but had retreated into the mountains because disease and death could not reach them there.

Gaia: The mother of the 'old gods' or *Titans* of Greek myth, Gaia was the Earth itself. Her husband was *Uranus*, who was jealous of his children, and hid them in Gaia's huge body, until she could bear it no longer. She gave her youngest son *Cronus* a sword, with which he disabled Uranus. Gaia was the 'mother of all things', but no particular stories were attached to her since she belonged to the dim past rather than to the gods of the present. Artists often represented her as rising out of the earth.

Gainjin: The first creatures in Papuan myth. They were larger than ordinary creatures and came from the sky to make everything in the world. When they had finished, they went back to the sky: only the crocodile and the snake stayed behind, and lived in the bush.

Galatea: One of the Greek nymphs called *Nereids*, who was loved by the shepherd Acis and by *Polyphemus* the *Cyclops*. Polyphemus, jealous of Acis' success in winning Galatea's love, crushed him under a rock, but Galatea turned him into a river.

Gandharvas: The Gandharvas were Hindu sky-gods, who controlled the stars and who guarded the *soma* which gave the gods eternal youth. Originally there was thought to be only one Gandharva but later writers speak of the '6333 Gandharvas'. They were singers and musicians, and the lovers of the *apsarases*. Their enemies were the *Nagas*, whom they overcame;

96

but the Nagas appealed to *Vishnu* for help. Vishnu appeared in the form of a hero, and killed the Gandharvas.

Ganesha: The Hindu god of wisdom, son of *Shiva* and *Devi*. His appearance is remarkable: he is usually shown as a small, stout man, pot-bellied and red-skinned; he has an elephant's head, but only one tusk, and he has four hands. His 'vehicle' or mount is a rat. There are various legends as to why he had an elephant's head: one is that *Devi* was taking a bath, and told Ganesha to prevent anyone from coming in. Her husband *Shiva* tried to enter, but Ganesha would not let him, and so Shiva cut off his head. Devi was furious, so Shiva replaced Ganesha's head with an elephant's. He lost his tusk in a similar fight when a visitor, *Parashurama*, came to see Shiva: Shiva was asleep, and Ganesha was guarding the door. Parashurama had an axe which Shiva had given him, and Ganesha was unable to stop him cutting off one of his tusks with this.

Ganges: The Indian river Ganges was supposed to flow from the toe of *Vishnu* and was brought to earth at the prayer of *Bhagiratha*, to cleanse the ashes of his ancestors. *Shiva* caught the river as it fell, because its weight would have been too much for the earth; and it ran from his brow in seven streams.

Ganymede: The son of Tros, king of Troy, whom *Zeus* carried off in Greek myth, disguised as an eagle, to be cupbearer to the gods. Tros was given a stud of marvellous horses by way of compensation for his son's disappearance.

Gaokerena: The tree of life in Iranian myth, the fruit of which made men immortal. *Angra Mainyu* sent a lizard to destroy it, but *Ahura Mazda* set ten fish to guard it; as they swim round it one of them always faces the lizard.

Garang and Abuk: The first man and woman in the myths of the Dinka of Sudan. God made them in miniature and put them in a pot; when it was opened they grew to normal size. He gave them one grain of corn each day to pound and make into food, and this was enough, until Abuk, the woman, was greedy and tried to pound more, using a longer stick. With this, she hit the sky; so God moved the sky, and himself, much further away from men.

97

Garm: The hound who guarded the Norse underworld, which the god *Tyr* is to fight at the day of *Ragnarok*; possibly another name for *Fenrir*.

Garuda: The 'vehicle' on which the Indian god *Vishnu* rides, half man, half eagle. Garuda has a white head and red wings like those of an eagle, and a golden body and limbs like those of a man. He is able to swallow evildoers of all castes, except for the highest, the Brahmans; he once swallowed a Brahman by mistake, but the Brahman burnt his throat and he had to let him go. Garuda is the great enemy of all snakes, with whom he is continually at war: Kadru, the mother of serpents, once captured Garuda's mother, and to ransom her he stole the *amrita* from the gods. *Indra* managed to get it back, but only after the Garuda had smashed his weapon, the thunderbolt. In Tibetan Buddhist myth there is a whole race of Garudas, with the same appearance and the same hostility to the snakes or *Nagas*.

Gaya Maretan: The first man in Iranian myth: he lived for thirty years before being destroyed by *Angra Mainyu*. His body became all the various kinds of metals, and from gold the first human couple were produced.

Geb: Egyptian god of the earth, one of the *Great Ennead*; husband of *Nut* and father of *Isis*, *Osiris*, *Seth* and *Nephthys*. He is sometimes shown as a goose. See *Ra*.

Gefion: Norse goddess to whom unmarried girls went when they died. She also appears in a story from the early history of Denmark, which is a myth explaining how the island of Zealand, on which Copenhagen stands, came to be separated from the mainland. *Odin* sent her to look for land on which to settle, and King *Gylfi* of Sweden offered her as much land as she could plough around in a day and a night. So she went to *Jötunheim*, married a giant, and had four sons by him, whom she turned into oxen. With their help she ploughed round what is now Zealand, and separated it from Sweden. She later married a son of Odin, called Skjold (see also *Scyld*), and lived there with him.

She was a goddess of fertility, like *Freyja*, and also possessed a magic necklace like *Brisingamen*.

Geirrod: 1. A giant in Norse myth. *Loki*, borrow-

98

ing *Freyja*'s shape as a bird, was captured by Geirrod, who recognized him in spite of his disguise by the look in his eyes. He shut him up without food for three months, until Loki promised to lure *Thor* to Geirrod's hall without either his hammer or his magic belt. Loki managed to persuade Thor into going, but on the way a friendly giantess warned him that he was running a dangerous risk, and provided him with different magic weapons: a staff, another belt and iron gloves. When Thor reached Geirrod's kingdom, Geirrod's daughters attacked him first: one caused a river to flood and nearly drowned him, but he hauled himself out, using the branch of a rowan tree which grew on the bank. He reached Geirrod's hall, but when he sat down in a chair, it rose from the floor and nearly crushed him against the roof. Geirrod's other daughters were underneath it, pushing it against the ceiling, but Thor brought the chair down with the help of his magic staff and broke their backs. Geirrod flung a ball of red-hot iron at him, but Thor caught it in his gloves and hurled it back. Geirrod tried to hide behind a pillar, but the iron went through the pillar and killed him.

King *Gorm* of Denmark and his servant Thorkill later visited Geirrod's hall after a long and perilous journey, and found it desolate and filthy, full of monsters and phantoms; there were three women with broken backs, who, so Thorkill told his companions, were Geirrod's daughters. There were treasures as well, but when some of the company tried to pick them up they turned into poisonous snakes and magic weapons which killed them. Thorkill himself was tempted by other treasures, but all the inhabitants of the hall witches and monsters, attacked them when he touched them, and they barely escaped with their lives.

2. A prince favoured by *Odin*; his half-brother *Agnar* was *Frigg*'s favourite, and they were rivals for a kingdom. Frigg tricked Geirrod into torturing Odin when he once visited him in disguise: Geirrod had Odin placed between two very hot fires and asked him all kinds of questions about the world and the gods. Odin's answers and his visions under torture are told in the poem *Grimnismál*. When Geirrod at last learnt who his guest really was, he unsheathed his sword and hurried forward to cut his bonds; but he tripped and fell on his own sword, and was killed.

Gerd: The beautiful daughter of a giant, whom the Norse god *Frey* once saw when he sat on

Odin's seat *Hlidskjalf*. She lived in the underworld, and her arms were so white that they lit up the whole earth and sky. Frey sent his servant Skirnir to woo her; after a long and dangerous journey he arrived at her home, but she would not listen to his pleas. Only when he threatened to put her under a strange spell which would make her waste away with longing did she agree to become Frey's bride and to meet him nine nights later in a magic grove.

Geryon: One of the monsters slain by the Greek hero *Heracles* in the course of his labours. He dwelt on an island in the stream of *Ocean* at the world's edge, where he tended great herds of cattle, which Heracles carried off. He was said to be either three-headed or three-bodied.

Giants: 1. In Greek myth, the war against the giants, like the wars with the *Titans* and the *Aloadai*, was one of the troubles which *Zeus* had to overcome after he seized power from *Cronos*. The giants were the children of Earth (*Gaia*), who caused a herb to grow which would make them invincible. But Zeus gathered the herb himself. In the battle, the giants advanced on the gods, hurling rocks and whole oak trees which they had set on fire, but they were defeated in the end and imprisoned under volcanoes.

2. In Norse myth, the giants are the evil opponents of the gods; they are often called *frost-giants* because they live in a cold realm, and they are also said to dwell in mountains. Their home lies to the north, and is called *Jötunheim*, 'the giants' world or *Utgard*, the outer regions. Like *dwarfs*, the sun is fatal to them, and turns them into stone. See *Fenja and Menja*, *Geirrod*, *Hymir*, *Thiazi*, *Thrym* and *Utgard Loki*. *Aegir* was part giant, part god, as was also *Loki*.

Gilgamesh: Hero of a great epic poem from ancient Babylon. At the beginning of the poem, Gilgamesh is shown as a powerful, tyrannical king, whose pride angered the gods. Aruru, the goddess who created Gilgamesh, was told to create a rival to him, and she shaped Enkidu out of clay. He was a wild being, who ran on the hills with the deer and other game, and who was immensely strong. Gilgamesh heard of his existence and lured him down to the plains by sending a woman to find him, to whom he made love. Enkidu found that the wild beasts ran away from him and that he was no longer as strong as he was before he had met her; and she persuaded him to come down to Gilgamesh's city of Uruk. Here he met Gilgamesh and wrestled with him: Gilgamesh threw him, but they made peace and became firm friends.

Gilgamesh and Enkidu then wanted to win glory for themselves, and set out to conquer the giant Humbaba or Huwawa, who lived in the forest of giant cedars. Despite bad omens and the huge size of the giant, they laid him low and destroyed the forest, so that he begged for mercy. Gilgamesh was inclined to let him go, but Enkidu did not trust Humbaba, and so they killed him. When they presented the head to *Enlil*, the god was angry, and cursed them both.

Gilgamesh's fame was such after this exploit that the goddess *Ishtar* herself sought his hand; but he rejected her, saying that she had always been a fatal curse to her lovers, who had been changed into beasts or killed. Ishtar was furious and persuaded *Anu* to make the bull of heaven to bring famine and plague to the land which Gilgamesh ruled. The plague carried off Enkidu, and Gilgamesh mourned him bitterly, setting up a great statue to his memory. Overcome by fear of death, Gilgamesh now set out to find *Utnapishtim*, 'the Far Away', the man who had survived the great flood, and to whom the gods had given eternal life in the garden of *Dilmun*. He passed many dangers, including the monsters who were half man, half scorpion at the mountain of Mashu, and reached the garden of Siduri, 'the Woman of the Vine', at the sea's edge. She directed him to Urshanabi, Utnapishtim's ferryman, who would take him across the 'waters of death' to Utnapishtim (rather as *Charon* ferried souls across the *Styx* in Greek myth). Although Gilgamesh destroyed the magic stones which ensured a safe voyage, he managed to cross the waters, and reached his goal. But Utnapishtim could not help him in his quest for eternal life, and as they talked Gilgamesh went to sleep. For each day that he slept, Utnapishtim's wife baked a loaf, and when he awoke saying that he had only slept for a moment, Utnapishtim showed him seven loaves, each mouldier than the last, and pointed out his weakness. Utnapishtim then sent him on the way home, but told him how to obtain a plant which grew under water that would restore his lost youth. Gilgamesh dived down and picked the plant, but a serpent stole it from him later on his journey while he was bathing. He returned home, and there the texts of the epic come to an end.

Gimle: The hall in the home of the Norse gods, *Asgard*, to which the righteous went after death; it was very splendid, with a golden roof.

Ginnungagap: 'The space of magic deceit', it lay between *Muspell*, the land of fire to the south, and the cold desert to the north, according to Norse stories of the creation of the world. Here shadow and substance met, and it was here that gods, men and giants first appeared. See *Audhumla*, *Ymir*.

Gitche Manito: The Algonquin Indians of the east coast of North America believed that all things had their own spirits or Manitos, and that the world was created by the Great Manito, or spirit of life, called Gitche Manito. Gitche Manito was believed to be without form or shape and only indirectly concerned with man's fate.

Gjallarhorn: The horn of the Norse god *Heimdall*, which could be heard throughout the world, and which would be blown at the day of *Ragnarok*. Heimdall was the watchful god, and this was the horn of warning; the idea is similar to that of the archangel Gabriel and the last trumpet in Christian belief.

Glasisvellir: In Norse myth, the home of *Gudmund*, a mysterious giant king, brother of *Geirrod*, who ruled over a kind of *Elysian Plain* or land where there was no death. The name means 'Glittering Plains'.

Glauce: Second wife of the Greek hero *Jason*. Like *Heracles*, she was burnt to death by a poisoned robe which *Medea*, Jason's first wife, sent to her.

Glaucus: A Greek sea-god, said to have been once a fisherman, who found a magic herb which made him immortal. Some say that he designed and built the *Argo*.

Gleipnir: Fetter used to tie down the *Fenris-wolf* in Norse myth.

Glooscap, Gluskap, Gluskabe: The creator-hero in the myths of the Abnaki Indians of the north-eastern United States. From his mother's body, he made everything that was pleasant, while his evil twin brother Malsun made unpleasant things like rocks, bramble bushes and poisonous snakes. Malsun found out how to kill

Gluskap, which was by shooting him with an owl's feather. Malsun did this, but Gluskap brought himself back to life, and killed Malsun, who became a wolf. Gluskap then finished creating the world, and stayed for a time to give gifts to men. He also fought the wind-bird and broke its wing, so that the winds were not as violent as they once were; and he killed a giant frog which had swallowed all the water, releasing it again for everyone else. In some versions, he has an elder brother, Mikumwesa, who, although smaller and less impressive, is his superior as an archer. In the end, he set out in his canoe, travelling eastwards, and was never seen again. He is sometimes said to be the same as *Nanabozho*.

Goibniu: One of the Irish *Tuatha De Danann*, Goibniu was a god expert in the work of a smith. With Luchtine, the maker of spear handles, and Creidne who forged nails, he could make a spear in a moment: he would fling the red-hot spearhead into the doorpost, Luchtine would throw the handle after it so that the two were fastened together, and Creidne pinned the two together by throwing a nail from his tongs. No weapon made by him ever missed its mark.

In the otherworld, he provided a feast at which magic ale was served; guests who drank this never grew old.

He appears in Welsh stories as Gofannon.

Gokuraku-Jōdo: The Buddhist paradise of *Amida* in Japanese myth.

Golden Age: The rule of the Greek god *Cronus* (or *Saturn* to the Romans) was looked back upon as an age when men lived in peace and without fear of want. They did not have to till the land, and nobody owned property; illness was unknown, and warfare had not been invented. It was only with the rule of *Zeus* that these evils came about.

Golden Fleece: The Greek hero *Athamas* married *Nephele*, who bore him two children, Phrixus and Helle. Athamas later left Nephele and took *Ino* as his wife, who tried to kill Phrixus and Helle. She did this by persuading the women of the country where Athamas ruled that they should roast the corn which was to be used for seed the following year before they sowed it. This meant that the corn failed to come up, and a messenger was sent to the oracle at Delphi to discover the cause. Ino bribed the messenger to

say that Phrixus and Helle should be sacrificed to the gods. But Nephele sent a golden ram which carried the two of them off. Helle fell off as they crossed the sea, and the place is still called the Hellespont after her. But Phrixus reached Colchis safely, where he sacrificed the ram to *Zeus*, and gave the fleece to King *Aeetes*. Aeetes hung it up in a grove guarded by a dragon, where it remained until *Jason* and the Argonauts seized it.

Gollveig: A mysterious seeress from among the *Vanir* attacked by the *Aesir*; this may have been the cause of the Norse war of the gods. She was burnt three times at *Asgard* for her sorcery, but each time she came to life again. Gollveig may be another name for *Freyja*, but the poem *Voluspa* in which this story is described is very obscure, and the detail is not clear.

Gopis: In Hindu myth, the girls who looked after herds of cows near *Krishna*'s home, Gokula, to whom he made love; their dances and love-making are a favourite subject for Indian artists.

Gorgons: Three sisters who were represented in Greek myth as being able to turn men to stone with a mere glance of their eyes. Early artists showed them as hideous, but later they were portrayed as beautiful women, with a look of fear or agony in their eyes. Their names were Euryale, Stheno and *Medusa*: Medusa was slain by *Perseus*.

Gorm: King of Denmark whose story is told in Saxo's history. 'His heart thirsted to see marvels, either ones that he himself could experience, or those which were brought to him by travellers' tales.' He set out, guided by Thorkill, to find the house of *Geirrod*. Landing first on a shore of a strange land north of Norway, they found the country full of herds of cattle. Thorkill warned them to kill only as many as they needed to end their hunger, but the seamen insisted on having a great feast. As a result, they were attacked by monsters, and three of the company had to be left as a sacrifice for the gods of the place. They sailed on to Biarmaland, a region full of forests haunted by strange beasts, where it was always cold; here Thorkill warned them not to speak to the inhabitants, in case they offended them. At nightfall, a giant came to their camp, whom Thorkill addressed courteously; it was Gudmund, king of the region and brother of Geirrod. He took them to his home, which lay near the river which divided the world of men from the world of giants; but Thorkill warned his companions that if they ate or drank in Gudmund's hall or fell in love with his beautiful daughters they would never be able to escape. Thorkill managed to stop Gudmund from being angry with them for refusing his hospitality, though he was unable to prevent four of the company from being tempted, and they were driven mad. At length Gudmund agreed to show them the way to Geirrod's hall. On their return from this visit (see *Geirrod*) he once again tried to tempt them, and one of the king's best warriors, Buchi, fell in love with one of Gudmund's daughters. He tried to accompany the king on his journey home, but was drowned as they crossed the river on the border of Gudmund's kingdom. The king and his men only reached home safely by sacrificing to *Utgard-Loki*. Gorm also later sent Thorkill on a journey to find Utgard-Loki.

Govardhana: A mountain near the home of the Indian god-hero *Krishna*, which protected the *Gopis* and their herds. Krishna persuaded the Gopis to worship the mountain as their protector instead of *Indra*, at which Indra sent a great deluge: but Krishna lifted up Govardhana on his finger and the herds and their keepers sheltered underneath. Indra had to admit defeat and later became Krishna's ally.

Graces (Charites): Daughters of *Zeus* and Eurynome, whom the Greeks regarded as patrons of beauty. They were called Euphrosyne, Aglaia and Thalia, and artists drew them as three lovely girls dancing in a circle.

Graeae: The Greek spirits of old age, grey-haired from their birth, who had only one eye and one tooth between them. *Perseus* stole these when he visited them and only returned them when the Graeae gave him a magic bag and shoes which enabled him to fly, as well as a cap which made him invisible. These enabled him to kill the *Gorgon Medusa*.

Grandfather: The Cariri Indians of Brazil remember in their stories a friend of their god Touppart, whom Touppart sent down to earth to live with them. They called him 'Grandfather', and one day when they went hunting, they left their children with him. Instead of looking after them, he turned them into wild pigs called

peccaries and climbed up a tree into the sky with them. He then got the white ants to eat away the bottom of the tree, which fell. The hunters came back and tried unsuccessfully to put the tree up again so that their children could escape. In the end, the children made a rope from their loin-cloths and slid down it; but it was too short, and they bruised themselves as they fell off the end. Instead of Grandfather, Badze (Tobacco) was sent to earth, and the Cariri offer sacrifices to this instead.

On another occasion, the Cariri, who only had one woman among the whole tribe, begged Grandfather for more. So he sent them hunting, killed the woman and cut her in little bits, which he gave to them when they came back. He told them to hang the pieces in their huts, and when they next returned from hunting, each piece had become a woman and they were all busy getting a meal ready for the men.

Great Ennead: The nine great gods worshipped by the Egyptians at Heliopolis, the 'City of the Sun'. They were: *Ra, Shu, Tefnut, Geb, Nut, Osiris, Isis, Seth, Nephthys*.

Grimnir: Name assumed by *Odin* when he went to visit *Geirrod* (2).

Geirrod was tricked into torturing Odin, who was in disguise. When Geirrod realized the identity of his victim, he rushed to release him but tripped, fell on his sword and was killed.

Gua: Thunder-god of the Ga tribe of West Africa, and patron of blacksmiths. His temples are often at blacksmiths' forges. He is also a god of farming, because iron tools for farming are made by blacksmiths.

Gualicho: Evil spirit of the Patagonian Indians of South America.

Guayarakunny: Lord of the dead in Patagonian Indian myths from South America; he was also the creator of the world, and released the men and beasts on earth from the underground caverns to which the dead returned. When the beasts were let out, the Indians were so frightened by their horns that they shut the caves up, trapping the black cattle who came out last; and for this reason there were no black cattle in their country until the Spaniards brought them.

Gudanna: 'The bull of heaven' (the constellation Taurus) created by the Babylonian god *Anu* at *Ishtar*'s request to kill *Gilgamesh*. It was slain by Gilgamesh and *Enkidu*, even though its breath alone killed two hundred men each time it snorted.

Gullfaxi: 'Golden-mane', the horse of the giant *Hrungnir* in Norse myth, was given to *Thor*'s son Magni as a reward for moving the leg of the giant which fell on his father when he killed Hrungnir.

Gullinbursti: A boar with golden bristles, which could run faster than any horse, and whose bristles lit up the darkest night, it was one of the three treasures of the Norse gods. It belonged to *Frey*.

The three treasures were made by skilful dwarfs. *Loki* had made a wager with two brothers that they could not match the treasures which other dwarfs had made for the gods: *Sif*'s golden hair, made of real gold, Frey's ship *Skidbladnir*, and *Odin*'s spear *Gungnir*. If they succeeded, Loki's head was theirs. First the dwarfs made Gullinbursti, though Loki tried to stop them by changing into a horse-fly and stinging the dwarf who worked the bellows. Then they forged *Draupnir*, the great gold armband from which eight other armbands dropped every ninth night, and finally Mjollnir, *Thor*'s hammer, though the dwarf had to raise his hand from the bellows to brush away the fly which was still attacking him, and the hammer came out a little short in the handle. The gods considered Mjollnir the best of all their treasures, and Loki was told that he had lost his wager. When the dwarfs tried to cut off his head, he claimed that they were not allowed to touch his neck, and ran away. But Thor brought him back, and they sewed up his lips instead.

Gungnir: Great spear of the Norse god *Odin*, which was forged by two dwarfs, the master craftsmen who had made *Sif*'s hair out of real gold. Odin used to fling it over the army which was going to lose a battle at the beginning of the fight, and he also stirred up all kinds of strife among men and gods with it. (See p. 108.)

Gunnlod: The daughter of the giant *Suttung*, to whom the Norse god *Odin* made love in order to get back the mead of inspiration made from honey and *Kvasir*'s blood.

Gwydion: A Welsh prince who was turned by Math mab Mathonwy into a stag, a boar and a wolf, each for a year, for helping his brother Culfathwy to attack Math's maidservant. He brought up his nephew *Llew Llaw Gyffes*, and helped him with his magic powers.

Gwyn: Gwyn, son of Nudd, was a great magician in Welsh myth. He carried off Creidylad, daughter of King Lud; her betrothed, Gwythur, pursued him, but his overlord intervened and Gwyn and Gwythur were ordered to fight each other every May Day until doomsday, when the winner would have Creidylad.

Gylfi: A legendary king of Sweden. There is a story about him called *Gylfaginning*, the deception of Gylfi, which tells how he questioned three beings called High, Just-as-High, and Third about the gods and the universe. They sat in a splendid hall, and answered everything he asked; when he had finished, there was a great noise, and everything vanished, leaving Gylfi in the open country. This work tells us a great deal about the Norse gods and forms part of the *Prose Edda* written by Snorri Sturluson in the thirteenth century.

Gymir: Father of *Gerd* in Norse myth; perhaps a giant who ruled the underworld.

Gyoja: One of the Japanese *Sennin* who was a particularly powerful magician: one of his feats was to build a great bridge of rocks between two mountains by forcing spirits to work for him.

Hachiman: Son of the Japanese Empress *Jingo*, he was worshipped as the warriors' god, the 'god with eight banners'.

Hactcin: The Jicarilla Apache Indians of the south-western United States said that the hactcin were the first beings, who had always existed. They possessed the material from which the world was created, and made the world, the underworld and then the sky. The earth was shaped like a woman and faces upwards; the sky is shaped like a man and faces downwards.

Another version says the hactcin were the children of the earth and sky, and lived in the underworld, from which they came up on earth. Black Hactcin was the most powerful of them and became their leader: it was he who created animals. The hactcin dance could only be danced by men with long hair who had not been vaccinated: and anyone who watched it would have a crooked face afterwards. Only those who had danced the hactcin dance could safely talk about them.

Hadding: A Norse hero whose strange and often obscure history is told in Saxo's history of Denmark. He was brought up by a giantess, and when she was carried off by evil spirits because she had used magic to make a dead man speak, *Odin* took him under his protection. He was once rescued by Odin, riding on *Sleipnir*, when he was defeated in battle; and on another occasion, he killed a strange monster, only to be warned that he had killed a friendly spirit and would have to pay for it by making sacrifices of men to *Frey*. He also visited the underworld: one winter evening, the figure of a woman bearing hemlock (a kind of herb) appeared in the fire, and asked where such a herb grew in winter. Hadding could not answer and asked her to show him. She wrapped him in her mantle and took him down to the underworld, where he saw, first of all, richly clad men, then sunny fields where the hemlock grew, and finally a place where warriors fought eternally against each other, because they had been killed in battle. A great wall barred the way, and they could go no further; but the woman produced a cock, cut off its head, and threw it over the wall, at which it came to life again. After this mysterious ceremony, Hadding returned to earth. Odin continued to favour him, and taught him how to fight with his men in wedge formation.

Like the god *Njord*, he married a wife, Ragn-

hild, who recognized him by a mark on his leg, and who longed for the mountains while he preferred the sea. As so often in Norse myth, we do not have enough knowledge to tell what the real connection between Njord and Hadding was.

Hades: In Greek myth, the name both of the kingdom of the dead and of its ruler. The god Hades was the son of *Cronos* and *Rhea*; when *Cronos* was overthrown, he won the underworld as his share of the inheritance when it was divided between *Zeus*, *Poseidon* and himself. In contrast to many of the rulers of the underworld in other myths, Hades was severe and resisted all pleas for mercy, but he was in no way evil or a source of evil. He carried off *Persephone* to be his queen, but she only dwelt with him for four months of every year.

The kingdom over which he ruled had its entrance either in the far west (the route used by *Odysseus*) or through any dark cleft in the earth. The entrance was guarded by *Cerberus*, and to reach it the dead had to be ferried over the river *Styx* by the ferryman *Charon*. The main part of it was the Plain of Asphodel, where most dead souls went; there they wandered aimlessly, retaining only the shadow of their former appearance. The more fortunate went to the home of the blessed, the *Elysian Plain*, while the wicked were condemned to *Tartarus*. Odysseus, *Orpheus*, *Heracles*, *Psyche* and *Aeneas* all visited Hades while they were still alive and returned safely.

Hahgwehdiyu and Hahgwehdaetgah: Alternative names for *Yoskeha* and *Taweskare* in Iroquois Indian myths from the Great Lakes region.

Haimon: Son of the Greek King *Creon* of Thebes, and fiancé of *Antigone*.

Haitsi-aibeb: A Hottentot hero, who was able to transform himself into various shapes. He conquered the evil Gaunab in a fight by the deep hole into which the Gaunab used to throw passersby. Although he was twice thrown in, the hole supported him, and he climbed out. The third time it was the Gaunab who was thrown in and vanished. He later died of eating wild raisins, but came out of his grave and walked around: his son stopped him from going back to it, and he recovered. Many caves in South Africa were called 'Haitsi-aibeb's grave'.

Hamadryads: Greek nymphs or tree-spirits; hamadryads were the spirits of the trees themselves, some said, while the *dryads* merely lived among the trees.

Hanhau: In Maya myth, the god who was lord of the underworld, Mitnal, where the wicked were tortured and suffered hunger and cold.

Hanuman: The Hindu monkey-god, whose exploits form a large part of the epic *Ramayana*. Hanuman was the ally of *Rama* against *Ravana*, king of the *Rakshasas*; and his supernatural strength enabled him to leap from India to Ceylon in one jump. On other occasions he uprooted the Himalaya mountains and captured the clouds, and he is shown as immensely tall and splendid, with a huge tail. He also appeared as a spy, in the shape of an ordinary monkey. The Rakshasas once tried to kill him by setting fire to his tail, but he used it to burn down their city instead.

Hap: Another spelling of *Apis*.

Hapi: The Egyptian god of the Nile, shown with water plants on his head and a tray of offerings in his hands. He was given woman's breasts to emphasize his role as provider of water for the land and food for its people.

Hapy: An Egyptian god who guarded a dead man's lungs when they had been embalmed; he was shown with a dog's head. See *Osiris*.

Hari: One of the names of the Indian god *Vishnu*.

Harmachis: The Great Sphinx, which stands near the Pyramids, was called by the Egyptians Harmachis or '*Horus*-on-the-horizon'.

Harmonia: Daughter of the Greek gods *Ares* and *Aphrodite*. Married to *Cadmus* of Thebes, and transformed, like him, into a snake by the god *Dionysus*. Her necklace, a wedding gift from the gods, played a fatal part in the later history of Thebes: see *Amphiaraus* and *Alcmaeon*.

Harpies: Greek monsters, shown as birds with women's faces, who persecuted those against whom the gods bore a grudge. They may once have been spirits of the winds, as the names of some of them (Aello, 'stormwind', Ocypete, 'swing-wing', Celaino 'dark') show. Their most famous victim was *Phineus*; *Jason* and the Argo-

nauts drove them away from him, and *Zetes and Calais* pursued them until *Iris* told them to stop.

Harpocrates: A name for *Horus*.

Hastshehogan: The house-god in Navaho Indian myth, god of evening and the west.

Hastsheyalti: The 'talking-god' in Navaho Indian myth, god of the dawn and the east. It was he who created *Changing Woman*.

Hathor: Egyptian goddess of love and fertility, who was also *Sekhmet*, the goddess of war and destruction. She was the wife of *Horus*. She was also the 'queen of heaven', and since the sky was envisaged as a great cow (see *Mehturt*) Hathor was sometimes shown in that form. Her four tresses of black hair were thought to hang across the sky, marking the points of the compass. The 'seven Hathors' were the stars which we call the *Pleiades*; these goddesses foretold the fate of new-born children. See *Ra*.

Haumea: God of wild plants in Polynesian stories; in other Pacific stories he appears as the goddess Haumea.

Haurvatat: The goddess of water in Iranian myth, who represented happiness in moral terms. She was one of the *Amesha Spentas*.

Hawaiki: In Polynesian myths, the land of the spirits, sometimes also thought of as the home of their ancestors somewhere in the west.

Hebe: Goddess of youthful beauty in Greek myth, daughter of *Zeus* and *Hera*. She was said to have been married to *Heracles* after he became immortal.

Hecate: A mysterious but powerful Greek goddess, usually said to be the daughter of *Zeus* and *Demeter*. She was the queen of black magic and of evil ghosts, though she had once been a local fertility goddess. She was also the goddess of cross-roads, which have always had a magical meaning. *Medea* worshipped her and practised her arts. She is often shown as having three faces.

Hecatoncheires: Like the *Titans*, they were the children of the first Greek gods, *Uranus* and *Gaia*; they had a hundred arms and fifty heads each. But the three of them, Briareus, Cottus and Gyes, fought on *Zeus*'s side in his battle with the Titans.

Hector: The chief hero on the Trojan side in the *Trojan War*, son of King *Priam* and married to *Andromache*. He killed *Achilles'* friend *Patroclus*, at which Achilles took to the field once more and had his revenge by killing Hector. He dragged Hector's body in the dust, and refused to hand it over to Priam for burial until Priam came and begged for it himself.

Hecuba: Wife of the Trojan King *Priam*. According to Greek myth, after the fall of Troy, she was given as a slave to *Odysseus*. On the way back, her ship was driven ashore in Thrace, where she learnt that the local ruler, Polymestor, had killed her last surviving son, Polydorus, because he thought that he had great treasures with him. Hecuba killed Polymestor's children and blinded him; she was transformed into a dog.

Heidrun: The goat which fed on the leaves of the great world-tree of Norse myth, *Yggdrasill*. It gave mead instead of milk, and this supplied the great feasts which the gods held.

Heimdall: The Norse god who kept watch on *Bifrost Bridge* leading to the gods' stronghold of *Asgard*. He was said to be the son of nine sea-maidens, and may have been one of the *Vanir*. He could see for immense distances, and could hear so keenly that he could hear the sound of grass growing. He owned the *Gjallarhorn*, which would be blown at the day of *Ragnarok*: in the battle which followed he was to kill *Loki*, but would also be killed himself.

Hel: In Norse myth, Hel is the goddess of the underworld. She was daughter of *Loki*, and was sent by *Odin* down to *Niflheim*, a land of cold and decay, to rule over the dead. Her kingdom is sometimes also called Hel, just as *Hades* in Greek myth could mean either Hades himself or his realm. Hel was a place of horror rather than torment; according to some stories, only the old and those who died in bed went there. From Hel the Christian name of Hell is taken. See also *Balder, Hermod*.

Helen: Daughter of the Greek queen *Leda* and of *Zeus* in the form of a swan. She was born from an egg which *Nemesis* or Fate gave to Leda. She grew up to be the most beautiful of women, and even when she was very young attracted the

attention of *Theseus*, who carried her off. But her brothers *Castor and Pollux* rescued her. Later she was wooed by all the great men of Greece, among them *Odysseus*, *Menelaus* and others. Odysseus persuaded all the suitors to swear that they would not argue with Helen's own choice, and would stand by her husband if need be. Helen chose Menelaus, and by him she had a daughter, Hermione. While Menelaus was away, *Paris*, son of *Priam* of Troy, abducted her, and the *Trojan War* began as a result. One version of the story says that she and Paris went to Egypt on their way to Troy. The king of Egypt, Proteus, detained her until her husband came to fetch her, sending a phantom which looked like her to Troy. Only when Menelaus brought the phantom back to Egypt did it disappear; he then took the real Helen home.

Helenus: A Trojan seer, captured during the *Trojan War* by *Odysseus*; he revealed to the Greeks that only by *Philoctetes'* arrows could the city be taken. He had become a seer after his ears were licked by young serpents, which enabled him to understand the speech of birds.

Helios: The Greek sun-god, son of the *Titans Hyperion* and Theia. He was not much worshipped in Greece, where from the fifth century onwards he was held to be the same as *Apollo*; and in the *Odyssey* his father Hyperion is named as the sun-god. See also *Clytie*, *Phaethon*.

Heller: In the Tehuelche Indians' myths, Heller, the son of the sun, created the Tehuelche tribe and gave them Patagonia, the very south of South America, in which to live. When they die, they return to him.

Heng Ha Er Chiang: Guardians of Buddhist temples in China; they were two heroes in ancient times who had magic powers. Ha could breathe a poisonous gas, while Heng could destroy men with two columns of light which appeared from his nostrils. In Taoist myth they are called Ch'ing Lung (Blue Dragon) and Pai Hu (White Tiger).

Hephaestus: The Greek god of fire, called *Vulcan* by the Romans. He was the god of fire which had been tamed and put to good use, and was therefore shown as a smith, making marvellous pieces of metalwork for the gods, and occasionally for favoured mortals like *Achilles*. Achilles' mother *Thetis* obtained from Hephaestus a wonderful suit of armour for her son before he went to the *Trojan War*. He was the husband of *Aphrodite*, but was lame and clumsy, and an unlikely match for such a goddess. She was unfaithful to him, and he once caught her and *Ares* in an invisible net when they were making love, and showed them to the other gods before they could escape.

Heqet: Wife of the Egyptian god *Khnemu*. She was shown with a frog's head, and was the goddess of childbirth.

Hera: The greatest of the Greek goddesses, wife of *Zeus*, called *Juno* by the Romans. Originally she was the local goddess of Argos, daughter of *Cronos* and *Rhea*; but she came to be regarded as Zeus' official wife. Her children by him were *Ares* and *Hebe*. She was especially the goddess worshipped by women, and the patron of wedded love. She was furiously jealous of Zeus' many affairs, and retaliated by giving birth to *Hephaestus* without a father, while the mortal women whom Zeus loved were always persecuted by her. She was a powerful and stately figure, and was also the goddess of royal power. In the *Trojan War*, she was a strong supporter of the Greeks. There are few stories about her, apart from her continual conflicts with Zeus over his love affairs.

Heracles: Son of *Alcmena* and *Zeus*, Heracles is the greatest of the Greek heroes, with a large number of stories about him. The most important are the famous 'Twelve Labours' which he performed for King *Eurystheus* of Tiryns. He and *Asclepius* were among the very few mortals to be admitted to heaven because they had deserved it by their deeds during their lifetime.

Hera attempted to thwart his career from the beginning. She knew that he was fated to perform great deeds, but even before he was born began to plot against him. She tricked Zeus into promising that any child descended from him who was born on the day when Heracles should have been would rule everyone around him; then she delayed Heracles' birth so that Zeus' great-grandson Eurystheus was born first. Hera sent serpents to attack Heracles in his cradle, but he strangled these. As a boy, he was called Alkeides, and was brought up with his twin brother *Iphicles* as *Amphitryon's* son; but only Iphicles was really of Amphitryon's blood. He was taught by famous masters: Eurytus, grandson of *Apollo*, taught him archery, *Autolycus* taught

him wrestling, and *Polydeuces* (Pollux) fencing. At eighteen he killed the lion of Mount Cithairon, which was preying on Amphitryon's flocks, and soon afterwards he led the Thebans in a successful war against the men of Orchomenus. For this, he was given Megara, the daughter of the Theban king, as his bride. But Hera, still pursuing him, sent him mad some years later; he imagined that his wife and children were his enemies, and killed them all. Although he was formally purified by Megara's father, he insisted on going to consult the oracle at Delphi, which told him of his divine ancestry and real name, and commanded him to serve Eurystheus for twelve years. If he performed all the tasks set him, said the oracle, he would become immortal. About this time, he fell in love with Eurytus' daughter Iole, but her father and brothers would not let him marry her. In a rage, he hurled one of the brothers from the town walls of Tiryns. He tried to get the king of Pylos to purify him, but was refused; and even the oracle at Delphi would not help him until he had tried to seize the holy tripod of Apollo itself. Only a thunderbolt from Zeus prevented him from carrying it off. The oracle finally said that he must go into slavery for a year, and he was sold to *Omphale*, queen of Libya, who made him spin and sew and do women's work for the year. He then married *Deianeira*, and set out to serve Eurystheus. (This at least seems to be the usual way his story was told, though there are many different versions of it).

The Twelve Labours which Eurystheus set him are the most famous part of his story. They were as follows:

1. The Nemaean Lion. This was a monstrous lion sent by Hera against Heracles which could not be wounded by any weapon. His bow and sword made no mark on it, but he beat it with a club and then strangled it with his bare hands. His costume was always, after this, the lion's skin and a club. Eurystheus was so frightened when Heracles reappeared that he ordered him to stay outside the city in future, and built his bronze jar in which to hide

2. The Hydra. Heracles next had to fight this monster, and a giant crab as well. The Hydra had a hundred heads; every time one was cut off, another grew in its place. So Heracles first crushed the crab by trampling on it, and then called in his nephew Iolaos. Iolaos built a great fire, and each time Heracles cut off a head, Iolaos took a burning stick from the fire and scorched the stump so that it could not grow

again.

3. The Erymanthian Boar. This creature could only be caught alive, so Heracles chased it into a deep snow-drift in the mountains, and trapped it in a net.

4. The Hind of Ceryneia. This was a magical hind with antlers, which also had to be caught alive, because it was sacred to *Artemis*. Heracles pursued it for a year, and finally came across it while it was asleep; although Artemis protested, he took it to Eurystheus and then released it again.

5. The Stymphalian Birds. These man-eating birds lived in a thick forest round a lake. Heracles had first to drive them out of the forest, which he did with a bronze rattle which *Hephaestus* made for him; he then shot them.

6. The Augean Stables. King *Augeas* had great herds of cattle which he had inherited from his father the sun-god. Their stables had never been cleaned, so Heracles, who had to do this in a day, diverted a river through them and washed out all the dirt.

7. The Cretan Bull. This great beast, said by some to be the one on which *Europa* was taken to Crete, was captured alive by Heracles and brought to Eurystheus.

8. The Horses of *Diomedes*. Diomedes, king of the Thracians, used to feed his horses on human flesh. Heracles defeated him and fed him to his own horses, which then became quite tame and went back to eating grass.

9. The Girdle of the *Amazon* Queen. This was a magic girdle which gave its wearer strength in battle. Heracles defeated *Hippolyta*, queen of the Amazons and captured it from her, presenting it to Eurystheus.

10. The Cattle of *Geryon*. To capture these, Heracles had to journey beyond the stream of *Ocean*, which he crossed in a golden cup he had forced the sun to give him. Here he killed the monstrous dog and the herdsman who guarded the cattle, and finally slew Geryon himself. On the way back he set up the Pillars of Heracles on the Straits of Gibraltar, and after many adventures in Italy, including the battle with *Cacus*, he returned home.

11. Cerberus. Heracles was now sent to fetch Cerberus, the guardian of the entrance to *Hades*. He reached the underworld by frightening *Charon* into ferrying him across the river *Styx*, and he also fought with Hades himself. He brought Cerberus back to Eurystheus, who once more hid in his bronze jar.

12. The Golden Apples of the *Hesperides*. Once again, Heracles had to journey to the bounds of Ocean, where he persuaded *Atlas* to gather the apples for him, while he held up the sky in his place. Atlas gathered the apples, but refused to take up his burden again, so Heracles had to trick him into doing so.

Heracles was killed by a poisoned robe which his wife Deianeira sent him, thinking that it would win him back to her. He was made immortal, and married to the goddess *Hebe*. See also *Alcestis*, *Centaurs*, *Hylas*, *Jason*, *Philoctetes*.

Hermaphroditus: Son of the Greek gods *Hermes* and *Aphrodite*; he fell in love with the *nymph* Salmacis, and they prayed to be united for ever. The gods granted their prayer by making them one person, half man, half woman.

Hermes: The Greek messenger-god, called Mercury by the Romans. He was also a bringer of good luck, and acted as guide to dead souls on their way to *Hades*. He was the son of *Zeus* and *Maia*, and was very quick to grow up: he was born at dawn, at noon he invented the lyre, and in the evening he stole a tortoise. He killed it and used the shell as the sounding board for a lyre, which he made by stretching strings across it. After this, he went out and stole *Apollo*'s cattle, disguising the tracks. Apollo took him to Zeus, where he protested that he was so young that he did not even know what a cow was; but in the end he had to appease Apollo, which he did by giving him the lyre he had just invented. He appears in other stories as a trickster, whose pranks are usually good-humoured; and he helped *Odysseus* during his wanderings, having fought on the Greek side in the *Trojan War*.

One of the mortal women whom he loved was Herse; her sister Aglauros was jealous of their love, and when Hermes came to visit Herse she barred the way and said she would not move. Hermes said 'Very well, you *shan't* move!' and turned her to stone.

Hermod: Son of *Odin*, chief of the Norse gods, who rode down to *Hel* on Odin's horse *Sleipnir* to try to obtain *Balder*'s release. He rode down through the gate of Hel's kingdom, over the Echoing Bridge, where the girl who guarded Hel, *Modgud*, challenged him. She asked him why he, who came alone, made more noise than three companies of dead men, and then realized that this was because he was a living man and the others had been ghosts. He rode on to Hel's hall, where he found Balder seated at her right hand; Hel asked him why he, a living creature, had come to her realm, and Hermod explained that he had come to seek Balder. Hel agreed that he should be released, provided that all things on earth wept for him, and Hermod returned to *Asgard*.

Herus and Kantaneiro: Modern stories told by the Apache Indians of the border of the United States and Mexico relate how before the white men came to America, a man called Herus appeared mysteriously among the Apache. He brought a book with him, and told them to keep it and hand it down from family to family. But when he died, they followed their old custom of burning all a person's possessions with them at their funeral; and the book was lost. After that, things went badly until Kantaneiro appeared, who was a great warrior, even though he only carried a spear. Once he was attacked by the Mexican Indians – this was long before white men had arrived – and all his followers ran away. But he killed their officers with his loin-cloth, and drove the rest off. Kantaneiro also had a book, which he told the people to keep, but they would not listen, and burnt it.

Heru-Sma-Tauy: A name for *Ahy*.

Hesione: 1. Wife of *Prometheus*, the Greek god who created man, made out of clay.
2. Daughter of King *Laomedon* of Troy. In Greek myth, her father cheated *Apollo* and *Poseidon* who sent a sea-monster to ravage the lands of Troy. The monster could only be made to go away if Laomedon would give him Hesione to eat. He did so but Hesione was rescued by *Heracles*. She eventually married Telamon, king of Salamis.

Hesperides: In Greek myth, the daughters of Evening, living not far from Mount Atlas in North Africa. In their garden, they tended the golden apples which *Gaia* gave to *Hera* as a wedding present, and which made anyone who ate them immortal. *Heracles* stole the apples as one of his Twelve Labours. He achieved this by persuading Atlas to gather the apples for him while he held up the sky in Atlas' place; but eventually *Athene* took them back.

Hestia: The Greek goddess of the hearth, called *Vesta* by the Romans. She never married, and never moved from *Olympus,* where she guarded the sacred flame in the hearth of the gods.

Hiku: In Hawaiian myth, Hiku was brought up by his mother far away from other men. One day he decided to set out in search of other humans, and fired his magic arrow to settle where he should go. It fell at the feet of a girl called Kawelu, who hid it. Hiku searched for the arrow, and finally called out to it. It answered, and he found it at Kawelu's house. He and Kawelu fell in love, and married. But he had promised to go back to see his mother, and although Kawelu tried to prevent him, he left her. She died of a broken heart while he was away, and Hiku in despair decided to try to fetch her from the underworld. He made a great rope and his friends lowered him into the underworld, swinging down the rope as he went. The ghosts of the underworld saw him swinging on the rope, and wanted to try the same game. Eventually Kawelu's ghost appeared and came to swing on the rope, at which Hiku gave a signal to his friends, who pulled him and Kawelu back again. But the ghost did not want to leave the underworld, and became a butterfly. However, Hiku caught it in a coconut shell and restored it to Kawelu's body, so that she came to life again.

A similar story was told in New Zealand of Pare and Hutu; in this case, Pare died heartbroken because Hutu would not marry her, and the pair were only united after Hutu had fetched her from the underworld.

Hild: Hild was a Danish princess who was so distressed by the tragic conflict between her father and the man whom she loved that when they met in battle, she wove magic spells over the dead to bring them back to life, and so the battle never came to an end.

Hildisvin: One of the names of the magic boar of the Norse goddess *Freyja.* Freyja is the goddess of love but also of magic. As well as Hildisvin she owned a number of cats who drew her carriage, and the modern idea of a witch may be a distant memory of her.

Hina: The first woman in Polynesian myths, wife of *Tane;* their daughter, also called Hina (or Hine-tui-ne-po), became the goddess of death.

ie was a great explorer, and one day sailed to
ie moon in her canoe. She found it so pleasant
uat she stayed there, and spent her time making
bark cloth from the great banyan tree which can
be seen in the markings on the moon's face.

Hino: The 'thunderer' in the myths of the Iroquois Indians of eastern North America. He was
the enemy of all poisonous creatures, and with his
flaming arrows destroyed the huge serpent which
lived in the waters and ate men. He was married
to the rainbow. He was helped in his task by
many lesser thunderers, and by *Oshadagea*, the
deer-eagle.

Hippolyta: The queen of the *Amazons*, whom
the Greek heroes *Heracles* and *Theseus* defeated
on different occasions. Heracles took her magic
girdle, while Theseus married her and brought
her to Athens.

Hippolytus: The son of *Hippolyta* and *Theseus*
in Greek myth. After Hippolyta's death, Theseus
married *Phaedra*, who fell in love with her stepson. He took no notice of her, so she accused him
in a letter of trying to seduce her and then killed
herself. Theseus read her accusation, believed it,
and cursed Hippolytus. Now Theseus had been
granted three wishes by *Poseidon*, who took the
curse as being one of them and sent a sea-monster
which frightened Hippolytus' horses. They over-
turned his chariot and killed him; and Theseus
only discovered the truth when it was too late.
One version of the story says that he was brought
back to life by *Chiron* the centaur for a huge fee,
but Chiron was killed by *Zeus* for this.

Hiranyagarbha: The first of all beings in
Hindu myth, the 'golden egg' from which *Brahma*
emerged, and which represents life itself. After
emerging from the egg, Brahma created the
world, which will last for two thousand million
years.

Hiranyakashipu: One of the *Daityas* in Hindu
myth. *Shiva* granted him power over earth,
heaven and hell for a million years, but he refused
to acknowledge *Vishnu*'s power, and was furious
with his son *Prahlada* for trying to persuade him
that Vishnu was everywhere. Striking a pillar
in the palace, he asked if Vishnu could possibly
be in a pillar, at which Vishnu came out of the
pillar as a man-lion (*Narasimha*) and devoured
him. Vishnu took this shape because Hiranyakashipu could not be killed either by man or a

beast.

Hlidskjalf: The magic seat of the Norse god *Odin*, from which he could see out across all the worlds of men, giants and gods. *Frey* once sat on it, and saw *Gerd*, with whom he fell in love.

Hoder: A Norse god about whom little is known, except that he was blind. It was he who, with *Loki* guiding his hand, threw the mistletoe dart that killed *Balder*; in the other version of Balder's story, he appears as Hother, Balder's human rival for the hand of Nanna. He will join Balder, their quarrel forgotten, in the world which arises when the present one is destroyed.

Hoenir: The 'silent god' of Norse myth, he was the companion of *Odin* and *Loki* on their wanderings, and shared adventures such as Loki's capture by the giant *Thiazi* in eagle form or the ransoming of *Ottar*. He was sent as a hostage to the *Vanir* at the end of the war between the *Aesir* and the Vanir; but because he was so silent, the Vanir did not feel they had had a fair exchange even though he was tall and handsome. It was for this reason that *Mimir* was killed. However, silence may really have been a sign of wisdom, because at the creation of the world, Hoenir was said to have given the gift of intelligence to mankind. He is one of the few gods who will survive *Ragnarok*, after which he will 'wield the staff carved with runes'.

Högni: see *Sigurd*.

Hoho-demi: Ho-deri and Hoho-demi were the sons of *Ninigi*, first ruler of Japan. Ho-deri had a magic fishing-hook which his brother Hoho-demi once borrowed and lost. Ho-deri was furious, and insisted that he find it again, refusing any kind of compensation. With the help of one of the gods, Hoho-demi made his way to the palace of the sea-god *Wata-Tsu-Mi*; but there he fell in love with the sea-god's daughter, married her, and forgot his errand. Three years later he remembered, and the sea-god found the hook for him, and gave him advice on obtaining his revenge on Ho-deri. The sea-god also gave Hoho-demi two magic jewels which made the waters rise and fall; and when Ho-deri, jealous of his brother's success, tried to attack him, he was able to raise up a wave which swept Ho-deri away. Ho-deri submitted to him, and Hoho-demi became lord

of his lands. His wife came to join him; but when
she was about to have their first child, she warned
him not to watch, because she would have to
change into her real shape. Hoho-demi disobeyed,
and saw her become a huge shark; she saw that
he was watching and returned to the sea.

Horagalles: The thunder-god of the Lapps,
whose name probably derives from that of *Thor*,
and is really '*Thor karl*', old man Thor.

Horai: The goddesses of the seasons in Greek
myth. They have no tales attached to them, but
are simply figures representing the different
times of year.

Horus: The Egyptian god Horus appears in
myth in two forms. There is Horus the elder,
who was a sun-god in early myths, and later on
was thought of as the same as the god *Ra*; one
of Ra's titles was 'Ra-Horus of the two horizons'.
His other name was Herakhty. Then there is
Horus the younger, also associated with the sun,
as god of the rising sun, who was son of *Osiris*
and husband of *Hathor*. He was born after Osiris
had been killed and revived by *Isis*, and because
of this Osiris' enemy *Seth* tried to have him declared illegitimate and to claim Osiris' kingdom
for himself. As with Seth's claim against Osiris,
there was a trial before the *Great Ennead,* at which
both sides resorted to all kinds of trickery and
Seth attempted to defeat Horus by force. In one
episode Seth and Horus changed into hippo-
potamuses and had a contest to see who could
stay under water longest; while another trial
was suggested by Seth, and involved building a
stone boat and making it float. Seth's boat sank;
but Horus built his of cedar and plastered it to
look like stone, and it floated. In the end the
matter was referred to Osiris in the kingdom of
the dead over which he ruled, and he naturally
declared in Horus' favour. When the gods were
reluctant to carry out his judgement, he threatened to send his fierce-faced messengers, who did
not fear gods or goddesses, to fetch all the gods
who were unjust to Horus to his kingdom. At
this the gods quickly agreed; Horus was crowned
and Seth was given the position of thunder-god
as compensation.

Hou Chi: The Chinese god of the grain, in
particular of the grain called millet. He was
descended from *Huang Ti* and is shown as an old
man weaving a dress of leaves, whose raised right

hand sprouts into a millet-shoot.

Hou T'u: The Chinese earth-spirit goddess; thought of as the spirit of the earth itself rather than as a separate being.

Hraesvelg: The giant eagle who causes the winds, according to Norse myth. His name means 'corpse-eater', and at *Ragnarok* he devours the dead.

Hrimfaxi: The horse who brings night in Norse belief. His name means 'frosty mane', and dew is the foam from his bit as he gallops across the sky.

Hrimgerd: A Norse giantess who used to live in the sea and wreck ships; she was caught in the daylight and the sun turned her to stone.

Hrungnir: A Norse giant who challenged *Odin* to a horse-race; Odin, mounted on his eight-legged steed *Sleipnir*, beat him easily, but Hrungnir could not stop his horse in time and he found himself in *Asgard*, the gods' stronghold. The gods received him well, although giants were their deadly enemies, and he was allowed to drink out of *Thor*'s huge cups while Thor was away. When Thor returned, he found the giant was getting drunk and boasting that he would carry off the prettiest of the goddesses. Thor tried to attack him, but the other gods stopped him because Hrungnir was their guest. Instead, Hrungnir challenged Thor to a duel.

The other giants made a man out of clay, called Mist Calf, to help Hrungnir in the fight. Hrungnir had a stone heart and head, and was armed with a stone shield and a whetstone. Thor was helped by *Thialfi*, his servant, who tricked Hrungnir into standing on his shield in case Thor attacked him from below. Thor opened the duel by hurling thunder and lightning at Hrungnir, and when Hrungnir threw his whetstone, Thor replied with his hammer, which shattered the whetstone in mid-air and went on to kill Hrungnir. One piece of the stone lodged in Thor's forehead (see *Aurvandill*), and Hrungnir fell on top of Thor. No one could move him until Thor's young son Magni lifted him off.

Hsien: 'The immortals' in Chinese Taoist myth, represented as very old men and women, they were always young in spirit and enjoyed perfect good health. They also had some of the characteristics of fairies in western stories, and could not always be trusted in their dealings with men. See
124

also *Pa Hsien* for the stories of the eight mortals who had achieved immortality through their good works.

Hsi Wang Mu: Ruler of the female immortals (*Hsien*) in Chinese myth; sometimes called by western writers Queen of the Fairies. She was visited by King Mu in about 1000 B.C. In the garden of her palace in the *K'un-lun* Mountain she had a famous peach tree, which bore fruit once every three thousand years. This fruit made anyone who ate it immortal and she gave it to one of the early emperors of China.

Hu: One of the attendants of the Egyptian sun-god *Ra* in the boat which Ra sailed across the sky each day. (See p. 126.)

Huacas: Tribal gods of the peoples ruled by the Incas in Peru. After a deluge, the people of Cuzco (where the Incas later founded their first city), were washed down to Tiahuanaco, where they remained. God made other people from clay, and sent them out underground to repopulate the deserted regions. Wherever they emerged, they set up a temple, and the huacas, or first men, were later worshipped there, often in bird or animal form. (See p. 126.)

Huang Ti: The 'Yellow Emperor' of Chinese myth, one of the *Five Rulers*, at whose birth there were many remarkable signs. He was the son of the governor of a province of China, and succeeded his father. He defeated the enemies of China and was proclaimed Emperor after his victory. He became very expert in philosophy and taught his people so well that his kingdom became a paradise on earth. In his reign the 'feng huang' or phoenix appeared, as did the 'ch'i-lin' or unicorn, to pay homage to him.

Huang Ti'en: 'Imperial Heaven' in Chinese myth, source of the unchangeable laws by which man ought to try to live.

Huasa Mallcu: The spirit of the pampas or open plains, according to the Aymara Indians of Bolivia; he protects all animals, wild or tame, and often appears in the shape of a bird, the condor. (See p. 126.)

Huehueteotl: Another name for *Xiuhtecuhtli*.

Huginn: One of the two ravens of the Norse god

Odin, which he sent out each day in search of news; his name means thought. The other raven was Muninn, memory.

Huitzilopochtli: Aztec god of war and also of daytime; he was god of the south. He was the god of the Aztec nation, and occupied the central place in their capital at Tenochtitlan, symbolizing the Aztec rule over the other tribes of the region. His mother was *Coatlicue*; when he was born, his four hundred brothers, urged on by his sister, tried to destroy him, but he overcame them all, just as the sun chased the stars and the moon from the sky each morning. He was shown as a blue man, with a head-dress of hummingbird feathers.

Hunab Ku: The great god, without shape or form, who existed only in spirit, in the Maya myths.

Hunapu: The story of how man was created is told in the Maya epic *Popul Vuh*. The gods tried to make a being which would recognize and worship them, but their first efforts were useless, and led only to the creation of monkeys. Then a rival to the gods appeared, proclaiming that he was the lord of light, called Vucub-Caquix. The gods sent the twins Hunapu and Ixbalanque to fight him; these were the sons of Hun-Hunapu, a god who had been killed by the people of the underworld. The twins succeeded in overcoming Vucub-Caquix, but the sons of the latter continued the fight. The first, Zipacna, was only overcome after he had killed four hundred warriors, while the twins killed the second with birds roasted and covered with poisonous earth.

They then went to avenge the death of Hun-Hunapu and his brother Vucub-Ahpu, who had been killed by the Xibalba or people of the underworld after they had defeated him in a ball game. The Xibalba tested the twins by a series of trials, and even though Hunapu and his brother defeated them in a ball game, the struggle continued. Hunapu's head was cut off by the bat-god *Camazotz*, and Ixbalanque had to fashion a new one out of a turtle. The Xibalba challenged the twins to another ball game, thinking that Hunapu would be so handicapped that they would defeat them. But the twins arranged for a rabbit to run off with the ball, and while their opponents were looking for it, stole back Hunapu's real head. They then defeated the Xibalba again. As a final test the Xibalba challenged the twins to burn themselves to death and come alive again, which they did. They then performed miracles, cutting themselves to bits and coming together again, and persuaded the Xibalba to allow them to do this to them. But the Xibalba, once cut up, did not come back to life.

After this, the way was clear for the creation of man, and the first four men were made. But they were so like the gods that the gods were frightened, and put a mist on their eyes, so that they could not see the whole world at the same time as they had once been able to do.

Hunbatz and Hunchouen: When the Maya hero *Hunapu* and his twin Ixbalanque were born, their half-brothers, the flute-players Hunbatz and Hunchouen, were jealous of them and plotted to kill them: but Hunapu turned them into monkeys.

Hurakan: God of the whirlwind (hence the word 'hurricane') and thunderstorms in Maya myth. Hurakan and his helper Gucumatz made the earth, but had difficulty in making a creature which would worship them. First they made animals, but these could not speak; then they tried men made of wood and clay, and when they managed to make real men, they were too perfect, and the gods had to make their sight less clear, in case they came to know everything. In all this Gucumatz played the lesser part, and worshipped Hurakan for his skill.

Hyacinth: A Greek youth beloved by *Apollo* and Zephyrus. Hyacinth preferred Apollo, but Zephyrus had his revenge. Just as Apollo threw a discus in a contest with Hyacinth, he sent a gust which made it strike Hyacinth and kill him. From his blood there sprang the flower hyacinth; if you look carefully at it, you will see the Greek letters AI, AI, which mean 'Alas, alas!'

Hylas: In Greek myth, *Heracles'* page on the *Argo*; famous for his beauty, he was seized by some water-nymphs when the Argo's crew went ashore on an island in the Black Sea. Heracles, who was very fond of him, spent so long searching for him that the Argonauts left him behind and sailed without him.

Hymir: The Norse gods, as they feasted in their stronghold *Asgard*, once ran out of ale. Hearing that the sea-giant *Aegir* had plenty in his hall, they went to visit him, but he would only provide a feast if they found a vessel large enough to brew

mead in for them all. So *Thor* and *Tyr* set out to get one from the giant Hymir. As he often attacked strangers, they hid in his hall, inside one of the ale-kettles hung from the beam. His wife promised to plead on their behalf. When Hymir came in, he was furious, but was persuaded to accept them as guests. The next day, he suggested to Thor that they go fishing. They set out, but Hymir left the bait behind; so Thor went back to get it, and cut off the head of Hymir's biggest ox. Thor then rowed out to sea at an incredible speed, until Hymir begged him to stop, saying that they would soon be in the *Midgard-serpent*'s waters. Thor continued, and when he reached a suitable spot, threw out his line baited with the ox's head. The Midgard-serpent rose to the bait, and took it; Thor hauled with all his might, digging his heels through the boat until he was standing on the sea-bed. He heaved up the monster, and was about to strike it with his hammer when Hymir, terror-stricken, cut the line. Thor threw Hymir overboard and waded ashore, while Hymir had to swim for it. When they returned to Hymir's hall, Hymir challenged Thor to break his glass cup, and Thor struck it against the pillars of the hall without damaging it, but breaking the pillars. Hymir's wife then told him to hit the giant on the head with it, and it shattered. Thor was then told that he could take the kettle for brewing ale, so that he would go away and not do any more damage. Tyr tried to move it and failed, but Thor succeeded. Hymir then pursued them to get it back, but Thor killed him.

Hyperboreans: To the Greeks, these people dwelt beyond the north wind, *Boreas*; they were said to be worshippers of *Apollo*. They were perhaps a real people, living to the far north of Greece.

Hyperion: In Greek myth, either the father of the sun-god *Helios* or the sun-god himself. Hyperion was the child of *Uranus* and *Gaia*, and was one of the *Titans*; he was dethroned by *Apollo*. It was his cattle that *Odysseus'* men killed, for which *Zeus* destroyed their boat with a thunderbolt.

Iapetus: One of the children of *Uranus* and *Gaia*, called by the Greeks the *Titans*. He had two sons by Clymene, the daughter of Oceanus, who were *Atlas* and *Prometheus*.

Icarus: Son of the Greek master craftsman *Daedalus*. He escaped with his father from Crete, where *Minos* wanted to keep them, by using wings glued together with wax; but he flew too close to the sun, his wings melted, and he fell to his death.

Icheiri: Household gods of the Caribbean Indians of the West Indies; there was an altar to them in every hut, on which offerings were placed.

Ida-Ten: The Japanese Buddhist god who guarded the law and looked after monasteries and monks. When Buddha died, a demon stole one of his teeth as his body lay in its coffin, and ran off with it. His first stride covered forty thousand miles, and all the disciples of Buddha were so astonished that they did not try to pursue the demon, except for Ida-Ten, who retrieved the holy relic.

Idomeneus: Leader of the men from Crete in the *Trojan War*. He was caught in a storm on the way back, and vowed to sacrifice the first living thing that met him on his return to appease *Poseidon*. His son was on the shore to meet him when he returned; and for failing to sacrifice him, Idomeneus was driven into exile.

Idunn: Wife of the Norse god of poetry, *Bragi*; she was the guardian of the apples of immortality, which kept the gods young. She was once carried off by *Loki* at the command of the giant Thiazi (see *Apples of Youth*). The apples were kept in a box, rather than being plucked from a tree like the golden apples of the *Hesperides* in Greek myth.

Ifa: God of fortune-telling among the Yoruba people of West Africa. He acted as messenger between the gods and men, enabling men to find out what the gods had in store for them.

Ihuaivulu: Seven-headed monster-spirit of volcanoes according to the Araucanian Indians of South America.

Ilamatecutli: The 'old goddess' or mother of the gods in Aztec myth, another name for *Coatlicue*.

Ilmarinen: The Finnish sky-god, who appears in the epic *Kalevala* as a hero rather than a god: see *Vainamoinen*. Called Inmar by the Votiak people.

Ilos: Grandfather of the Trojan King *Priam*, from whom Troy got its Greek name, Ilion; the poem about the *Trojan War* by Homer is called the *Iliad* for this reason.

Ilyap'a, Illapa: The weather-god of the Incas of Peru, whose name meant 'thunder and lightning'. When the rainy season was late in starting appeals were made to Ilyap'a and processions were held with everyone dressed in mourning. Black dogs were tied up and left to starve until the god took pity on their howling and sent rain. He was thought of as a man in shining clothes, with a club in one hand and a sling for throwing stones in the other; when he threw a stone, the crack of his sling was the thunder, and the reflections from his clothes were the lightning. He drew water for rain from the Milky Way in the sky, and kept it in a jug. When he broke the jug, with a stone from his sling, the rains came down. After the Spaniards came to Peru, St James or

Santiago was said by the Incas to be the same as Ilyap'a, and ceremonies are still held in honour of Ilyap'a on St James's day, 25 July.

Imhetep: The Egyptian god of learning and medicine, identified by the Greeks with *Asclepius*. He lived under King Zoser who reigned about 3000 B C, and because of his wisdom was made a god after his death. He was said to have designed the step-pyramid at Sakkara, and to have been a great doctor, as well as the writer of a book of proverbs.

Inanna: The Sumerian 'queen of heaven', and fertility goddess. She was wooed by the shepherd Dumuzi (*Tammuz*) and Enkidu, a farmer. Dumuzi offered her milk and honey and woollen cloth, while Enkidu promised beans and grain and woven cloth. Although Inanna's brother, the sun-god *Uttu*, took Dumuzi's side, Inanna preferred Enkidu. But in later myth she had many other lovers; of whom the most important was Tammuz, the god she had once rejected, the lord of vegetation, who died and was revived each year. The sacred marriage of Inanna and Tammuz was an important annual festival. See also *Ishtar*.

Inapertwa: The aborigine tribesmen of Tasmania believed that human beings had once been Inapertwa, half-formed creatures with the general shape of men, but without limbs. Two sky-beings came down, and by cutting into the Inapertwa's bodies gave them arms and legs; then they made fingers and toes by cutting the ends of these; and finally they gave them mouth, nose and eyes by cutting their faces.

Inari: Japanese god of rice, shown as a fox holding two bags of rice. Ordinary foxes are his messengers. As god of rice, he was the bringer of wealth and good fortune, and became a very popular god, who helped in all kinds of problems.

Indra: The Hindu king of the gods, son of *Dyaus* and *Prithivi*, who rules the weather and gives rain. His weapons are the thunder and lightning, and he rides on a golden chariot drawn by two horses, or on the elephant *Airavata*. His particular enemy is the drought-demon *Vritra*, whom he overcomes with thunderbolts in order to make him release the rain which he tries to hoard. He is the great enemy of the *Asuras*, and fights them with the help of the *Maruts*. Among the gods, he is the rival of *Varuna*, whom he

supplanted as ruler of the gods and protector of mankind.

In later legends he is shown as drunken – he was especially fond of the *soma* – and fond of love-making, both of which led him into trouble. He was defeated and captured by *Ravana*'s son, and only released when the gods made his conqueror immortal. He was also defeated by *Krishna*, and suffered from a curse laid on him by *Durvasas*.

In Buddhist myth he appears as the *Dharmapala Vajrapani*. See also *Adityas*, *Ahalya*, *Garuda*, *Govardhana*, *Krishna*.

Indrani: Wife of the Indian god *Indra*.

Ing: A title of the god *Frey*; the royal dynasty of Sweden in early times were called the Ynglings after him, since they were supposed to be descended from him.

Inktonmi: Among the Sioux Indians of the American plains, Inktonmi was the hero of a number of tales similar to those told about *Nanabozho*.

Ino: Wife of *Athamas* in Greek myth; she nursed the god *Dionysus*, whom *Hera* hated, and for this both she and Athamas were driven mad. Athamas killed one of their sons, but Ino leapt over a cliff with the other. Dionysus took pity on her and turned her into a sea-goddess. See *Golden Fleece*.

Inti: The sun in Peruvian myths. The legends about Inti mostly date from the period after the Spanish Conquest and show Christian influence: there was said to be a trinity of Intis 'Lord Sun', 'Son Sun' and 'Sun-brother' like the Christian trinity. And Inti Huayma Capac (IHC) was said to be the same as God and Christ. (IHC are the Christian 'sacred initials'.) The sun warmed the earth, but it was subject to the same illnesses as people, and when it was ill drinking water would be contaminated. Rainbows were a sign that this was about to happen, and when they appeared people stored up as much water as possible. The earth's diseases were caused by evil spirits, who were the souls of wicked men who lived before the coming of Inti Huayma Capac. Most of the people who were alive when he came to earth made war on him and were burned to death.

Io: A Greek princess whom *Zeus* loved. *Hera* was jealous of her so Zeus disguised her as a cow to protect her. *Hera* discovered this, and asked Zeus for the cow, which he could not refuse without giving the plot away. She set *Argos* to guard it, but *Hermes* beguiled him to sleep and killed him. Hera then plagued Io with a gadfly, which drove her to wander as far as Egypt, where she bore a son. She was later worshipped as *Isis*.

Iolaos: Nephew and helper of *Heracles* in Greek him. (See p. 134.)

Iouskeha: In one Iroquois Indian myth, the god who looked after animals. At the beginning of the world, all the animals were shut up in a great cave, and only when Iouskeha released them were they able to come out into the world. He was also the god of harvests. Other branches of the Iroquois tribe called him *Yoskeha*, and made him a much more important god.

Iphicles: The half-brother of *Heracles* in Greek myth.

Iphigeneia: Daughter of the Greek King *Agamemnon*. Agamemnon sacrificed her at Aulis to appease *Artemis*, so that the Greek fleet could set sail for Troy. This was part of the curse on the house of *Atreus*; because of this *Clytemnestra*, Agamemnon's wife, murdered him on his return from Troy. In some versions Iphigeneia was snatched away by Artemis to become her priestess at Tauris, where all strangers were sacrificed to Artemis. Iphigeneia's brother *Orestes* arrived there some years later and put an end to the custom, taking his sister back to Greece with She was married to Zephyrus. (See p. 134.)

Iris: The Greek goddess of the rainbow and one of the messengers of the gods, especially of *Hera*. She was married to Zephyrus. (See p. 134.)

Irminsul: The 'pillar of the world', worshipped by followers of the early German sky-god, *Tiwaz*. Charlemagne destroyed a pillar of this kind, revered as the support of the universe, on the Holy Heath of the tribe of the Engers in 772.

Iruwa: Sun-god and chief god of the Chaga people of East Africa. A man once lost all his sons and swore that he would go to the place where Iruwa rose as the sun and shoot him in revenge. When he got there, he saw a great procession, with Iruwa in the middle, splendid and shining, and he hid himself in terror. But he was discovered, and Iruwa read his thoughts, saying

that he knew the man wanted to shoot him. However, he was forgiven, and sent back with great wealth, and more sons were born to him.

Ishtar: The Babylonian goddess of fertility, and of the evening star (Venus); the same as *Inanna*. She also appeared as a fierce war-goddess in Assyria and Egypt, whose sacred animal was the lion, and who encouraged soldiers in battle.

Her journey to Arallu, the underworld, is described in a Babylonian poem. She threatened to burst into *Ereshkigal*'s kingdom, but Ereshkigal craftily let her in on condition that she left some of her clothing at each of the seven gates through which she passed. As her jewels and garments were stripped from her, she left all her divine powers behind as well, so that when she finally came, naked, to Ereshkigal herself, she was in Ereshkigal's power, and Ereshkigal was able to put a curse on her and imprison her. So the god *Ea* sent a messenger to Ereshkigal, and she fell in love with the messenger. When he asked for permission to leave, she cursed him; at once the curse she had put on Ishtar lost its effect, and Ishtar was able to return to the land of the gods. But she had to find a replacement to take her place in hell, and she sent her lover *Tammuz*; he was later rescued by his sister.

Isis: The mother-goddess of ancient Egypt, she was daughter of *Geb* and *Nut*, and married her brother *Osiris*, in whose adventures she played a very important part, especially after he was killed by *Seth*. She was a great worker of magic, and one story tells how she gained her power. *Ra* was growing old, and, as old men do, used to dribble into his beard. Isis noticed this, and caught his saliva as it fell. She mixed it with earth, and made it into a serpent, which bit Ra, and caused him great pain. Isis refused to cure him unless he told her his secret magic name, which he reluctantly did. With this power, she was able to become the greatest of the goddesses.

Ismene: Sister of the Greek princess *Antigone*; unlike her sister, she did not attempt to defy *Creon*'s command not to bury their brother *Polyneices*.

Itiwana: The Zuni Indians of Mexico tell how their ancestors, on their journey up to the world from the regions below it, crossed a great lake. The first people to cross it lost all their children on the way. But two gods showed the rest how to cross, and told the first ones that their children were still alive in the underworld; their children were living happily below the lake. Their parents visited them there, and found them quite content; all the dead go there when they die.

Itzamna: Sky-god of the Mayas. He was son of *Hunab Ku* and traditional founder of their capital Mayapan: he was also said to have named all the places in their lands.

Itzli: God of sacrifice, and of the stone-knife used in human sacrifices, in Aztec mythology.

Ixion: A Greek ruler who murdered his father-in-law in a pot of red-hot coals. Only *Zeus* would purify him, but Ixion repaid him by trying to make love to Zeus' wife *Hera*. Zeus deceived Ixion by making a cloud image of Hera, which became the goddess *Nephele*; the children of Ixion and Nephele were the *centaurs*. Ixion was punished for his crimes by being bound to a burning wheel which turns forever in *Tartarus*.

Ixtab: Maya goddess who ruled the paradise of the blessed: those who have led good lives were rewarded with food and drink, and lived under the pleasant shade of the tree called Yaxche. Ixtab, for unknown reasons, was shown as a hanged woman with a noose round her neck.

Izanagi and Izanami: In Japanese myth, 'Male and female who invite', sent down by the gods of heaven to create life on earth. They made land by stirring the water which covered the earth with a spear; a drop hung on the end of the spear, and became an island when it fell again into the water. Here Izanagi and Izanami lived. Their children were the gods of the sea, the woods and all such things, but everything was covered by a great mist until the wind-god was born and blew the mist away. When the fire-god was born, however, Izanami was burned by him and died. She was the first person to die, and she went down to the underworld, *Yomi-No-Kuni*. As she went, she became old and ugly, and when Izanagi tried to follow her, she asked him not to look at her. But he disobeyed, and as a punishment she tried to imprison him in the underworld too, sending the *Shikome* or furies to pursue him. He escaped, and blocked the entrance to Izanami's new world with a great stone. Izanami swore to claim a thousand of Izanagi's subjects each day; but Izanagi said he would create fifteen hundred each day. So Izanami became goddess of death. and Izanagi lord of life. 135

J

Jagannath: A Hindu title meaning 'lord of the world', applied to the image of *Krishna* worshipped at Puri in Orissa State. When Krishna was killed, his body was left under a tree; his bones were later collected, and the local king was told by *Vishnu* to make an image and put the bones inside it. The image was made by the architect of the gods, *Vishvakarman*, on condition that he was left entirely alone while doing the work. But the king could not wait until he had finished, and the image had no hands or feet. The king prayed to *Brahma*, who gave the image eyes and a soul, and made it famous. The image is housed in a huge wheeled carriage, and is pulled to a lake nearby once a year, as part of the sacred ritual. This carriage has given us our word 'juggernaut'; excited worshippers used to hurl themselves under its wheels, believing that they would go at once to heaven.

Jamshid: Another name for *Yima* in Iranian myth: he appears under this name in Fitzgerald's translation of the *Rubaiyat* of Omar Khayyam as a legendary king of the past ('the courts where Jamshid gloried and drank deep').

Janus: The Roman god of the gates of the city and of the opening of the year; January is called after him. He frustrated a plot to betray the city of Rome to its enemies the Sabines, so his temple in the city was always open in wartime in case he needed to go out and help the Romans. In Rome's later years as an empire, the temple was very rarely closed because peace was so unusual.

Jarnsaxa: A Norse giantess loved by *Thor*, and mother of his son *Magni*.

Jason: Son of *Aeson*, king of the Greek colony of Iolchos in Thessaly. His step-uncle *Pelias* seized the throne when his father died, and Jason was brought up by the *centaur Chiron*. He returned to the court wearing only one sandal, to the terror of Pelias, who had been warned by an oracle to beware of someone wearing only one sandal. On his way to the court, he had helped an old woman by carrying her over a stream; this was the goddess *Hera* in disguise, and she therefore favoured him. Pelias sent Jason to search for the *Golden Fleece*, hoping he would be killed on the way. The expedition, in the ship *Argo*, attracted many great heroes, including *Heracles, Castor and Pollux, Meleager, Laocoon, Zetes and Calais.*

The Argo and its crew, called the Argonauts

by those who later told their story, set off northwards from Iolchos. After some minor adventures they arrived at the kingdom ruled by Cyzicus which was being attacked by six-armed giants who were born from the earth. Heracles defeated these with his deadly arrows, and the Argo left. But they were driven back by the wind, and when they landed again they were mistaken for invaders. In the fighting, Cyzicus was killed. Then Heracles' oar broke, and they landed at Kios, where *Hylas* was seized by *nymphs* and Heracles had to be left behind since he refused to give up the search for him. In the kingdom of the Berbyces, their next port of call, the king, who always challenged strangers to a boxing match, was defeated and killed by Pollux. Sailing up the Bosphorus they reached the kingdom ruled by Phineus, who had used his prophetic powers to betray the secrets of the gods, and was plagued by the *Harpies* in punishment. These creatures would not let him touch any food that was set before him, but devoured it or made it uneatable. Zetes and Calais drove them off, but were prevented by *Iris* from killing them. In return, Phineus told them how to get through the Clashing Rocks or Symplegades, which came together whenever a boat tried to pass, and which barred the way to the Black Sea. The Argonauts were to release a dove, and if this got through, they were to row as hard as they could when the rocks reopened. The dove's tail-feathers were just touched by the rocks, but *Athene* helped the Argo through: after which the rocks never moved again.

Further adventures led them to Colchis, on the far side of the Black Sea, where *Aeetes*, owner of the Golden Fleece, lived. Here his daughter *Medea* fell in love with Jason as soon as she saw him, because *Eros*, the god of love, had been bribed by Hera to shoot his arrow at her. She gave Jason a magic ointment which protected him through the trials which Aeetes devised. Firstly, he had to plough a field with huge firebreathing wild oxen. Then he had to sow it with the teeth of *Cadmus*' dragon. Just as Cadmus had done, Jason defeated the armed men that sprang up out of the earth by making them fight each other. Aeetes suspected treachery, but Medea and Jason removed the Golden Fleece, killing the dragon that guarded it, and escaped. Medea's brother *Absyrtus* was sent after them; he was treacherously killed on Jason's ship when Medea pretended that she wanted to talk to him. *Zeus* was angry with them for this, and they wandered across the Mediterranean, until they came to

Circe's island. Circe, not knowing that it was her nephew that they had killed, purified them. They voyaged on to Corcyra, where Jason and Medea were married, and then home by way of Crete, where Medea killed the giant *Talus*.

At Iolchos, Medea plotted against Pelias, who had sent Jason on the expedition. She persuaded his daughters that if they used certain herbs, they could renew their father's youth by plunging him in a cauldron of boiling water, and she proved this with an old ram; but she gave them the wrong herbs on purpose, and they killed their father. For this both Jason and Medea were exiled to Corinth, where, some years later, Jason abandoned her for *Glauce*, daughter of the king of Corinth. Medea sent the bride a poisoned robe, which killed her, and then killed her own children by Jason. She escaped to Athens; Jason died soon afterwards when part of the Argo, which he had put in *Poseidon*'s temple nearby, fell on him as he sat under it.

Jigoku: Hell in Japanese Buddhist myth. Its ruler was *Emma-o*, who judged the dead and assigned them to one of its sixteen regions, until their sins had been punished for a suitable length of time, after which their souls were reborn on earth.

Jimmu Tenno: Legendary founder of the Japanese imperial dynasty, great-grandson of *Ama-terasu*.

Jingo: Japanese empress of the third century AD who was supposed to have crossed the sea and conquered Korea. This she did with the help of two magic jewels given to her by the sea-gods. With one she was able to raise the sea-water; with the other she could lower it, and she crossed the sea by using the two as necessary. She was the mother of *Hachiman*, the warrior-god. (See also *Hoho-demi* for another story about the same magic jewels.)

Jizo: Japanese god who protected children and anyone who suffered. He appeared in various forms, and often helped warriors in battle in his shape as Shogun-Jizo. There is a different form of Jizo for each of the separate paths that men's souls take after death.

Jörd: A name meaning literally 'earth', perhaps a title of the Norse goddess *Frigg*, wife of *Odin*.

138

Also, an Anglo-Saxon charm for use before ploughing the earth and planting the new crop runs: 'Hale be thou, Earth, mother of men; be faithful in God's embrace, filled with food for the use of men.'

Jötunheim: The home of the Norse giants, separated from the worlds of men and of gods, and generally thought of as a cold and dismal place. *Thor* once went there disguised as *Freyja* in order to win back his hammer.

Jumala: The creator and greatest of gods in Finnish myth, later identified with *Ukko*.

Juno: The goddess whom the Romans identified with *Hera*. She had been a moon-goddess. On the Capitol, the hill in the centre of Rome, geese were kept which were sacred to her, for they had once warned the Romans of a surprise attack on the city and she was worshipped as the goddess who gave warning of the future. It was because she was the protectress of women, particularly in childbirth, that she was regarded as the same as Hera. The month of June gets its name from her.

Jupiter: The greatest of the Roman gods, who was later identified with *Zeus*. He was the 'smiter' or the god of lightning, and in the early days of Rome was regarded as the chief god of the federation of Latin cities to which Rome belonged. The *flamen dialis* or Roman high priest was Jupiter's priest, and he was later worshipped as the 'greatest and best of gods', *deus optimus maximus*, abbreviated in inscriptions to D.O.M.

The largest planet in the Solar System is named after him.

Kachinas: In the mythology of the Hopi Indians of the Mexican border, kachinas are the spirits which inhabit and control everything in nature.

Kaitabha: A demon which tried to attack the Hindu god *Brahma* as he was born from the lotus in *Vishnu*'s navel: Vishnu slew him and his companion Madhu.

Kala: A title of the Hindu god *Yama* meaning 'time'.

Kalevala: The land ruled by *Vainamoinen* in Finnish myth, which gives its name to the Finnish national epic.

Kali, Kalika: 'The black': *Devi*, wife of the Hindu god *Shiva*, in her terrifying appearance.

Kaliya: A five-headed serpent king, who devastated the country near the house of the Hindu god-hero *Krishna*. Krishna jumped into the pool where he lived and overcame him by his divine power, forcing him to go and live in the ocean.

Kama: The Hindu god of desire, similar to the Greek *Eros*: like Eros, he is shown as a handsome youth carrying a bow. His 'vehicle' is a parrot, and he is lord of the *apsarases*. *Shiva* once reduced him to ashes because he distracted him when he was at his devotions. He was reborn as a son of *Krishna*.

Kame and Kayuruke: The Caingang Indians of Brazil tell how animals were created by two brothers Kame and Kayuruke who appeared from inside a mountain. They made jaguars from ashes and coals, and the tapir from ashes only. The tapir's ears were very small, so when they ordered him to eat meat, he did not hear properly, and ate leaves and branches instead. Kayuruke also made the great anteater, but did not finish it: that is why it has no teeth and a long thin tongue, which is a bit of stick which Kayuruke hurriedly pushed into his mouth. Kayuruke made all the useful animals, Kame all the harmful ones; and when they had finished, they decided that the jaguars were too dangerous and they would have to kill them. So they made the jaguars get on a tree trunk with the idea of pushing it out into the river, where they would drown. But some of them clung to the river-bank, roaring at Kame and Kayuruke, and Kame was so frightened that he did not dare to push them in: so there are still jaguars around.

The people of Kame and Kayuruke intermarried with the Caingang Indians, and it was Kayuruke who taught the Caingang how to sing and dance, an art he learnt from the great anteater who lived in the depths of the forest.

Kami: The gods or 'higher beings' in Japanese myth. As in China, the *kami* include not only what westerners would think of as gods, but also the forces of nature, described as the *kami* of mountains or rivers, and great men who lived in the past. *Kami* are divided into *Amo-no-kami*, the heavenly *kami*, and *Kumi-no-kami*, the *kami* who live on earth.

Kami-mi-masubi: 'Miraculous-producing-goddess' in Japanese myth, who appeared after *Kuni-Toko-Tachi* and *Taka-Mi-Masubi* at the beginning of the world.

Kami-nari: The goddess of rolling thunder; trees split by lightning were sacred to her in Japan and could not be cut down.

Kan-xib-yui: In Maya myth as recorded in the *Book of Chilam Balam*, Kan-xib-yui recreated the earth after the four *Bacabs* had destroyed it and thrown down the sky. He raised the sky on five trees, one at each corner and one in the centre; and when the sun, moon and stars awoke, the world began.

Kappa: Japanese evil spirit, rather like a monkey but with a dent in the top of its head. It lived in pools, and came out to attack men and women. There was always water on top of its head, and if this was spilt, its strength disappeared. As it was very polite, in spite of its evil ways, the best way of overcoming a Kappa was to bow to it: it would then bow back, losing both the water and its power.

Kartikeya: The Indian god of war, son of *Shiva* and the *Ganges*; his great enemy was Taraka, a *Daitya*, who had acquired great power by prayer and fasting and who threatened the power of the gods. He is shown riding a peacock, holding a bow and arrow: he is six-headed, with twelve arms and legs.

Kasyapa: One of the seven Hindu great sages or *maharishis*, who was the father of many kinds

of living creatures as well as human beings. Among his human or divine children were the *Adityas* and *Vaivasvata*. He himself was the grandson of *Brahma*.

Kawa-no-kami: The Japanese river-gods, each river having its own particular spirit.

Keresaspa: An early hero of Iran, whose enormous strength and massive club enabled him to conquer many evil creatures, including the dragons Srvara and Kundrav. He also killed giants as well as human enemies, but eventually he was bewitched by Khnathaitu, whom he married. She converted him to the worship of idols, and he neglected to worship the sacred fire. He was wounded in a battle, and lies in a deep sleep until the end of the world. Then he will appear and kill the demon *Dahhak*.

Keret: A Canaanite legend tells how Keret, prince of Ugavit, mourned his wife. The god *El* told him to besiege Udum and demand Hurrya the king's daughter which he did successfully, and she was surrendered to him. But he had failed to complete a vow he had made to a goddess called Athirat, and became sick. During his illness, the crops failed and the land became waste; and justice was no longer done. His eldest son tried to persuade him to give up the throne, perhaps in the hope of lifting the curse on the land; but Keret revived, thanks to the help of El, and continued to rule.

Keri and Kame: In South American Indian myths, Keri and Kame were sons of a jaguar, Oka, and a magically-made woman. They were born in the sky-world, but the jaguar's mother, Mero, killed their mother. In revenge, they lit a fire which in turn burnt Mero and both of them to death. Keri and Kame brought themselves to life again and descended to earth as men. They set the sun and moon in their places, after stealing them from the vultures who owned them. They separated heaven and earth, and stole water from the great snake to make rivers. From the fox they stole the fire which he kept in his eye. Then they taught humans how to live together, and, their work done, climbed a mountain and vanished.

Khensu: Son of the Egyptian gods *Amen* and *Mut*, Khensu represented the king's spirit and power, and was shown as a young, handsome prince. He was also god of the moon, and his head-dress is usually a full moon supported on a crescent moon.

Khepra: The Egyptian sun-god in the shape of the scarab-beetle. The scarab-beetle makes a ball of dung as its food, and rolls it away until it can find a hole in the ground in which to eat it; and it lays its eggs in similar balls of dung, though the ancient Egyptians do not seem to have known this. Because a living beetle appeared to come directly from this ball of dung, without any other parents to be seen, the Egyptians regarded it as self-created. The sun-god, too, who rolled the ball of the sun across the sky each day, was self-created because he was also the creator-god; so the beetle became the symbol of the sun-god, and was worshipped under the title Khepra.

Khnemu: In Egyptian myth, the god who shapes men's bodies on his potter's wheel. His wife was *Heqet*, the goddess who gave these bodies life. Early myths about them say that they created not only men but the gods and the universe as well.

Khshathra Vairya: The Iranian god of metals, who also represented the state of mind which worshippers tried to reach, the 'desirable kingdom' of righteousness; he was one of the *Amesha Spentas*.

Kibuka: The war-god of the Baganda people of East Africa. He was sent by heaven to help the Baganda in a battle, but was told not to have anything to do with women. However, some women prisoners were taken, and he made love to one of them. She escaped, and told the enemy how to kill him in the next battle, by firing arrows at the clouds above the battlefield. When they did this, Kibuka was killed.

Kichijōten: Japanese goddess of luck, consort of Bishamon-ten (see *Shichi Fukujin*).

Kinharingan: According to the Dusun tribe of Borneo, it was Kinharingan who made the earth, with the help of his wife Munsumundok. The two of them appeared on an island in the middle of the waters, and walked across the waters till they came to the home of Bisagit. Now Bisagit was the smallpox, and he agreed to give Kinharingan the earth he needed to create the world if he could

143

have half Kinharingan's people. Kinharingan agreed, and he and his wife made the earth and sky, sun, moon and stars. They killed one of their children and buried the pieces of its body in the earth; from these plants and animals grew. But when they created men, Bisagit claimed half of them, and the Dusuns say that he comes every forty years.

Kinnaras: In Hindu myth, creatures with men's bodies and horses' heads, who live in the realm of *Kuvera* and are great musicians.

Kintu: The first man in the myths of the Ganda tribe of East Africa. He was alone in the world with a cow, and lived off milk and cheese. One day the children of the sky-god Gulu came to where Kintu was living, and Nambi, Gulu's daughter, insisted that she wanted to marry Kintu. But her brothers were suspicious of him and did not want her to marry him; so they stole his cow, to see what he would do. He survived on bark for a time, but Nambi rescued him and took him to heaven.

In order to test Kintu, Gulu shut him up with a huge amount of food and ordered him to eat it; but Kintu found a hole in the house floor and threw the food into it. With the help of a hornet, which went and sat on his cow's horn, he picked out his own cow from a great herd of cattle. So Gulu gave him Nambi as his wife, and sent them back with all kinds of seeds, a banana tree and chickens, which had not been seen on earth before. But he warned them not to turn back, even if they left something behind, because if they did, Death, who was away when they left, would have returned, and would insist on going with them. Kintu found he had left the corn for the chickens behind, and went back; so Death came back to earth with him. Although Gulu sent another of his sons to catch him and bring him back, Death escaped and stayed on earth.

Kishimojin: In Japanese Buddhist myth, a female demon who was converted by Buddha and became the goddess of children and of birth.

Kōbō Daishi: Japanese priest who founded a local sect of Buddhism which included the worship of some of the native Japanese gods at the end of the eighth century AD. He was a great worker of miracles, and could control all kinds of spirits.

Kompira: The Japanese name for *Kuvera*, the Hindu god of wealth. He was also protector of sailors: in a storm they would cut off their hair and throw it in the sea as they prayed to him to calm the winds.

Krishna: An Indian hero of the epic period, the centuries preceding the birth of Christ in Western history. He later came to be regarded as a god, either the eighth *avatar* of *Vishnu*, or as Vishnu himself. He is the most popular god in modern Indian religion, and a whole series of myths about his life have developed, some of them in quite recent times.

From his youth (like *Heracles*) he showed signs
Krishna and his brother *Bala Rama* were said to have been born from two hairs of Vishnu, one dark (*Krishna* means black), the other light. Krishna's mother was Devaki, wife of one of the *Pandava* family. Vishnu had brought Krishna into the world because of the evil deeds of Kansa, who had become ruler of the Yadava people, and had banned the worship of Vishnu. Kansa had been warned by an oracle that Krishna would be born to Devaki and would be his enemy, and tried to kill all Devaki's sons as soon as they were born. However, Vishnu protected Krishna and he was brought up as the son of a cowherd and his wife, Nanda and Yashoda.

From his youth (like *Heracles*) he showed signs of heroic powers: he strangled an ogress who tried to poison him by giving him her milk when he was only a baby, and he destroyed two demons, Shakata and Trinavarta, who attacked him. Trinavarta took the shape of a whirlwind and tried to seize Krishna, but Krishna hurled him against a rock. As he grew up, Kansa, who had been told that a cowherd's son would destroy him, sent other demons to attack him, but he defeated them all by his powers. A crane-demon swallowed him, but Krishna became so hot that he had to disgorge him, while he split open a snake which swallowed him by making himself steadily bigger until the snake burst. It was at this time that he also killed the demon *Kaliya*.

As he grew up, he showed his defiance of the other gods as well as of the demons. He once persuaded the wives of some Brahmans (priests in Indian society) who were preparing a sacrifice to give it to him and his companions instead, because they were hungry, and this disrespect for the gods was not punished, because Krishna was a greater god than the others. He won an argument with *Indra* when he persuaded the cowherd with whom he lived to worship the mountain

Govardhana which sheltered them instead of Indra: and Indra ended by paying homage to Krishna.

Krishna appears in his youth as a kind of god of love, and his affairs with the cow-girls or *Gopis* are one of the most famous parts of his story. He started by teasing them and stealing their clothes while they bathed, and later danced with them, in a dance which lasted for six months. Each girl thought that Krishna was in love with her alone, but he finally went off with one of them, *Radha*, and the others set off in pursuit. But Radha insisted that Krishna should carry her and, annoyed at her pride, he left her. All the girls pleaded with him to come back, and he now used his magic powers to make them all believe that he was dancing with each of them alone. Although the dance went on for half a year, when the girls returned home they found that no one had missed them.

Kansa had now definitely discovered that Krishna was his enemy and the man who would kill him, so he sent more demons against him, again without success. He then invited Krishna to his capital, Mathura, hoping to kill him by treachery in a wrestling match. But Krishna was warned, and after a triumphant arrival at Mathura, he defeated all the wrestlers and killed a savage elephant which Kansa had kept to send against him as a last resort. He then killed Kansa himself, who was threatening to kill Krishna's mother Devaki, and seized his throne. But Kansa's relations continued to attack him, using methods just as evil as Kansa's, and he had to fight seventeen battles with Kansa's father-in-law Jarasandha before he was able to achieve peace.

He now asked *Vishvakarman* to build a city for him in a single night: this was called *Dvaraka* and here Krishna ruled for the rest of his life. He married the beautiful Rukmini, whom he snatched away on the morning that she was to marry a man whom she hated. His name was *Shishupala*, but he was really a demon who appears elsewhere as *Hiranyakashipu* and *Ravana*. Although Krishna frequently had him at his mercy, he had once promised his mother to pardon him a hundred times. Shishupala and Jarasandha now made an alliance, and Krishna enlisted the help of *Bhima* against them. After a long struggle, Bhima tore Jarasandha in half, and Shishupala, having used up all his pardons, was killed by Krishna with a discus, the magic weapon Sudarshana which never failed.

Krishna also overcame the *Asura Naraka*, who

had stolen some of the gods' treasures, including *Aditi*'s earrings, *Indra*'s canopy, and carried off the *apsarases* and *Gandharvas* from heaven. Krishna tried to exchange the earrings and canopy for the magic tree from Indra's realm, but Indra refused. Once again Indra was defeated, and Krishna obtained the tree, which one of his wives had asked him to get, though he returned it a year later.

Krishna took part in the great battle between the Pandavas and the Kauravas, though he did not actually fight, but merely gave advice: much of what he taught is contained in the book called *Bhagavad Gita*, which was his advice to *Arjuna*.

But he himself did not have much more time on earth. Because his son had mocked some Brahmans, the Yadava people over whom he ruled were cursed with destruction, and although Krishna tried to avert disaster by sending them on a pilgrimage as a penance, they took to drinking on the way back, and started to fight among themselves. They were all killed, and Krishna himself prepared to leave the world. As he sat in meditation, a hunter threw a spear at his foot, which as *Durvasas* had foretold, was the place where he would be fatally wounded. Warning the few Yadavas left at Dvaraka that the city would sink into the sea at his death, he returned to his heavenly place as Vishnu.

Krishna appears frequently in Indian painting, particularly in pictures showing his love-affair with the Gopis and with Radha.

Kuan Yin: The Chinese goddess of mercy, originally a male Buddhist *Bohdhisattva*. According to the Chinese version of her story, which mixes Buddhist tradition with native Chinese ideas, when she was on earth, she was Miao-shan, youngest daughter of a king of Siam. Her father wished her to marry, but she insisted on going into a Buddhist convent. He finally allowed her to go on condition that she did all the cooking and washing for the other five hundred nuns. But the gods took pity on her, and her work was done magically for her. Her father discovered this, and set fire to the convent in his anger. Miao-shan miraculously put out the flames; her father tried to have her head cut off, but the sword broke, and she was strangled instead. But when she reached the realms of the dead, she recited the holy books, and the ruler of the dead was unable to make any of the inhabitants of hell suffer. So he sent her back into the world, where she gained great spiritual wisdom and was made

immortal by the Buddha. Meanwhile her father had become ill, and the only medicine that would cure him had to be made from the hands and eyes of a living person. Miao-shan gave her hands and eyes so that he could be cured; the medicine worked, and he was converted to Buddhism, while she was miraculously made whole again.

Kuan Yu: In the official religious calendar of China, Kuan Yu was the war-god; but popular myths made him the 'great judge', who protected people from wrongs and evil spirits. He also predicted the future by means of numbered slips shaken in hollow bamboos. The number on the first slip to fall out was looked up in a special book of verses, and the message which corresponded to the number foretold the future.

In real life, he was a commander in the civil wars of the second and third centuries A D, who was both a great warrior and a just and good ruler. He was named as god of war during the Ming Dynasty, in the reign of the Emperor Wan Li (1572–1602). In 1914 *Yo Fei* was given equal rank with Kuan Yu.

K'uei-Hsing: Chinese god of examinations. The imperial examinations for the civil service were very important in China, as they were the chief means by which an ambitious man could make his way in the world. K'uei-Hsing is said to have come first in one of the most important of these examinations when he was alive, but he was very ugly, and the Emperor refused to confirm his place when he saw him. So K'uei-Hsing threw himself in the sea in despair, but was rescued by a giant turtle.

Kukulcan: The storm-god of the Mayas of central Mexico: his name means 'feathered serpent' and the stories about him are broadly the same as those about the later Aztec god *Quetzalcoatl*. He was said to have been a human king, and to have built the great religious citadel at Chichen Itza.

Kullervo: Hero of a tragic episode in the Finnish epic *Kalevala*: his father and uncle quarrelled before his birth, and as a result Kullervo was sold into slavery. His parents were killed, and Kullervo later met his sister without knowing who she was. He made love to her; she discovered who he was, and she killed herself. His uncle destroyed his home, and Kullervo too killed himself when he arrived at the ruined house.

Kuma: In the creation myth of the Yaruro Indians of Venezuela, Kuma, the moon-goodess, is the most important figure. She made the world with the help of Puana, the water snake (who made the water) and Itciai, the jaguar (who made the land): Puana taught her son Hatchawa many useful arts such as how to make fire, how to hunt and fish. It was Hatchawa who brought mankind out of the underworld by giving them a rope to climb up; but the rope broke when a woman who was expecting a child tried to climb it. So some people were left behind in the underworld, where the evil spirit Kiberoth is their queen. Kuma rules over a paradise in the west where everything on earth has a giant counterpart.

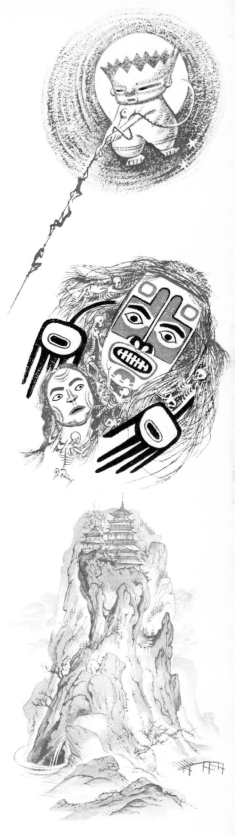

Kumush: In Modoc Indian myths of the Pacific coast of North America, Kumush was a sky-god who had a daughter. He made ten dresses for her, one for each stage of her life; but when she was almost grown up, she demanded the most beautiful of all, her burial dress, and died. Kumush went with her to the land of ghosts, but grew tired of living there. So he decided to bring life back to earth, and took the skeleton-spirits of the dead with him. Twice he tried and failed, but the third time he reached the earth and sowed it with the bones of the spirits; and from these came men, who repeopled the earth.

Kuni-toko-tachi: First god in Japanese myth, who appeared in the chaos at the beginning of the world; his name means 'he who always stands over the world'.

K'un-lun Mountain: The Chinese paradise, a mountain at the centre of the earth ruled by *Hsi Wang Mu*. On top of the mountain is a marvellous nine-storeyed palace built of jade, in the gardens of which grows the peach tree of immortality. Here the Immortals themselves live, and the only men who are admitted are those whom the gods have rewarded during their lifetime with the fruit of the peach tree. There is an actual range with this name in the west of China.

Kura-Okami: The Japanese god of rain and snow.

Kururumany: Creator-god in the myths of the Arawak Indians of Guyana.

Kuvera: Leader of the spirits in Indian myth.

149

partly an opponent of the gods and hence evil, but also given power and treasures by them. He ruled the northern kingdom or Himalayas and is god of wealth and guardian of treasure, rather like Plutus in Roman myth. He was the owner of a magic chariot, and half-brother of *Ravana*. See also *Kinnaras*.

Kvasir: When the Norse gods, *Aesir* and *Vanir*, met to make peace at the end of the war between them, all the gods spat into a vessel. From the contents of this they created the wise dwarf Kvasir, who could answer all questions. Kvasir was later killed by two other dwarfs, who made his blood into mead. Anyone who drank of this was inspired with poetry and wisdom. This mead came first into the hands of the giant *Suttung*, but was won for the gods by *Odin*.

However, in the story of *Loki*, which seems to come after this legend in sequence, it was Kvasir who discovered how to capture Loki, because he was 'the wisest of the Aesir'.

Kwannon: The Japanese regarded the Chinese goddess *Kuan Yin* as a male *Bodhisattva* or future Buddha, like the Indian original *Avalokiteshvara*. He is the god of infinite mercy, and helps all men: he is worshipped in many different forms, including the thousand-handed Senju Kwannon, each of whose hands has an eye in the palm of it, and who represents the ever-watchful god. There is also Bato Kwannon, who fights demons, and has a horse's head instead of a crown, as well as other forms with special religious meanings, often complicated by their use of obscure symbols.

Labraid: Brother-in-law of *Fand* in Irish myth; one of *Cuchulainn*'s adventures was to help him against his enemies.

Laertes: Father of *Odysseus* in Greek myth.

Laestrygonians: In Greek myth, cannibal giants in whose country *Odysseus* landed in the course of his travels; they received him kindly at first, but then treacherously attacked his men and devoured all of them except those in his own ship.

Laius: King of Thebes in Greek myth, whose throne was usurped while he was still a child. While in banishment he was given shelter by *Pelops*, but he kidnapped Pelops' beautiful son Chrysippus. This repayment of good by evil led to the curse on his family. He regained his kingdom and married *Jocasta*, but was warned by an oracle that if he had a son by her, the son would kill him. When *Oedipus* was born, he was left on a hillside to die; but he survived to fulfil the prophecy, as his own story tells.

Lakshmana: One of the heroes of the Indian epic *Ramayana* and half-brother to *Rama*. He accompanied Rama throughout his wanderings, and helped him in his war against *Ravana*. He was forced to interrupt Rama, who was talking to *Yama* about his death, by the sage *Durvasas*, though he knew that to interrupt such a sacred interview would mean his own death. However, Durvasas made such threats that he had to do so, and the gods carried him to heaven.

Lakshmi or Shri: In Hindu myth, the goddess of fortune and wife of *Vishnu*. She appeared when the ocean was churned by the gods in their search for the *amrita*, and came out of the foam, like *Aphrodite*. She carries a lotus, and is shown as a very beautiful woman. In each of his *avatars*, she was Vishnu's wife or mistress: so *Sita*, *Radha* and Rukmini, wife of *Krishna*, are all Lakshmi in other forms.

Landvaettir: Guardian spirits of a place or country in Norse belief. When King Harald Gormsson of Denmark wanted to invade Iceland, he sent a magician to spy out the land. The magician changed himself into a whale, but the Landvaettir prevented him from landing, though he tried in four different places. Another version of the story of Thorhall and the *disir* tells how he

was staying with his friend Hall, just before
Christianity came to Iceland. One day as he was
sitting in bed, looking out of the window, Hall
saw him smile, and asked him what he could see.
'I see mounds opening and the Landvaettir and
other spirits packing and preparing to depart.'

Laocoon: In Greek myth, the priest of *Apollo* at
Troy; he declared that the *Trojan Horse* was a
trick, and should be destroyed. But he and his
two sons were killed by two huge red-crested
serpents which appeared out of the sea, and the
Trojans took this as a punishment for his lack of
respect for the gods. So they hauled the horse
into the city, only to discover that Laocoon had
spoken the truth.

Laomedon: Father of King *Priam* of Troy in
Greek myth. He hired the gods *Poseidon* and
Apollo to build the walls of Troy, but refused to
pay them when they had finished. Poseidon sent
a sea-monster to plague him in revenge, and
Heracles agreed to kill it, in return for Laomedon's
marvellous horses (given to his grandfather as
compensation for *Ganymede*). But once again
Laomedon refused payment when the task was
done, so Heracles raised an expedition against
Troy and captured it.

Lao T'ien Yeh: 'The Father of Heaven' in
Chinese myth, often identified with *Yu Huang*.
Lao T'ien Yeh created men, by making them out
of clay, and leaving them to dry in the sun. But
just then there was a heavy rain-storm, and he
hastened to put the clay figures under cover.
Some were damaged, and they became sick men,
while those which were unharmed became
healthy men.

Lao Tzu: The first great writer on the Taoist
philosophy, who was a contemporary and rival
of Confucius. Like Confucius, he was later worshipped by the Chinese as a sage. His disciples
Chuang Chou and Lieh Tzu were also
worshipped.

Lapiths: A people who lived in Thessaly, beyond the northern border of Greece. They were
the enemies of the *centaurs*, and were often at war
with them. During a time of peace they invited
the centaurs to the wedding of their chieftain
Pirithous to *Hippodameia*; but the centaurs got
very drunk and tried to carry off all the women,
including the bride. A fierce battle followed, in

which the centaurs were defeated.

Lares: Spirits worshipped by the Romans, which were in charge of each household, and which also presided over cross-roads.

Latinus: When the founder of the Roman nation, *Aeneas* landed in Italy, Latinus was king of Latium. Aeneas met him and fell in love with his daughter Lavinia, but events led to a quarrel between the Trojans and Latins, and in the war which followed Aeneas defeated Latinus. However, peace was made on generous terms, and Aeneas married Lavinia. From him the Latin language was said to have got its name.

Leda: Queen of Sparta in Greece, she was visited by *Zeus* in the form of a swan, after which Fate presented her with an egg from which *Helen* was born. She was also the mother by him of *Pollux* (Polydeuces); her other children were Pollux's twin *Castor*, whose father was Tyndareos, and who was not immortal, and *Clytemnestra*, later wife of *Agamemnon*.

Legba: Son of God in myths from Dahomey in West Africa. He was originally God's messenger on earth, but he grew tired of being blamed for whatever God did to men. So by a trick he made God move away from the world: he got an old woman to throw her dirty water at the sky each time she washed until God grew tired of this. Leaving Legba to report to him what went on in the world, God went away, and Legba was worshipped and honoured as God's representative, though he was a trickster and mischief-maker, and did just as he pleased, without troubling about taboos or morals. He later taught men how to read oracles, particularly the palm-nut patterns thrown by the diviners using 'Fa' oracles.

Lei Kung: Chinese thunder-god; he was hideously ugly, with a bird's head and claws, and blue skin. He carried a mallet with which he made thunder. His wife *T'ien-Mu* made the lightning with two mirrors. He punished anyone guilty of a crime which had not been detected, and also pursued evil spirits.

Lemminkainen: A Finnish hero whose adventures are told in the epic *Kalevala*. He is portrayed as a rough and often brutal man whose boldness led him into misfortune. He won Kylliki

as his bride by carrying her off, and she made him promise not to go to war as long as she did not go dancing with the other girls. But she forgot her vow, and Lemminkainen rejected her, going in search of the maid of Pohja instead, whom *Vainamoinen* and *Ilmarinen* were already wooing. Although he succeeded in the first task set him by Louhi, the girl's mother, which was to capture the elk of the god *Hiisi*, he was killed by an enemy when he tried to shoot the swan of *Tuonela*, which lived on the whirlpool on the edge of the kingdom of death. His mother learnt of his death because a brush he had left with her began to bleed; she sought him and pulled his body in pieces from the river of Tuoni. By praying to the gods, she restored him to life and returned home with him. Because he was not invited to the wedding feast of the maid of Pohja and Ilmarinen, he made war on *Pohjola*, but was eventually beaten off by a great frost. He had his revenge when he helped Vainamoinen and Ilmarinen to steal the *sampo* talisman from Pohjola.

Ler: In Irish myth, the children of Ler were turned into swans by their step-mother because she was jealous of them; and their song was such that anyone who heard it was made happy. Their father tried to disenchant them, but could not; only when St Patrick came to Ireland and baptized them did they become human again. They were already over three hundred years old, and they died as soon as they regained their human form.

Lethe: One of the five rivers of *Hades* in Greek myth; anyone who drank of its waters forgot everything he knew about the past; the dead drank of the water to forget their earthly life.

Leto: One of the Greek *Titans*, mother of *Apollo* and *Artemis*, whose father was *Zeus*. *Hera* was jealous of her and sent a monster called *Python* to pursue her. She also decreed that her children should not be born anywhere where the sun shone. So *Poseidon* shaded the island of Delos with a huge wave and Apollo and Artemis were born there. The island is sacred to them both, and there are temples to them which were very important centres of their worship.

Leza: Supreme god of the Central African peoples, who created the world and gave the tribes their customs. He ruled the sky, and it was he who made rain; when he blew, it was windy and when he beat his rugs, it thundered. He was said to be growing old, and did not hear prayers as easily as he used to.

Liber: A minor Roman god, sometimes said to be the same as *Dionysus*.

Lif and Lifthrasir: In Norse myth, the survivors of the great winter or *fimbulvetr* and the day of *Ragnarok*; during these disasters, Lif and his wife shelter in the world-tree *Yggdrasill*, and when the new world comes into being, they emerge to repeople it.

Lilith: In Hebrew myth, a giantess who was the first wife of Adam; she appeared afterwards as a terrible demon, who attacked men and children by night.

Linus: The music teacher of the Greek hero *Heracles*; when Heracles misbehaved while he was giving him a lesson, he tried to punish him, but Heracles killed him. Brought before the king, Heracles pleaded self-defence and was sent to herd cattle for a year.

Llew Llaw Gyffes: Son of the Welsh princess Arianrhod; he was brought up by his uncle *Gwydion* because Arianrhod would have nothing to do with him. She put a spell on him so that he would never have a name unless she gave it to him. But Gwydion made a ship by magic, and loaded it with leather, which he also made by magic. He and the boy sailed to Arianrhod's castle, and made shoes for her; they fitted badly and she went to see them at work on their ship. While she was there, the boy threw a needle at a wren and hit it. She said 'The fair one has hit it with a skilful hand', and that was his name, Llew Llaw Gyffes, 'fair-skilful-hand'. When she realized what she had done, she made another spell, that he should never have armour or weapons unless she herself gave them to him. But Gwydion outwitted her again: they came into her castle in disguise, and he used magic to make a host of men who attacked the castle from without. Arianrhod armed them both, and Gwydion at once dispersed the phantoms and told her whom she had armed. Again she put a spell on Llew Llaw Gyffes, that he should never marry a woman 'of the race that is now on earth'. Gwydion made a bride from flowers, the most beautiful girl anyone had ever seen, called

Blodeuedd. But she proved untrue to Llew Llaw Gyffes, and fell in love with Gronw Bebyr instead.

She managed to discover how Llew Llaw Gyffes might be killed: if he stood in a bath-house on a river-bank with one foot on the back of a he-goat and one on the edge of the bath, he could be killed with a spear that had been made Blodeuedd told Gronw, who made the spear, and then she persuaded Llew Llaw Gyffes to show her the exact position in which he could be killed. As soon as he was standing on the edge of the bath with one foot on the goat's back, Gronw stabbed him. He gave a dreadful scream and vanished in the form of an eagle. But Gwydion tracked him down and changed him back into human shape; he was fearfully thin, and it took a year to nurse him back to health. Blodeuedd was turned into an owl, and Gronw was given the same blow that he had once given Llew Llaw Gyffes: Gronw put a stone to protect his back, but Llew Llaw Gyffes drove the spear through the stone and killed him.

Lludd and Llevelys: When King Lludd ruled Britain, the kingdom was afflicted by three plagues: a people called the Coranieid who could hear every whisper; a great cry on May-Eve which made cattle barren and crops fail to grow; and a mysterious disappearance of food from the king's household, as much as a whole year's supply at a time. Lludd consulted his brother Llevelys, king of France, through a great bronze horn, so that the Coranieid should not hear him, and was told to bruise certain insects in water, and pour this over all his people when they assembled: it would kill only the Coranieid. The cry was caused by two dragons fighting underground at the exact centre of Britain, Oxford; he was to drug them with mead and bury them in a pit at Dinas Emrys. The disappearance of the food was due to a magician, who enchanted everyone to sleep; Lludd was to keep awake by getting into a cold bath whenever he felt sleepy and thus staying awake to capture the magician. Lludd carried out these instructions, and the kingdom was freed from the plagues.

Llyr: The Welsh name for the Irish sea-god *Ler*. He was the original of Shakespeare's King Lear.

Lodur: A mysterious Norse god about whom little is known except that he helped *Odin* and *Hoenir* to create man, giving man senses and outward form.

Loka: In Hindu myth, a division of the universe or 'world'. The three *lokas* are earth, heaven and hell, though more complicated divisions give seven or eight *lokas*, corresponding to spiritual stages.

Lokapalas: The eight guardians of the points of the compass in Hindu myth, who each ride on an elephant, also called a Lokapala. The Lokapalas are: *Indra* (east), *Agni* (south-east), *Yama* (south), *Surya* (south-west), *Varuna* (west), Vayu (north-west), *Kuvera* (north) and *Soma* (north-east).

In Buddhist myth there are only four Lokapalas, corresponding with the main points of the compass.

Loki: Loki is the most puzzling of the Norse gods. He was not strictly a god at all, being the son of a giant, and despite his handsome appearance he was cunning, treacherous and deceitful. He was tolerated in *Asgard*, the gods' home, despite his often harmful tricks, and feared for his outspoken tongue. One poem describes how Loki taunted the gods with their misdeeds and failings, and was only silenced when *Thor* threatened him with his hammer.

He was a great shape-changer, taking on bird, fish or animal forms; and he was also a master thief. On different occasions he stole the *Apples of Youth*, the necklace *Brisingamen,* Thor's hammer and gloves. He was involved in many of the adventures of the gods in the outside world: the retrieval of Thor's hammer, the encounter of Thor with *Utgard-Loki*, the making of the treasures of the gods (see *Gullinbursti*), and the ransom of *Ottar*. It was he who caused the death of *Balder*, and who kept him in *Niflheim* by disguising himself as the giantess *Thokk,* and refusing to weep for him. For this the gods at last took vengeance on him. He fled from Asgard, and the gods pursued him, but lost him. He built a house with doors which looked out in all directions, and when the gods at last caught up with him, he changed into a salmon. *Kvasir* saw the pattern of a net in the ashes, and realized that Loki had been working out how he might be caught. With this new invention, Loki was indeed captured at the third attempt. One of his sons was killed, and his entrails were used to bind Loki to three huge flat stones. A snake was tied above him to drop its poison on his face; but his wife Sigyn sits by him catching the poison in a bowl. When she goes to empty it, Loki writhes in torment, and

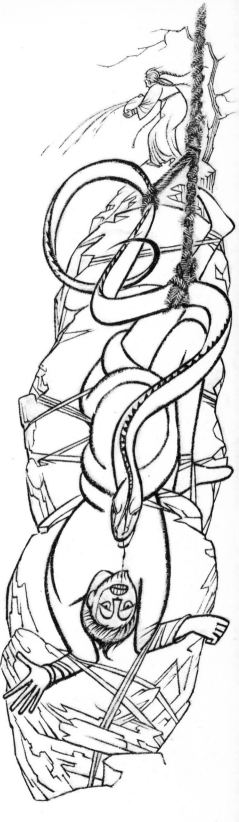

the result is an earthquake. At *Ragnarok*, he will burst his bonds and will help *Surt* against the gods, steering the ship *Naglfari. Heimdall*, his old enemy, will kill him.

Loki could change his sex as well as his appearance, and once as a mare lured away the stallion *Svadilfari* which was helping to build *Asgard*; their offspring was *Odin's* horse *Sleipnir*. He also gave birth to the monsters *Fenris-wolf* and *Midgard-serpent. Hel* was his daughter. See also *Utgard-Loki.*

Lotan: A seven-headed serpent in Canaanite myth, destroyed by *Baal* (compare *Hydra*). He is the original of the 'leviathan' of the Bible.

Lotus Eaters: In Greek myth, inhabitants of one of the lands visited by *Odysseus* on his wanderings. They lived off the fruit of the lotus tree, which made anyone who ate it forget his home and friends, and wish only to live in Lotus-land.

Lucina: The Roman goddess of childbirth, identified with *Eileithyia.*

Lugh: Although Lugh was the grandson of the *Fomorian Balor*, he became the chief of the *Tuatha De Danann*, their rivals for Ireland. Before the second battle of Moytura, he arrived at the stronghold of the Tuatha De Danann, and said

Lu Hsing: The Chinese god of salaries. To receive a salary was regarded as good fortune, as it meant that the man who was paid in this way was a member of the imperial civil service, the highest ambition of all educated men.

Luk, Lukelang: The highest god and father of *Olifat* in the myths of the Caroline Islands in the Pacific. He created the earth and its plants, and human beings were descended from his daughter Ligoapup, Olifat's sister.

Lung Wang: The dragon-king in Chinese myth, who ruled the dragon-race; he and his people controlled water, whether in the rain, rivers, lakes or seas. The dragon-king himself was a huge creature, over five hundred yards long, when he appeared in dragon form; but more often he and the other dragons appeared as humans. According to some stories, there were four dragon-kings, each ruling his own sea.

Luonnotar: In Finnish myth, the 'maiden of the sky' who came down from the heavens and became Mother of the Waters. She created the world with the help of a duck which made its nest on her knee. From the duck's eggs earth and the sky were made, and Luonnotar shaped the hills and shores. She was the mother of *Vainamoinen*. She was also called Ilmatar.

Lycomedes: King of the Greek island of Skyros. *Achilles* was brought up at his court, disguised as a girl; but he was discovered by *Odysseus* and *Diomedes*. *Theseus* took refuge with Lycomedes, but was murdered by him.

Lycurgus: A Greek king who opposed the god *Dionysus* and attacked him while he was still young and defenceless. Dionysus took refuge in the sea, where the nymph *Thetis* cared for him; Lycurgus was blinded by *Zeus* in punishment and put in a rock-walled prison.

Maat: The principle of truth in Egyptian myth, on which the god *Ra* lived; also the goddess of truth and justice.

Macuilxochitl: Aztec god of music and dancing.

Maenads: Women who worshipped the Greek god *Dionysus*; their wild dances sent them into a kind of trance, in which they were able to kill wild animals with their bare hands and could not be harmed by fire or weapons. See *Pentheus*.

Magni: Son of the Norse god *Thor*; see *Hrungnir*.

Mah: 1. The Iranian moon-god.
2. The Assyrian earth-goddess, sister of *Enlil*. It was she who created man from clay, making the first seven men and seven women. She was the same as the Sumerian *Ninhursag*.

Mahadeva: 'The great god', a name of *Shiva*, in Hindu myth. Mahadevi is his wife's title. See *Devi*.

Mahapurusha: 'The great spirit'; a name of *Vishnu*, in Hindu myth.

Mahendra: A name of *Indra*.

Maia: Daughter of the Greek god *Atlas*, and one of the *Pleiades*. She was the mother of *Hermes*, his father being *Zeus*, but was also the wife of *Vulcan*. The month of May derives its name from her.

Maiso: In the stories of the Paressí Indians of the Matto Grosso of Brazil, the first being was Maiso, the stone woman. Her son, Dukavaitore, and his wife Urahiulu were the parents of the stars; then they produced the parrots and snakes; but it was not until Maiso made magic over Urahiulu that she had a son. Even though this first man was hairy and had a tail, he was the ancestor of all the Paressí.

Maitreya: The next Buddha, who is at present a *Bodhisattva*, in Buddhist myth.

Makara: A sea-monster, on which the Hindu god of the ocean, *Varuna*, rides. It corresponds to the sign of Capricorn in our Zodiac.

Makonaima: Creator-god of the Orinoco Indians of South America. He created the world, which was at first a paradise, where all the birds and animals could speak, and Sigu, his son, ruled over it. There was a secret tree which Makonaima made, from which all cultivated plants came; and when Sigu managed to find it, he decided to cut it down and spread its seeds throughout the world. But the tree-stump flowed with water, until the whole world was flooded, and Sigu had to retreat up a tall tree. Half the animals came with him, while the others were sealed in a cave. Sigu used the nuts from the tree to find out how deep the water was, as there was also a great darkness; and when he at last heard no splash, he came down. But the birds and animals could no longer speak, and men had to labour to gain their food.

Mama Cocha: Sea-goddess of the Indians of the west coast of South America, worshipped for the food she provided.

Mama Huaco: Wife of Ayar Auca: see *Paccari-Tambo.*

Manannan Mac Lir: The Irish god of the sea, 'horseman of the crested waves', Manannan was ruler of the other world called the Land of Promise, Tir Raingiri, and husband of *Fand.* His brother was *Bran,* and his foster-son was *Lugh:* Manannan gave Lugh his magic armour. When he appeared to men, as he did to King *Cormac,* he was always splendidly clothed. His pigs could be killed and eaten, and the bones thrown back in the sky: and, like *Thor's* goats, they would be alive again next day.

In Welsh myth, he appears as *Manawydan.*

Manawydan: In Welsh myth, Manawydan was the son of *Llyr,* brother of *Bendigeidfran.* After Bendigeidfran's death, *Pryderi* gave him his mother *Rhiannon* as his wife. Not long after, as Pryderi and his wife Cigfa feasted with Manawydan and Rhiannon, there was a great clap of thunder and a sudden mist; and when the mist cleared, there was no one in the whole country except the four of them. They spent a year pleasantly enough, but after that they grew weary of being alone and went into England, where Manawydan and Pryderi made marvellous saddles to make a living. But they made them so well that the other saddlemakers drove them away, because they could do no business. They moved on to another town, where they made shields; and the same happened, because their shields were so marvellously coloured. Again they journeyed on, and

set up as shoemakers. When, once again, they were driven out, they decided to go back to Wales.

One day when they were out hunting, they came to a strange building. Pryderi went inside, and found a golden bowl on a marble slab, with four chains attached to it which vanished upwards into the air. When he touched it, he could not move. Manawydan waited for him until evening; when Rhiannon found him she asked what had happened. Manawydan explained and she followed Pryderi, but like him was spellbound by the golden bowl. There was a peal of thunder, and they vanished together with the golden bowl and the whole building. Manawydan and Cigfa were now left alone.

Once more Manawydan went into England as a shoemaker, and was driven out. He went back to Wales and planted three fields with wheat; and the wheat produced a splendid crop. But before he could reap it, it was all destroyed, field by field. He kept watch over the third field to see what was destroying it, and saw a horde of mice swarming over it and devouring it. When he tried to catch them, they were too quick for him, except for one, which he caught. Furious, he decided to solemnly hang it; and as he prepared to do so, a bishop rode past, and offered him first of all twenty-four pounds if he would not do it, and then anything he desired if he would spare the mouse. At last the truth came out: the bishop was a wizard who had wrought the spells on Manawydan, and the mouse was his wife. Manawydan obtained the lifting of the spells in return for sparing her, and the wizard said that the spells were a revenge on Rhiannon, because she had rejected a friend of his who had wanted to marry her before she married *Pwyll*. By her arts she had lured him into a bag at a great feast, and pretended that he was a badger: all the men at the feast had beaten him, calling the game 'Badger in a Bag'.

Manco Capac: Manco Capac and *Mama Ocllo*, children of the Sun, were the founders of the Inca race of Peru. The Sun took pity on men, because they were leading a savage life, and sent his children to earth. They appeared on an island in Lake Titicaca, and set out to teach mankind civilisation, journeying northward across the high plateau of the Andes mountains. They carried with them a long golden rod, and tested the soil with this, to see if it would sink completely into the ground. When they reached Cuzco, the rod sank in and they founded a city there. See also the version of the story given under *Paccari-Tambo*, where Manco Capac is called Ayar Manco.

Later writers tried to explain part of the story by saying that Manco Capac was a king who appeared before his subjects in a cloak of gold which glittered in the sun. His subjects were so impressed that they worshipped him as a child of the Sun.

Manitou: The 'great spirit' in Algonquin Indian myths from North America. Manitou created the heavens and moved everywhere in the form of the winds, but he did not play a very active part in what went on. In everyday life the lesser manitous, spirits of particular things, were more important.

Manjushri: One of the *Bodhisattvas* in Buddhist myth. Like *Brahma* he was said to have been born from a lotus. The Chinese emperor was regarded as Manjushri in human form. He was reputed to have conquered *Yama*, the god of death, and is shown sword in hand in memory of his victory.

Mantis: The chief character of the myths of the Bushmen of S. W. Africa. The mantis is a kind of stick-insect, which feeds on smaller insects, and is often called the 'praying mantis' because of the position it takes up when waiting for its victims: but the mantis worshipped by the Bushmen was a much more powerful creature. He created the moon by throwing one of his old sandals into the sky. But he was also a trickster: one story tells how he pretended to be a dead hartebeest, and when the carcass was cut up, the parts complained when they were carried home. The children who were carrying them – men would have known better – dropped the pieces in terror; the pieces came together, and changed from a hartebeest into a man, who chased the children home.

Mantis could also bring dead things to life, and make objects talk: yet he was not always wise enough to avoid defeat, and his son-in-law Kwammang-a and grandson the Ichneumon often had to teach him what to do. Mantis usually pretended that he always knew but had forgotten. He did not fit logically into the usual divisions of gods, heroes and men, but was very much a mixture of all three. He is also called *Cagn*.

Manu: In Hindu myth, the title of the first

162

fourteen rulers of the world, each of whom reigned or will reign for 4,320,000 years. The first Manu was Svayambhuva, who produced the ten *Prajapatis* or *maharishis*, from whom mankind is descended. The Manu of the age in which we live is *Vaivasvata*, son of the sun, and there are still seven Manus to come.

Maponos: In Celtic myth, Maponos is the god of youth who appears in Irish stories as *Oengus Mac Oc*. A Welsh story tells how he was imprisoned in Caer Loyw when he was three days old. Arthur, who needed his help on a magical quest, only found him by asking the oldest of all living creatures, the salmon of Llyn Llyw, where he was, for he had been so long in prison that no other creature had heard of him.

Mara: The evil spirit or tempter in Buddhist myth.

Marduk: The god of the city of Babylon, son of *Ea*. He took over *Enlil*'s part as storm-god, and was shown in his festival at the New Year as the god who overcame Chaos and created the universe. The festival was an elaborate one, lasting for twelve days. The first four days were holidays, and were not counted in calendars, because Marduk was said to be imprisoned in the underworld. On the fifth day, the king surrendered his crown to Marduk, and received it back again only after being reminded that he was Marduk's servant. On the seventh day, *Nabu* was said to free Marduk, and the remainder of the festival celebrated Marduk's return.

It was Marduk who pursued and overcame the storm-bird Zu who once stole the great tablets of fate, on which the destinies of men were written, and which were the sign of the gods' power. He also defeated the evil spirits who put out the light of *Sin*, the moon-god, because he showed up their wicked deeds at night. See also *Apsu and Tiamat*.

Marpessa: Wife of the Greek hero Idas, she was carried off by the god *Apollo*. Idas dared to take aim with his bow at the god himself, and *Zeus* had to intervene. Marpessa was allowed to choose between god and mortal; she preferred to stay with Idas, because Apollo, being immortal, might grow weary of her when she grew old.

Mars: The Roman name for *Ares*; Mars was at first a god of war and of agriculture, and the month of March was named after him. His warlike associations may have come from the fact that in March the army was put into commission again, being disbanded for the winter months when the weather made fighting impossible. The planet nearest to the Earth is named after him.

Marsyas: A Greek *satyr* who picked up the flutes which *Athene* had thrown away because they distorted her face when she played them. Athene thrashed him for taking them, but he was undeterred and went on to challenge *Apollo* at flute-playing. Apollo agreed, on condition that whoever won could do what he liked with his opponent. Apollo won, and skinned Marsyas alive.

Maruts: The Hindu gods of winds and storms, who accompanied *Indra*, whose sons they were sometimes supposed to be. They had thunder and lightning as weapons, and were brilliant in appearance, wearing golden armour and riding in a golden chariot drawn by deer.

Mataora: In Polynesian myth, Mataora married Nuvarahu, who was one of a people called the Turehu, who lived in the underworld. At first the pair lived on earth, but they quarrelled one day and Nuvarahu went back to her own people. Mataora followed her, and found her at her father's house. Her father was tattooing someone by cutting marks on his skin and colouring them, a skill which was not yet known on earth; and Mataora watched him. But the other Turehu laughed at Mataora, because the marks on his skin were only painted on, and rubbed off easily. Mataora agreed to be tattooed properly, and later went back up to earth with Nuvarahu: but when they passed out of the gate from the underworld, the Turehu who guarded it locked it, saying that in future living men would not be allowed to go down there, but only the spirits of the dead.

Matsya: The fish *avatar* of *Vishnu* in Hindu myth.

Maui: The greatest of the magical heroes of the stories of the Polynesians, Maui lived not long after the beginning of the world: he had two or more brothers of the same name, but he was the youngest and cleverest. His brothers tried to hunt with spears without barbs, which came out when they struck their prey, and they thought they could catch eels in pots which had no trap-

door to hold the eel in. Maui invented both barbed spears and doors for eelpots, but the others could not understand why he was so successful. He helped *Tane* to raise the skies, and to set the world in order, but his actions were often mean as well as good. It was believed that he fished up the islands of the ocean, but his brothers broke the spell, terrified by the size of Maui's catch, and the islands broke apart. In those early days people did not have enough time to tend their gardens (or, in some versions, to cook their food); so Maui trapped the sun in a noose and beat him until he was crippled and could only move slowly, so that he took longer to complete his day's journey.

Maui also won fire for mankind. He and his brothers saw fire for the first time when they were out fishing; it was made by some birds on the shore. When they went up to it, the birds put the fire out, and every time Maui tried to approach them they did the same, until he put a dummy in his place on the boat and hid on shore. The birds thought he was still in the boat and made a fire again, but Maui caught one of them and threatened to kill it unless it told him the secret. It tried to give him the wrong answer, but in the end it revealed which kinds of wood had to be used and Maui let it go.

Because his father left out some words when he gave him his name, Maui was not immortal, and he died trying to obtain immortality from the goddess *Hina*.

Mawu-Lisa: The great god and goddess of the Ewe people of West Africa: Lisa is the sun, and Mawu the moon, though this is sometimes changed round, and Mawu is the sun-god, particularly of the rising sun, among some tribes.

Maya: One of the titles of *Devi*, the Hindu goddess, in her terrible aspect as *Durga*: 'Maya' means illusion, and in this form Devi is mistress of spells and deception. The name is also used to imply the idea that everything we know about through our senses is only an illusion.

Medea: Daughter of King *Aeetes* of Colchis, she was an enchantress and priestess of *Hecate*. When the Greek hero *Jason* arrived at Colchis on his quest for the *Golden Fleece*, she fell in love with him and helped him to win it. She laid the ambush in which her brother *Absyrtus* was killed, and caused *Pelias'* death in revenge for his ill-treatment of Jason. After this she fled with Jason to

Corinth, where Jason abandoned her in favour of *Glauce*, daughter of the king of Corinth. But Medea killed Glauce with a poisoned robe, and then killed her two children by Jason (though some say that the people of Corinth killed them in revenge for Glauce's death). She escaped in a winged chariot, and took refuge in Athens, where she tried to poison *Theseus*, which is the last that we hear of her.

Medhbh: Queen of Connaught, and wife of *Ailill*; her jealousy of him over his famous white bull led to her expedition to Ulster (defended by the hero *Cuchulainn*) to fetch the *Brown Bull of Cuailgne*.

Medusa: One of the *Gorgons* of Greek myth, she had once been beautiful until she and *Poseidon* made love in one of *Athene*'s temples. For this Athene changed her hair into a wreath of snakes. *Perseus* killed her and from her body the winged horse *Pegasus* sprang, while the drops of her blood became the poisonous snakes found in Libya.

Mehturt: The Egyptian sky-goddess: in one version of their myths, the sky was thought of as a huge cow called Mehturt, along whose belly *Ra* the sun-god travelled each day in his boat. Mehturt was identified with the goddess *Hathor*.

Melampus: Greek seer who once saved some young snakes; these licked his ears in gratitude, and he was able to understand the speech of all creatures. He was imprisoned by Iphiclus for trying to steal his cattle; but, overhearing some woodworms saying that the prison would soon fall down, he prophesied this correctly, and was set free out of respect for his powers of foretelling the future.

Meleager: Son of Oineus, the Greek ruler of Calydon. When he was born, the *Fates* decreed that he would live as long as a certain piece of wood in the fire remained unburnt. His mother seized this and put it out, and kept it safely. Oineus forgot to sacrifice to *Artemis* at the appointed time, and the goddess sent a great boar to ravage Calydon. Meleager gathered a band of huntsmen to pursue the boar, among them the huntress *Atalanta*, whom he loved. It was she who first wounded the boar, and he awarded her the spoils. His mother's brothers tried to take them from her, and Meleager killed them. His mother, maddened by her brothers' death, took

the fated piece of wood and plunged it into the flames, and Meleager died.

Melpomene: The Greek *muse* of the lyre or of tragedy.

Menelaus: Brother of the Greek leader *Agamemnon* and husband of *Helen*, who chose him from among all the greatest men in Greece. *Odysseus*, who had been one of the suitors, made all the others swear to abide by her choice. From this oath came the alliance of the Greeks against Troy, when *Paris* of Troy carried Helen off. Menelaus was not very prominent in the war itself, and on the way home, like the rest of the Greeks, his ship was driven off course and he arrived in Egypt. According to some versions, it was here that he found the real Helen again, Helen of Troy being only a ghost. When he tried to leave Egypt, he was becalmed for a long while, until the sea-nymphs took pity on him. They told him that his only hope was to capture the sea-god *Proteus* and question him. Proteus came each day to count his flocks of seals and other sea-creatures, so Menelaus was given sealskins in which to disguise himself and his companions. Proteus appeared and they seized him; he changed himself into all kinds of shapes, but they managed to keep a hold on him. At last he told Menelaus that he had forgotten to sacrifice to the gods before leaving Egypt and must go back and do so. After his death, because he was the son-in-law of *Zeus*, he went to the *Elysian Plain*.

Menglod: Daughter of a giant of the underworld, she was a servant of the Norse goddess *Freyja*. The hero Svipdag won her by going through the ring of fire which surrounded the hall where she lived, and answering the questions which the giant Fjolsvid put to him.

Meng P'o: Goddess of the Chinese underworld; after souls had undergone punishment there, and were about to be reborn, they were given a drink which Meng P'o brewed to make them forget all previous existences.

Menoeceus: Son of King *Creon* of Thebes in Greek myth; when *Tiresias* the seer declared that the gods could only be appeased for the killing of the sacred dragon by *Cadmus* if one of the royal family gave his life, Menoeceus stood on the walls of Thebes and stabbed himself; he fell into the lair where the sacred dragon had once lived.

Mên-Shên: The 'door-gods' in Chinese myth, who protected men from evil influences. The Emperor T'ai Tsung was once much troubled by spirits each night, and two of his ministers offered to stand at his palace gate each night to ward them off. This worked very well, but the ministers grew very tired and ill; so pictures of them were painted and set up, which proved just as effective. The two ministers became the two Mên-shên.

Menthu: Egyptian god of war, shown as a man with a hawk's head. Because this was also the symbol of *Ra-Horus*, Menthu was confused with him, and his sacred bull *Buchis* was called 'the soul of Ra'.

Mercury: The Roman god who protected merchants and traders, identified with the Greek *Hermes*.

Meri and Ari: Meri (Sun) and Ari (Moon) appear in the stories of the Tupinamba Indians of Brazil as brothers who quarrelled with each other and caused mischief. They once stole all the fire belonging to the Indians, and for this the Indians killed Ari. Meri revived him; but on another occasion Ari killed Meri and was unable to bring him back to life. Meri rose by his own power, and hid from Ari, who did not know how to get his own food, and nearly starved. So Meri turned into a fish and let himself be caught by Ari. Meri and Ari were warned by the Indians never to break the bottles which they owned; but they ignored this warning. The Indians pursued them and caught them: then they blew them up into the sky, where they remain to this day.

Meru: A mountain at the exact centre of the world, on which the heaven of the Indian god *Indra* is to be found; here the gods dwell, and also the spirits of heaven. It is a kind of Indian equivalent of *Olympus*, and just as Olympus was a real mountain, so Meru was said to lie north of the Himalayas.

Meskhent: The Egyptian goddess of birth.

Mesta: Egyptian god who guarded the embalmed liver of a dead man. See *Osiris*.

Metis: Daughter of Night in Greek myth, she was the first wife of *Zeus*; but she was fated to

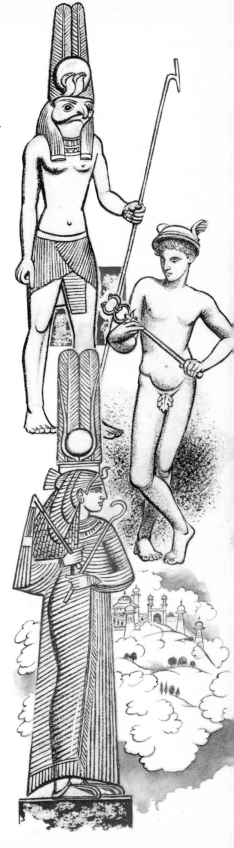

169

bear a god who would rule the gods, so Zeus swallowed her and *Athene* was born from his head.

Mictlantecuhtli: Aztec god of the underworld and of the north, where those who had not earned a place in the heavens led a shadowy, colourless life, rather like that of the ghosts in the Greek *Hades*. See *Chiconamictlan*.

Midas: King of Phrygia in Turkey; he was given asses' ears by *Apollo* for judging in *Pan*'s favour when he and Apollo had a musical contest. The king wore a turban to hide this, but his barber had to know the secret. Being a talkative man, he could not bear to keep it to himself, so he finally dug a hole in the ground and whispered into it: 'King Midas has asses' ears', but reeds grew from the spot and endlessly repeated it whenever the wind blew through them.

Midas once found *Silenus* asleep on the banks of a river, where he had been tied up by some peasants while he was drunk. Midas released him, and *Dionysus*, grateful for Midas' kindness to his follower, offered him a wish. Midas asked that everything he touched might turn to gold; but he soon regretted this, because even his food turned to gold, and he was in danger of starving. Dionysus sent him to wash in a sacred river, and the spell was lifted.

Midgard: The world of men in Norse myth. It is divided from *Jötunheim*, the land of giants, by a wall made from *Ymir*'s eyebrows, and is surrounded by deep sea, in which the *Midgard-serpent* lies.

Midgard-serpent: The giant serpent which lies in the ocean and encircles the world of men in Norse myth. It was the offspring of *Loki*, and was flung into the ocean by *Odin*, where it lies coiled in a circle, biting its own tail. *Thor* once fished it up when he was visiting the giant *Hymir*. At *Ragnarok* Thor will kill it, but he himself will be overcome by its poison, and when it emerges from the sea the world will sink under the waves.

Midir: One of the Irish *Tuatha De Danann*, and lord of the fairy mound called Bri Leith in Co. Longford. He won Etain, the loveliest girl in all Ireland, as his bride, with the help of *Oengus Mac Oc*. But when he returned home with her, his first wife Fuamnach turned her into a pool of water, then into a larva on the pool which became a butterfly. Oengus Mac Oc found her and made her a glass bower filled with precious herbs which he then carried about with her inside and the butterfly grew very beautiful by living on the scent of the herbs. But Fuamnach was still jealous, and lured Oengus away from the bower. She then blew Etain out of it, and drove her across Ireland until she fell through the smoke-hole in the roof of Etar the Warrior's house. She fell into his wife's cup; and Etar's wife swallowed her. Etain was magically reborn as her daughter, with the same name. When she grew up, she married Eochaid of Tara, but Midir claimed her. He played Eochaid at chess for her, and lost; as a penalty he had to build Eochaid a great causeway across a bog in Co. Meath. When he had finished, he returned and beat Eochaid at chess, claiming a kiss from Etain as his prize. A month later he returned to take his reward, but all the doors were bolted because Eochaid was holding a feast. Midir magically entered the hall, and carried off Etain through the smoke-hole, changing her and himself into two swans, which circled overhead and then vanished.

Milanion: Another name for Hippomenes: see *Atalanta*.

Miming: A Norse forest-god who guarded the sword which could kill *Balder*, which *Hoder* (Hother) obtained from him by force. Perhaps the same as *Mimir*.

Mimir: One of the *Aesir* gods in Norse myth, famous for his wisdom. He and *Hoenir* were sent as hostages to the *Vanir* when the Aesir made peace with them. When the Vanir thought that they had been tricked because Hoenir was so silent, and the exchange was therefore not a fair one, they took their revenge by cutting off Mimir's head and sending it to the Aesir. *Odin* sang spells over it, so that it told him secret things. But Mimir was also the guardian of a spring of wisdom, below the root of *Yggdrasill* which lay in the land of the frost-giants. Odin gave one of his eyes for the right to drink from it, because it gave such powers of knowledge and understanding.

He also appears as a master-smith, who taught *Sigurd* how to forge the sword Gram, and, if he is the same as *Miming*, as the owner of a magic weapon.

Min: An early Egyptian fertility-god who was identified with *Amen*: he was worshipped by the

171

half-civilized tribes of the eastern desert, who celebrated his festivals by a strange pole-climbing contest.

Minerva: The Roman goddess of wisdom, perhaps originally a local Italian deity. She was in particular the patroness of schools, poetry and learning. She was identified with the Greek *Athene*.

Minos: Son of *Zeus* and *Europa*, he was king of Crete; the civilization of Crete before the Greeks overran it is called Minoan after him.

He prayed to *Poseidon* to send a bull from the sea as a sign of his power as king, promising to sacrifice it to the god; but when it appeared, it was so splendid that he sacrificed another bull in its place. In revenge, the god caused Minos' wife Pasiphae to bear a son who was half bull, half man; he was called the *Minotaur*.

Minos' son Androgeus had been killed by some allies of the Athenians, so in revenge he attacked Athens and Megara, the town where Androgeus had died. Megara could not be taken until its king lost a certain lock of purple hair on his head; but the king's daughter fell in love with Minos as she watched him from the city walls, and cut off the lock of hair as a gift for him. Minos refused to have anything to do with her, but the city fell nonetheless, and he put her to death. Minos exacted a yearly tribute of seven young men and seven girls from Athens, who were sacrificed to the Minotaur, until *Theseus* put an end to the custom by killing the Minotaur.

Minos followed the master-craftsman *Daedalus* (who had made the maze in which the Minotaur lived) to Sicily; but the daughters of King Cocalos drowned him as they bathed him. After his death he ruled among the dead, acting as their judge, because he was one of the three just men of early days; the others were *Aeacus* and *Rhadamanthus*.

Minotaur: In Greek myth, son of Pasiphae, wife of King *Minos* of Crete, and of *Poseidon* in the shape of a bull. It was kept in a maze or labyrinth built by *Daedalus*, where it lived on human sacrifices until *Theseus* killed it, with *Ariadne's* help.

Miroku: Japanese name for the Buddha *Maitreya*, the 'Buddha-to-be'.

Mithras: Originally an Iranian god who was

one of the *Yazatas*, Mithras became a very important god in the Roman Empire. When *Ahura Mazda* was creating all things, he made a great ox. Mithras fought with this great ox and killed it, releasing its spirit to become guardian of all animals, while from its body all living things were created. So Mithras was the lord of life, which he defended against the attacks of *Angra Mainyu*; the latter first used drought, then a flood, and finally fire, in his attempts to destroy it, but Mithras foiled him each time. In the Roman Empire, and particularly in the Roman army, the worship of Mithras was very popular. There were elaborate ceremonies, and no woman was admitted; but despite this outward show of ritual, there was strong emphasis on the good behaviour in this world needed to reach Mithras's heaven. All worshippers were regarded as equal and as brothers. In the worship of Mithras the background of the Iranian myths remained, but Mithras rather than Ahura Mazda was the centre of attention, the saviour by whom mankind was freed from evil.

Mitnal: see *Hanhau*.

Mitra: In Hindu myth, the sun as ruler of earthly things, his opposite being *Varuna*, ruler of spiritual things. Between them, they give justice to the world, guard it from evil spirits, and punish those who do wrong. Mitra is one of the *Adityas*.

Mixcoatl: Aztec god of the clouds; his name means 'Cloud Snake'; he was the lord of the stars, and also god of numbers.

Mnemosyne: Said to be one of the *Titans* in Greek myth, her name means 'memory', and she is an idea rather than a goddess. The *muses* were her children by *Zeus*.

Modgud: Guardian of the bridge at the entry to the Norse kingdom of the dead, ruled by *Hel*; it was she who challenged *Hermod* when he rode in search of *Balder*.

Mo-Li: In Chinese Buddhist myth, the four hero-brothers Mo-Li replaced the Celestial Kings or *Lokapalas* as temple guardians. They carried a sword, an umbrella, a guitar and a snake. If the first lifted his sword, huge whirlwinds arose; the second hid the sun by raising his umbrella; the third directed the winds by playing his guitar, while the fourth let loose the snake to swallow

up their enemies.

Mondamin: In Chippewa Indian myths, Mondamin was a boy sent down from heaven, who was killed by a human hero. From Mondamin's grave grew the first maize plant, and he was worshipped as the god of corn.

Montezuma: The Papago Indians of Southern Arizona believed that their lands had once been occupied by another race, whose leader was Montezuma. At first Montezuma ruled his people well, but later he mistreated them, and they killed him. But he came to life again four days later, so they killed him again. This happened three times: the fourth time Yellow Buzzard killed him with his iron bow and he was dead for four years. He tried to win back his people by creating huge birds and monsters, which terrified them. He then killed the monsters, including one called a Ho'o'ke which ate children; but his people did not trust him. So he asked the chiefs nearby for advice; and in the end the chief of the underground world said that Montezuma would only regain power if the underworld people came up and killed his tribe and took over their lands. This was what happened. At the end of his life Montezuma went south to Mexico, and there he was shut up alive in an underground house.

Morning Star: The Blackfeet Indians of the central North American plains regarded the Morning Star as an important power in heaven, second only to the sun, his father. Morning Star was a handsome young man, and married a beautiful Indian girl, Soatsaki. She went to live with him in heaven, where her mother-in-law, the moon, gave her a pick with which to cultivate her fields. The moon warned Soatsaki not to dig up a certain turnip, but her curiosity got the better of her. Through the hole she made, she saw her home, and longed to return. The sun punished her for disobeying her mother-in-law by sending her and her son back to earth.

But Soatsaki died soon after she returned to earth, and her son Poia (Scarface) grew up very poor, with an ugly scar on his face. He tried to win the daughter of the chief of the tribe when he grew up, but she would not have him. So he went on his travels, and crossed the ocean to the sun's home. Here he rescued his father, Morning Star, from seven huge birds which were attacking him; and the sun took away his scar in return for his courage. He went back to earth, married the chief's daughter, and returned with her to her father's home.

Morrigan, The: One of the three great goddesses of the Irish *Tuatha De Danann*, the others being Macha and *Badb*. She was goddess of war, and just as the fortunes of war were uncertain, so she was fickle and spiteful, not to be trusted. She also appears as a sea-goddess: she was said to have drowned a prince of Leinster by 'flinging her white mane against his coracle'.

Moshanyana: The Sotho people of South Africa tell how everyone in the world, and all the animals, were swallowed up by a monster called Kholumolumo, except for a woman who was expecting a baby. After eating all the people, Kholumolumo got stuck in a mountain pass. When the woman's baby was born, it became a man in a few moments; and this hero was called Moshanyana. He killed the monster easily, because it could not move, and cut it open to let out all the people, who made him their chief.

But in due course some men grew jealous of him; and although he escaped by magic three times when they tried to kill him, he allowed himself to be killed the fourth time.

Mot: The Canaanite god of death and the underworld, enemy of *Baal*.

Mugdala: A Hindu sage who was famous for his patience and good temper. *Durvasas* once went to test his self-restraint, and devoured all Mugdala's food six times without provoking any anger from him. For this he offered him immediate entry to heaven, and a messenger came from the gods to fetch him. But he asked the messenger about heaven, and when he learnt that it too would one day come to an end, he preferred not to go there. Instead, he meditated until he had achieved *nirvana*, or the absence of all desires and feelings.

Mundilfari: In Norse myth, Mundilfari named his two children Sun and Moon, because they were so beautiful. The gods were angry at this, and made his daughter, Sun, drive the chariot of the sun, and his son, Moon, drive the chariot of the moon.

Murungu: The supreme god of many of the East African peoples, who ruled over the sky, and controlled the sun and moon, which he

created, along with everything else. He lived on four sacred mountains, but at the same time was everywhere and invisible.

Muses: In Greek myth, the goddesses who inspired writers and artists, daughters of *Mnemosyne* and *Zeus*. They were worshipped at Pieria near Mount *Olympus* and at Mount Helicon; 'the Pierian spring' came to mean in poetic language a source of inspiration. Later writers gave them each a special domain: *Calliope* looked after epic poetry, Clio history, Euterpe flute-playing or tragedy, Melpomene lyre-playing or tragedy, Terpsichore dancing, Erato music, Polyhymnia dancing, Urania astronomy and Thalia comedy.

Mushussu: One of the eleven dragons of *Tiamat* overcome by the Babylonian god *Marduk*; it was often shown on doorways as a kind of guardian spirit.

Muspell: At the beginning of the world, according to Norse belief, there were two worlds, separated by *Ginnungagap*; to the north was a land of frost and ice, while that in the south was a world of fire, Muspell. At the world's end, on the day of *Ragnarok*, *Surt* and his host, the sons of Muspell, will ride out of Muspell to do battle with the gods on the plain of *Vigrid*.

Mut: Wife of the Egyptian god *Amen*, usually shown as a queen, but originally a devouring vulture-goddess. She was mother of *Khensu*.

Myôô: In Japanese Buddhism, each of the five great Buddhas has his double in his myôô who carries out his wishes.

Myrrha: The mother of *Adonis*, also called Smyrna, in Greek myth.

Myrtilus: The charioteer of King Oenomaus in Greek myth. See *Pelops*.

Nabu: The god of writing and speech in Babylon, who communicated with men on behalf of the gods, rather like *Hermes*.

Nagas: The snake people in Hindu myth, who were snakes with human heads. They were always at war with the *Gandharvas* for the land of Nagaloka which lies beneath the earth and which is filled with great treasures.

They also appear in Tibetan Buddhist myth, with the additional power of causing plagues and famines among men.

Nagenatzani and Thobadestachin: The Navaho Indian myths tell how after the first man and woman had made men, the men became proud, and their ancestors decided to punish them by making monsters to persecute them: the giant Yeitso, the man-eating antelope Delgeth, the ogre who threw people over a cliff and the birds who devoured men. But after a time the first woman felt sorry for men; so she adopted a daughter, Estanatlehi, who grew up in four days into a beautiful girl. Estanatlehi married the sun, and had twin sons, Nagenatzani and Thobadestachin. They grew up as quickly as their mother, and set out in search of their father the sun. When they reached his home, he put them to various tests, and eventually recognized them as his sons. With the sun's help they destroyed Delgeth, the man-eating antelope, who lived in the middle of a huge plain. To get near him, Nagenatzani burrowed until he was underneath Delgeth, and then made four burrows branching off the first one. When he shot Delgeth through the heart, the antelope ripped up the burrow with his horn, but Nagenatzani hid in each of the four branches in turn until the beast stopped ploughing up the ground and lay still.

Next he went to kill the man-eating birds who lived on a high cliff. These birds seized men and killed them by dropping them on top of the cliff for their young to eat. Nagenatzani allowed himself to be caught by one of the birds, but cushioned his fall with a bag full of blood. He frightened away the young birds, and killed their parents with thunderbolts; and the young birds he turned into the eagle and other birds of prey. With the help of the Bat-woman, he got down from the cliff, and rewarded her with some feathers from the birds he had killed. These changed into song-birds when she walked through the fields carrying the feathers.

Then Nagenatzani killed the ogre who threw

people over a cliff, and also other monsters who lured men into a palace full of treasures in order to kill them. Finally he and his brother destroyed the remaining giants by means of a magic chant and their work was completed.

Naglfari: A ship made from dead men's finger and toe nails, in which the Norse god *Loki* and his company will set sail against the other gods at the day of *Ragnarok*. Because it was built of the nails which were not cut after death, a dead man's nails were always carefully cut to delay the building of Naglfari.

Nahusha: A great Indian king, who by his virtues became master of the world, even though he did not pay proper respect to the Brahmans or priests. When *Indra* was in disgrace for having killed a Brahman, Nahusha took his place in heaven and a thousand *rishis* drew his chariot. But he once touched one of them, *Agastya*, who cursed him, saying 'Fall, you snake!' and Nahusha became a snake, though Agastya later put a limit to the time he had to spend in that shape.

Naiads: Greek *nymphs*, who were the spirits of lakes, rivers and springs.

Nakali: A hero in the myths of the Miskito Indians of Central America who went down to the underworld in search of his wife; on his return, he described the bridge by which the land of the dead was reached. It was the width of a single hair, and below sat a monstrous bird with a cooking pot. Anyone who had been tight-fisted or had not given food to those who asked for it fell off the bridge into the pot.

Namuci: One of the greatest of the *Asuras*: *Indra*, the Hindu god, was able to conquer them all except Namuci, who conquered Indra but let him go on condition that he did not kill him either by day or night or with a weapon that was wet or dry. So Indra killed him at twilight (neither day nor night) by cutting off his head with magic foam (neither wet nor dry).

Nanabozho, Nanabush: In the myths of the Algonquin tribes of the north-eastern United States Nanabozho was the creator and giver of life, though not the supreme god.

As the Great Hare, he was the creator of the earth and everything in it, and he taught men useful skills such as fishing and hunting. One day when he was hunting with his pack of wolves, they disappeared into a lake; he tried to follow them, but the water from the lake overflowed and covered the whole world. The Great Hare asked first the raven and then the otter to find him some earth with which to make land again, but they could not. The musk-rat finally found some; and the Great Hare made the land from it. He made trees to plant on the land by firing arrows at logs and setting them up so that the arrows became branches.

Another version tells how at the beginning of the world all the animals, including the Great Hare, drifted on a raft on a vast waste of water. There was nowhere for them to land, so they asked the beaver to dive down and find some earth at the bottom of the water. He disappeared for a long while, and finally reappeared, almost dead, without having reached the bottom. The otter dived next, also without success, and next the musk-rat was sent. He vanished for a whole day and night, and then floated up to the raft, belly upwards and paws clenched. The animals examined his paws and in the last one they opened, they found four grains of sand. From these the Great Hare created the dry land. When it seemed large enough, he sent the fox to look at it, and see if it would do. The fox found it just big enough for him to be able to catch his prey easily, and said that it was all right; but the Great Hare soon discovered that he had been tricked, and went on adding to the land; the Algonquins believed that he was still at work extending it.

Nanabozho was also said to have been the eldest of four brothers. The second, Chipiapoos, was his constant companion, but he hated the youngest, Chakekenapok, because he had killed their mother when he was born. His first deed, as soon as he was old enough, was to take revenge on Chakekenapok, whom he cut into pieces, which turned into flint.

Because Nanabozho and Chipiapoos were good magicians, evil spirits tried to attack them. Nanabozho was immune to their efforts, but he warned Chipiapoos not to leave their home without him. One day Chipiapoos ignored this warning and was drowned by the evil spirits in an ice-covered lake. Nanabozho was inconsolable, and in the end the evil spirits, to avoid his anger, taught him the secrets of magic medicine and brought Chipiapoos back to life. However, he could not be completely revived, and was sent to rule over the land of the dead, while Nanabozho introduced humans to the arts of the medicine

man, and to the uses of herbs and roots.

Nanabozho destroyed the monster Mashenomak by allowing himself to be swallowed by it and then stabbing its heart. He and all its other victims cut their way out into the daylight as soon as it was dead.

He also obtained fire for men, by going in his canoe across the sea to the east, where an old man lived. The fire burned in his sacred wigwam, tended by his two daughters. Nanabozho took the form of a rabbit, and the two daughters took him into the wigwam because he was wet and cold; but he seized a burning log from the fire and ran off with it.

When he had finished his work, Nanabozho retired to a distant land, either in the west or north, in the Village of Souls, which men occasionally managed to visit. The Cree and the Ojibwa or Chippewa Indians of Canada have different versions of the cycle, though the broad outline is similar. Nanabozho appears elsewhere as Michabo, Manabozho, *Wisakedjar* and similar names. Some of the stories used by Longfellow in his poem *Hiawatha* belong to the stories about Nanabozho rather than to the real Hiawatha, a seventeenth-century Indian chief.

Nanauatzin: The sun-god in Aztec myth. He was the lowest of the gods, despised by the others because of his pock-marked face. When the gods asked themselves who was to rule the world, Tecuciztecal volunteered, but in order to become the sun he had to sacrifice himself in a fire. He hesitated to do this, and Nanauatzin took his place. Shamed by this, Tecuciztecal also sacrificed himself, and became the moon. But at first sun and moon were equally bright, and the light was too strong even for the gods. So they threw a rabbit in Tecuciztecal's face, and this shaded his light: the rabbit can still be seen in the moon.

Nanderuvucu: The 'great ancestor' of the Apapocuva Indians of Brazil, who lived in a distant paradise and did not care greatly about the world. But long ago he had destroyed it and created it again, and one day he would destroy it again.

Nandi: The milk-white bull on which the Hindu god *Shiva* rides; his image is always outside Shiva's temples, and he is the guardian of all four-footed creatures.

Narada: In Hindu myth, the chief of the

Gandharvas and inventor of the lyre. He is a *Prajapati* and *maharishi*, and appears as one of the great worshippers of *Krishna*.

Naraka: 1. The Hindu equivalent of hell, to which the souls of the wicked are sent for punishment.

2. One of the most violent and evil of the *Asuras* in Hindu myth, who carried off the treasures of the gods and the *apsarases* to his castle of Pragjyotisha, where *Krishna* eventually overcame him and retrieved them.

Narcissus: The most handsome young man in all Greece, Narcissus was indifferent to love. The nymph *Echo* wasted away for his sake, and he was punished by falling in love with his own reflection in a pool. He was so entranced by the sight of himself that he could not move from the spot; when he wasted away and died, he was turned by the gods into the flower that bears his name, which always hangs over pools as if to look at its reflection as he once did.

Nareau: Nareau the elder ('Ancient Spider') and Nareau the younger ('Young Spider') were the creator-gods of the Gilbert and Ellice Islands in the Pacific. Nareau the elder, who existed before anything else, took a seashell and made heaven and earth from it. But they were not properly separated, and Nareau the younger had to enlist the aid of the eel, Riiki, and other creatures, to force them apart. Nareau the younger then made the sun, moon and stars, and a great tree, which stood on the island of Samoa. From this tree came the first men.

Naum: 'The mother of the mind' in the myths of one of the Maya tribes of Central America. She created mind and thought, and was wife of the chief god Patol.

Nausicaa: Daughter of King Alcinous of Phaeacia, she met *Odysseus* wandering naked and exhausted on the beach after his shipwreck, which *Poseidon* had caused. She led him to her father's palace, even though all her companions fled in fear at the stranger's wild appearance; here he was given clothing, royally feasted and lent a ship to return to Ithaca.

Na Ye'Nez Nane: In the religion of the White Mountain Apache of the south-west United States, Na Ye'Nez Nane ranked second only to

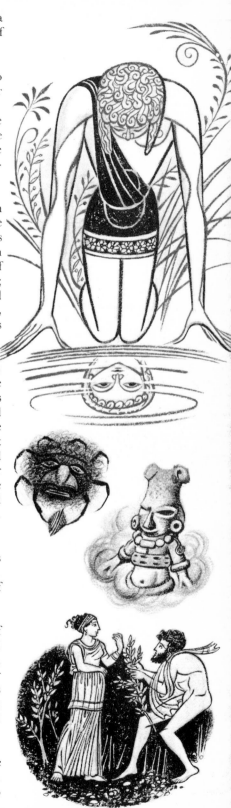

the sun. Everything that he did was good for his people, except at the very beginning, when the sun offered him the choice of things like horses and firearms, which he refused. These went to the white men instead, which was why the Europeans conquered the Indians. Na Ye'Nez Nane was the son or grandson of Isdzana-Ne-He, the greatest of the goddesses who produced the crops each year.

Ndengei: Snake-god from Fiji in the Pacific. His son Rokomoutu made the land, while Ndengei hatched two eggs from which the first man and woman came. Ndengei controlled day and night; when he slept, it was dark, but a black dove woke him each morning. His nephews were boatbuilders, and they grew tired of waking up each day and working. So they shot the dove, but Ndengei sent a great flood and they were separated, and had to become the servants of other tribes instead of working on their own.

Nefertem: Son of the Egyptian god *Ptah* and the goddess *Sekhmet*.

Nehalennia: An ancient goddess of fertility and navigation worshipped in what is now Holland, shown as a woman seated in a chair with a bowl of apples by her. She was the particular patron of sailors crossing to Britain, in the period before the Viking Age.

Nehebkhau: A serpent-god believed by the Egyptians to live in the underworld. He sometimes provided food for the dead, but was also ready to attack the wicked.

Neith: Egyptian goddess who helped to guard the body of a dead man after it was embalmed.

Nekhebet: The guardian goddess of the province of Upper Egypt: she was wife of the Nile god *Hapy*.

Nemesis: The child of Night, she was a minor Greek goddess worshipped near Athens; her name means 'retribution', the repayment for crimes or sins.

Neoptolemus: The son of *Achilles*; he fought on the Greek side in the later stages of the *Trojan War*. He married Hermione, the daughter of *Helen* and *Menelaus*, despite *Orestes'* rivalry for her hand. Orestes murdered him at Delphi and carried off Hermione. See also *Andromache*.

Nephele: In Greek myth, a cloud-creature made by *Zeus* to deceive *Ixion* when he tried to make love to *Hera*; she was the mother of the *centaurs*, and also of Phrixus and Helle (see *Golden Fleece*).

Nephthys: Wife of the Egyptian god *Seth*; she helped *Isis*, her sister, after Seth had killed *Osiris*. Some versions of the story make her the second wife of Osiris himself, which would explain her part in the search for him rather better, since if she was Seth's wife, she would be unlikely to help his enemy.

Neptune: The Roman god of the sea, identified with the Greek *Poseidon*; his wife was *Amphitrite*. He is usually shown holding a trident, the weapon used by tunny-fishers. One of the outer planets of the Solar System is named after him.

Nera: Irish hero from Connaught, who during a feast at court, went out and cut down a corpse from the gallows because it complained that it was thirsty; he gave it a drink and put it back on the gallows. But he went back to find that the court had been raided by the hosts of the dead from the fairy mound nearby. He followed the fairy warriors back to their mound, where he was given the task of supplying the fairy king with firewood. But he was warned in a vision that the fairy warriors would attack the court of Connaught again unless he warned the king and queen, *Ailill* and *Medhbh*. Taking primroses, bracken and wild garlic as a sign that he had been to the underworld, he delivered his message at their court, and they destroyed the fairy mound; but Nera was left inside it, because he had stayed at the fairy court and was now one of the dead.

Nereids: Greek *nymphs* of the sea, daughters of *Nereus* and *Doris* a sea goddess. *Thetis* and *Galatea* were Nereids.

Nereus: A Greek sea-god, helpful and gentle unlike the easily angered *Poseidon*, god of the raging sea in all its fury. He was often a friend and adviser to the Greek heroes.

Nergal: Babylonian god of death and destruction; he lived in the underworld, *Arallu*, where he judged the dead. His chief weapons were

plague and war, and he was also a fire-god, representing the sun as he travelled underground at night (see *Shamash*). He is also called Irra, and under this name appears as an evil god who loves war for its own sake. See *Ereshkigal*.

Nerthus: The goddess of the German tribe of the Suebi in the first century A D. Her worship was described by the Roman historian Tacitus: 'There is nothing particularly noteworthy about these people in detail, but they are distinguished by a common worship of Nerthus or Mother Earth. They believe that she interests herself in human affairs and rides through their peoples. In an island of Ocean (in the North Sea) stands a sacred grove, and in the grove stands a cart draped with a cloth which none but the priest may touch. The priest can feel the presence of the goddess in this holy of holies, and attends her, in deepest reverence as her cart is drawn by kine. Then follow days of rejoicing and merry-making in every place she honours with her advent and stay. No one goes to war, no one takes up arms; every object of iron is locked away; then, and then only, are peace and quiet known and prized, until the goddess is again restored to her temple by the priest, when she has had her fill of the society of men. After that, the car, the cloth and believe it if you will, the goddess herself are washed clean in a secluded lake. This service is performed by slaves who are immediately afterwards drowned in the lake.'

This parade of the goddess is similar to that of the god *Frey* in later centuries in Sweden. Carts that may have been used in such processions have been found in the ship burial at Oseberg and at Dejbjerg.

Nesaru: Sky-god of the Plains Indians of North America. He created men, whom he sowed like maize seeds; but they were trapped under the earth, with all the other animals. First the badger, then the mole tried to dig their way into the light, but the light was too strong. Then the mouse managed to burrow out, though the light took off the long snout which he used to have. All the people and animals followed, and the thunder helped by shaking the earth so that it was loose. Nesaru taught men how to live together in tribes, while the Corn Mother, who had come up with them from below ground, taught them how to grow food.

Nestor: The elder statesman of the Greek army

184

during the *Trojan War*, his advice was always wise and sensible, though he was a little inclined to ramble on about the past. He acted as a peacemaker in quarrels.

Nidaba: The grain-goddess of the Babylonians; according to her worshippers, it was she who brought civilization to mankind.

Nidhogg: In Norse myth, a flying dragon, 'corpse-tearer', who bore away the dead in his pinions; the Nidhogg serpent also gnaws at the root of the world-tree *Yggdrasill*, and is at war with the eagle that perches in the tree's branches.

Niflheim: The world of the dead in Norse myth, where *Hel* had her kingdom.

Night: In Greek myth one of the primeval goddesses, sprung from Chaos itself. She was ancestor of numerous goddesses including the *Fates* and the *Hesperides*.

Nine Heroes: The Chinese poet Ch'u Yuan celebrated nine heroes in his *Nine Songs*, who as a result became famous throughout China. They were: Tung Huang Ta'i, the Eastern Emperor; Yun Chung Chun, the god of clouds; Hsiang Chun, god of waterways; Hsiang Fu-Jen, the daughter of the Emperor *Yao*; *Ssu Ming*; Tung Chun, god of the sunrise; Ho Po, god of the yellow river; Shan Kuei, a mountain spirit, who rides a leopard and is a kind of female *Dionysus*; Kuo Shang who died for his country, fighting an army 'as thick as the dark clouds'; Li Hun, the god of ceremonies, who when he was a man was killed because he insisted on carrying out a ceremony according to the rules.

Ningirsu or Ninurta: Sumerian war-god, who was also a great hunter; his emblem was an eagle with outstretched wings. His name was altered by the Hebrews to Nimrod, and he appears in the Book of Genesis as 'a mighty hunter before the Lord'. In early Sumerian myth, it was he, not *Marduk*, who defeated *Tiamat*, and overcame the bird *Zu*, which became his eagle symbol.

Ningyo: A Japanese mermaid, who often appeared to warn fishermen of danger. Her tears are pearls. If a woman can catch and eat one, she will always be young and beautiful.

Ninhursag: The earth-goddess in Sumerian

myth, originally the wife of *Enki*. It was she who created man from clay; the goddess Aruru, who created *Enkidu* from clay in the *Epic of Gilgamesh*, may be the same.

Ninigi: First ruler of Japan, worshipped as a god. He was grandson of the sun-goddess *Amaterasu*. When he arrived on earth, he brought the sacred treasures of the emperors of Japan with him, the sword which *Susa-no-wo* gave to Amaterasu, the mirror which once lured her out of the cave, and the heavenly jewels. He married Ko-no-hana-sakuya-hive, daughter of *O-yama-tsuni*, the mountain god. His sons were *Hoho-demi* and Hoderi and they and their descendants (the present rulers of Japan) are also regarded as gods.

Niobe: A Greek queen who boasted that she was superior to the goddess *Leto*, because she had seven sons and seven daughters, while Leto had only one of each, *Artemis* and *Apollo*. At this, Artemis killed all her daughters and Apollo all her sons. Niobe wept over them until the gods turned her to a pillar of stone; but even in this shape her tears continued to flow.

Niparaya: The invisible creator in the myths of one of the California Indian tribes. He was challenged by the evil god Wac-Tupuran, who rebelled against him; but Niparaya won, and Wac-Tupuran was thrown out of heaven and shut in a cave.

Nisien and Efnisien: The half-brothers of *Bendigeidfran*: Nisien would make peace between armies at the height of a battle, while Efnisien could make twin brothers fight each other.

Njord: The chief of the clan of gods called *Vanir* in Norse myth. He was sent as a hostage to *Asgard* at the end of the war with the *Aesir*, together with his son *Frey*; his daughter *Freyja* also went with them. He was the lord of the winds and of the sea, and helped men in their sea-faring and fishing. It was he who brought men wealth, and there used to be a phrase in Iceland about very rich people, who were said to be 'as rich as Njord'. He lived in Noatun, 'enclosure of ships', and was married to *Skadi* but the marriage was not a successful one, because she was a mountain goddess, and longed for the hills, while Njord could not bear to be away from the sea for long. So after nine nights they went back to their separate homes. Njord was particularly worshipped on the west coast of Norway, and in pagan days oaths in law-courts usually included his name, so he was held in high honour.

Nohochacyum: The creator-god in Maya myth: his name means 'grandfather'. He was always at war with Hapikern, an evil god who tried to destroy mankind.

Nokomis: The Algonquin Indian name for the earth, meaning 'grandmother': Nokomis was the grandmother of *Nanabozho*. In one version of the story of Nanabozho, both his mother and twin brother died when he was born and Nokomis placed a bowl over him to protect him. When she lifted it off again, he had taken the form of a white rabbit.

Nootaikok: The Eskimo god of icebergs, who lived in the sea; it was he who sent seals to the hunters, and prayers were said to him for this.

Norns: The Norse equivalent of the Greek *Fates*. They dwelt by the Well of *Urd*, or fate, near the root of *Yggdrasill* which grew out of *Asgard*; and they tended the world-tree, watering it each day. There were three of them, named Fate, Obligation and Being. In particular they ruled the fate of new-born children, as a late folk-story from Christian times tells. One day a stranger calling himself Nornagest came to King Olaf, and told how three Norns had been present when he was born. Two promised good fortune, but the third was angry because she had been pushed off her chair by the crowd of people in the room, and said that he would only live as long as a lighted candle by the bed stayed unburnt. The eldest Norn put the candle out, and gave it to his mother, who later gave it to him. Olaf persuaded Nornagest to become a Christian, and he now lit the candle, saying that he was already three hundred years old. As the flame went out he died.

Notus: The Greek spirit of the south wind, called *Auster* by the Romans.

Nuadu Argetlam: The king of the *Tuatha De Danann* of Ireland: he was called Argetlam because he had a silver hand, made for him by the god of healing, *Dian Cecht*. Yet Nuadu himself seems to be the same as the Romano-British god of healing, Nodens, who had a great temple at Lydney in Gloucestershire.

Nun: The god of the watery universe at the beginning of creation, according to Egyptian myth. He was later identified as *Ptah*, the god of forms, and he, and *Ra*, were said to have created the world.

Nut: Egyptian goddess of the sky, one of the *Great Ennead*: wife of *Geb* and mother of *Osiris*, *Isis*, *Seth* and *Nephthys*. She was the goddess of the night sky, and was the mother of the stars.

Nü Wa (or Nü Kua): Sister and successor of the Emperor *Fu Hsi* in Chinese myth. Like him, she was half serpent, half woman. She created human beings out of clay, and was goddess of marriage and its rituals. Kung Kung, one of the princes who ruled under her, rebelled against her, and she defeated him in battle; in despair he hurled himself against a mountain and killed himself. But the mountain was demolished, the pillar which supported the north-west of heaven was damaged and the corners of the heavens fell off. Nü Wa repaired the heavens with jewels, and used the feet of a tortoise to repair the pillars.

Nyame (Nyankopon): The supreme god of the Ashanti people of West Africa. He appeared as the sun (Nyankopon) and also as the moon-goddess. He created three realms, the sky, the earth and the underworld. He ruled over the sky, while a fertility-goddess ruled the earth, and an earth-goddess the underworld. Among the neighbouring Ga tribe, he was called Nyonmo, and was chiefly a rain-god.

Nyame or Nyankopon used to be much closer to earth. But an old woman used to pound food in a mortar, and the pestle she used banged against Nyame. So he moved further away, and it became difficult to approach him with requests. The old woman and her children decided to do something about this, and piled up all the mortars they could find. The pile nearly reached where Nyame was, but they could not find one more mortar to complete it. So they took one out of the bottom of the pile to put on top; and the pile came crashing down, killing many of them.

Nymphs: Greek nature-spirits, who inhabited wild places. Among them were *dryads*, *hamadryads*, *Nereids* and *Naiads*. They were always shown as young and beautiful, and fond of dancing and music; but they were also able to grant prophetic powers to humans, and if made angry, could drive men mad.

Oannes: A god in Sumerian myth, half human, half fish, who emerged from the sea and taught men how to write, and also introduced them to the arts and sciences. He showed them how to build cities and temples, and how to till the fields. Each night he disappeared into the waters again.

Obatala: Sky-god of the Yoruba people of West Africa. Some of the stories about him gave him the same powers as *Olorun*, but Obatala was a god who took an active part in men's affairs, while Olorun remained at a distance. His wife was the earth-goddess *Odudua*.

Ocean: In Greek belief, this was the stream which surrounded the flat circular plain of the inhabited world. It was worshipped in the person of a god, one of the *Titans*, son of *Uranus* and *Gaia*. Beyond the stream of Ocean lay the kingdom of *Hades*; only heroes such as *Odysseus* and *Heracles* dared to cross the stream.

Od: The husband of the Norse goddess *Freyja*; all that is known about him is that his disappearance was the reason why Freyja wept tears of red gold.

Odin: Odin is the chief of the Norse gods. He was one of the three sons of *Bor*, and with his brothers *Vili* and *Ve* killed the frost-giant *Ymir*. He was the leader of the *Aesir*, and lived in the hall Valaskjalf in *Asgard*, where he had the seat *Hlidskjalf*, from which he could look out over all the worlds, of gods, men and giants, at once. *Valhalla* was another of his halls; here the *Valkyries* served warriors who had fallen in battle with mead from the goat *Heidrun*. For Odin was above all god of strife and battle; with his spear *Gungnir*, he stirred up quarrels between kings, and he began battles by hurling his spear over the opposing armies. His spells could make even the bravest men blind or panic-stricken in battle, and this sudden numbness was called the 'battle-fetter'; a man might overcome it once or twice, and fight on, but it always returned and he would be slain. A spear thrown over the enemy army with the words 'Now I give thee to Odin' was supposed to bring victory. He helped great heroes, such as *Sigurd* and *Hadding*, but, just as the fortunes of war are uncertain in real life, so Odin was regarded as fickle and likely to betray his favourites. He was the god of battle, magic and death and his eight-legged horse, *Sleipnir*, carried him to the realms of the dead.

He was married to the goddess *Frigg*, and his sons included *Balder, Vali, Hermod* and *Vidar*. *Thor* was his eldest son, and in some ways his rival.

Odin was also a great traveller. He appeared among men as an old one-eyed man wearing a broad-brimmed hat and carrying a traveller's staff, and he also journeyed in the company of *Loki* and *Hoenir*, with whom he created mankind. With them he encountered the giant Thiazi in eagle form (see *Apples of Youth*), and was involved in the ransom of *Ottar*. But behind this simple love of travel and adventure lay deeper things. For Odin behaved like one of the 'shamans', the explorers of the other world, and he was deeply skilled in magic and hidden knowledge. He had once learned the secret of writing the alphabet of runes which the Norse people used, by hanging on a tree, pierced by a spear, for nine days and nine nights. His ravens, *Huginn* and Muninn, thought and memory, roamed throughout the world and brought him news of all that happened, just as a shaman had his messengers in animal form. He could take the shape of bird or beast, and travel to the ends of the earth in a few moments.

His other source of wisdom was either *Mimir*'s head or the well of Mimir. The two versions of Mimir's legend both have in common the fact that it is from Mimir that Odin gains his knowledge, either by singing spells over his head when it is sent to him by the *Vanir*, or by giving one of his eyes in exchange for a drink from the spring guarded by Mimir.

Odin was also god of poetry; it was he who won the mead made from *Kvasir*'s blood for the gods, and the warrior inspired by him in battle was compared with the poet inspired by him to make songs and stories.

In the days after the Norsemen had become Christian, Odin was believed to ride at the head of the *Wild Hunt* on his eight-legged horse Sleipnir. The idea of a host condemned to ride the skies forever was known to the pagan Norsemen, because 'those slain by violence go to the Furious Host, and souls of heroes go to Odin in Valhalla'. Perhaps because he himself had once hung on a tree, Odin was also god of those who died by hanging, and sacrifices were made to him by hanging and piercing with a spear, of which the most important was that at the great temple at Uppsala, where nine creatures of every kind, including men, were said to be sacrificed every nine years.

When he travelled in *Midgard*, the world of men, he often adopted other names, such as Grimnir (when he went to visit *Geirrod*), but he was also called 'All-Father', 'the One-eyed', or 'Father of Battle'.

At the day of *Ragnarok* he will be devoured by the *Fenris-wolf*, who will be slain by his son Vidar in revenge. Although he inspires battles, the battle of Ragnarok will be the first in which he himself takes part.

Odrörir: One of the vessels in which *Kvasir*'s blood was collected; in Norse myth it is a cauldron of poetic inspiration and wisdom, like those found in Celtic myth.

Odudua: The earth-goddess of the Yoruba people of West Africa, wife of *Obatala* the sky-god.

Odysseus: Odysseus is the hero of the saga called the *Odyssey* by the Greek poet Homer. Odysseus is one of the many heroes of the *Iliad*; and the *Odyssey* deals with his adventures on the way home after the *Trojan War*. He was the son of Laertes, king of Ithaca. In his youth, he had been one of *Helen*'s wooers, and it was he who had arranged the oath of loyalty to the man whom she chose, which was to lead to the Trojan War. When *Menelaus* won Helen, Odysseus returned home and later married *Penelope*. At the outbreak of war, he was summoned by a messenger from Menelaus, but he had been told that if he went he would only return home with great difficulty, so he pretended to be mad, ploughing his fields with an ass and a horse instead of oxen. But the messenger put Odysseus' son *Telemachus* in Odysseus' path, and he swerved to avoid him; so he had to admit that he was sane. Once he joined the Greek army, he was one of the most active leaders in the campaign. It was he who was responsible for finding *Achilles* and for bringing *Philoctetes* back to the army; his other exploits included the theft of the *Palladion*, a sacred image of *Athene* which guarded Troy, and an expedition inside the walls of Troy disguised as a beggar in order to spy out the land.

After Troy had fallen, Odysseus set out for home. He first landed among the Cicones, whose city he tried to raid, but was beaten back with heavy losses. Then he almost reached Ithaca, but the weather turned against him, and his ships were driven on to the land of the *Lotus Eaters*. The inhabitants lured his crew to stay

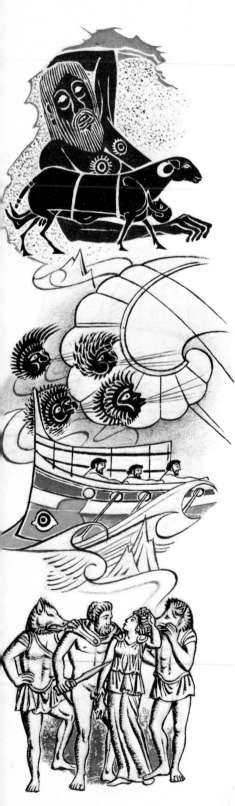

with them by giving them the lotus fruit, whose taste made men forget all desire to reach home. Odysseus rescued those of his crew who had tasted the fruit and set sail again. He next reached an island of the land of the *Cyclops*, where everything grew wild in great plenty; here his men feasted on wild goats and were ready to sail on when Odysseus insisted on exploring the mainland to see what the inhabitants were like. So he landed and went with twelve companions to one of the caves and awaited its owner, in the hope of a friendly welcome. But when the one-eyed giant *Polyphemus* to whom the cave belonged returned, he closed the cave with a vast rock. He killed and ate two of Odysseus' men for supper, and did the same for breakfast. Odysseus had cunningly told him that his name was Nobody; so when the giant returned that evening, he took his revenge by putting out Polyphemus' eye with a glowing stake, and, as he had planned, Polyphemus' neighbours took no notice of his cries that 'Nobody was blinding him', thinking he had gone mad. Odysseus and his remaining companions escaped by tying themselves underneath Polyphemus' sheep as he let them out of the cave the next day; but as they sailed off, Odysseus cried out to Polyphemus and told him his real name. The Cyclops prayed to his father *Poseidon* that Odysseus should only come home after long wanderings, alone, in a foreign ship, and even then find trouble in his own home.

Once more Odysseus almost reached home, for he landed at the island of *Aeolus*, lord of the winds, who tied all the winds in a bag except the one which would send him back to Ithaca, and gave the bag to Odysseus. The crew thought that there was treasure in the bag, and while Odysseus slept, having steered all the way until they could see Ithaca, the crew opened the bag. The winds rushed out and blew them back to Aeolus' isle; and Aeolus refused to help them again. From here Odysseus and his men sailed to the land of the *Laestrygonians*, who wrecked all the ships except his own, and devoured the crews. Odysseus managed to escape to Aeaea, the island where the goddess *Circe* lived. Here further troubles awaited him. Sending half his men to explore, they met Circe, who changed them into pigs. Only one escaped and told Odysseus what had happened. Odysseus set out alone to rescue them, and on the way met the god *Hermes*, who gave him the herb moly, counter-charm to Circe's magic, and told him what to do. Circe, terrified when her magic failed to work, changed back his companions into their proper shape, and feasted them all royally. Odysseus stayed with her for a year, but when he wanted to leave, she told him that he would have to go down to *Hades* to consult the prophet *Tiresias* before he could journey further. She gave him detailed instructions as to how to find his way, beyond the stream of *Ocean* and on to the banks of the *Styx* itself. Here he was to sacrifice, and to question Tiresias when he and other ghosts came up to drink the blood of the offering. Odysseus followed her instructions, and at the edge of Hades he saw Tiresias, who told him that he would only come home easily if he did not touch the cattle of the sun-god on the island of Thrinacie; and in any case he would have to go on a long journey as a penance after he returned. After Tiresias had spoken, Odysseus let other ghosts drink the blood and spoke with them; he learned how many of the heroes of Troy came to be in Hades, having met their death on the way home. Then he returned to Circe, who now told him how to avoid the first dangers he had to face, the *Sirens* and *Scylla* and *Charybdis*. The Sirens were beautiful women who lured sailors onto the rocks of their island by their sweet songs; so Odysseus blocked the ears of his crew with wax, and had himself bound to the mast, so that he could hear but could not answer their call. Next they came up to the cave of the monster Scylla, who seized six of his crew with her six heads, but they avoided the whirlpool Charybdis, and landed on the island of Thrinacie. Here they were stranded for a month by the south wind, and rather than starve, Odysseus' men waited until he was elsewhere and then slaughtered the sun's cattle. When Odysseus returned from making a private offering to the gods, he was horrified to discover what they had done, and for their sins *Zeus* struck the ship with a thunderbolt. Only Odysseus survived by clinging to the mast for nine days, during which he escaped from Charybdis once again. He was washed ashore on the island of Ogygia, where the goddess *Calypso* lived; she detained him for seven years, but at last gave him materials to build a boat. Poseidon was still angry with him, and he had only gone a little way when the god shipwrecked him. He managed to reach land, on the island of Phaeacia, where the king's daughter, *Nausicaa*, found him on the beach. Here he told his story to King Alcinous, who provided him with a ship to take him home; and so at last he reached Ithaca.

Here, with Athene's help, he killed the suitors

who were trying to persuade his wife Penelope that he was dead. They had moved into the palace, where they spent the time in feasting and in insulting Odysseus' son Telemachus, who was not old enough to stop them. When Odysseus arrived, he was in disguise, and he managed to arrange matters so that the suitors were to hold an archery contest to decide who should win Penelope's hand. None of them could string the great bow which had belonged to Odysseus, so Odysseus himself, still in his beggar's disguise, did it; with it, he killed the suitors. Penelope still refused to believe that the beggar was Odysseus himself, until he told her the secret of their great bed which he himself had built out of an olive-tree that grew in the courtyard, making a room round the trunk, so that it could not be moved unless the tree was cut down. At last she recognized him, and they were reunited for a little while.

Then Odysseus set out to do his penance; carrying an oar on his shoulder he crossed to the mainland and walked inland until he met a man who thought that the oar was a winnowing fan, used to separate the chaff from wheat, because he lived so far from the sea that he knew nothing of ships. Here he founded a shrine to Poseidon. He returned home, and died after a peaceful reign, as Tiresias had told him: 'Death will come to you out of the sea, Death in his gentlest guise. When he takes you, you will be worn out after an easy old age, and surrounded by a prosperous people.'

Oedipus: Son of King *Laius* of Thebes and his queen Jocasta in Greek myth. An oracle had told Laius that his son would kill him, so Oedipus was left to die on a mountainside on the border between Thebes and Corinth. Here he was found by a Corinthian shepherd, and brought up as the child of *Merope*, wife of the king of Corinth, Polybus. When he grew up, he consulted the oracle at Delphi, to find out who his real parents were, and was told that he would kill his father and marry his mother. So he decided never to go back to Corinth, in case Polybus and Merope were his real parents. On his journeyings he met Laius, and quarrelled with him when Laius's servants told him to clear the road so that the king could pass: in the fight which followed, he accidentally killed him. He then arrived at Thebes, which was plagued by the *Sphinx*, a monster which killed anyone who could not answer its riddle. Since the king was dead, anyone who could rid the city of the monster was to marry Jocasta and rule as king. The Sphinx's question was: 'What goes on four feet, and two feet and then three feet, and the more feet it uses the slower and weaker it is?' Oedipus correctly answered, 'Man, who goes first on all fours, then upright, and then in old age with a stick.' The Sphinx killed herself, and Oedipus completed the oracle by marrying Jocasta. They had two sons, *Eteocles* and *Polyneices*, and two daughters, *Antigone* and *Ismene*. On the death of King Polybus of Corinth, Oedipus was asked to be king of Corinth, and the truth about his real parents came to light. Oedipus blinded himself in despair, and Jocasta hanged herself. Oedipus lived on at Thebes, while *Creon*, his uncle, ruled until his sons were of age. They looked after him, but one day they gave him his food in dishes that had belonged to King Laius. He cursed them for this, and prayed that they would never live in harmony. It was this curse that brought about the war of the *Seven Against Thebes*. The Greek playwright Sophocles wrote about Oedipus before his death at Colonus, showing him as a heroic figure who had reached peace of mind despite his trials.

Oengus Mac Oc: Son of the Irish gods the *Dagda* and Boann, he was brought up by *Midir*. He was lord of the land of youth, and is perhaps the same as *Maponos*.

Oengus once pined away because of a girl he had seen in a dream; so his parents searched for the girl and found that she was called Caer, and lived in one of the fairy mounds in Connaught. Mac Oc went in pursuit of her, and came across her and her maidens in the form of swans on a loch. He called to her, and persuaded her to become his bride.

Ogma: The Irish god of eloquence and learning; a great warrior as well. He was the inventor of Ogham letters, which were similar to runes. See also *Ogmios*.

Ogmios: The Gaulish god of eloquence, he was portrayed as an old bald-headed man with the same attributes as *Heracles* – a lion skin, bow and club, but he was also shown 'drawing a multitude by chains of gold and amber attached to their ears, and they follow him with joy'. The picture was explained as follows: he achieved feats like those of Heracles through his eloquence, he was old because experienced speakers are the

most persuasive, and his hearers wore chains because he bound them to him by his eloquence.

Ogun: God of blacksmiths among the Yoruba people of Nigeria. As maker of iron weapons he was also the god of war and of hunting, and it was he who cleared the forests which covered the earth at the beginning of time with his iron axe.

Oisin: Son of the Irish hero *Fionn*, who was said to have written many of the poems about the *Feinn*, Fionn's followers. He did not die, but went to the land of youth; however, he longed to see how the Feinn were in his absence, and went back to Ireland. He was warned not to get off his horse, but he did so, and became an old man. St Patrick converted him to Christianity before his death.

Ō-kuni-nushi: Japanese god of medicine and magic, who was also one of the early rulers of the province of Izumo. A white hare which lived on an island off the coast of Izumo wanted to cross to the mainland, so it tricked all the crocodiles in the sea into lining up so that it could count them, because it said there were more hares on the island than crocodiles in the sea. It ran across their backs but just as it got across, it laughed at the crocodiles for being so stupid. The last crocodile seized it and skinned it of all its fur. Just then Ō-kuni-nushi and his eighty brothers passed, on their way to seek the hand of the local princess. The eighty brothers told the hare to wash in the sea and lie in the wind to make its fur grow again, but this of course only made its skin crack and blister. Ō-kuni-nushi, the youngest, saw this and told it to wash in fresh water and to spread bulrushes on the ground and roll on the soft ends. The hare thanked him, and said that he would win the princess. His brothers heard this and killed him; but his mother persuaded the gods to bring him back to life.

To protect him from his brothers, he was sent to live with *Susa-no-wo*, but he fell in love with the god's daughter Suseri-hime. Susa-no-wo tried to kill him, first by sending him to sleep in a room full of snakes, then in a room full of poisonous insects; but in each case Suseri-hime gave him a charm which saved him. Then Susa-no-wo shot an arrow into the middle of a hayfield and sent Ō-kuni-nushi to look for it. When he was in the middle of the field, Susa-no-wo set light to the dry grass, but a mouse found the arrow for Ō-kuni-nushi and showed him a hole in which to hide from the fire. Ō-kuni-nushi then returned to Susa-no-wo's house, and managed to tie him to one of the rafters by his hair while he was asleep. He escaped with Suseri-hime and took Susa-no-wo's sword, bow, arrows and harp. Although the harp struck a branch as they escaped, and woke the god, it took Susa-no-wo some time to untie himself. He pulled the house down around his ears, according to one account, and Ō-kuni-nushi got away. However, Susa-no-wo forgave him, and with the god's weapons he defeated his brothers and ruled Izumo. He was helped as ruler by the dwarf-god *Sukuna-bikona*, who arrived in a drifting boat and departed just as mysteriously. But later he was replaced by *Ninigi*, the grandson of the sun-goddess *Amaterasu*. As compensation, he was sent to rule over the invisible world of spirits and magic.

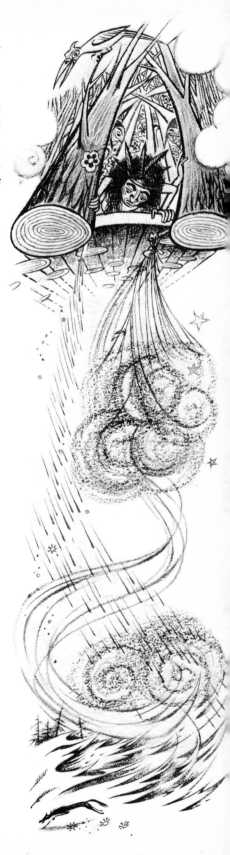

Olelbis: The creator-god in myths of the Wintun Indians of the Pacific coast of North America. He lived in Olelpanti or heaven with two old women, and built himself a great sweat-house in the sky, with huge oaks as its pillars and flowers woven into screens as its walls. The first people who lived in the world quarrelled and set fire to everything in it; so Olelbis summoned the wind and waters to put out the fire. A few men and women had escaped to Olelpanti, and Olelbis sent them back to earth, which he now repaired. Flowers sprang up from the seeds which fell from the flowers on his sweat-house; beasts and birds were made from the feathers and body of the Wokwuk, a huge bird; and the clouds were captured and prevented from going back to the north, where the wind and waters had come from.

Olelbis intended that men should live forever; when they grew old they were to climb up to heaven and drink and bathe in two springs there. He set two buzzards the task of building a ladder from earth to heaven, but as they worked *Coyote* came past and said: 'If you build the ladder, men will never know joy or love, because life will always go on just the same; they will grow old and become young again, and they will always be alone. Far better to have joy when they are born and grief when they die; then they will know love and friendship.' The buzzards stopped work, but warned Coyote that he too would die; so he tried to reach heaven by flying, but fell from the sky and was killed.

Olifat: Hero of stories from the Caroline Islands in the western Pacific, Olifat was the son of the sky-god and a mortal woman. When he was born his father warned his mother that he should not be allowed to drink from a coconut through a hole bored in the top. One day Olifat did this, and saw his father in the sky as he put his head back to get the last drops out. He at once set off for heaven on a column of smoke, and when he got there found his father building a house. He helped to dig the post-hole, but no one recognized him except his father, who pretended not to know him, and as a sacrifice was needed for the post to be erected, the other helpers decided to kill him. But Olifat guessed this and made room for both himself and the post at the bottom of the hole, so when they put the post in on top of him he was safe. With the help of some ants, he tunnelled up through the post and sat in the rafters of the house. He shouted suddenly at the men down below, and they were terrified, because they thought he was dead. His father acknowledged him as his son, and Olifat eventually returned to earth.

Olokun: God of the sea among the Yoruba people of West Africa. He once tried to compete with the great god, *Olọrun*, to see who could dress most splendidly. But Ọlọrun sent the chameleon as his messenger on the day of the contest, and whatever Olokun put on, he found that the chameleon was wearing the same when he went outside to go with him to meet Ọlọrun. So he gave up, because if Ọlọrun's messenger was so finely dressed, he could not hope to match Ọlọrun himself; and he went to live in a great underwater palace.

Ọlọrun: 'Owner of the sky', supreme God of the Yoruba people of Nigeria. He was the creator, and also the judge of what men do, but he was a distant being, who did not take a close interest in human affairs.

Olympus, Mount: Home of the Greek gods, identified with the mountain of the same name in north-west Greece.

Omacatl: *Tezcatlipoca* in his form as god of feasts.

Ometeotl: Maya supreme god-goddess, who was both male and female at once. The name means 'the being at the centre', and he was

198

thought of as the still point at the centre of a moving ring, where everything is balanced and at rest. In Aztec myth, there were two beings, the god Ometecutli and the goddess Omecuiatl, who were the source of all life, instead of the two gods in one.

O-Mi-T'o Fo: Chinese name of *Amitabha*, ruler of the Western Paradise or *Sukhavati*.

Omphale: Queen of the Libyans, to whom *Heracles* was sold as a slave, in Greek myth,

Onatha: The spirit of wheat, daughter of the earth-goddess *Eithinoha* in Iroquois Indian myth. She was carried off by the spirit of evil while she was searching for dew, but was rescued by the sun.

Oni: Fearsome Japanese demons who seized wicked men when they died, and carried them off to the other world in a flaming cart. They were huge flat-faced giants with three eyes, three fingers on each hand and three toes on each foot. But as well as being terrifying, the oni who appeared on earth were also stupid and could often be deceived when they tried to interfere in human affairs. Their great enemy was *Shoki*.

Ops: A Roman goddess identified with the Greek *Rhea*.

Orcus: The Roman name for *Hades*.

Oreads: Greek *nymphs* who lived among oaks and pine trees on the mountains; they were very long-lived but not necessarily immortal, and some said that they died when trees died.

Orestes: Son of *Agamemnon* and *Clytemnestra*, in Greek myth. With his sister *Electra's* encouragement, he revenged his father's death by killing his mother and her lover *Aegisthus*. For this he was pursued by the *Furies* to Athens, where a formal trial was held, with *Apollo* speaking for Orestes while the Furies claimed him as their rightful prey. The voting was equal, but *Athene*, who was presiding, gave her casting vote for acquittal. She appeased the Furies by giving them a temple in Athens.

He competed with *Neoptolemus*, *Achilles'* son, for the hand of Hermione. When she rejected him in favour of Neoptolemus, he murdered his rival and carried her off.

Orion: A great hunter in Greek myth, the son of *Poseidon* and *Euryale*. He was a giant, like other sons of Poseidon. He pursued Pleione and her seven daughters the Pleiades, but the gods stopped him by turning both him and the Pleiades into constellations in the sky; though other stories say that he was killed by *Artemis*, who was jealous of his skill in hunting.

Orishala: Creator-god of the Yoruba people of West Africa. At the beginning of the world, there was water and marsh everywhere, and Orishala was told by *Olorun* to make firm ground. Olọrun gave Orishala a pigeon and a hen and a snail shell full of earth. Orishala emptied the earth in a heap, and the two birds started to scratch around it; they soon spread the earth over much of the marsh and it became dry land. Later Orishala made plants and animals; but when it came to human beings, he could only shape them, and Olọrun made them come alive. He would not let Orishala see how he did this, and when Orishala tried to spy on him, he made him fall fast asleep. Orishala occasionally grew angry when he made a human being and remembered that he did not know how to make them come alive, and that is why some people were deformed.

Ormuzd: Another name for *Ahura Mazda*.

Orpheus: Son of the Greek god *Apollo* and one of the *muses*, he was a skilful musician, whose playing had miraculous effects. Beasts and trees would listen to his singing, and fountains would be still at the sound of his lyre. He married *Eurydice* who died of a snake-bite when being pursued by *Aristaeus*. Orpheus charmed his way down to *Hades* with his music, and obtained her return on condition that he did not look back at her before she reached the daylight. He forgot this and looked back too soon; so she was lost to him forever. He wandered alone, and no longer honoured *Dionysus* and women as he had once done, so in punishment for this lack of respect was torn in pieces by the *maenads*. His head was washed up on the island of Lesbos, still singing; and an oracle was founded there in his honour.

Some early versions of the story say that he was successful in rescuing Eurydice, while others say that he only brought back her ghost.

Oshadagea: The great eagle in the myths of the Iroquois Indians who helped *Hino*, the thunderer: he protected all green things on earth from the evil fire-spirits by spreading dew on the earth from a lake which he carried in the hollow of his back.

Osiris: Egyptian fertility-god who gradually replaced the old sun-gods, *Ra*, *Amen* and *Khepra*. His annual death and revival were connected with the Nile floods, which deposited the mud which made the land fertile again. The full story of his legend is given only by the Greek writer Plutarch, so it may have been affected by similar legends from the Near East: but this is what he has to say.

Osiris, son of *Geb* and *Nut*, ruled Egypt with his twin sister *Isis* as his queen, and was a just and good king, who taught men religion and farming, and how to grow vines. His wicked brother *Seth* decided to seize the throne, and plotted to kill Osiris. He did this by making a beautiful chest large enough for Osiris to get into; and he brought this to court one day. Jokingly, he said that Osiris could have it if he could fit himself into it; and no sooner had Osiris lain down in it that Seth nailed the chest down and sealed it with lead. It was thrown in the Nile, and carried out to sea. Isis, mourning her dead husband, went in search of his body, and found it on the coast of Lebanon. She brought it back, still in the chest; but Seth found it one night when he was hunting by moonlight, and seized the body, which he cut into fourteen pieces and left in different places. Isis patiently searched for them, burying each piece where she found it. Osiris reappeared from the world of the dead, and told his son *Horus* to attack Seth and revenge his death. Horus defeated Seth in battle and became king himself.

From Egyptian sources, we learn that Osiris was brought back to life after Isis had recovered the pieces of his body. *Anubis* embalmed him, and then Isis, with *Thoth*'s help, recited magic spells over him until he was restored to life. Hence Osiris was the god who offered hope of life after death to his worshippers.

Even after his revival Seth continued to attack him, and challenged his claim to the kingdom of Egypt before the nine gods or *Great Ennead* at Heliopolis, but the gods judged in favour of Osiris.

Osiris appeared chiefly as god of the dead, ruling a shadowy kingdom in the west (where the sun sets). Here he received the souls of the dead and judged them. At his great court of

judgement all the gods were present, including the Great Ennead themselves. Anubis and Thoth were his chief helpers: as the dead man made his declaration of innocence, Anubis weighed his heart against the feather of truth in a huge pair of scales. In order to make sure that the dead man was acquitted, his body was carefully embalmed in the same way as that of Osiris, and he was buried with a papyrus describing his trial before Osiris (the so-called 'Book of the Dead') which made sure that the right answers were given. During the embalming, special gods were asked to protect parts of the body (see *Mesta, Hapy, Tuamutef, Qebehsenuf*), so that nothing went wrong when the dead man came to life again in the next world. In particular, these gods guarded against serpents and crocodiles who tried to waylay the dead man on his journey.

Ottar: The Norse gods *Odin*, *Loki* and *Hoenir*, on their travels in the world of men, once saw an otter near a waterfall eating a salmon. Loki killed it with a stone, and boasted that he had caught both otter and fish with one throw. The three travellers stopped for the night at the house of Hreidmar, only to discover that the otter had been his son Ottar in disguise. Hreidmar threatened to kill the gods unless they covered the otter-skin with gold. Loki had to get the gold from the dwarf *Andvari*, who tried to disguise himself as a fish: but Loki caught him and made him give up his treasure. When the gold was placed on the skin, it covered it completely except for one of the whiskers; so Loki made Andvari give up the gold ring which he wore on his finger. Andvari was very reluctant, saying that he could not become rich again without it, and when he was forced to hand it over, he put a curse on it, saying that it would bring disaster on all who owned it. This came true, for Hreidmar's sons killed their father to get the treasure. *Fafnir*, one of the sons, turned himself into a dragon, and guarded the gold, only to be slain in turn by *Sigurd*.

The theme of the golden ransom and the magical ring were used in a different plot, and were connected with the building of *Asgard*, by Wagner at the beginning of his cycle of operas *The Ring of the Nibelungs*.

Oxomoco: In Aztec myth Oxomoco and Cipactonal were the first man and woman, created by the four gods *Camaxtli*, *Quetzalcoatl*, *Tezcatlipoca* and *Huitzilopochtli*. Oxomoco and Cipactonal

were said to have invented the calendar.

Oya: Goddess of the Niger river in West Africa, and wife of the thunder-god *Shango*.

Ō-yama-tsuni: Japanese mountain-god; *Ninigi* was offered the choice of Kono-hana-sakiuja-hine or Iwa-naga-hime, the mountain-god's daughters, as his wife. He chose the first, whose name means 'lady who makes the trees bloom', and as a result his children only lived a little while, like flowers; if he had married Iwa-naga-hime, 'the lady of the everlasting rocks', they would have lived for a very long time.

P

Paccari-Tambo: 'The House of Origin' in the myths of the Inca peoples of Peru. It was from the three caves at Paccari-Tambo (near Cuzco) that four pairs of brothers and sisters, children of the sun, emerged from the underworld. They were the ancestors of all the Incas: their names were Ayar Manco and Mama Ocllo; Ayar Auca and Mama Huaco; Ayar Cachi and Mama Ipacura; Ayar Uchu and Mama Rawa. When they appeared, richly dressed and armed with slings, the country was full of warring tribes. But the Ayars and their four sisters conquered them and slowly made their way towards Cuzco, looking for good land on which to settle. One of the Ayars, Ayar Cachi, angered the others, because he was always boasting and showing off; for instance, he climbed a mountain called Huanacauri one day, and amused himself by hurling huge boulders, which made great deep valleys in the country around. The other brothers persuaded him to go back into the cave from which they had all come, and then walled him up. He later appeared as a spirit to the others when they had chosen a place to settle, and told them that it was the wrong site and they should go on to Cuzco. Ayar Cachi's spirit also told them that he was to be worshipped as a god; and either he or Ayar Auca turned into a stone pillar on the mountain Huanacauri, which the Incas regarded as holy. Ayar Manco and Mama Ocllo eventually reached the site of Cuzco, where they married and founded the Inca race. Ayar Manco was also known as *Manco Capac*; under this name he appears in a different version of the myth, in which Paccari-Tambo was merely an inn where he stayed.

Pachacamac: A creator-god of the peoples of Peru before the Inca period, worshipped only at a temple called Pachacamac near what is now Lima. One of the few surviving myths about him tells how he created a man and a woman, but gave them no food, so the man died of starvation. The sun took pity on the woman and taught her how to live on plants. She had a son by him, whom Pachacamac killed; from his body came all the cultivated plants. The woman had another son by the sun, and Pachacamac killed her out of jealousy. But the second son survived and drove Pachacamac into the sea. Pachacamac is possibly another name for *Con* or *Viracocha*.

Pa Hsien: Eight supernatural beings in the Taoist myth of China, all of whom had once been mortal, but achieved immortality through their good works. The usual list is as follows:

1. Li T'ieh-Kuai, a god of healing, who took the form of a beggar with an iron staff and gourd. He would sit in the marketplace and sell miraculous drugs, withdrawing into the gourd at night.

2. Chung-Li Ch'uan, perhaps a disciple of Li T'ieh-Kuai, who attained immortality through an ascetic existence in the mountains.

3. Lü Tung-Pin, who as a youth dreamt that he would have a successful career but meet a miserable end, murdered by robbers. He decided to renounce the world instead, and when he became immortal he went about punishing the wicked and rewarding the good. He also slew dragons with a magic sword.

4. Lan Ts'ai-Ho, who is shown as a young flute player carrying a basket full of fruit. He appears in Chinese art with the first three immortals, enjoying a convivial evening.

5. Chang-Kuo Lao. A recluse of mysterious and magical powers, said to be an impersonation of the 'primal vapour', or force which caused life itself.

6. Han Hsiang-Tzü. A young scholar who preferred the study of magic to the usual Chinese preparations for the civil service. He rejected the advice of his uncle, who disapproved of magic, by instantly producing two miraculous flowers with poems on the leaves.

7. Ts'ao Kuo-Chiu. Brother to an eleventh-century emperor, he attempted to persuade his dissolute brother to reform, saying 'You may escape the law, but you can never escape the invisible net of Heaven over all things'. He was introduced by Chung-Li Ch'uan and Lü Tung-Pin into the company of immortals.

8. Ho Hsien-Ku. A girl from Canton who dreamt that she would attain immortality by eating powdered mother-of-pearl. She became ethereal and vanished, reappearing only to men of great virtue.

Pakrokitat and Kukitat: Pakrokitat was the creator, according to the myths of the Serrano Indians of California. From his left shoulder was born Kukitat, his younger brother, who was always quarrelling with him. Pakrokitat made man, but Kukitat thought that men should have webbed feet and eyes in the back of their heads. In the end Pakrokitat left this world and retired to a world of his own, Panamam in the island of Payait, which he made. Kukitat caused death to come into the world, but Pakrokitat made the

souls of the dead come to his world after they had visited the three beautiful goddesses. When Pakrokitat left the world, Kukitat made men divide into nations and fight each other; but they grew tired of him and killed him; and when his body was being burnt, a coyote or prairie dog came and stole his heart.

Palladion: An image of *Pallas*, sacred to the Greek goddess *Athene*. During the *Trojan War* it was stolen from Troy by *Odysseus* and *Diomedes*, because the city could not be taken while the Palladion remained within its walls.

Pallas (Athene): The Greek goddess *Athene* was so called either from a giant whom she killed, or from her playmate Pallas, daughter of *Triton*, whom she killed in a quarrel.

Pan: Greek god of the fields and meadows, son of *Hermes*. He is always shown with the horns, ears and legs of a goat. He was a playful creature, unless disturbed in the heat of noon while he was resting; but he was also the cause of 'panic', a fear without any reason which would seize a large number of people.

He loved the *nymph* Syrinx, who refused to listen to him; as he pursued her, she was turned into a bed of reeds, from which Pan cut his 'pan-pipes'. Another of his loves was *Echo*.

There was a strange story of his death told in historical times, under the Emperor Tiberius in the middle of the first century AD. A ship was becalmed by the island of Paxi in the Aegean Sea, when a voice called the ship's pilot by name. He ignored the call for a time, but at length answered, and the voice continued, 'When you arrive at the next island, tell them that great Pan is dead.' He did so, and in answer there came a great hubbub of mourning and shouts of amazement.

Pan once challenged *Apollo* to a music contest, in which the judge awarded the prize to Apollo; but King *Midas* dissented, and it was in punishment for this that Apollo gave him asses' ears.

Pandavas: The descendants of Pandu, whose war with the Kaurava princes is the basis of the Indian epic *Mahabharata*.

Pandora: A beautiful girl created by the Greek gods at *Zeus'* order to achieve his revenge on *Prometheus*. *Hephaestus* formed her, *Athene* gave her life, *Aphrodite* endowed her with beauty and

206

charm, and *Hermes* taught her guile and trickery. She was sent to Prometheus' brother Epimetheus, who accepted her despite Prometheus' warnings. She brought a box with her, which she opened, and out of it came all evil and disease, with only Hope at the bottom as a compensation.

P'an Ku: In Chinese myth, there is only one version of the creation story, while most mythologies have several. In this P'an Ku, the great creator, brought order into the world when it had been chaos. He was born from an egg, which separated to form the earth and sky. He grew up to become a giant, and when he died, the various parts of his body, which filled the entire space between heaven and earth, became different natural objects. Other stories agree that he was a giant, but describe him as having horns and tusks, and thick hair; but he was very wise and not only controlled the forces of nature but taught men how to make tools and how to govern themselves. When he had given them his instructions, he vanished.

Papa: The earth-goddess in Polynesian myth: see *Rangi*.

Parashurama: The sixth *avatar* of the Hindu god *Vishnu*.

Pariacaca: Rain-god of the Chincha Indians of South America, who, like his four brothers, was born from an egg which appeared mysteriously on a mountainside.

Paris: Son of King *Priam* of Troy, it was foretold of him when he was born that he would be the downfall of Troy. He was left to die on Mount Ida, where a she-bear cared for him; some shepherds found him and brought him up. He was called Alexander, until he went to Troy to take part in some games; he was recognized by his skill and returned to his father's household.

At the wedding feast of *Peleus* and *Thetis*, Eris or Strife threw an apple into the guests; on it was written 'Let the fairest take it'. *Hera*, *Athene* and *Aphrodite* all claimed it, but *Zeus* ordered that the most handsome man alive, Paris, should judge. Each offered him gifts in return for the prize: Hera promised royal power, Athene success in battle, Aphrodite the loveliest woman in the world as his wife. He gave the apple to Aphrodite, who rewarded him by helping him to carry off *Helen*, thus causing the *Trojan War*. This episode,

called the judgement of Paris, was a favourite with painters, the most famous version of it being that by Rubens. Paris did not play a very distinguished part in the war, although towards the end of it he killed *Achilles*. He himself was killed by the arrows of *Philoctetes* before the sack of Troy.

Parjanya: The rain-god in Hindu myth, later regarded as the same as *Indra*. He was one of the *Adityas*.

Parvati: One of the titles of *Devi*.

Pashupati: One of the titles of *Rudra*.

Patala: In Hindu myth, the worlds below the earth in which the *Nagas* and other spirits lived, many of them evil spirits such as *Daityas* and *Yakshas*. There are said to be seven Patalas in all, and they were just as delightful as the heavens: they are not to be confused with *Naraka* or hell.

Payatamu: In Navaho Indian myth, Payatamu was the god of the summer fields, a little man crowned with flowers and playing a flute, who made the flowers blossom and the butterflies come out. He loved the corn maidens, but they were frightened of him, and hid, so that there was a famine; but they were eventually persuaded to return, and appeared to the ancestors of the Indians, teaching them a ritual which was to be held every four years in their honour. Then they vanished, never to be seen again.

Pegasus: A winged horse which sprang from the body of the Greek *Gorgon Medusa* when *Perseus* killed her. *Bellerophon* tried to tame it, but was unable to do so until *Athene* appeared to him in a dream and gave him a magic bridle; when he awoke, the bridle was really there, and with it he tamed Pegasus.

Peko: Esthonian god of barley, worshipped on the evening of Whitsun each year with a night-long feast. Similar to the Norse *Byggvir*, Peko particularly guarded the crops against hail.

Pele: Hawaiian fire-goddess and ruler of volcanoes. She fell in love with a chieftain called Lohiau and sent her younger sister Hi'iaka to woo him for her. Hi'iaka met many magic adventures on the way, but was able to overcome them and to set out for Pele's home with Lohiau. But Pele, who was always quick-tempered, had to wait so long that she suspected Hi'iaka of having married Lohiau herself; and she killed Hi'iaka's best friend in her rage. Hi'iaka, however, returned safely with Lohiau, even though Lohiau had declared that he loved her and not her sister. As they parted on the edge of Pele's volcano, they kissed, and Pele in fury burnt Lohiau to ashes, though she could not harm Hi'iaka. But Hi'iaka brought Lohiau back to life and went back to his home with him, where they married.

Peleus: Son of the king of Aegina, Peleus married the Greek goddess *Thetis*. She was fated to bear a son who would be greater than his father, so the gods married her to a mortal, though Peleus had first to wrestle with her to win her. She turned into all kinds of shapes – lion, snake, and other creatures, as well as fire and water – but with the help of the gods he held her fast. She bore him sons, but killed the first six trying to make them immortal by throwing them in the fire. Peleus saved *Achilles*, but she deserted him in a fury. Other versions say that she dipped Achilles in the *Styx*, making him invulnerable except for the heel where she had held him.

Pelias: Greek king of Iolchos, uncle of *Jason*, killed by *Medea*.

Pelops: Son of the Greek King *Tantalus*. He wooed *Hippodameia*, who could only be won if the man who wished to marry her could carry her off and avoid being killed by her father Oenomaus, who pursued the suitor with a spear. Twelve suitors had failed before Pelops; but he bribed Myrtilus, Oenomaus' charioteer, to put in a waxed lynch pin to hold the wheels. It melted as the wheel turned, and Oenomaus was thrown and killed. But Pelops drowned Myrtilus instead of paying him, and for this his descendants, *Atreus* and his family, were cursed.

Penates: Each Roman home had its household gods, who included the penates or guardian spirits of the provision cupboard. The penates were also worshipped at Lavinium in their own temple; *Aeneas* was said to have brought them from Troy and when an attempt was made to move their images to Rome, they mysteriously disappeared and were found again at their old home at Lavinium.

Penelope: Wife of *Odysseus*; during his long

absence at Troy and on his wanderings, she was besieged by suitors who tried to persuade her that he was dead, and that she should remarry. They wasted Odysseus' property in riotous living, while she put them off by weaving a great winding-sheet for her father-in-law *Laertes*. When this was finished, she said, she would make up her mind as to which of them she would marry; but everything that she wove during the day she secretly unravelled at night. Her secret was finally betrayed by one of her maids, just before Odysseus himself returned. When Odysseus arrived, disguised as a beggar, he got his son *Telemachus* to suggest to her that the question should be settled by an archery match: anyone who could string Odysseus' great bow and shoot through a line of axes should win her. None of the suitors could even string, the bow; Odysseus, still in his disguise, asked to do it, and used the bow to kill the suitors, beginning with their ring-leader Antinous. Penelope still doubted that it was really Odysseus, until he had told her the secret of their bed, which, as he and she knew, was built into a living olive-tree and could not be moved from the bedroom.

Penthesilea: Queen of the *Amazons*, beautiful and brave, who led her women against the Greeks before Troy; she was killed by *Achilles* who mourned her death nonetheless.

Pentheus: King of Thebes who declared the Greek god *Dionysus* to be an imposter. When the women of the city went out to hold a festival in Dionysus' honour, Pentheus tried to stop them. In revenge, Dionysus appeared to him in disguise and persuaded him to go out dressed as a woman and to spy on them. He was unmasked and torn apart by the frenzied women or *maenads*, among whom was his own mother, *Agave*.

Perkuno: The thunder-god of Prussians, his sanctuary was at Romove, where a fire was continually kept alight before an image of him in a hollow oak. Only the high priest could enter the shrine where the fire was kept.

A great king, perhaps a god, once imprisoned the sun in a strongly-built tower, and it was not seen for several months until Perkuno broke the tower with his great iron hammer, which the Lithuanians kept at his shrine and worshipped down to the fifteenth century.

Persephone: Daughter of *Demeter* and *Zeus*. She

was carried off by the Greek god of the under-world, *Hades*, who lured her by making a most beautiful flower grow in the fields where she was playing with her companions. When she picked it, he appeared in a chariot and carried her off to his underworld kingdom. Demeter searched for her everywhere, and eventually found her. The gods persuaded Hades to release Persephone, but he gave her a magic pomegranate. Once she had eaten it, she had to return to him; and in the end it was agreed that she should spend four months of each year as queen of Hades. During this time Demeter mourned for her absent daughter, and the earth was bleak and bare.

Perseus: Son of *Danae* and *Zeus*, in Greek myth. An oracle foretold that he would kill his grand-father Acrisius, so when he was born, both he and his mother were set adrift in a chest. This was washed up on the island of Seriphos, where the king's brother looked after them both. But the king himself, Polydectes, fell in love with Danae, who repulsed his advances. When Per-seus grew up, Polydectes tried to get Perseus out of the way so that he could no longer protect his mother, and sent him to fetch the head of the *Gorgon Medusa*. With *Athene*'s help and advice, he went first to the *Graeae*, and stole their one eye and one tooth. As ransom, they gave him a cap of darkness, shoes of swiftness and a wallet in which to put the Gorgon's head so that it would not turn him to stone. He reached the Gorgons' home, and found them asleep; so he looked at the reflection of Medusa in his polished shield and killed her. Because he was invisible by virtue of the cap of darkness, the other two Gorgons could not see him, and he escaped. On the way home he rescued *Andromeda* from a sea-monster which he turned to stone with the Gorgon's head, and returned to save Danae from Polydectes. He later accidentally killed Acrisius with a discus, and for this went into exile in Asia, where his son Perses became the king of the Persians, who took their name from him.

Perun: The most important of the gods of the Russians in pagan times. He was god of thunder and oaths were sworn by him as with *Thor* and *Zeus*. See also *Perkuno*.

Phaedra: Daughter of King *Minos* of Crete and sister of *Ariadne* in Greek myth; *Theseus*, king of Athens, married her after his first wife *Hippolyta*, queen of the *Amazons* had died. In Theseus'

absence, she fell in love with *Hippolytus*, Theseus' son by his first marriage. Hippolytus repulsed her, and she hanged herself, leaving a letter saying that Hippolytus had tried to seduce her. Theseus read the letter and cursed Hippolytus; *Poseidon*, who had granted Theseus three wishes, heard this and sent a monster from the sea which frightened Hippolytus' horses. They threw him, and he was killed. It was only afterwards that Theseus discovered the truth.

Phaethon: Son of the Greek god *Helios* and of Clymene. He was brought up by his mother and, when he was old enough, set off in search of his father. He arrived at Helios' palace, where his father recognized him and offered him any wish he liked. Phaethon asked to drive his father's chariot, the chariot of the sun, for a day in his father's place. His father tried to persuade him to ask for something else, but he insisted. He was unable to control the horses of the sun, which bolted with him, and *Zeus* had to kill him with a thunderbolt to stop the earth from being burnt up.

Philoctetes: Greek hero who inherited the bows and arrows of *Heracles* from his father Poias. The Trojan seer *Helenus* told the Greeks that these were essential to the capture of Troy, but as Philoctetes had been left behind on the voyage to Troy, because he was suffering from snakebite, *Odysseus* and *Diomedes* had to be sent to fetch him. When he arrived at Troy, one of the sons of *Asclepius* healed him; Philoctetes later killed *Paris* and so helped to win the siege.

Philomela: Sister of Procne, who was the wife of King Tereus of Thrace, in Greek myth. Tereus made love to her, but was afraid that his wife would find out. So he cut out her tongue; but Philomela wove a tapestry showing what had happened to her. In revenge Procne killed her son by Tereus, Itys, and cooked him for Tereus to eat. Tereus tried to kill both his wife and her sister, but the gods prevented him, changing Philomela into a swallow, Procne into a nightingale and Tereus into a hoopoe. This is the original Greek version. The Roman version changed the names round, and made Procne the swallow, and Philomela the nightingale. In English poetry Philomela is the nightingale.

Philyra: Mother of *Chiron* the *centaur*.

Phoebe: One of the Greek *Titans*, daughter of *Uranus* and *Gaia*. She was goddess of the moon, and was mother of *Leto*. Because of her association with the moon, she was often confused with her granddaughter *Artemis*.

Picus: A minor Roman god, who appeared as a woodpecker, which was the bird of *Mars*. He was married to the *nymph* Canens, and was turned into a woodpecker by *Circe* when he rejected her advances.

Pierides: The nine daughters of Pieros challenged the Greek *muses* to a singing contest. A jury of *nymphs* voted unanimously for the muses, who turned the Pierides into jackdaws. Later the muses were themselves called Pierides.

Pi-Hsia Yuan-Kun: The 'Holy Mother' (Sheng Mu) of Chinese myth, guardian goddess of women and children. Her attendants brought children to earth and guarded them from eye diseases. She is the Taoist equivalent of *Kuan Yin*.

Pillan: The fire-god of the Araucanian Indians of South America, who was the greatest of all the gods, as well as being war-god. He ruled over the world of the gods as a supreme chief, and all kinds of spirits were under his command.

Pirithous: Chieftain of the *Lapiths*, he was a friend of *Theseus* in Greek myth. It was at his wedding with *Hippodameia* that the battle of the Lapiths and the *centaurs* took place. With Theseus, he tried to carry off *Persephone*, but they were caught, and punished by *Hades* by being eternally fastened to chairs, though Theseus was later rescued by *Heracles*.

Pluto: The Roman name for the Greek god of the underworld, *Hades*.

Pohjola: Home of the dead in Finnish myth, probably the same as *Tuonela*; it lay in the Arctic Ocean to the north of Finland, beyond a great whirlpool. Its ruler was Louhi, mother of the maid of Pohja. See also *Vainamoinen*.

Polyneices: Leader of the *Seven Against Thebes*, son of *Oedipus*, in Greek myth. He and his brother *Eteocles* killed each other during the fighting; his sister *Antigone* tried to bury him against her uncle *Creon*'s orders, and he had her put to death.

Pomona: The Roman goddess of fruit and fruitfulness, shown crowned with all the riches of the earth; wife of *Vertumnus*.

Poseidon: The Greek god of the sea, called by the Romans *Neptune*. He was son of *Cronos* and *Rhea*, and won the sea as his portion when *Zeus*, himself and *Hades* cast lots for their father's inheritance. He was lord of storms and earthquakes, and the stories about him show him as ruler of the sea in its violent moods. He was always ill-tempered and difficult to please, and this appears particularly in his pursuit of *Odysseus* after the latter had blinded his son *Polyphemus*. He was known as the Earthshaker. Curiously, he was also lord of horses, and he sometimes appeared in the shape of a bull. In the *Trojan War*, he supported the Greeks, because *Laomedon*, king of Troy, had once cheated him over his reward for building the walls of Troy.

Prajapati: In Hindu myth, a name meaning 'lord of creatures'. It is applied to *Brahma* as the creator of things, but also to other gods. The *Prajapatis* are also the sages who were the ancestors of men, sometimes said to be the same as the *maharishis*.

Priam: King of Troy during the *Trojan War*; shown as a reluctant fighter, anxious to make peace with the Greeks. He had numerous sons by *Hecuba*, *Hector* and *Paris* being the most important. He was killed by *Neoptolemus* at the sack of Troy.

Priapus: A minor Greek god of fertility and of gardens, shown as a misshapen dwarf; he was the son of *Aphrodite*. Statues of him were put in corners of gardens to bring good luck to the owners.

Prithivi: The earth in Hindu myth; worshipped with the sky as *Dyaus*-Prithivi. See also *Prithu*.

Prithu: The Hindu *rishis* at the beginning of the world made Vena its king; but he was wicked and prevented sacrifices being made, so they killed him with blades of grass. To obtain another king, they created two sons from his body; one had all his evil ways, while the other, Prithu, was perfect. He compelled the earth to yield food, by giving her a calf which caused her to give milk. This he transformed into all kinds of food for his people.

214

Prometheus: Son of the *Titans Iapetus* and Clymene in Greek myth. Prometheus created man, made out of clay, and *Athene* gave Prometheus' creation life. *Zeus* disliked mankind and oppressed them, depriving them of fire; but Prometheus stole fire from the hearth of heaven, which he hid in a hollow stalk, and brought to man. Zeus was furious at this, particularly as Prometheus had already cheated him over the sacrifices offered by men to gods. There was an argument as to which part of the sacrifice belonged to the gods, so Prometheus divided up an ox that had been offered; but he disguised all the best parts by wrapping them in the skin and made the worst parts look attractive. Zeus picked the worst half, and so the gods are always given the worst half. Zeus attempted to take his revenge by the creation of *Pandora*; when this failed *Hephaestus* and two giants carried Prometheus to the Caucasus mountains, where he was chained to a mountain-top, and an eagle came each day to tear at his liver. He finally gained his freedom by revealing to Zeus the oracle about *Thetis*, and *Heracles* released him.

Proserpina: The Roman name for *Persephone*.

Proteus: A minor Greek sea-god, who herded the sea-creatures, and was able to change his shape at will. *Menelaus* had a famous encounter with him.

Pryderi: Son of *Pwyll* and *Rhiannon*: see also *Manawydan*.

Psyche: A certain Greek king had three most lovely daughters: the youngest, Psyche, was so beautiful that people worshipped her instead of *Venus*. This made Venus jealous, and she sent *Cupid* down telling him to use his arrows to make her fall in love with some ugly old man. But Cupid saw her and at once fell in love with her himself. He persuaded *Apollo* to give an oracle which said that she must be led to a mountain-top and abandoned there, because a black serpent had fallen in love with her and would destroy the kingdom if this was not done. So the king, accompanied by a sad procession, led Psyche, dressed in mourning, to the mountain-top. But Cupid had built a marvellous palace there for her to live in, which he could visit without Venus knowing about it. Psyche soon found this; and voices guided her to her chamber and servants,

all of them invisible, produced a marvellous banquet. At midnight Cupid came to her, but left before dawn, so that she could not see him. This happened each night; but she grew lonely during the day and asked if her sisters could visit her. They were jealous, and aroused her suspicions until one night she lit an oil lamp to see who her husband was. She spilt a drop of oil on him; he woke up, and left her at once, saying that he could never return. Venus learned of the affair, and vowed to have her revenge on Psyche. Psyche wandered in search of Cupid, but was summoned by Venus, who made her do three impossible tasks: to sort a huge heap of corn and sand, in a single night; to fetch wool from magic sheep which no-one could approach because they were so fierce; and to get water from a fountain which was impossible to reach. All this she did: an ant summoned his kin to sort the corn, a reed told her how to gather the wool from thorn bushes where the sheep grazed, and an eagle fetched the water for her. Venus was even angrier, swearing that Psyche must be a witch; and she sent her to fetch a fresh supply of beauty for her, from *Persephone* in *Hades*. Psyche tried to throw herself off a tower in despair; but the tower itself spoke and told her what to do, warning her not to open the box which she would be given. She managed the journey safely, but could not resist opening the box: at once a deep sleep overcame her. In the end Cupid himself intervened, and revived her. Then he begged *Zeus* to let him marry her, and the Father of the Gods agreed; Venus was won round, and the gods made Psyche immortal.

Ptah: The god of creative work in Egyptian myth, patron of artists and craftsmen. Ptah was said to have made all the images of gods in the Egyptian temples, and some of his worshippers said that he had made the gods, including *Ra* himself, and the whole universe. The Greeks identified him with *Hephaestus*. His wife was *Sekhmet*.

Ptah-Seker-Osiris: A god of funerals in Egyptian myth; although shown as a dwarf with bandy legs, he represented the three great gods after whom he was named.

Pulekukwerek: In the myths of the Yurok Indians of north-western California, Pulekukwerek is the great protector of mankind. He stole night so that men could rest, and he had the sky

woven and set with stars. His other deeds included the killing of cannibals and monsters who
attacked people through 'accidents' while they
were playing or working.

Puntan: The creator in the myths of the Mariana
Islands; he and his sister lived before anything
else, and when he died he told his sister to make
the earth from his body, the sun and moon from
his eyes, and the rainbow from his eyebrows.

Pururavas: An Indian hero who fell in love
with the *apsaras* Urvasi. She married him on condition that she was never separated from her two
rams and that she never saw him naked. But the
Gandharvas were jealous, and one night stole the
rams. Pururavas leapt out of bed naked to pursue
them, and Urvasi vanished. Pururavas at length
found her again, but was only allowed to see her
once a year. This went on for eight years, and in
reward for his patience the Gandharvas granted
him any wish he might desire. He wished to be
reunited with Urvasi forever, and this was duly
fulfilled.

Purusha: In Hindu myth, *Brahma* in his form
as the original creator and eternal spirit.

Pushan: One of the twelve *Adityas* of Hindu
myth, according to some legends the sun himself.
He is the sun which encourages life and growth.
At *Daksha*'s sacrifice, *Shiva* knocked out all his
teeth, so offerings to him consisted of a kind of
porridge, as he could only eat gruel.

Pwyll: Pwyll was prince of Dyfed in Wales. He
once went hunting, and met another huntsman
whose hounds killed the stag his own pack were
pursuing. They quarrelled, but made their peace
when Pwyll agreed to change shapes with the
stranger, Arawn, king of *Annwn*, and to fight his
enemy Hagfan for him. Pwyll would rule Annwn
for a year while Arawn in Pwyll's shape would
rule Dyfed. At the end of the year Pwyll killed
Hagfan in single combat, and Arawn and he
changed shapes again.
 Pwyll later married *Rhiannon*, and she bore
him a son who disappeared at birth. Rhiannon
was suspected of killing her son; but he was found
outside a stable by Teyrnon, a nobleman who
had a mare which always gave birth to a foal on
the evening before May Day. The foal always
vanished and Teyrnon went out to find out why.
He saw a great claw come into the stable and

seize the foal, and when he cut off the arm behind it, and went outside, he found the child. Eventually the child was recognized as Rhiannon's son, and Rhiannon was released from the punishment inflicted on her.

Pygmalion: A king of Cyprus who made a beautiful statue and fell in love with it. He prayed to *Aphrodite* to give him a wife who was as beautiful as the statue, so the goddess made the statue itself come to life.

Pyramus: The Roman poet Ovid tells how Pyramus lived next to Thisbe in the city of Babylon. He was as handsome as she was lovely, and they fell in love. But their parents would not let them marry or even meet, and they could only whisper to each other through a crack in the wall between their houses. So they planned to meet at the tomb of Ninus, outside the city. Thisbe arrived first, but met a lioness and fled, leaving her cloak behind. This was torn in pieces by the lioness, which had just killed its prey, and in doing so stained it with blood. Pyramus found the blood-stained pieces, and thinking that Thisbe was dead, killed himself; she returned to find him dying and also stabbed herself. From their blood the mulberry fruit gets its deep red colour; it was once white, but a mulberry grew near the spot where they died and was sprinkled with blood.

Python: A dragon that lived at Delphi, which persecuted the Greek goddess *Leto* before her children were born. It was slain by *Apollo* while he was still very young. At the Pythian games, there was a flute-playing contest in which the subject of the piece was the struggle between the god and the monster.

Qamaits: In the myths of the Bella Coola Indians of the Pacific coast of North America, Qamaits was the great goddess who lived in the upper heaven, on a desolate plain. Behind her house was the lake where the *Sisiutl* lived. She had long ago fought the mountains and made them smaller, so that men could live on the earth; but she was not worshipped by men, because whenever she visited the earth, sickness and death followed.

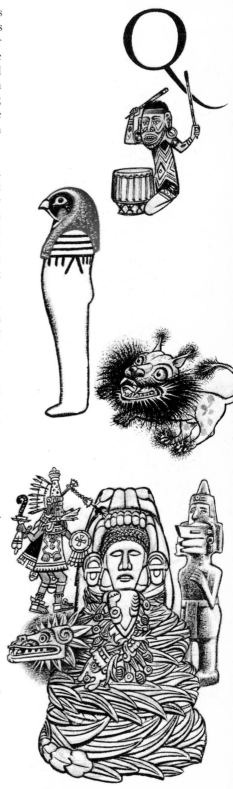

Qat: In Polynesian myth, Qat was born from a stone which split apart of its own accord. Qat created the first three pairs of men and women by carving them out of a tree, and beating a drum to make them dance. His rival Marawa saw this and did the same, but when his figures began to move he buried them in a pit. When he dug them up a week later, they had rotted; and so death first came to men.

Qat had to buy night from the god of night, because at first there was only day, and there was no time for rest; he stopped the night from going on forever by cutting it with a hard red stone, which is the dawn.

Qebehsenuf: Egyptian god who guarded the intestines of a dead man after he had been embalmed; he was shown with the head of a falcon. See *Osiris*.

Qiqirn: An Eskimo spirit which took the shape of a huge dog; but it had no hair except round its mouth, on its feet and on the tips of its ears and tail. It terrified dogs, which went mad while it was near them; but it was very frightened of men, especially of *angukoqs*, or men wise in spirit matters.

Quetzalcoatl: In Aztec myth, the 'plumed serpent', god of the wind, and of the west. He was a gentle and compassionate god, who taught wisdom and knowledge to those who followed him. He ruled Tlillan-Tlapallan, the paradise of those who had succeeded in leaving behind earthly desires and who lived only for spiritual pleasure.

It was Quetzalcoatl who, with the help of *Tezcatlipoca*, destroyed the all-devouring earth serpent which existed before all things and shaped heaven and earth from it. But just as the earth had once been a devouring serpent, so it occasionally longed again for blood; and hence the Aztecs offered human sacrifices to it.

Quetzalcoatl journeyed to the home of the sun, by means of a magic bridge made by Tezcatlipoca, and brought back one of the sun's musicians to teach music to men on earth.

He was, like Buddha, a real king who became the centre of mythical stories, though we know nothing of his historical life, not even roughly when he lived. He seems to have been a great lawgiver and founder of a religion which was later woven into other beliefs, rather as Buddhism was mixed with all kinds of myths about other non-Buddhist gods.

In the mythical story of Quetzalcoatl, he was the son of *Coatlicue*, one of the five moon-goddesses, and of the sun. Quetzalcoatl's half-brothers killed his father the sun, because he had seduced their mother; but Quetzalcoatl took his revenge by overcoming all four hundred of them when he was nine years old. When Quetzalcoatl grew up, he refused to kill any living thing, despite the temptations of evil gods, and led a pure and holy life. His chief enemy was Tezcatlipoca, the earth-god, who finally brought about his downfall. First Tezcatlipoca showed Quetzalcoatl his reflection in his magic mirror, making him appear old and wrinkled. Quetzalcoatl was so horrified that he withdrew from worldly affairs, leaving his kingdom to his enemy. But Tezcatlipoca returned, and using his mirror showed Quetzalcoatl a new image of himself, as a handsome youth. Quetzalcoatl was so delighted that he yielded to the evil gods who tempted him with wine. He and his sister Quetzalpetlatl got drunk together, and made love. When Quetzalcoatl was sober again, he was overcome with regrets, and decided to kill himself. First he did penance for four days, and then threw himself on a funeral pyre. His heart was carried up into the sky by a flock of birds, and it became the planet Venus.

Later, more elaborate forms of the myth describe how Tezcatlipoca drove Quetzalcoatl to despair and killed all the people of his kingdom by assuming a variety of disguises. First he tempted Quetzalcoatl with wine, and then seduced his daughter. He defeated Quetzalcoatl's people in battle, and then bewitched them with music and magic. Finally he killed them all except a handful with plagues and poisoned maize. Quetzalcoatl abandoned his kingdom and set out with the few remaining people for Anahuai, the symbolic 'place in the centre', where everything was still, and where he would find spiritual knowledge. His followers died on the journey; and after climbing up into the mountains and performing various ritual acts, such as the building of a ritual ball court, he departed across the sea on a raft of serpents. See also *Five Suns*.

The other gods were often regarded as aspects of Quetzalcoatl, particularly *Xipe Totec*; and Quetzalcoatl himself was later identified with the sun-god of the Aztecs, *Huitzilopochtli*.

Quirinus: A Roman war-god, probably inherited by them from the Sabine people whom they conquered in the early days of the city. He gave his name to one of the seven hills of Rome, the Quirinal. *Romulus* was identified with him as a god.

R

Ra: The Egyptian sun-god in his most common
form, as a man with a falcon's head. On his head
are the disc of the sun and the sacred cobra. He
was often regarded as the same as *Horus*, under
the name 'Ra-Horus, the dweller on the Horizon'. Each day he appeared from behind the
great mountains of the dawn, and sailed across
the sky in a boat, accompanied by Horus and
Thoth. He was said to age through the day,
starting as a child in the morning and ending as
an old man each evening. Each night, Ra journeyed through the underworld in another boat,
pulled by the spirits of the dead, before reappearing in the east. At the beginning of the world Ra
was alone in a watery universe, whose spirit was
the god *Nun*. He first created *Shu*, the god of the
air, and *Tefnut*, the goddess of moisture. Their
children were *Geb*, god of the earth and *Nut*,
goddess of the sky, who lay embracing each other
closely. Shu separated them, and lifted up Nut
so that her head was in the west and her feet in
the east, while Geb remained below as the earth.
Early in the work of creation, Ra's Eye left his
head, to take care of Shu and Tefnut; so Ra had
to make another one to take its place. The first
Eye returned and was angry with Ra for having
made another one, and Ra wept. He made his
first Eye into the sacred serpent which appeared
on his head; and from his tears as they fell on his
body, Ra created men. But when he had made
them, they began to rebel against him, saying
that he was old, even though they put their com-
plaint into respectful language: 'The King (may
he live and prosper and have good health) has
become old. His bones are silver, his flesh gold,
and his hair real lapis lazuli!' Ra read their
thoughts and decided to destroy some of them,
as an example. He sent his Eye in the form of
Hathor, goddess of love and fertility to attack
men. But Hathor enjoyed her brutal work so
much that she became *Sekhmet*, the goddess of
war and destruction, and Ra could not stop her.
So he made imitation blood from red ochre and
beer, and flooded the country with it; Hathor-
Sekhmet drank it, and became so drunk that she
could not see men, and the rest of mankind was
saved.

Each pharaoh was regarded as the son of Ra,
and part of his title often indicated that he and
Ra were one and the same. In particular, the
pharaohs wore the sacred serpent of Ra, the
golden cobra, as their crown. After a pharaoh's
death, he was said to be reunited with Ra.

Radha: The favourite of the Hindu god *Krishna* among the *Gopis*; her love for the god is a frequent theme in Indian art.

Ragnarok: In Norse myth, the day on which the present world and its gods will meet their end. First there will be three winters of great and vicious wars throughout the world. Then will follow the *fimbulvetr*, the great winter of biting cold, whirling snow and freezing winds, when the sun will give no heat, and there will be two more like it. Two wolves will swallow the sun and moon, and the stars will vanish from the heavens. Great earthquakes will follow across the whole of the earth, mountains will fall, and all fetters will be broken, including those that bind the fearsome *Fenris-wolf*. The *Midgard-serpent*, driven mad with rage, will try to come on dry land.

Then the forces of evil will gather: the Fenris-wolf, his jaws gaping so wide that they span heaven and earth, his nostrils breathing fire, the Midgard-serpent, spreading poison over the whole world, and the armies of the fire- and *frost-giants*. The dreaded ship *Naglfari* will be launched, and in it *Loki* will sail to the attack, while the sons of *Muspell* ride out from the south, led by *Surt*. They will gallop over *Bifrost Bridge*, which will break under them, to meet the gods in the plain of *Vigrid*. One by one the gods will fall before the monsters they attack: *Odin* will be swallowed by the Fenris-wolf, *Thor* will die as he kills the Midgard-serpent, *Heimdall* and Loki will kill each other. But Odin's son *Vidar* will tear the Fenris-wolf apart, and although Surt will destroy the world with fire, a new world will arise after the terrible struggle is over. The sons of the gods, Vidar and *Vali*, Modi and *Magni*, will rebuild *Asgard* and call it Idavoll, and Thor's sons will possess his hammer *Mjollnir*. *Balder* and *Holder* will come from *Hel* and live there peaceably together. A new sun will appear in the heavens, and from the world-tree *Lif and Lifthrasir* will emerge from their hiding place to repeople the world. 'Earth will rise out of the sea and be green and fair, and fields of corn will grow that were never sown, and the spirits of those already dead will continue to dwell in splendid halls in heaven.'

Rahu: When the Hindu gods 'churned the ocean' to find the *amrita*, a *Daitya* called Rahu managed to drink some of it by disguising himself as a god. The sun and moon saw him, and *Vishnu* cut off his head and two of his four arms.

But as the head had drunk the amrita it was already immortal, and so Vishnu made it into a planet. Here he gets his revenge on the sun and moon by pursuing them and swallowing them at intervals, causing eclipses.

Raiden: Japanese god of thunder, usually shown as an *oni* or demon.

Rainbow Snake: The Australian aborigines have a great number of names for the great snake who appears as the rainbow, and who has many special sacred pools. He is very powerful, and must not be angered. He controls the rain and the revival of trees and flowers each spring.

In one myth from north-west Australia, his rival is his son the *Bat*, called Tjinim, who stole his women and stabbed him so that he bled endlessly. In the end he went down to the sea and vanished into it carrying all the fire in the world with him, which went out as he disappeared. Fire had to be made again in a new way, by rubbing sticks together.

Rakshasas: In Indian myth, evil spirits who attack mankind, either as ghosts, vampires, man-eaters or monsters. Some are beautiful, and tempt holy men. In *Rama*'s war against *Ravana*, Ravana led an army of Rakshasas.

Rama: Hero of the Indian epic *Ramayana*. His full name was Ramacandra, and he was the seventh *avatar* of *Vishnu*, brought into the world to combat the evil *Ravana*. His three brothers and constant companions, *Bharata*, *Lakshmana* and Shatrughna, were also partly divine. When they were still boys, they helped the sage *Vishvamitra* to overcome a *Rakshasa*, and Vishvamitra taught them many things in return, and gave Rama divine weapons. As his bride, Rama won Sita, daughter of the king of Videha, by bending the great bow of the god *Shiva*: none of the other suitors could bend it at all, but Rama bent it so strongly that it broke. Because of a plot at his father's palace, Rama was replaced as heir to the throne by his brother Bharata; and Rama went into exile for fourteen years. When Bharata inherited the throne, he refused to accept it, but went and sought out Rama instead. Rama refused to break the exile imposed by his father, and Bharata finally agreed to return and rule as regent. Rama now incurred the hatred of the Rakshasas, because one of them, jealous of Sita, had tried to attack Sita and had been driven off by Lakshmana, who cut off the Rakshasa's ears and nose. Rama and his brothers defeated one army of Rakshasas, but the enemy gained the help of Ravana, the Rakshasa king of Sri Lanka (Ceylon). Ravana managed to carry off Sita, and Rama set off in pursuit. He managed to make an alliance with the king of the monkeys, Sugriva, and his general *Hanuman*, the monkey-god. Hanuman, as son of the wind, could fly and change his shape at will, so he spied out the land before the army attacked Ravana's capital Lanka. Using a magic bridge, the monkey army crossed to Ceylon, and after a series of battles slaughtered the Rakshasas, Ravana among them. Sita was rescued, but Rama refused to believe that she had not gone with Ravana of her own accord. She protested, and after an ordeal by fire, in which she walked through the flames unharmed, her innocence was proved, and Rama returned with her to rule his kingdom.

A sequel tells that Rama's doubts were still not satisfied, and he banished Sita. In exile, she gave birth to Rama's two sons, Kusha and Lava. They remained with her until they were about sixteen, when Rama decided to carry out the great 'horse sacrifice' to assert his superiority over other kings. The horse was let loose, as custom required, and Shatrughna was sent after it with an army. But Kusha and Lava seized the horse, and defeated in turn Shatrughna, Lakshmana and Bharata. Rama himself now came against them, but recognized them as his sons, and peace was made. Sita forgave Rama, and the great sacrifice was performed.

Ran: Norse sea-giantess, married to *Aegir*. She was said to trap seafarers in a net, and drag them down to her hall. If a man was drowned, he was said to have gone to Ran, and if his ghost appeared at his own funeral feast, she had given him a good welcome.

Rangi: The sky-god in Polynesian myth. He and *Papa*, the earth-goddess, created the gods *Tane-Tangaroa*, *Tu*, *Rongo*, *Haumia* and *Tawhiri*, but kept them held closely to them so that they lived in darkness. These gods decided to push Rangi and Papa apart in order to escape, though Tawhiri, the wind-god, objected. All of them tried in turn, but only Tane, the forest-god, succeeded; and he propped heaven up so that light could come between heaven and earth. Tawhiri attacked him and felled his trees, and stirred up

the ocean, Tangaroa's kingdom. Haumia and Rongo, the plant-gods, hid with Papa, and in the end it was Tu, the war-god, who conquered his brothers and put the trees, birds, animals, fishes and plants to his own use.

Rata: The Polynesian hero Rata was the son of Wahieroa and the nymph Tahiti Tokerau. His mother had rejected a man called Puna in favour of Wahieroa, but Puna revenged himself by killing Wahieroa and making Tahiti Tokerau his slave. When Rata grew up he determined to avenge his father, and set about cutting down a tree to make a canoe to reach Puna's home across the sea. He used a magic axe, but cut down a sacred tree by mistake. The wood spirits set it up again, but he cut it down once more and frightened them with a great shout when they came back to replace it. They helped him to build the ship, and Rata set out with the wood spirits as crew. When they approached Puna's home, Rata destroyed the sea-monsters which had eaten his father, and recovered the parts of his body. He killed Puna, despite his guard of lizards and cocks who were always on the alert, and rescued his mother.

Ratatosk: A squirrel which lived on the Norse world-tree *Yggdrasill*, and which ran up and down it bearing messages of hate between the eagle perched at the top and the serpent *Nidhogg* which gnawed its roots.

Rati: The wife of the Hindu god *Kama*, goddess of love.

Ratri: The Hindu goddess of night, regarded as gentle and peaceful.

Ravana: The evil king of the *Rakshasas* in Hindu myth. He worshipped *Brahma* so faithfully that Brahma made him immune to attacks by the gods; but his evil deeds were such that *Vishnu* declared that since he had not asked for protection against men and beasts, he would suffer from them instead. In order to defeat him Vishnu assumed his seventh *avatar* as *Rama*.

Raven: In the myths of the North American Indians of the Pacific coast, Raven occupies a similar place to that of *Coyote* and *Nanabozho* elsewhere to the south and east, appearing both as a creator and as a cunning spirit-creature: he was said to be very greedy, and to be forever

226

seeking food.

Renenutet: The Egyptian goddess of young children and their mothers.

Reshpu: A war-god from Syria, whose worship was introduced into Egypt during one of the periods when Syrian invaders ruled there.

Rhadamanthus: Son of *Zeus* and *Europa*, he was one of the three just men of early mankind in Greek myth. He was either the judge of the wicked or lord of the *Elysian Plain*.

Rhea: A grandiose but rather indistinct mother-goddess in Greek myth, wife of *Cronos* and mother of *Zeus*. She played an important part in the struggle between these two gods. The Romans identified her with Ops.

Rhiannon: Wife of the Welsh prince *Pwyll*. She was perhaps a goddess (Rigantona) in pagan Britain, whose story has come down in a Christian version which makes her a queen instead. See also *Manawydan*.

Ribhus: In Hindu myth, three brothers who became gods through performing good deeds. They were the craftsmen of the gods, and made the chariot of *Indra*.

Rishi: The Hindu name for a poet or sage: *maharishis* are 'great sages'. In particular, the *Prajapatis* were *maharishis*, though other names were later added to the list.

Romulus and Remus: The twin sons of Rhea Silvia and the Roman god *Mars*. Rhea Silvia was a distant descendant of *Aeneas*, and was a Vestal Virgin. Because she was not supposed to have children, their grandfather ordered them to be drowned, but the men sent to do this abandoned them on the edge of the river Tiber instead, where a she-wolf found them and fed them. A herdsman, Faustulus, brought them up. At first they made a living by attacking robbers and recapturing their spoils, but their true birth was soon discovered. However, when they planned to build a new town on the spot where they had been found as children, they quarrelled as to whom the new city should be named after, and Romulus killed Remus. It was he who built the new city, which he called Rome. All Roman documents were dated from the year in which

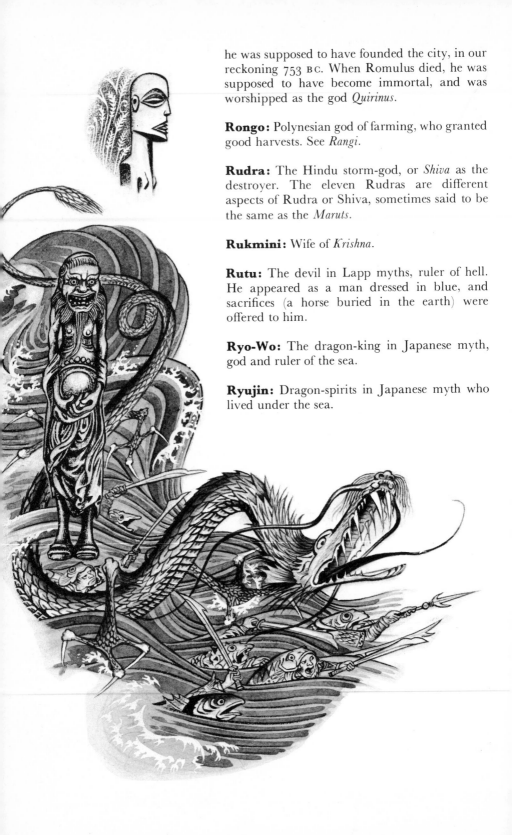

he was supposed to have founded the city, in our reckoning 753 BC. When Romulus died, he was supposed to have become immortal, and was worshipped as the god *Quirinus*.

Rongo: Polynesian god of farming, who granted good harvests. See *Rangi*.

Rudra: The Hindu storm-god, or *Shiva* as the destroyer. The eleven Rudras are different aspects of Rudra or Shiva, sometimes said to be the same as the *Maruts*.

Rukmini: Wife of *Krishna*.

Rutu: The devil in Lapp myths, ruler of hell. He appeared as a man dressed in blue, and sacrifices (a horse buried in the earth) were offered to him.

Ryo-Wo: The dragon-king in Japanese myth, god and ruler of the sea.

Ryujin: Dragon-spirits in Japanese myth who lived under the sea.

Saa: One of the attendants of the Egyptian god *Ra* in the ship in which he crossed the heavens each day.

Sadhyas: Minor Hindu gods who guard the rites and prayers of the greater gods.

Sagara: An Indian king who tried to perform the *asvamedha* or horse sacrifice to show his superiority over other kings. The horse was released, but his sixty thousand sons, whom he sent to follow it, offended the gods by their wild ways, and the horse was carried off to *Patala*. Sagara's sons followed it, but were reduced to ashes by Kapila, and only when Sagara's grandson had made amends was the horse released. *Bhagiratha* later purified the ashes of his ancestors in the river *Ganges*.

Sakpata: God of smallpox in Dahomey, called Shokpona among the Yoruba. His priests tried to protect the people from his attacks, both by prayers and by medicinal means; some of their practices show considerable knowledge of the nature of the disease. Smallpox was regarded as a great disgrace, and the victim was isolated from the village. Tuberculosis and leprosy were also treated by Sakpata's priests.

Sampo: In Finnish myth, a magic talisman, covered in marvellous designs, which the smith *Ilmarinen* wrought to win the maid of Pohja, Louhi's daughter. See *Vainamoinen*.

San Ch'ing: The three great gods of Taoist belief in China: T'ien Pao, 'the eternal' ruler of the jade heaven, son of *P'an Ku*; Ling-Pao T'ien-tsun, ruler of all supernatural beings and of the 'Superior Heaven'; and Shen Pao, who on earth was the great teacher *Lao Tzu* and rules the 'Highest Heaven'. *Yu Huang* sometimes takes T'ien Pao's place.

Sarama: The dog of the Hindu god *Indra*; her puppies were the four-eyed Sarameyas, watchdogs of *Yama*.

Saranyu: In Hindu myth, wife of *Vaivasvata*, the sun, and mother of the *Ashvins*.

Sarasvati: A river-goddess, who in later Hindu myths became the wife of *Brahma* and goddess of speech and learning. She was the inventor of language and writing.

Satet: The Egyptian goddess of the first cataract of the Nile, who shot the water down the cataract like a bow from an arrow, and so was shown carrying bow and arrows.

Saturn: An ancient Roman deity who was later identified with *Cronos*. He was the lord of the *Golden Age*, when men did not have to work and everything was peaceful, though his name seems to mean the 'sower'. Saturday is named after him, and the Roman equivalent of Christmas, the Saturnalia, were held in his honour at the end of December. The second largest planet of the Solar System, between Jupiter and Neptune, is named after him.

Satyrs: Greek spirits of wild-life and the woods. Early artists showed them as men with horses' tails, but later, in imitation of *Pan*, they became more goatlike. They were fond of dancing and love-making, but were shy and cowardly. They were among the attendants of *Dionysus*.

Savitri: 1. A name for the morning and evening sun in Hindu myth; Savitri orders night to come near, so that men and beasts can rest.

2. The Indian story of Savitri tells how the princess Savitri married Satyavan, although she was told that he would die in a year's time. Satyavan went out one day to cut wood and collapsed; Savitri tried to help him but saw *Yama*, god of death coming to fetch his spirit. When Yama set off with Satyavan's soul, Savitri followed them: and Yama offered to reward her devotion by granting any wish she made, except only her husband's return to life. She extracted three such wishes from him, and continued to follow the god and his victim, until Yama finally relented and returned Satyavan to her.

Saxnot: The god whom the East Saxons in Essex regarded as the founder of their dynasty; he seems to have been a war-god, his name being 'sword-companion', and he may be *Tiwaz* under another name.

Sceaf: A Norse child-god who came across the sea to Denmark in a boat with a sheaf of corn beside him and founded a kingdom there. Other traditions say that he landed on the island of Scani with a boatload of weapons, and was made king: in either case, the story seems to be the same as that of *Scyld*.

230

Scyld: Early king of Denmark who arrived in his kingdom as a child sent from across the sea and bearing rich gifts: see also *Sceaf*. In *Beowulf*, an Old English poem, he is called Scyld Sceafing (son of Sceaf), and they are probably the same person. He also appears as a son of *Odin*, called Skjold, who married *Gefion*.

Scylla: Greek monster, the daughter of Phorkys and *Hecate* who, when *Poseidon* fell in love with her, was turned into a six-headed sea-creature by Poseidon's wife *Amphitrite*. She lurked in a cave on the Straits of Messina, between Sicily and Italy, and whenever a ship passed would seize six of its crew and devour them.

Sedna: The great mother of the sea in Eskimo myth. There were once, long ago, a giant and his wife, who had a daughter. When she grew up, she ate as much meat and flesh as she could find, and her father and mother could never give her enough. One night she attacked them while they were asleep and started to eat their arms and legs. So her parents seized her and threw her into the sea, first cutting off her fingers. Her fingers became all the creatures which lived in the sea, and she herself ruled over them. When the Eskimos were short of food, they would send their magician or Angakok to beg for fish; he would go into a trance and his spirit would travel to Sedna's palace, where he would try to attract her attention and get a favourable answer.

Another version of the legend makes Sedna an Eskimo girl who was carried off by a bird-spirit. Her father rescued her, but the bird-spirit returned and demanded his bride. The father refused, and the bird-spirit disappeared in fury. A great storm arose, and the father sacrificed Sedna to appease the angry spirits of nature.

Sedu: Guardian spirits in Assyrian myth, placed beside gateways to turn back evil spirits: they are shown as huge winged bulls, just as the lamassu in Sumeria, who were also guardians of gateways, were shown as winged cows.

Segais: An Irish supernatural spring in the Land of Promise from which the rivers Shannon and Boyne flow. It was surrounded by hazel trees, whose nuts fell into the water and were eaten by the Salmon of Knowledge, which lived there.

Seides: Stones worshipped as gods by the Lapps, which were used as oracles and which were

decorated with greenery. If a question was put to a seide, the questioner tried to lift the stone. If it grew heavier until he was unable to lift it, the answer was negative. With large stones, the questioner's hand stuck to the stone until he guessed the true answer. Seides were regarded as human beings turned to stone, and could occasionally resume their human form.

Seker: An Egyptian god of funerals.

Sekhmet: The Egyptian goddess of war, *Hathor* in her form as destroyer. Sekhmet came into being when Hathor was sent to destroy mankind by *Ra*. She refused to stop, because she enjoyed her work so much, and thus became Sekhmet goddess of violence as well as Hathor goddess of love and fertility.

Selene: One of the several Greek goddesses associated with the moon. She was the daughter of the *Titans Hyperion* and Theia. Like *Helios*, she drove a chariot, but it was pulled by two instead of four horses. She was identified with *Artemis*; and it was she who loved *Endymion*.

Semele: In Greek myth, daughter of *Cadmus* of Thebes, and mother of *Dionysus*. *Zeus* was her lover, and *Hera*, jealous of her, persuaded her to beg Zeus to appear to her in his real form. Zeus reluctantly agreed when Semele asked him, but his thunderbolt destroyed her even though he tried to protect her.

Sennin: The immortals in Japanese myth; like the Chinese immortals *Hsien* they were usually mortals who had acquired magic powers by their virtue. If they married human beings, they lost their magic power: this happened to Ikkaku Sennin, who was so powerful that he shut up all the dragons in a cave, causing a great drought, because the dragons controlled the rain. The king heard of this, and sent a beautiful girl to Ikkaku Sennin. He fell in love with her, and the dragons were able to escape, ending the drought. The realm of the Sennin, Senkyo, was in the mountains, where they walked and talked together on pleasant terraces among the pine trees. See also *Gyoja*.

Senx: In the myths of the Bella Coola Indians of the Pacific coast of North America, Senx, the Sun, lived in the lower of the two heavens, in the 'house of myths'. He and Alkuntam created man. He crossed the sky each day on a huge broad bridge; in winter he walked on the left hand side, nearer the horizon, in summer on the right, higher up in the sky.

Septu: An Egyptian god of war, whose help was specially valuable when the Egyptians fought against the Syrians and Hittites from the Middle East.

Sequana: A Gaulish nature-goddess, patron of the river Seine: her shrine was at the river's source, and was regarded as a place of healing.

Serapis: The Egyptian state god under the Greek rulers of the third and second centuries BC. His name derived from *Osiris-Apis*, and his myths adopted much of the basic story of Osiris.

Seshat: The Egyptian goddess of writing and written records. She was also the goddess who wrote out men's fates, as well as recording what had happened, and was called the librarian of the gods.

Seth: Egyptian god, often regarded as evil, who murdered *Osiris* and tried to gain his kingdom from *Horus*. He was identified by the Egyptians with the god *Baal* worshipped by their enemies the Hittites: like Baal, he was a storm and thunder-god. Even though evil by nature, he was still recognized as a god, and was the god whom soldiers worshipped. He was confused with *Aapep* in the later myths, and when the Greeks came to Egypt they called him *Typhon*.

Seven Against Thebes: In Greek myth, *Eteocles* and *Polyneices*, sons of *Oedipus*, agreed to rule in Thebes for alternate years, while the other went into exile. At the end of the first year, Eteocles refused to surrender the throne to Polyneices, who gathered an army led by his father-in-law *Adrastus*. The other five chieftains who made up the Seven were *Capaneus*, Hippomedon, Parthenopeius, *Tydeus* and *Amphiaraus*. Tydeus was sent to urge Eteocles to surrender peacefully, but was sent away with a scornful answer, and ambushed by the Thebans as he left. He fought his way out, killing all his opponents, and the war began. Each of the champions was given one of the seven gates of Thebes to attack, but the defenders put them all to flight. Only Adrastus escaped alive; Eteocles and Polyneices killed each other in the battle, and their uncle

233

Creon became king of Thebes. *Theseus* is said to have taken immediate revenge on the Thebans at the pleas of Adrastus and the mothers of the dead heroes, defeating them completely and giving the dead honourable burial; but other versions say that it was only when the sons of the Seven attacked some years later that Thebes was overthrown and ruined.

Shakra: King of the gods in Buddhist myth: a name of the Hindu god *Indra*.

Shakuru: The sun in Pawnee Indian myth, regarded as the chief assistant of *Tirawa-Atius*, whose power Shakuru brought down to earth. The great dance in his honour was the most important religious festival of the year.

Shamash: The Sumerian sun-god, also called Uttu, the golden healing-god who drove away disease with his wings. He crossed the sky each day, and made a similar journey across the underworld each night. Because he saw everything on earth, he was the god of justice, and in the famous code of laws issued by King Hammurabi, the text begins with a picture of the king standing before Shamash.

Shango: God of thunder of the Yoruba people of West Africa. His wives were the great rivers of the district, while he was called the stone-thrower, and stones said to be his thunderbolts were kept in his temples. He was an early king of the Yoruba who had the power of calling down fire from heaven; but when he did so, it killed his family, and he hanged himself out of grief.

Sheng Jen: The 'holy beings' in Chinese Taoist myth, highest of all beings, represented as men of unlimited powers and virtue.

Shên I: 'The great archer' in Chinese myth. He appeared to the emperor *Yao*, and told him that he was a great archer, and could fly; and he proved it by shooting an arrow into the top of a pine-tree and leaping on the wind to go and fetch it. He once saved the earth from being burnt up. One day all the ten suns decided to appear in the sky at once, and Shên I shot down nine of them. His wife, *Ch'ang-O*, stole the potion of immortality which he had been given by *Hsi Wang Mu*, and drank half of it before he discovered her; as a result she could only travel half-way to the heaven of the immortals, and

234

could only reach the moon, where she stayed. Here Shên I used to visit her twice a month, but had to live in the Palace of the Sun for the rest of the time.

Shen Nung: The Earthly Emperor in Chinese mythology, one of the *Three Emperors*, who invented all kinds of tools for farming and set up markets for food, as well as studying plants and their uses in medicine.

Shesha: In Hindu myth, Shesha is king of the serpent race or *Nagas*. He has a thousand heads, and sheltered *Vishnu* during the creation of the world while he rested from his work. He is a world serpent like the *Midgard-serpent*, and supports either the earth or the seven *Patalas* beneath it, over which he rules. His yawning is the cause of earthquakes.

Shiang Ti: 'Supreme Ruler' in Chinese myth, lord of *Huang Ti'en*; but he was thought of not as a human being but an idea or spirit.

Shichi Fukujin: The seven gods of good fortune in Japanese myth. They were as follows:
1. Ebisu, the fisherman, round-faced and smiling. With his rod he caught sea-bream, regarded as a lucky fish.
2. Daikoku, identified with *Ō-kuni-nushi*, who was a god of wealth; he was shown standing on two rice bags and carrying another bag. He possessed a hammer which would produce anything his worshippers wanted.
3. Bishamon-ten, the same as the Buddhist god *Kuvera* or Kubera. See *Kompira*.
4. *Benten*.
5. Fuku-roku-ju, who gave men not only wealth but also long life; he had a very long head and was accompanied by the symbol of long life, a white crane.
6. Jurōjin, giver of health and long life, accompanied by a deer.
7. Hotei, the god of children, shown as a fat, cheerful monk; his bag is full of treasures which he gives to people who refuse to worry about life.

Shih-Tien Yen-Wang: The ten rulers of the otherworld in Chinese myth. There were ten law-courts, each presided over by one of the ten '*Yama*-kings'. In the first, the soul was examined and sent to one of the eight courts of punishment according to its misdeeds during life. The tenth court dealt with souls which had completed

235

their punishment and sent them to be reincarnated. In the eighteen halls where the souls were punished 'the punishment fitted the crime': misers, for instance, were made to swallow molten gold, while liars had their tongues cut out. When suitable punishment had been handed out, the soul was given the brew of oblivion to drink, which made it forget its previous existence before being reborn into its new form.

Shikome: The Japanese furies, who lived in *Yomi-No-Kuni*.

Shina-Tsu-Hiko: The Japanese god of the wind, who was born of the breath of *Izanagi*. He and his wife Shina-tsu-hime, who blew the mist off the land at the beginning of the world, filled the space between heaven and earth.

Shishupala: The evil cousin of *Krishna*, the Hindu god-hero, whom Krishna killed. He was said to have lived on earth before, as *Hiranyakashipu* and *Ravana*.

Shiva: Shiva is the Hindu god of destruction and renewal of life. Because to the Indian mind everything is eternal, anything which is destroyed must reappear in another form, so Shiva rules over both events. He is shown in his terrible aspect as destroyer as the enemy of the other gods, but also as the 'one great god', *Mahadeva*, who is the real ruler of all things. So he appears as the great ascetic, who can perform all kinds of yoga and can achieve great spiritual knowledge. In his peaceful aspect, he is lord of cattle and leader of revels and dances. He is shown as a five-faced man with four arms, with a third eye in the middle of his forehead. This third eye, when opened, is very destructive; with it he once reduced the god *Kama* to ashes, and at the end of one of the years of *Brahma*, Shiva destroyed the universe with it.
His wife is *Devi*, who also has a pleasant and terrible aspect. See also *Bhrigu, Daksha, Ganges, Kama, Nandi*.

Shiwanna: The spirits who bring rain, according to the Keres Pueblo Indians of California; they are among the most important of the *kachinas*, and are represented in many of the ritual dances of the tribes.

Shojo: Japanese mythical being rather like the Greek *satyr*; he was always drinking sake or rice-wine, and his face was red as a result. He carried

236

a ladle with which to drink, and was gaily dressed; he often danced wildly when he was merry.

Shoki: In Japanese myth, the chief enemy of the *oni* or devils; he acted as guardian of the Chinese imperial palace against such creatures, and was promoted to a kind of archangel figure. He is the same as the Chinese god *Chung K'uei*.

Shokpona: Another name for *Sakpata*.

Shou Hsing: The Chinese god of long life, identified with the star Canopus. His companions were a stork or a turtle, both supposed to be very long-lived. It was he who decided the date of each man's death; on very rare occasions he could be persuaded to alter this date and so prolong a man's life.

Shri: A name of *Lakshmi*, wife of the Hindu god *Vishnu*.

Shu: Egyptian god of the air, one of the *Great Ennead*; husband of *Tefnut* and father of *Geb* and *Nut*. See *Ra*.

Sibu: Supreme god of the Indians of Central America, who gave the seed from which men and animals were born to Sura, a lesser god. But the evil god Jaburu stole the seed and ate it, and killed Sura. So Sibu killed Jaburu with poisoned chocolate, which made him swell until he burst. He brought Sura back to life and gave him back the seed which he had taken from Jaburu's body.

Sibyls: Prophetesses in ancient Greece and in Rome. The first sibyl was *Marpessa*, whom the god *Apollo* inspired to give marvellous though obscure forecasts of the future. As many as ten sibyls lived at different times, though no two writers agree on the exact list; and it was quite a common title in the lands to the east of Greece. The most important was the Cumaean Sibyl, who lived at Cumae near Naples in southern Italy. Like Marpessa, Apollo loved her, but she rejected him, even though he offered her immortality if she would yield to him. Instead, she was granted the gift of living for as many years as she could hold grains of dust in her hands, but she was not given eternal youth. As she neared the end of her very long life, she shrank until she was so small that she was hung in a bottle. When children asked her what she wanted, she used to

answer, 'I want to die'.

It was the Cumaean Sibyl who guided *Aeneas* to the underworld, and she was the supposed author of the Sibylline Books, which foretold Rome's future. These books were collected in the early days of Rome, under King Tarquin, and were destroyed in a fire in 83 BC. They were collected again from other sources in 76 BC and edited on the Emperor Augustus' instructions in 18 BC. They were used on great occasions to discover what ought to be done, though the answers they gave were so obscure that they could be interpreted as necessary.

Sif: The wife of the Norse god *Thor*. Her hair was once cut off by *Loki* in a mischievous mood, and dwarfs forged new hair of real gold, which looked exactly like natural hair, for her.

Sigmund: The story of Sigmund is the beginning of the Norse saga about the Volsungs, descended from Sigmund's father Volsung. Volsung was killed in a battle with King Siggeir, and Sigmund and his nine brothers were captured. Signy, their sister, who was married to King Siggeir, begged that they should be put in the stocks rather than killed, and this was done; but each night a she-wolf came and killed one of them, until only Sigmund was left. With Signy's help, Sigmund killed the wolf; he escaped into the forest and lived there in hiding. Signy followed him, and they had a son, Sinfjotli. In order to train him, Sigmund and he used to hunt in the form of wolves, and eventually they managed to take their revenge on King Siggeir, and burnt his hall, Signy dying in the fire. Sigmund became lord of a kingdom, and married again. Sinfjotli killed his stepmother's brother in a quarrel; she poisoned him, though Sigmund tried to prevent it. So Sigmund married a third time, but before his son by his new wife, Hjordis, was born, Sigmund was killed in battle. Hjordis kept the pieces of his magic sword, which *Odin* had given him long before, and gave them to their son *Sigurd* when he grew up.

Sigurd: Son of *Sigmund* the Volsung in Norse myth. He was brought up by the dwarf Regin, who taught him all kinds of things. When he grew up, Regin told him the story of *Ottar*, and how *Fafnir* had changed himself into a dragon and was guarding the gold. Sigurd asked Regin to make him a sword, and with it promised to kill father Sigmund's sword, Gram, which Regin

238

good enough for him, and he broke them easily.
Only when his mother gave him the pieces of his
father Sigmund's sword, Oram, which Regin
forged together again, was he satisfied. But first
he avenged himself on the men who had killed
his father. Then he and Regin went to kill Fafnir;
when this was done, Regin asked him to give him
the dragon's heart to roast, but some of the blood
fell on Sigurd's hand, and he put his thumb in
his mouth to cool it, because the blood had burnt
him. At once he understood what the birds
around him were saying; and he learnt that
Regin was proposing to kill him. So he killed
Regin instead, seized Fafnir's treasure, and
following the birds' advice rode off to seek
Brynhild, who lay asleep in a cave surrounded
by fire. He found her clad in mail, and learned
that she was a *Valkyrie* who had disobeyed *Odin*
and had given victory to the wrong man in battle.
Odin had sent her down to *Midgard* as a mortal,
but she had sworn that she would only marry a
man without fear, who could penetrate the fire
and awaken her. Sigurd and Brynhild swore
that they would marry each other, but for the
moment they parted. However, Sigurd was given
a drugged drink by Grimhild, mother of the
beautiful Gudrun, and fell in love with Gudrun,
forgetting Brynhild. He wooed and won Brynhild in disguise for his brother-in-law Gunnar,
and Brynhild came to live in the same household.
But Sigurd remembered his oath to her, and she
discovered that it was not Gunnar who had won
her. She urged Gunnar and his brothers to kill
Sigurd, but when the deed was done, she killed
herself, and the two of them were burnt side
by side.

Such, in brief outline, is the story which
Wagner used to shape his four great musical
dramas, *The Ring of the Nibelungs*. The story of
Sigmund and Signy (Siegmund and Sieglinde)
forms the second opera, *Die Walküre*; Wagner
cleverly adapts the tale so that it is Brunnhilde's
(Brynhild) refusal to let Siegmund die that
brings about her fate (Odin kills Siegmund himself). The youth of Siegfried and his winning of
Brunnhilde forms the third opera, and the last
opera (*Götterdammerung, Twilight of the Gods*) deals
with the death of Siegfried, after which Fafnir's
treasure is returned to its rightful owners and the
world of the gods comes to an end.

(Although Wagner's title *The Ring of the
Nibelungs* is closer to the title of the German
version of the story, *Das Nibelungenlied*, his plot
is basically that of the *Saga of the Volsungs*, the

Norse version of which is given in outline above.)

Silenus: A Roman god or spirit; he was rather like a *satyr*. Some poets thought there were several Sileni. He was older than the satyrs, but like them was a constant companion of *Dionysus*. Although he had a kind of simple wisdom, he often drank too much, and is often shown by artists drunk, with a cup in his hand.

Sin: The moon-god of Sumeria, who was chiefly worshipped at the city of Ur. He was the god who marked the passing of time with his waxing and waning, and was important to travellers on long journeys across the desert. See also *Marduk*.

Sirens: Beautiful but evil creatures in Greek myth, sometimes shown as birds with women's heads. They sang enchantingly to any sailors who passed their island, so that they forgot to steer their boats and were wrecked on the rocks around the island. *Odysseus* contrived to sail past them and still listen to their song, by filling his crew's ears with wax and having himself tied to the mast. At this the Sirens drowned themselves in a rage, because no-one had ever escaped them before; but other versions of the story dispute this, because *Orpheus* had saved the Argonauts when they passed the same island by playing even more sweetly than the Sirens sang.

Sisiutl: The great double-headed snake, spirit of the waters, in the myths of the Indians of the Pacific coast of North America; it lived in a lake in heaven behind the house of *Qamaits*, and was so hard-skinned that no knife could cut its skin. It was prayed to by medicine-men, and could help men.

Sisyphus: Son of the Greek god *Hermes* and king of Corinth, he inherited from his father great skill in trickery, and was granted the gift of changing the appearance of anything he stole and of always escaping capture. He escaped Death himself, first by tricking him and tying him up; *Ares* released Death, who was more successful the next time, and actually got Sisyphus down to *Hades*. But Sisyphus had told his wife *Merope* to throw out his body unburied when he died. When he arrived in Hades, he went to Hades himself and asked to be allowed to go back and punish Merope for such disrespect to the dead. Hades gave his consent, provided he returned as soon as he had punished her. Sisyphus

240

was careful not to do anything of the sort once he was back on earth, and he only died of old age, many years later. But his trickery earned him the punishment of rolling a great stone up a hill in *Tartarus*; every time he was about to reach the top, it rolled back to the bottom again.

Sita: The wife of the Indian hero *Rama*.

Skadi: A Norse mountain-goddess, who married the sea-god *Njord*. Neither could bear to live away from their home, since Skadi hated the sea, and Njord was bored by the mountains; so after nine nights they separated, and Skadi went back to hunting and skiing in the hills. She was the daughter of the giant *Thiazi*, who had got the *Apples of Youth* from *Loki*; and she was allowed to choose one of the gods in marriage as compensation for her father's death, provided that she only looked at their feet when she made her choice She chose Njord thinking that he was *Balder*, the most handsome of the gods.

Skanda: A name of *Kartikeya*, the Hindu war-god.

Skidbladnir: A magic ship owned by the Norse god *Frey*, which could hold all the gods at once, but when not in use could be folded up and put in a small pouch. It always had a favourable wind, so could travel very swiftly in any direction.

Skinfaxi: The horse which drew the chariot of Day in Norse myth; his shining mane lit up the earth and sky.

Sleipnir: The horse of the Norse god *Odin*, born to *Loki*, when he took the form of a mare and lured the stallion *Svadilfari* away from the building of *Asgard*. He had eight legs, and was the swiftest of all horses. When Odin journeyed to *Hel*, to find out why Balder had such troubled dreams, and when *Hermod* went there to obtain Balder's release, they rode on Sleipnir; and it has been suggested that Sleipnir is a symbol of the bier on which a coffin was put, which, carried by four men, could be said to have eight legs.

So: Thunder-god of the Ewe people of West Africa. His sacred animal was the ram, and his weapon the axe. When lightning struck, it was the god throwing a stone axe from heaven. He punished people who did not respect the gods.

and the trees which he struck are those where witches gathered at night.

Soma: Soma was the Hindu god of the drink soma which produced strange dreams and visions, rather as *Bacchus* in Greek myth was god of wine. Soma was brewed from the juice of a plant, perhaps a mushroom; its effects were regarded as a kind of magic inspiration. It was also called *amrita*.

Sosondowah: A great hunter, who, according to the Iroquois Indians of eastern North America, pursued the elk of heaven up into the sky after it had once strayed down to earth. He was captured by the dawn, who made him her watchman. He saw a girl called Gendenwitha far below on earth, and fell in love with her. So he went down to woo her disguised as a bird, taking different forms in spring, summer and autumn. At last he carried her off to the sky in the shape of a giant hawk. But the dawn was angry with him for being away for so long, and tied him to her doorpost, turning Gendenwitha into the Morning Star, which shines above his head, where he cannot reach her and so must always long for her.

Sothis: Egyptian goddess of the dog-star, Sirius: later regarded as the same as *Isis*.

Spenta Armaiti: The Iranian earth-god, who represented devotion in moral terms; he was one of the *Amesha Spentas*.

Sphinx: In Greek myth, the daughter of *Typhon* and *Echidna*, the Sphinx had a lion's body, woman's face, and wings. Anyone who could not answer her riddle was killed by her, until *Oedipus* gave the correct answer.

Sphinxes are Egyptian in origin, where they were symbols of the god *Horus*; the most famous is the Great Sphinx at Giza, near the Pyramids.

Ssu Ling: The four spiritual creatures of Chinese myth: the ch'i-lin, the feng-huang, the tortoise and the dragon. The ch'i-lin was like a unicorn, with a deer's body, ox's tail, horses' hooves and a single horn. It appeared only before the birth or death of a great man. The feng huang or phoenix was a bird with beautiful feathers and an enchanting cry; it too appeared only when good fortune was at hand: it was the symbol of the south point of the compass. The tortoise was regarded as long-lived and righteous; when a thousand years old, it acquired the power of human speech. Tortoise shells were used to foretell the future: they were thrown on the fire, and the cracks that appeared were meant to foretell coming events. With the snake, the tortoise was lord of the north. The dragon was also a bringer of good fortune, and the sign used to indicate the power of the emperor: it was the creature which symbolized the east. Dragons were lords of water, both in the sea and rivers and in the rain-clouds. Another, earlier tradition gives the white tiger as lord of the west, and calls the snake coiled round a tortoise the 'black warrior' of the north, underlining that the animals were really symbols.

Ssu Ming: Chinese god, the 'Master of Fate', who acted for the Heavenly Power *Shiang Ti* in dealing with men. He ruled over life and death, protecting good men and punishing the wicked.

Ssu Ta T'ien Wang: The four Buddhist *Lokapalas* who became kings of heaven in native Chinese myth. They guarded the temples and each ruled over the point of the compass. They were: To Wen (*Vaishravana*) the black warrior, god of autumn, ruler of the treasures of the north; Tseng Chang (Virudhaka) the red god of summer, ruler of the south; Chih Kuo (Dhrirashtra) god of spring, whose colour was blue and ruled the east; Kuang Mu (Virupaksa) the white god of winter, ruler of the west.

Starkad: A Danish hero whom *Odin* particularly favoured, but whom *Thor* hated because his mother had preferred a giant to himself as a husband. So when it came to the time when Starkad's future was to be decided, Thor cursed him and Odin gave him blessings. Thor said he would have no children, while Odin said he would live for three generations. Thor replied by saying he would do hideous treachery once in each generation. Odin gave him the best of weapons and armour, but Thor said he would never have lands. Odin countered this by saying he would have many possessions, but Thor cursed him with a longing for yet more than he had. Odin promised victory in every battle; Thor sent him dreadful wounds; Odin granted him the gift of poetry, Thor that of forgetting all he ever composed. Odin ended by saying that the bravest and noblest men would be his friends, while Thor said that the common people would hate him.

243

This curious story reflects a deep rivalry between Odin and Thor: Odin is the devious, magical god whose gifts are not always what they seem, while Thor treats his worshippers honourably, giving them all the things he denied to Starkad.

Styx: A river surrounding the Greek underworld, *Hades*; its name means 'repellent'. The dead had to cross it to reach Hades, and the only method of doing so was by paying *Charon* to ferry them across. The gods themselves used to swear by the Styx; it was a very sacred oath, and if a god swore falsely by the Styx, he was punished by a year's unconsciousness and nine years' banishment from Heaven.

Sui-Jen: One of the Three Emperors in Chinese myth, granter of fire and ruler of heaven.

Sukuna-bikona: Dwarf-god who helped *Ō-kuni-nushi* to rule the Japanese region of Izumo. He was so small that he could stand on a man's palm, but was unable to walk. One day when the grain in his fields was ripening he climbed one of the stalks to look at it. The stalk sprang back, and he was thrown all the way to Tokoyo-no-kuni, the land of eternity.

Sul: A British goddess who presided over hot springs, particularly at Bath, where she was worshipped as Sul Minerva. A fire burned perpetually in her temple: according to a Roman writer, it never 'grew old', but turned into shining globes when the fire wasted away. It was perhaps a coal fire, which was strange to the Romans.

Sumur: The nomads of central Asia believed in a 'world mountain' called Sumur, which rose out of the north until its peak reached to the North Star. Some stories said that it was square, and had three great steps in it; and on its summit stood a huge tree, the world-tree, which is a birch with golden leaves. The great snake *Abyrga* lay wound around the mountain.

Sun Hou-Tzu: The Chinese monkey-god, whose lengthy adventures are told in the story translated under the title *Monkey* by Arthur Waley.

Sunjata: Culture-hero of the Manding people of West Africa. He was the son of Fata Kung Makhang, king of Manding, and one of his wives

244

Sukulung Konte. Sunjata was Fata Kung Makhang's eldest son, and his father had promised to give his kingdom to his first son. But the messenger bringing the news of Sunjata's birth was slow in announcing it, and another son's birth was announced first. As a child, Sunjata was a cripple and only crawled until he was seven, but was very strong; when he came of age, he put on a huge pair of trousers which were said to belong to the future king of Manding. Soon after this, his father died, but Sunjata refused to take any of his belongings except for the *griots* or bards of his father's court. But he had nothing to pay them with, so he stole what they needed and gave it to them, thus earning his name Sunjata, 'stealing lion'. Sunjata's brothers plotted against him, and he had to leave Manding, with his mother and sister. At the court of a neighbouring king, he again passed tests which showed that he would be king of Manding, and he learnt from his mother that he was really the eldest son.

In the meanwhile Sunjata's brothers had been killed by Sumanguru. Sunjata returned to Manding and raised an army against Sumanguru; but refused to start fighting until the hero Tira Makhang arrived. Tira Makhang came on a bier, wrapped in a shroud, declaring that he would either kill Sumanguru or be killed by him. The fighting began but Sumanguru was invulnerable and Sunjata was in danger of defeat. So Sunjata's sister went to Sumanguru and pretended to be in love with him. She learnt his secrets: he was the son of a djinn, and he had two mothers. Only by killing his father, with an arrow tipped with a white cock's spur, could Sumanguru's strength be destroyed. In order to escape he would then change into different animals in turn, and he told her all the shapes except the last one. Sunjata's sister escaped from Sumanguru and told Sunjata Sumanguru's secrets. One of Sunjata's warriors shot the magic arrow, and next day Sumanguru's town was destroyed by Sunjata's men. Sumanguru tried to escape, but Sunjata followed him in each different shape he took, until the last one, which Sunjata did not know, and so Sumanguru got away. Sunjata became king of Manding and founded the great empire of Mali.

In other versions Sumanguru is a rival claimant for the kingdom of Manding, and tries to kill Sunjata while he is still a boy, but is unable to do so; omens always predict that Sunjata will be king in the end.

245

Some make Sunjata's birth mysterious. One story tells how a giant buffalo laid waste the king's lands, and two hunters went to kill it. The younger hunter helped an old woman to carry a basket, and in return for his kindness she told him that she took the form of a buffalo each night. As she was destined to die in a few days, she told him how to kill her, and also to ask for the king's ugliest daughter as a reward. But when he had done all this, he found that his wife had strange powers, so he gave her to a great magician. Sunjata was her son by the magician, and grew up to become king of Manding.

There are numerous variations in other parts of the story, as it is a very popular epic, and widely told in West Africa.

Surt: A fire-giant, associated with the sons of *Muspell*, who at *Ragnarok*, the Norse day of judgement, will defeat the gods and 'cast fire over the earth', consuming it in flames. An underground cavern in the lava in Iceland is called Surt's Cave.

Surya: The Hindu sun-god, whose other names are *Savitri* and *Vaivasvata*, the rising sun; he was father of the *Ashvins*. He was married to the daughter of *Vishvakarman*, who found his light so overpowering that she left him; but her father seized the sun and cut away one-eighth of its light, and she was able to return to her husband. From the parts that were cut away the weapons of the gods were made, *Vishnu*'s discus, *Shiva*'s trident, *Kartikeya*'s lance and *Kuvera*'s treasures.

Susa-no-wo: The Japanese storm-god, brother and great rival of *Ama-terasu*, the sun-goddess. He was ruler of the sea, but neglected his kingdom and tried to take over his sister's territory. He destroyed her rice-fields and disturbed her worshippers, so that she retired into a cave and refused to come out. When she was persuaded to return, Susa-no-wo was punished and sent to wander on earth as a human being. When he first reached earth, he met an old couple and their beautiful daughter, who were sitting and weeping. They told him that the girl was the last of their eight children, because a great serpent appeared each year and ate one of them. Susa-no-wo offered to rescue the girl, if he could marry her, and they agreed. When the serpent appeared Susa-no-wo put a large bowl of very strong rice-wine in front of each door of the house. The serpent drank these and fell asleep,

so Susa-no-wo was able to kill it. In its tail he
found a magic sword which he gave to Ama-
terasu: the sword was called Kusanagi, and is
said to be the same as the one called by that name
today which is kept with the imperial treasure.
He founded a kingdom at Izumo on the coast of
Japan, which was later taken over by Ō-kuni-
nushi. The sword, together with a jewel and a
mirror are the three symbols of sovereignty.

Suttung: When *Kvasir* was killed, according to
Norse myth, the two dwarfs who slew him made
mead from his blood, which inspired anyone who
drank it to become either a prophet or a poet.
But the two dwarfs also killed the father and
mother of the giant Suttung, and in revenge he
lured them into a boat, rowed them out to a rock
which was submerged at high tide, and left them
there. However, they managed to persuade him
to save them by offering him the magic mead in
exchange for their lives.

   The gods were anxious to obtain the mead, and
Odin himself set out to win it. So he went to the
farm of Suttung's brother Baugi, and offered to
sharpen the scythes of his men as they reaped the
harvest. He sharpened them so well that they
quarrelled over the stone he had used, which
they all wanted. They began to fight, and killed
each other. Odin offered his services to Baugi in
their place, saying that he could get the harvest
in single-handed, if he would give him a drink of
his brother's mead in return. Baugi agreed to
this; but when they went to Suttung to get the
mead, Suttung refused to give his brother any.
So Baugi bored a hole in the mountain where
Suttung lived, and Odin changed himself into a
serpent and crawled in. He made love to Suttung's
daughter *Gunnlod*, who gave him three drinks
of the mead; and he swallowed it all. Then he
became an eagle and flew back to *Asgard*; once
he was safely within the walls he spat the mead
into three great vessels, and from this store he
gives inspiration to poets.

Svadilfari: The magic stallion who helped a
giant to build the home of the Norse gods,
Asgard. When the work was almost completed,
Loki took the form of a mare and lured him away.
Odin's horse *Sleipnir* was born as a result.

Svantovit: The chief god of the tribes living on
the river Elbe in eastern Europe. Little is known
of the myths about him; he was said to fight
those who opposed his worship, mounted on a

sacred white horse which was kept at his temple. He was highly regarded as a god of victory: three hundred soldiers were always in his service, and their booty was given to the temple. The great idol of Svantovit at Rügen was destroyed by King Waldemar of Denmark in 1168.

Svarga: In Hindu myth, the heaven of *Indra*.

Svarog: One of the gods of the Slavs, said to be the same as *Hephaestus*; he was perhaps their chief god.

Swan Maidens: Three sons of the king of Finland, one of whom was Volund or *Wayland*, were at their hunting lodge deep in the forest when they met three girls on the shores of a lake; near them there lay their swan-forms which turned them into birds. The youths seized these and took the girls as their brides; but after seven years they managed to get the bird-forms back and flew off, never to reappear.

Tagaro: Hero of stories from the New Hebrides in the Pacific, Tagaro was said to have been responsible for all the good things in the world, while his rival Suqe-mata produced all the bad things. To decide whether plants could be eaten by men, he and Suqe-mata tossed them in the air as soon as they were made, and if Tagaro caught them, they were edible, while if Suqe-mata caught them they were poisonous.

Tagaro married a girl from the sky, who could make plants ripen by touching them. But Tagaro's brothers scolded her for picking fruit before it was ready, and she fled back to the sky. Tagaro shot an arrow into the sky, which stuck there; he then shot another hundred arrows each into the end of the one before, to make a bridge. He climbed up into heaven and fetched his wife, who unwillingly followed him down. When they were halfway back she cut the bridge in two with an axe. She climbed back into the sky, while Tagaro fell to the earth.

Taikomol: 'He who walks by himself', the creator in the myths of the Yuki Indians of California. The first world which he made floated on the waters, which had always been there; but after a little while, it sank. The next world was dark, and there were no animals to eat, so people ate each other. So Taikomol burnt it, and made another. This new world was not very secure so he balanced it by making three great animals, an elk, a coyote and a deer, lie down at one end of it. When they move, there is an earthquake. Then Taikomol made men, and taught them to dance. One day, a man made a wrong step in the dance, and died. Taikomol buried him, and brought him to life again the next day, but no one would dance with him because of his smell. So after that people stayed dead when they died.

Taiowa: The great creator in the myths of the Hopi Indians of Arizona. He created Sotuknang and ordered him to make the universe. Sotuknang made water, land and air, and then Tokpela, the first world. In it he made Kokyangwuti, or spider woman, who helped him by creating the twins Poqanghoya and Palongawhoya. These two formed the earth, its mountains, rivers and seas, and helped to keep it in good shape and order. Then Kokyangwuti made all living things, and, last of all, mankind; but she could not make men speak and had to ask Sotuknang to help.

But after a time, men grew disobedient, and listened to Mochni, the mocking-bird and Kato'-

ya, the snake, instead of Palongawhoya, the voice of the creator. So the first world was destroyed by fire, and with it all the men who had been disobedient. Those who were left lived underground with the Ant People until Tokpa, the second world, was ready. In this world men and animals lived apart; and it did not last long, because men began to trade with each other, and to quarrel. So the twins Poqanghoya and Palongawhoya stopped controlling the world and it spun over and over in disorder and everything froze. Only a few good men escaped, going below ground again to live with the Ant People; and in due course Sotuknang reshaped the world. But this lasted even less time; and at the end of it Sotuknang did not even trouble to destroy it, but simply flooded it, while the good people were sealed up in hollow reeds by Kokyangwuti, and floated on the surface of the water. When the waters went down, they made rafts from their reeds, and travelled eastwards in search of the fourth world. They landed on various islands, but each time they were told to continue, until they came to a line of great cliffs. They tried to land, but could not find a place until they turned southwards and found a sandy bay. Here Sotuknang met them, and told them that they had reached Tuwaqachi, the Fourth World, which was not easy and beautiful like the previous worlds. And from their landing place, the 'place of emergence', the clans wandered across the land until they finally settled in Arizona.

T'ai-Yo Ta-Ti: The Emperor of the Eastern Peak in Chinese myth, ruler of the world and of men. A man's spirit came from him and returned to him at death.

Taka-mi-masubi 'High-producing-god' in Japanese myth, who appeared after *Kuni-toko-tachi* at the beginning of the world, and helped to create it.

Talus: A bronze giant who guarded Crete, made by the Greek god *Hephaestus* and given to *Minos*. He walked round the island three times a day, and threw anyone whom he caught into a fire. *Medea* killed him by enchanting him to sleep and drawing the bronze pin in his heel which sealed in his blood, so that he bled to death.

Tammuz: Sumerian god of corn and vegetation, who died each winter and revived in the spring. He was loved by *Ishtar*, the fertility-goddess, and her journey to *Arallu* was in search of him. He was later identified with *Adonis*. See *Inanna*.

Tane: Polynesian god of the trees: it was he who separated earth and sky at the beginning of the world. He was also the creator of man. In one story he did this by making a clay model of what he wanted; when it was complete he stood it up and gave it life, calling it Tiki. He also made Iowahine, Tiki's wife, in the same way.

Another version of the story tells how he took different goddesses as his wives, but they never produced real children, only stones, grasses and such like. So he made a woman out of earth, *Hina* or Hine-ahu-one, and married her. Their first child was an egg, from which the ancestor of all the birds came, but then they had a daughter followed by a son, and Tane was content. Tane later married his daughter, but when she found out that he was her father, she killed herself and went to the underworld to become goddess of night, Hine-nui-te-po. When he tried to bring her back to the world, she refused, saying that she would stay there and drag his descendants down there as well. See *Rangi, Tangaroa*.

Tangaloa: A myth from the Pacific island of Samoa tells how Tangaloa created the world. In the beginning there was only a great stretch of water, and Tangaloa's bird, Tuli, could find nowhere to rest. So Tangaloa threw a rock into the sea and it became an island; then he made the other islands of Samoa. The bird complained that there was no shade, so Tangaloa planted a vine; and when the vine grew, he made men from it. Tangaloa is called *Tangaroa* elsewhere in the Pacific.

Tangaroa: In the myths of the Polynesians Tangaroa is the creator of the world. In Tahiti he was said to have made the sky from the shell of the egg in which he sat and contemplated before he began creation. He had to create the world in the dark, because the shell was held down on the earth by a great octopus. *Tane* eventually pulled earth and sky apart, and only then was there light.

Tano: The great river-god of the Ashanti people of West Africa, spirit of the river of the same name. His wives and children and relations were the gods of other rivers and streams of the region. He was second son of *Nyame*, and managed to cheat his eldest brother Bia of his share of Nyame's

lands, so that he received the rich lands of Ghana, while Bia got only the less prosperous area to the west. Tano once had a singing-match with Death, but could not defeat him, and had to allow Death to come with him to the town where mankind then lived.

Tantalus: A Greek king who tried to test the wisdom of the gods by serving them the flesh of his son *Pelops* to see if they could tell what it was. The gods realized at once what they were being offered except for *Demeter* who was brooding over the loss of *Persephone* and absent-mindedly ate a shoulder. Pelops was brought to life again by the gods and given an ivory shoulder as a replacement; and Tantalus was condemned to eternal punishment in *Tartarus*, where he stands up to the chin in a pool surrounded by fruit-trees; he is always hungry and thirsty, but when he tries to eat the wind blows the branches out of his reach and the water vanishes when he tries to drink it. He also lives in eternal fear, because a rock is balanced precariously above his head, about to crush him.

Tapio: The Finnish god of the forest: with his wife Mimerkki or Mielikki and daughter Timlikki he controlled the forests and the wild creatures that lived in them.

Tara: In Tibetan Buddhist myth, the saviour goddess, the female partner of *Avalokiteshvara*, who also appeared in other forms.

Taranis: A Gaulish god mentioned by the Roman poet Lucan. Lucan was horrified by the way in which human victims were burnt, several at a time, in wooden cages as a sacrifice to him. His symbol was the sacred wheel, but little else is known about him.

Tarksya: A name of the *Garuda* bird, in Indian myth.

Tartarus: Part of the Greek underworld, *Hades*, where the very wicked are punished: see *Danaids*, *Ixion*, *Sisyphus*, *Tantalus*, *Tityus*.

Tarvos Trigaranus: A bull-god worshipped by the Gauls in Roman times; an altar now in Paris shows him with three cranes, but nothing is known about his myths.

Tathenen: An Egyptian earth-god; *Ptah* in a different form.

Tatsuta-hime: Japanese goddess of the autumn, her name means 'lady who weaves the brocade', because the autumn leaves are like a rich tapestry.

Taurt: An Egyptian goddess of good luck and of childbirth popular among ordinary men and women. She was shown as a strange monster, a mixture of lioness, hippopotamus and crocodile.

Tawhaki: Maori hero whose father was seized by evil spirits when he went in search of a birth-gift for his new-born son. Tawhaki grew up to be very handsome, and although he had many rivals, he always outwitted them. His rivals once disguised themselves as fish and tore all his skin off when he was taking part in a diving competition; but his grandmother gathered the pieces of skin and stuck them back on again. His rivals laughed at him because he had no father, but eventually Tawhaki found out what had happened to him: his eyes had been put out and he had been thrown into a pit. Tawhaki set out to avenge him, and on the way met his blind grandmother, who sat at the entrance to the other world, which was reached by a swinging vine which led to the sky. Tawhaki first teased her by stealing her supper, but then restored her sight. She told Tawhaki and his brother Kaviki how to climb the vine, but Kaviki, who was not very clever, seized the wrong end and was swept off across the sky. Tawhaki rescued him and then climbed up from the roots of the vine. In the sky he found his way to the spirits and released his father; then he tricked the spirits into sleeping until it was daylight by blocking up all the places in their house where light could get in. They thought it was still night, but Tawhaki suddenly let the light in, which destroyed them all, because they could only live in darkness.

Tecuciztecal: Aztec moon-god. See *Nanauatzin*.

Tefnut: Egyptian goddess of moisture, one of the *Great Ennead*; wife of *Shu* and mother of the god and goddess *Geb* and *Nut*. She was always shown as a woman with a lion's head. See *Ra*.

Tejeto: The Caingang Indians of Brazil say that fire was brought to men by Tejeto, who turned himself into a white bird and threw himself into a stream which flowed past the house of the Master

253

of Fire. The Master of Fire's daughter picked him out of the water and put him near the fire to dry. He stole an ember, and the Master of Fire came after him. Tejeto hid in a crack in the cliffs, but the Master of Fire pushed his bow up into the crack trying to kill him. So Tejeto made his nose bleed and rubbed the blood on the end of the bow. The Master of Fire thought he was dead, and left him alone; and Tejeto carried the fire to men.

Tekkeitserktok: Eskimo earth-god, who was also lord of hunting, and to whom all deer belonged. Sacrifices were offered to him before the hunting season.

Telegonus: In Greek myth, son of *Odysseus* by *Circe*. In some versions of Odysseus' story, Odysseus was killed by Telegonus by mistake, when Telegonus came to Ithaca in search of his father.

Telemachus: In Greek myth, son of *Odysseus* and *Penelope*. He plays a large part in the *Odyssey*, first in searching for his father and later in helping him to kill his mother's suitors.

Tellumo, Tellurus, Tellus: Roman earth-deities; Tellus corresponds to the Greek *Gaia*.

Telyaveli: A god of the Lithuanians, who was a great smith: it was he who forged for *Perkuno* 'the sun as it shines on earth, and set the sun in heaven'.

Temaukel: The Ona tribes of Argentina believed in a god called Temaukel, whom they referred to as 'that one there above', because he lived above the stars and took little notice of men, except to inflict epidemics on them and to kill the occasional evil-doer.

Tengu: In Japanese myth, demons who were the spirits of proud men or men who died seeking revenge; they tried to harm mankind and stirred up all kinds of warfare and quarrels.

Tenjin: The Japanese god of calligraphy or beautiful writing and of poetry. He was a minister, Sugiwata Michizane, of the emperor, who was unjustly exiled; after his death, his spirit, known as Tenjin, revenged itself on his enemies by bringing them misfortune.

Tennin or Tennyo: Angels who lived in the heaven of *Amida* Buddha, Gokuraku Jōdo, in

Japanese myth. (Tennin are male angels, Tennyo female.)

Teotihuacan: Home of the gods in Aztec myth.

Tepeu: Creator-god of the Quiché Indians of Central America; their myths, recorded in the book *Popul Vuh*, told of him as one of the two beings who existed before everything else, the other being *Gucumatz*. Tepeu took no part in the work of creation after the heaven and earth had been formed, but left the work to *Hurakan* and Gucumatz.

Tepeyolhotli: Aztec god of earthquakes: his name meant 'heart of the mountain', and he was shown as a jaguar, which had to be given sacrifices in order to prevent earthquakes.

Terminus: Roman god of boundaries, worshipped in the form of the boundary stone itself; he was important in the early days of Rome when it was still largely a farming community.

Terpsichore: *Muse* of flute-playing or dancing.

Tethys: One of the Greek *Titans*, a goddess of the sea. Homer calls her the 'nurse of the gods'.

Teutates: A god of the Gauls, perhaps a kind of patron spirit of the tribe: like other Gaulish gods he was reputed to be offered human victims, who were drowned by being plunged head first into a vat.

Tezcatlipoca: Aztec god of night and of all material things, called 'god of the smoking mirror' because he carried a magic mirror which gave off smoke and destroyed his enemies: he was god of the north. As lord of the world and the natural forces in the world, he was the opponent of the spiritual *Quetzalcoatl*, and sometimes appeared as a tempter, urging men on to evil. But he rewarded goodness and punished evil; he tested men's minds with temptations, rather than trying to lead them into wickedness. He was also god of beauty and of war, the lord of heroes and lovely girls: he once seduced the goddess of flowers, Xochiquetzal, wife of the god *Xochipilli*, because such a lovely goddess was a good match for him as the handsome, warlike god.

Yet he appeared most frequently as a magician, a shape-shifter and a god of mysterious powers.

255

His animal symbol was the jaguar, which was sometimes believed to take human form, like the werewolf of European folklore. See *Five Suns*, *Quetzalcoatl*.

Thalia: *Muse* of comedy.

Thamyris: A Greek bard who claimed that he could outsing even the *muses*. For this boast they blinded him and made him forget his skill.

Themis: One of the Greek *Titans*, perhaps the original wife of *Zeus*. She is difficult to distinguish from *Gaia*, and there are close parallels between the three early pairs of gods in Greek myths, *Uranus* and *Gaia*, *Cronos* and *Rhea*, *Zeus* and Themis. She was the mother of *Prometheus* according to some versions.

Theseus: Early king of Athens, one of the greatest of Greek heroes. He was the son of *Aegeus* of Athens and Aithra, daughter of the king of Troizen. Aegeus left Aithra before Theseus was born, but hid a pair of sandals and a sword under a rock. He told Aithra that if she had a son she was to send him to Athens as soon as he could move the rock and recover the sandals and sword. When Theseus grew up, he regained the tokens as soon as he could, and set out. The usual way to Athens was by sea, because the land was full of brigands and robbers. Theseus chose to go by land, because he wanted to find adventures. First he met and overcame Periphetes, who killed travellers with a huge club; Theseus took the club and used it as his own weapon. Then he came to the home of Sinis, who used to tie down two bent pine saplings, and strap passers-by onto them, one leg to each sapling. He then cut the ropes holding the saplings, which sprang up and tore them apart. Theseus inflicted the same treatment on him, and continued on his way. He next met Sciron, who made travellers wash his feet on the edge of a cliff; as they knelt, he kicked them into the sea. Theseus dodged him and hurled him over the cliff instead. Lastly, he came to the home of Procrustes, who laid travellers on a bed and either stretched or cut them off short to make them fit. Theseus laid him on his own bed, and cut off his head as it stuck out over the end.

So he reached Athens in safety, having cleared the road for other travellers. His father recognized and welcomed him; but it was the time of the annual tribute paid to King *Minos* of Crete in retribution for the death of his son Androgeus. Seven young men and seven girls were sent to Crete, where they were shut up in the *Minotaur*'s labyrinth, and were either devoured by the monster or lost their way and starved to death. Theseus volunteered to go with them, as one of the seven young men. If he returned safely, his ship was to use a white sail, if he was killed the sailors were to hoist a black sail which they had used on the outward voyage. When he reached Crete, *Ariadne*, the king's daughter, fell in love with him. She gave him a sword and a ball of thread, and laying the thread so that he could find his way out again, he reached the heart of the maze and killed the Minotaur. He then traced the thread back, and escaped with the other intended victims, taking Ariadne with him as well. They landed on the island of Naxos, where he abandoned Ariadne and sailed on without her. As they approached Athens, he forgot to hoist the white sail, and his father threw himself off a cliff because he thought that Theseus had died.

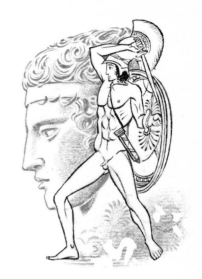

Theseus therefore became king of Athens, where he ruled wisely and well. He sheltered both *Oedipus* and *Heracles* in their exile. He fought a number of wars, including one against the *Amazons*; he defeated them, and married their leader *Hippolyta*. His later years were marred by the tragedy of the death of their son *Hippolytus* through the scheming of his stepmother *Phaedra*, Theseus' second wife. Some say that his reign ended when the Athenians rebelled against him, because he was too just and severe for them, and that he died in exile; others tell how he and his friend *Pirithous* the *Lapith* went down to *Hades* and tried to carry off *Persephone*. Hades caught them and bound them fast forever to two chairs; however, Theseus was later released by Heracles and was eventually killed by *Lycomedes*.

Thetis: Daughter of the Greek sea-god *Nereus* who was fated to bear a son who would be greater than his father. Both *Zeus* and *Poseidon* were in love with her, but *Zeus* discovered the prophecy from *Prometheus* in time, and she was married to the mortal *Peleus*, king of Iolcus, to whom she bore seven sons. She killed six of them in her efforts to make them immortal by holding them in a fire, but Peleus saved *Achilles*; she had to content herself by making him invulnerable by holding him in the waters of the *Styx*, and she then left Peleus in fury. It was at their wedding feast that Eris threw the apple which led to the judge-

ment of *Paris* and to the *Trojan War.*

Thialfi: Servant of the Norse god *Thor.*

Thor: The Norse god of thunder, called by the Anglo-Saxons Thunor. Thursday is named after him; in Germany he was called Donar, and Thursday is called Donnerstag.

He was the eldest son of *Odin*, and his mother was Fjorgyun or Earth. He was huge, red-bearded and red-eyed, and was immensely strong. Each day the gods met at the Well of *Urd*, and while the others rode there, Thor came on foot, wading through any rivers that lay in his path. He rode across the sky in a wagon pulled by two goats. Thunder was the noise made by this wagon as it rattled along. He was the great enemy of the frost-giants, and defended *Asgard* against them. His power was increased by his three treasures: the hammer *Mjollnir*, which always returned to his hand when he threw it, a belt of power which doubled his strength, and iron gloves with which he grasped his hammer. The hammer was his special sign, and is one of the commonest images in Norse art. Little hammers in a shape rather like a cross were carried as charms in the tenth century because Thor's hammer was used to bless new-born children and marriages and to protect houses against fire, or theft. Once Thor found that his hammer was missing, and sent *Loki* in search of it. Eventually Loki found it hidden deep in the earth by the giant Thrym. Thrym would only return it if he was given the goddess *Freyja* as his wife. The gods were furious, and Freyja shattered her famous necklace *Brisingamen* in her rage. But *Heimdall* suggested that Thor should dress up as Freyja and go with Loki to the giant's home, pretending to be the bride. Thrym was taken in by the disguise when they arrived, but when they sat down to the wedding feast, Thor's huge appetite nearly gave them away, because he ate a whole ox and eight salmon. Loki quickly explained this by telling Thrym that 'Freyja' had been so anxious to come and marry him that she had not eaten for eight days. Then Thrym tried to kiss his bride, but was so terrified by a glimpse of Thor's fiery red eyes glowing through the veil that he retreated. Loki's excuse was that 'Freyja' had had no sleep for eight nights because she longed so much for the wedding. At last the hammer Mjollnir was brought in to bless the wedding; as soon as Thor had it in his hands he stood up and killed Thrym and the other giants, and

258

returned safely to Asgard.

In some ways Thor is the rival of Odin, as in the story of *Starkad*. He is the god of law and order, and the champion of ordinary people against Odin's wild warriors; he keeps faith, while Odin does not, and oaths were sworn by the sacred armring of Thor. Odin's worshippers were killed in battle or touched with a spear before death, and were burnt when they were dead. Thor's worshippers were buried in mounds, where Thor protected them. He and Odin represent two sides of human nature in the same way as *Apollo* and *Dionysus* in Greek myth, the division is the same, though Thor is nearer to *Zeus* as a thunder-god.

He was a fierce opponent of Christianity when it came to Iceland. While the other gods were generally regarded as surrendering without a fight, Thor once wrecked a Christian missionary's ship by 'blowing out his beard' at it; and one of his followers said that he challenged Christ to single combat, and Christ did not dare to accept the challenge.

See also *Geirrod, Hymir, Midgard-serpent, Utgard Loki*.

Thorgerd Hölgabrud: A guardian-goddess of the rulers of northern Norway who was particularly worshipped by Jarl Hakon in the tenth century; perhaps the same as *Freyja*.

Thoth: Egyptian god of wisdom and magic, who played an important part not only in the judgement of the dead (see *Osiris*) but also in *Seth*'s attempts to oust Osiris and *Horus*, when Thoth presented Osiris' case and supported Horus before the *Great Ennead*. He was also the god of the magical power of writing, and god of judgement, distinguishing between right and wrong words.

In early times, he was the moon-god, because the moon's changing appearance gave knowledge of the passing of time. *Khensu* later became god of the moon, and he and Thoth were often thought of as the same god.

Thunderbirds: Most American Indian myths associate thunder with birds, and the belief is also found in Asia. The thunderbird haunted the realm of winds and clouds immediately above the earth, and was an invisible spirit. The lightning was the flashing of his eyes, the thunder the noise of his wings. There were also lesser thunderbirds, such as the golden eagle. Mountain

Indians believed the thunderbird to be a small red bird, which shot lightning arrows from its wing, the thunder being its wing rebounding. For the Pacific Coast Indians it was a vast creature with a lake on its back from which the rain came; it ate whales and left their bones on mountain-tops.

T'ien: Heaven or the sky in Chinese myth, which was worshipped at the end of the year and beginning of the new year. The Chinese emperors were always known as 'Son of Heaven'.

T'ien Fei or T'ien Hou: Chinese goddess of the sea. When she lived as a human being she had supernatural powers and used them to protect her brother when he went to sea.

Tiermes: Thunder-god of the Lapps, also called Horagalles: reindeer were sacrificed to him; and great carved wooden hammers were given as offerings.

Tiki: The first man in Polynesian myth: see *Tane*.

Tiphys: In Greek myth, pilot who accompanied *Jason* on the *Argo*; he was endowed with superhuman skill.

Tirawa-Atius: The 'power above' in Pawnee Indian myth. He created the heavens, and put a race of giants on earth: but he killed the giants because they were too proud, replacing them with men. He supported the sky, putting a great buffalo in the north-west corner: it lost one hair each year and when all its hairs fell out, the world would end.

Tiresias: Greek prophet from Thebes who lived for seven generations. He once saw two snakes coupling, and killed the female; he was at once turned into a woman, and only became a man again when he found another pair of snakes and killed the male. *Zeus* and *Hera* once argued as to which sex got more pleasure from making love; when Tiresias, from his experience of both, declared that women did, Hera blinded him in a rage, but Zeus gave him the gift of prophecy and a long life. He advised the Thebans during *Oedipus'* troubles and during the war of the *Seven Against Thebes*; and when he died he was the only dweller in *Hades* who was allowed to keep his memory and the power of speech (though other

spirits could speak after tasting a blood sacrifice).
Here *Odysseus* questioned him as to how he should
reach home.

Tir na Nog: The Land of Youth in Irish myth,
the same as the world in which the inhabitants
of the fairy mounds lived.

Tirthankaras: 'Perfect saints' in the Jain mythology of India. There are 720 of them, twenty-four
in each age of the ten continents of the universe.
The twenty-four of this world in the present age
are the gods of the Jains.

Tishtrya: The spirit of the dog-star, Sirius, in
Iranian myth. As the star which appeared in
high summer, Tishtrya was said to bring cooling
showers by fighting the demon *Apaosha* who
had carried off the waters, and forcing Apaosha
to release them. They attacked each other in the
shape of horses: Tishtrya became a beautiful
white horse with golden harness, while Apaosha
appeared as a bald black horse. At their first
encounter Tishtrya was beaten back, but he
attacked again and drove Apaosha away from
the sea Vourukasha where the waters were
stored. He made the sea overflow, and the rains
descended. This battle was usually said to be
repeated each year, but some versions of the
myth say that this battle only took place once,
long ago, and Tishtrya used the water from
Vourukasha to destroy all kinds of evil creatures
which *Angra Mainyu* had created.

Titans: Children of the first Greek gods, *Uranus*
and *Gaia*; their names are usually given as *Ocean*,
Crius, *Coeus*, *Hyperion*, *Iapetus*, Theia, *Rhea*, *Themis*,
Mnemosyne, *Phoebe*, *Tethys* and *Cronus*. They all,
with the exception of Themis, fought against
Zeus in a battle which raged for ten years; in the
end Zeus and his allies won, and the Titans were
bound.

Ti-Tsang Wang: Chinese god (the Indian
Kshitigarbha) who delivered souls from the kings
of the ten hells and sent them instead to paradise.
He had once been a priest of *Brahma*, but was
converted to Buddhism and became a Buddha
himself, with special powers over the dead.

Tityus: In Greek myth, Tityus attacked *Leto*,
mother of *Apollo* and *Artemis*: for this he was
chained in *Tartarus*, where vultures peck eternally
at his liver.

Tiwaz: The god of the sky and of war among the early German peoples, called Tiw or Tig in England; from him we get our name for Tuesday. He may also have been known as Irmin, and the sacred pillar *Irminsul* was part of his worship. He is remembered as the god *Tyr* but among the Norse gods his place as god of law and justice was taken by *Thor*. A further complication is that his name is very like that of *Zeus*, so presumably he was a sky-god in early times.

Tlacolotl: Maya god of evil, shown as a horned owl; he was the source of all disasters, because he had been thrown down from heaven, and took his revenge by harming men at random.

Tlaloc: Pre-Aztec rain-god later adopted by the Aztecs, ruler of a pleasant heaven, Tlalocan, the land of water and mist. Here the dead passed their time in earthly enjoyments, with abundance of food and flowers and beautiful things. After a time they were reborn on earth, and repeated the cycle of death and return to Tlalocan unless they wished to reach the more spiritual heaven of *Quetzalcoatl*. Tlaloc was also the lord of growing plants and crops: his name meant 'He who makes thing sprout'. See also *Five Suns*.

Tlaltecuhtli: The Mexican 'lord of the earth', a toad with jaws gaping waiting for human sacrifice and the victims of war, on which it fed his open mouth also swallowed the setting sun each evening.

Tlazolteotl: The earth-goddess in Aztec myth, shown with a death's head mask: she ruled over unpleasant things such as dirt and sin. She was the mother of Cinteotl, the corn-god.

Tloque Nahuaque: The supreme god in late Aztec myth, always present but invisible. He seems to have been the result of philosophical thinking about the nature of God, like the Egyptian *Aten*.

To-Kabinana and To-Karvuvu: In Polynesian stories, To-Kabinana and To-Karvuvu were brothers; the first was clever, the second stupid. To-Kabinana made many good things, but To-Karvuvu spoilt them by making bad imitations: To-Kabinana made beautiful women, his brother tried to imitate him and made ugly ones. To-Kabinana made porpoises, while his brother made sharks. When To-Karvuvu was told to go and look after his mother, he roasted and ate her because he had misunderstood what his brother said, and so brought death into the world.

Tonacacihuatl: Wife of the Aztec god *Tonacatecuhtli*, sometimes said to be the same as *Xochiquetzal*.

Tonacatecuhtli: The food-giving god in Aztec myth, who set the world in order at the creation, dividing sea and land: sometimes said to be the same as *Ometeotl*.

Tonapa: Legendary teacher of the Incas, who after a time of war and troubles appeared in Peru and performed many miracles, teaching the inhabitants about *Viracocha*. The early Spanish missionaries regarded him as the apostle St Thomas.

Tonatiuh: Aztec sun-god and god of the present age (see *Five Suns*), who ruled over the heaven reserved for warriors, Tonatiuhican. This may originally have been the highest spiritual paradise, for those who had fought against worldly temptations and overcome them.

Torngasak: The 'good spirit' of Eskimo myth, representing everything in nature which is helpful to man.

Triptolemos: The messenger sent by the Greek goddess *Demeter* to teach men how to plant corn, in gratitude for the return of her daughter *Persephone*.

Trita: In Iranian myth, the discoverer of *haoma*, the *soma* plant, and the great healer who asked *Ahura Mazda* to provide him with means of conquering sickness and was given all kinds of medicinal plants.

Triton: A kind of Greek merman; it is not clear whether there was only one or many. He was in many ways the marine equivalent of *Silenus*. He is always shown blowing a conch-shell, with which he commanded the waters.

Troilus: Son of King *Priam* of Troy; although he appears in Homer's *Iliad*, the story of his love for *Chryseis* or Cressida which has inspired a number of famous works is an invention of the Middle Ages and was first written down about AD 1200.

Trojan War: When the Greek Prince *Menelaus* married *Helen*, her other suitors, who included most of the leading men of Greece, swore to abide by Helen's choice, and to help her husband if need be. After *Paris* eloped with Helen to Troy, this oath led to an alliance of all the Greek princes to recover her. The Greek fleet, under the leadership of Menelaus' brother *Agamemnon*, gathered at Aulis. Here, because Agamemnon had offended *Artemis*, the army was delayed until he had sacrificed his daughter *Iphigeneia* to the goddess. When, after various other adventures, they finally reached Troy, they built a great camp, and from this vainly tried for nine years to take the city, defended by *Priam* and his sons under *Hector*'s leadership.

At the beginning of the tenth year, the famous quarrel between Agamemnon and *Achilles* took place. Agamemnon had seized the slave-girl Briseis, allotted to Achilles as booty, because he had had to return *Chryseis*, who had been given to him as a result of the same raid. Achilles refused to fight on the Greek side, and retired to his tents. Only when Hector drove the Greeks back to their ships and threatened to set them on fire did Achilles relent a little, and allowed his friend Patroclus to fight in his place. Patroclus was killed by Hector, and Achilles at last took up arms again in order to avenge his death. He killed Hector, but refused to give up his body to Priam for burial. After twelve days he was finally persuaded to change his mind when Priam himself came to him and begged him for it. Achilles was killed by Paris, who shot him in the heel with a poisoned arrow.

The Greeks now sent for Achilles' son *Neoptolemus* and for *Philoctetes*, but they were still unable to take the city. At last a plan was made to gain entrance by a trick. With *Athene*'s help a huge wooden horse (the Trojan Horse) was made, large enough to hold a number of men. This was then left outside the city filled with warriors, with a dedication saying that it was sacred to Athene, and the fleet sailed away. The Greeks left one man behind, who said that his comrades had tried to kill him in a quarrel; in revenge he was ready to tell them the secret of the horse. If it was ever taken inside the city, he said, Troy could never be captured; and for this reason it had been built too big to go through the gates. The Trojans, despite the warnings of *Laocoon* and *Cassandra*, broke down the walls and dragged it inside. The next night the fleet returned, the horse was opened, and the warriors inside let their comrades into the city. After a short but fierce fight the Greeks took Troy and burnt it, killing the men except for a few, such as *Aeneas*, who escaped, and taking the women away as slaves.

Trolls: In Norse myth, beings with magic power, particularly evil and monstrous creatures, such as the giants, Grendel and other beings which attack men and houses at night.

Ts'ai Shen: The Chinese god of riches, who controlled an elaborate divine ministry of wealth.

Ts'ang Chien: Inventor of the art of writing in Chinese myth; his signs were based on the marks made by birds walking in the sand, and there were 540 of the signs altogether.

Tsao Chün: Chinese god of the hearth; each household has its own Tsao Chün, and according to his annual reports to heaven, made on the twenty-third day of the twelfth month, that household will have good or bad luck, so sacrifices are offered to him each month. He was originally the god of fire and of the furnace in which metals were forged.

Tsui'goab: The rain-god of the Hottentots, called Tsui'goab or 'wounded knee' because he was wounded there when he fought and killed his great rival Gaunab. He himself died, but came back again; this happened several times. He created the first man and woman; but his real power was as god of rain, which he controlled. He also gave health and riches to his worshippers.

Tsuki-yo-mi: Japanese moon-god.

Tu: War-god of the Polynesian islands; human sacrifices were offered to him. See *Rangi*.

Tuamutef: Egyptian god who guarded the stomach of a dead man after it had been embalmed. He was shown with a jackal's head.

Tuat: The underworld in Egyptian myth, through which the sun-god *Auf* passed each night.

Tuatha De Danann: In Irish myth, the last of the divine races who inhabited Ireland. Their

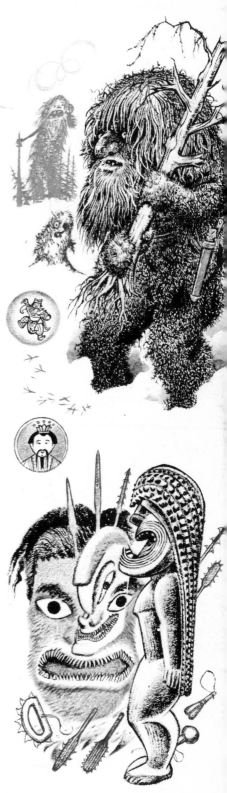

name means 'tribes of the goddess *Danann*'. They invaded Ireland under their king *Nuadu*, and defeated the people living there, the *Fir Bolg*, at the first battle of Moytura. They were magicians, and when they first appeared in Ireland it was in a magic mist, led by their druids.

They ruled Ireland in alliance with the *Fomorians*, until the meanness of the latter led to the second battle of Moytura and the driving out of the Fomorians. The Tuatha De were in turn defeated by the *Sons of Mil* at the battle of Tailtiu; but they deprived their enemies, by magic, of all milk and corn, until they agreed to divide Ireland with them. The lower half, the underground, was given to the Tuatha De who lived in the fairy mounds or *side*.

Tuchaipa: Among the Yuman tribes of southern California, Tuchaipa and Kokomat were two brothers born at the bottom of the sea. Kokomat was blinded by the salt water as he rose to the surface. Tuchaipa created everything good, but Kokomat's attempts to imitate him produced evil or clumsy creatures. Web-footed birds were the result of his efforts to imitate Tuchaipa's creation of mankind. But Tuchaipa offended his daughter, Frog, and she killed him. The mourning for the dead Tuchaipa was an important part of Yuman religion.

Tucupacha: Creator-god of the Tarascan people of Central America; he made a man and woman of clay, but they were dissolved when they went bathing, and he had to make a second pair, of ashes and metal: their descendants peopled the world.

Tuirenn: The children of Tuirenn, in Irish myth, were at war with Cian. They surprised him alone but he turned himself into a pig. The children of Tuirenn became hounds and chased him: when they caught him, they stoned him to death; but he prophesied that the weapons used to kill him would tell his son Lug of his death. And so it happened: Lug was told of his death by the earth and he demanded payment from the children of Tuirenn, making them fetch magic treasures which were hard to obtain. The last of the tasks was to raise three shouts on Miodhchaoin's hill, where all noise of this kind was forbidden by Miodhchaoin. When they shouted, Miodhchaoin attacked them, and only a magic skin which Lug owned could cure them. But he refused to help them, and so avenged himself for his father's death when they died in torment.

Tukma: The Juaneño Indians of the coast of California told how the world, the sea, animals and plants were created by Night or Tukma. He fastened the earth by means of a huge black stone, the tosaut. The ocean was over-crowded, until a fish dived down and brought up the tosaut, which was filled with a bitter fluid. This was emptied into the ocean, and it spread until it reached its present size. After this, Tukma created Ehoni, the first man, whose grandson was *Wiyot*. (In other versions of the story, Wiyot was the first man.)

Tung Wang Kung: Ruler of the male immortals (*Hsien*) in Chinese myth.

Tuonela: Finnish otherworld, under the earth, also called *Pohjola* or Manala. It was surrounded by a black river on which neither sun nor moon shone, which was sometimes said to be turbulent rapids. A black swan was said to swim on the river. Souls were transported over it in a boat. *Vainamoinen* once visited Tuonela. The grave is described as a man's 'house in Tuonela'.

T'u-Ti: In Chinese myth, the local god, who was worshipped when good weather was needed or when other homage to nature needed to be paid. Such gods were often people who were famous in the district while they were alive.

Tvastri: A name of *Vishvakarman*, the great artist and craftsman of the Hindu gods, whose skill lay chiefly in metalwork: it was he who made *Indra*'s thunderbolts on his forge. He was also the god who gave things their form and created the physical world and everything that is beautiful.

Tyche: Greek name for the mother-goddesses who protected the various cities in the Middle East: there were different Tyches for Damascus, Antioch and Palmyra, for instance.

Tydeus: One of the *Seven Against Thebes*, son-in-law of the Greek king *Adrastus*. When he was mortally wounded *Athene*, who favoured him, intended to make him immortal; but he had a furious temper, and when she came to him she found him gnawing the head of Melanippos, who had given him the wound and whom he had killed. Revolted by the sight, she left him to die.

267

Typhoeus or Typhon: A monster born after the battle of the Greek *Titans* with *Zeus*, child of *Tartarus* and *Gaia*. It had a hundred snake's heads with five eyes in each, and it made strange noises which could only occasionally be understood. It attacked the world and *Olympus* itself, and Zeus hurled it back with a thunderbolt. As it fell, the earth was scorched, but it was not defeated. Seizing Zeus' sickle, it maimed Zeus and threw him in a cave, taking the muscles of his hands and feet which it had cut out. *Hermes* stole these back and Zeus got safely back to heaven. Here he took up his thunderbolts again, while the *Fates* lured Typhon into eating mortal food, which weakened it. Zeus finally defeated the monster and buried it under Mount Etna. See also *Seth*.

Tyr: An early Norse god of war, whose earlier name was *Tiwaz*; his original place as the sky-god may have been taken over by *Odin*. Like Odin, he could give victory in battle, and swords were marked with the rune letter T so that the god Tyr would bring their owners success in battle. Also like Odin, he fights a giant hound – in this case, the dog which guarded the gates of *Hel* – at the day of *Ragnarok*. It was he who brought up the *Fenris-wolf*, and who lost his hand when he bound it with the fetter *Gleipnir*.

Ukemochi: Japanese goddess of food. She was once visited by *Tsuki-Yo-mi*, and offered him a feast which she produced out of her own mouth. Offended at this he killed her; but when he told his sister *Ama-terasu* she was horrified and said she would never see him again, which is why the sun and moon appear at different times.

Ukko: Thunder-god of the Finns. When seed was sown in the spring, a great drinking feast was held in his honour, to make sure that rain and a good harvest followed. Food was offered to him by being put in a chest and carried to his sacred mountain. In the epic *Kalevala* he appears as the greatest of the gods and ruler of heaven.

Ulgen: Among the tribes of central Asia, Ulgen is said to have created the world, making the earth in the shape of a disc, which he supported on three great fish, one under the centre, and one each to east and west. When he came to make earth – because at first there was only water – he could not think how to begin, until Man appeared. Ulgen asked who he was, and Man said that he had come to create earth as well. Ulgen was angry and told him to find some earth-matter, if he was so clever. Man took the shape of a diver-duck and dived down into the water and came back with a piece of earth in his mouth. Some of this he gave to Ulgen, who made dry land with it, but he kept the rest until Ulgen made him spit it out, when it became marshes and swamps. Man later became the devil, Erlik, and was lord of the dead, while Ulgen was lord of the living.

Ull: A Norse god about whom little is known except that he may have been one of the *Vanir*, and was a great archer and skier.

Ulysses: The Roman name for *Odysseus*.

Unkulunkulu: In Zulu myth, Unkulunkulu is both the first man and the creator, the 'great one of old'. He created everything, and gave the world its order, showing men how to live together.

Upuaut: The Egyptian god who guarded the dead on their way to the hall of *Osiris*: he was closely associated with *Anubis*.

Urania: *Muse* of astronomy.

Uranus: First of the Greek gods, his name means

Heaven or Sky. He was not much worshipped as a god, but appeared in the myths about the early days of the gods. He was married to *Gaia* or Earth, by whom he had the *Titans*. The youngest of these, *Cronos*, overthrew him and took his place. The outermost planet of the Solar System is named after him.

Urd: Each day the Norse gods used to assemble to take council at the Well of Urd, where they settled disputes and discussed common problems. Urd was one of the *Norns* and her name means 'fate'. From her name we get our word 'weird', which has come to mean strange or mysterious, because fate seemed to be strange and mysterious.

Ushas: The goddess of the dawn in Hindu myth, eternally young and beautiful.

Utgard: In Norse myth the name of the outer regions, which were thought to lie to the east of the home of the gods, and to be inhabited by giants.

Utgard-Loki: The Norse god *Thor* was once on his travels with *Loki*, driving his chariot harnessed with goats. They lodged at a farmhouse, and Thor killed the goats to provide food. He told the farmer and his family to keep the bones and put them with the skins; but the farmer's son cracked one of the bones with his knife to get at the marrow. During the night, Thor blessed the bones with his hammer, and the goats came to life again; but one was lame. Furious, Thor raised his hammer against the farmer and his family; but they managed to appease him by sending the son and the daughter, Thialfi and Roskva, as his servants, to go with him. Then Thor set off with them on an expedition into the land of giants. The first night that they spent there, they found themselves in the middle of a great forest, and searching for somewhere to sleep, they came across a huge hall with no-one in it. They went to sleep, but were awoken at midnight by a terrible roaring noise and an earthquake, and Thor advised them to move into a side hall which he had found. When morning came, they saw an enormous giant sleeping not far off, snoring loudly, and Thor realized that this was the cause of the earthquake and strange noises in the night. The giant stood up, and asked Thor if he had moved his glove; when Thor looked he realized that what they had thought was a hall was the

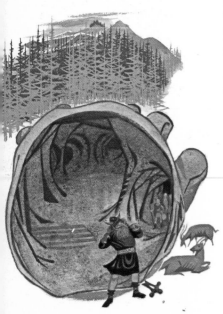

giant's glove, and the side hall was the thumb of it. They agreed to go on their journey in the giant's company, and to share their food with him, as they were a little short of provisions. So Skrymir, the giant, went on ahead, carrying all the food, and the next night they found a great oak tree under which to shelter. Skrymir went to sleep without eating anything, but told Thor to undo his bag and help himself. Try as he might, Thor could not begin to undo the bag; in a rage, he picked up his hammer *Mjollnir* and hit the sleeping giant. To his amazement, Skrymir merely woke up and asked if a leaf had fallen on him. Thor said that that was what must have happened; but he was determined to get his revenge, and at midnight he swung Mjollnir with all his might on the top of the giant's head. Skrymir, waking up again, asked if an acorn had fallen on him, even though Thor could have sworn that the head of the hammer went right into his skull. So Thor tried again, and thought that he sank the whole hammer in the giant's temple; Skrymir merely asked if a twig had dropped from the tree above. In the morning, Skrymir went off to the north, but first showed them the way to *Utgard*. He warned them that there were much bigger men than himself there, and that they should not try boasting in such company.

Thor and his companions reached Utgard; but they could not open the gate, and finally had to squeeze through the bars. Eventually the king, Utgard-Loki, noticed them, and recognized Thor. He said he was surprised that he looked so small, and asked what his companions were good at, because they only welcomed guests who had some special skill.

So Loki said that he could eat faster than anyone else; and Utgard-Loki called for Logi to come and compete with Loki. They were given a huge trencher full of meat, and they each started at one end; they reached the middle at the same time, but Loki had only eaten the meat, while Logi had eaten the bones and the trencher as well.

Thialfi then came forward and said that he was a very good runner. Utgard-Loki called for Hugi to race against him. They went outside, and found a good place to run: the first time Hugi finished in time to turn round and come back to meet Thialfi, the second time there was the distance of an arrow fired from a bow between them, and the third time Thialfi had only got halfway when Hugi finished.

Now it was Thor's turn, and Utgard-Loki said

that he expected some great feat, after all that he
had heard about Thor. Thor chose to try his skill
at drinking, and a horn that was used by Utgard-
Loki's men was given to him. It was long, though
not very big; he took a deep breath, and being
very thirsty, drank as hard as he could, but there
was little difference in the level of the liquid. The
next time it had gone down a little when he had
finished drinking; and the third time he thought
he had made some difference to the amount in
the horn.

'You're not as strong as I thought you were,'
said Utgard-Loki; 'try lifting my grey cat off the
floor.' Thor put his arm round it, as it was quite
large; it arched its back when Thor tried to lift it,
and all he could do was get one of its paws off
the ground. Thor then said that he would like to
try a wrestling match, because he was really
angry now. Utgard-Loki said that his old foster-
mother, Elli, would be a good match for him.
The harder Thor tried to throw her, the firmer
she stood and it was Thor who was forced down
onto one knee. So Utgard-Loki stopped the contest. Thor and his companions were well entertained, and they stayed at Utgard that night.

Next morning, Utgard-Loki went to see Thor
and his companions off and Thor was depressed
by his failure the previous night. 'On the contrary,' said Utgard-Loki, 'I shall never let you
in here again, and I would never have let you in
last night if I had known that you were so strong.
For I worked magic spells on you. I was Skrymir,
and the bag you tried to open was bound with
iron. If you go back to where you tried to hit me,
you will find a great hill with three huge square
pits in it, because I put the hill between you and
me, and those are the holes the hammer made.
When Loki tried to race Logi at eating, he was
competing against fire, which burnt up the
trencher as well as the meat. Thialfi was running
against my thoughts; and the horn you were
drinking from had one end in the sea. When you
began to empty it a little at the third attempt,
we were all terrified, because the sea started to
go down. The cat was the *Midgard-serpent*, and
you nearly wrenched it from the sea-bed where
it lies; and the old woman was Old Age herself,
which overcomes everyone.' Thor raised his
hammer to strike Utgard-Loki, but he vanished;
he turned to destroy Utgard, and there was only
a broad grassy meadow to be seen.

Utgard-Loki also appears in the story of King
Gorm. Gorm particularly honoured Utgard-Loki,
and once despatched his counsellor Thorkill to

seek him and consult him as to the future. Thorkill, suspecting treachery, insisted that those who had suggested that he should be sent should come with him, and Gorm agreed. After a dangerous voyage into a region where there was no day, the sun never shone and the stars never appeared, they reached the cavern of two giants, a squalid place full of rotting filth and snakes. Thorkill was told to journey for four days until he came to a land where no grass grew. Here Utgard-Loki lay, in a filthy cave. They found the spot, and discovered him, a huge monster, bound in chains, and surrounded by poisonous snakes. Thorkill managed to pluck one of the gigantic hairs from his beard, but only five of the company survived the poison dripped on them by the snakes. Their return journey led them to Germany, where Thorkill became a Christian. When they at last returned to Gorm, the king died of horror when he learnt that his favourite god was a monster.

In both stories the figure of Utgard-Loki has a great deal in common with Loki; in the encounter with Thor he is the trickster and arch-deceiver, and in the second story he is the bound giant, living in a poisoned world.

Utnapishtim: The Sumerian equivalent of Noah, the only survivor of the great flood which covered the earth. The god *Enlil*, angered by the tumult made by mankind, decided to flood the world, but *Ea* warned Utnapishtim to make a boat and gather his family and animals into it. When the waters rose, the boat floated for seven days as the rains fell; on the seventh day, they ceased, and the boat went aground on a mountain. Utnapishtim offered a sacrifice to all the gods except Enlil, because Enlil had caused the flood; Enlil was angry but the other gods told Enlil that he had been wrong to flood the earth. He forgave Utnapishtim and made him immortal; sending him to live in the garden of *Dilmun*.

Uzume: Japanese goddess of mirth: see *Amaterasu*.

V

Vac: The goddess of speech in Hindu myth, who helped *Prajapati* in the work of creating the world.

Vafthrudnir: *Odin*, chief of the Norse gods, once challenged the giant Vafthrudnir to a contest of knowledge. Each wagered that he would die if he was unable to answer all the questions put to him. After a long struggle, Odin at last asked Vafthrudnir, who did not know who his opponent was, what Odin had whispered in *Balder*'s ear as he lay on his funeral pyre. Vafthrudnir realized that he was being questioned by Odin, and admitted defeat.

Vaikuntha: The paradise of the Hindu god *Vishnu*.

Vainamoinen: Son of *Luonnotar*, the creator-mother, in Finnish myth. The epic *Kalevala* tells of his adventures, beginning with his creation of plants. He was old from the day he was born, and was the greatest of all singers, able to sing spells which destroyed all his enemies. He won Aino from her brother Joukahainen, who had dared to challenge him to a singing-match, but Aino refused to marry such an old man, and drowned herself. He then sought to marry the daughter of Louhi, lady of *Pohjola* but had to admit that he could not make the *sampo* talisman which she demanded in return, and sent *Ilmarinen* to woo the girl instead. Ilmarinen made the *sampo*, but the girl refused to marry him for the moment. *Lemminkainen* and Vainamoinen both tried to win her in the meanwhile: Vainamoinen began to build a ship in which to reach Pohjola again, but was unable to complete it for want of three magic words. So he questioned the sleeping giant Antero Vipunen, who swallowed him. Vainamoinen tortured him from inside until he released him and taught him the spells. But when he had built the boat and reached Pohjola, the girl chose Ilmarinen instead, and a great wedding feast was held.

She died not long after, and Ilmarinen married her sister. She made him so angry that he turned her into a seagull and vowed revenge on Louhi, her mother. With the help of Vainamoinen and Lemminkainen, Ilmarinen set out to take the sampo. On the way they killed a huge pike and Vainamoinen made a harp from its jawbone. With this he lulled Louhi to sleep, and the three heroes made off with the sampo. Louhi pursued them, and in the battle which followed the sampo was broken. Vainamoinen managed to seize most of the pieces and planted them in his kingdom, where they brought prosperity. But Louhi still sought to destroy him, and sent a bear to attack his herds. He killed it and sang such songs to celebrate his victory that the sun and moon came to listen. Louhi seized them and locked them up, and put out all the fires in Vainamoinen's land of Kalevala. Ilmarinen and Vainamoinen sought new fire from *Ukko*, and although it nearly destroyed them, Ilmarinen made a new sun and moon from it. But they would not shine, so the two heroes went to Pohjola and forced Louhi to release the old ones. Vainamoinen was eventually overcome by a child (Christ) magically born to a girl called Marjatta (the Virgin Mary), and departed from his land, to come again when he should be needed, an ending which reflects the triumph of Christianity over the old paganism.

Vaishravana: A name of the Hindu god *Kuvera*.

Vaitarani: The river which was the boundary of hell in Hindu myth, a swift-flowing stream which runs with blood and filth.

Vaivasvata: *Manu* of the present age in Hindu myth. See *Vishnu*. 1. Matsya (the fish *avatar*).

Vajra: The thunderbolt carried by the Hindu god *Indra*, shown as a circular disc with a hole in the centre.

Vajrapani: One of the *Dharmapalas* of Buddhist myth, a form of the Hindu god *Indra*.

Valaskjalf: The hall of the Norse god *Odin* which contained the seat *Hlidskjalf*.

Valhalla: The hall of the Norse god *Odin*, where he offers hospitality to all those slain in battle and chosen by him. Each night they feast on a boar which is revived each morning, and on mead from the goat *Heidrun*. Each day they fight, and the dead are revived each evening to join in the feasting. They are served by *Valkyries* who also act as guides to those chosen for Valhalla and escort them to it. Odin chooses the greatest champions to go there, because he needs their help on the day of *Ragnarok*. The hall itself is filled with shields and mailcoats, wolves and eagles roam in it, and it has hundreds of doors so

that when *Heimdall* sounds his trumpet on the fatal day, the warriors can all rush out at once to attack the enemy.

Vali: The son of the Norse god *Odin* who was to avenge the death of *Balder* by killing *Hoder*. He is one of the gods who will inherit their world after the day of *Ragnarok*.

Valkyries: In Norse myth, the attendants of the warriors in *Valhalla*. They were warlike women, who wore armour and rode splendid horses, and they carried out Odin's orders on the battlefield, giving victory according to his wish. Their appearance was a sign that battle was about to begin, and they also wove a web of fate deciding the outcome of battles, rather as the *Norns* wove individual fates before birth.

Vamana: The Hindu god *Vishnu* in his fifth *avatar* as a dwarf.

Vanir: In Norse myth, the group of gods originally opposed to the *Aesir* and later allied to them. The chief of them was *Njord*, and his children *Frey* and *Freyja* were the most important. They may represent the gods of an earlier race who were combined with those of later invaders of Scandinavia. Similar divisions are often found in myths, as for example in the Irish stories about the *Tuatha De Danann* and the *Fir Bolg*.

Varaha: The Hindu god *Vishnu* in his third *avatar* as a boar.

Varuna: God of the sky or universe in Hindu myth, and spiritual ruler. His counterpart is *Mitra*, temporal ruler. In early legends, he appears as one of the greatest gods, but later stories make him a less important figure, one of the *Adityas*. Even later, he was regarded as the god of seas and rivers, and he is shown riding on a *Makara*. In the early legends he appeared as all-powerful and all-knowing, the god who arranged the workings of the universe; he decreed each man's fate and judged them according to his laws, which men could never discover; their only hope was to fear and worship Varuna. He is depicted with a noose, with which he binds offenders.

Vasishtha: A great Hindu sage (*maharishi*) and one of the ten *Prajapatis*. His great rival was another sage, Vishvamitra. He and Vishvamitra competed to become priest to King Kalmashapada; but Vasishtha's eldest son Saktri once met the king in the road, and refused to give way to him, saying that by law a king should give way to a member of the Brahman class. The king struck him with a whip, and Saktri cursed him, saying that he would become a man-eater. At this the king devoured Saktri and all Vasishtha's other sons. Vasishtha tried to kill himself out of grief, but whatever he tried, failed. He threw himself over a cliff, but the rocks at the bottom became soft and cushioned him; a forest fire refused to burn him; the sea refused to drown him, and rivers dried up when he threw himself into them. So he returned to Kalmashapada and exorcised him from his curse.

In other legends, the rivalry between Vasishtha and Vishvamitra takes the form of a battle over a cow of plenty which Vasishtha owned. Vishvamitra tried to seize it, but the cow, which produced anything Vasishtha needed, supplied him with an army, and Vishvamitra was driven off. They were also supposed to have fought as two monstrous birds, and their struggle was so fierce that *Brahma* had to put a stop to it lest the universe should be destroyed.

Vasuki: Another name of the Hindu serpent-king *Shesa*.

Vasus: The gods of nature and the elements in Hindu myth; there are eight in all, representing water, fire, earth, light and wind; and the moon, the pole star and dawn.

Vata: The Iranian god of the winds.

Vayu: The Hindu lord of the winds, a god who rides with *Indra* in his chariot. He was king of the *Gandharvas* and father of *Bhima* and *Hanuman*, the monkey-god.

Ve: One of the brothers of the Norse god *Odin*, who helped him and Vili to slay *Ymir*. Nothing else is known about him.

Vediovis: An early name for Jove or *Jupiter*; perhaps originally the Etruscan god of lightning.

Veles: A god of the Russians in pagan times, who was the patron of flocks and of harvests. The last ears of wheat at harvest were left 'for Veles' beard'.

Venus: Originally the Roman goddess of

gardens, she was later identified with the Greek *Aphrodite*. The Romans did not think of her at first as a love-goddess, but as the goddess who made things grow if they were sown and cultivated; later she took on the same character as Aphrodite.

Verethraghna or Bairam: Iranian god of victory. He was born in the ocean, and overcame two great dragons of evil, *Azhi* and Vishapa, and chained them to a mountain. He appeared in ten different shapes, from a great wind to a fine golden-horned bull, including a camel, boar, a swift bird, a ram and lastly as himself, a hero in fine garments.

Vertumnus: A minor Roman fertility god, husband of *Pomona*.

Vesta: The Roman goddess of the hearth, identical with the Greek *Hestia*. The Vestal Virgins who guarded her shrine at Rome were originally the daughters of the king; later there were six of them, from noble families, who were not allowed to marry until they had served for thirty years. If the fire which they tended went out, the Vestal Virgin responsible was whipped and had to rekindle it with a special wooden borer and board, a very primitive method of making fire.

Vidar: Son of the Norse god *Odin* who avenges his father's death by tearing the *Fenris-wolf* in half, at the day of *Ragnarok*. He does this by putting his heel on the wolf's lower jaw, protected by a special shoe made of the scraps of leather which are pared away when the heel of a shoe is shaped by a cobbler. These scraps had to be thrown away to help in the making of Vidar's shoe.

Vidyadharas: The attendants of the Hindu god *Indra*, good spirits who inhabit the air and help men.

Vigrid: Plain where the Norse gods will fight their last battle against the forces of *Surt* and the sons of *Muspell* on the day of *Ragnarok*.

Viracocha: Supreme god of the Incas of Peru. He was the creator and made the earth, sky, stars and mankind, though his two sons Ticci Viracocha and Imaymana Viracocha also played a part. In some myths, there is no distinction between father and sons, and Viracocha seems to have meant 'the creator' in general, whether he was one god or several. Ticci Viracocha was said to be a tall man, clad in white and robed like a Catholic priest.

After Viracocha made the world, it passed through five ages, rather like the idea of *Five Suns* in Aztec myth. The first was the age of gods, followed by those of the giants, the savages, the warriors and finally that of the Incas, ended by the arrival of the Spaniards.

Another version says that Viracocha's first creation, a world of giants who lived in darkness, because there was no sun, was destroyed by him in a great flood, and he began his work again. The moon was originally brighter than the sun, but the sun made it dimmer by throwing ashes at it. When Viracocha had finished, he set out across the western sea, promising to send his messengers to teach his people (see *Tonapa*).

There are many parallels between Viracocha and the Aztec god *Quetzalcoatl*.

Vishnu: One of the three great gods of Hindu myth, the others being *Brahma* and *Shiva*: Vishnu is the preserver, and Brahma sprang from a lotus which grew from Vishnu's navel, while Shiva came out of Vishnu's forehead. As preserver of creation, Vishnu has taken on human or other forms at intervals in order to rescue the world from some great evil, or to provide some great benefit. These forms or incarnations are called *avatars*, and are usually said to be ten in all.

1. Matsya, the fish *avatar*. In this incarnation, Vishnu took the form of a golden fish with a single horn in order to save the Manu Vaivasvata from the great flood at the beginning of the present age. In this shape, he not only warned Manu of the flood, but towed his ship to safety when it was nearly wrecked on the Himalayas.

2. Kurma, the tortoise *avatar*. When the *amrita* was recovered from the ocean, Vishnu helped by becoming a tortoise, whose back was used as a support for the stick with which the sea was churned.

3. Varaha, the boar *avatar*. The demon Hiranyaksha had worshipped Brahma so faithfully that he was told that no creature that he named would be able to attack him; but once he had obtained this protection, he terrorized mankind and dragged the earth down to his haunts at the bottom of the sea. But Hiranyaksha had forgotten to ask for protection against boars, so Vishnu took the form of a boar, killed Hiranyak-

279

sha and dragged the earth up into its proper place again.

4. Narasimha, the man-lion *avatar*. *Hiranyakashipu*, brother of Hiranyaksha, had also been promised by Brahma that he would not be killed by day or night, inside or outside a house, by man, beast or god. Protected by this, he banned the worship of the gods, and set himself up as a god instead. But his son Prahlada insisted on worshipping Vishnu, saying that Vishnu was everywhere and all-powerful. Hiranyakashpu argued with him at twilight on the threshold of his house, and struck one of the pillars of the doorway, asking if Vishnu could possibly be in a pillar. Vishnu came out of the pillar as a man-lion, and devoured him; it was neither day nor night, he was neither in his house nor out of it, and Vishnu appeared as neither man nor beast.

5. Vamana, the dwarf *avatar*. Bali was a king who honoured the gods and ruled well, but had the great fault of being too ambitious. But his goodness made him irresistible, and the gods eventually had to yield the heavens themselves to him. So Vishnu took the form of a dwarf, and asked Bali, who was renowned for his generosity, for as much land as he could cover in three paces. Bali granted this, but Vishnu at once grew to such a size that in two paces he covered the earth and heavens, and regained all Bali's lands. As compensation, Vishnu gave him the *Patalas*, which he would have taken in the third pace, and Bali now rules there.

6. Parashurama. The rest of Vishnu's *avatars* were in human shape. In the first of these he was born as the son of a Brahman hermit, Jamadagni, who owned a marvellous cow. At this time the Kshatriyas or warriors were tyrants, and persecuted the Brahmans, and one of their kings seized Jamadagni's cow. Parashurama killed him, but his sons took revenge by killing Jamadagni. In the wars which followed Parashurama destroyed all the Kshatriyas, and then retired to the mountains to end his days as a hermit.

7. Rama. See under *Rama*.

8. Krishna. See under *Krishna*.

9. Buddha. The Hindus regard Buddha as an incarnation of Vishnu, just as Buddhist myths include some of the Hindu gods as minor gods in the Buddhist heavens. The version of his teaching is very different, because Vishnu took this shape in order to lure wicked men to their own destruction.

10. Kalki. The future incarnation of Vishnu. He will appear at the end of the present age as a

man riding on a white horse, and will destroy the wicked with a fiery sword, preparing the way for the end of the world and its renewal in the next age.

Vishnu's wife is *Lakshmi* or *Sri*, and he rules over the heaven *Vaikuntha*, made of gold and jewels. Other legends make *Aditi* either his wife or mother.

See also *Bharata*, *Bhrigu*, *Gandharvas*, *Ganges*, *Garuda*.

Vishvakarman In Hindu myth, the architect of the universe, the same as *Tvastri*. It was he who reduced the splendour of *Surya*, the sun, to whom his daughter was married, because his brightness was too much for her. See also *Jagannath*.

Vohu Manah: God of domestic animals in Iranian myth; on a moral level he represented good thoughts, and was one of the *Amesha Spentas*.

Vritra: The demon of drought, with whom the Hindu god *Indra* is constantly at war.

Vulcan: The Roman god of fire; although he represented destructive fire (his temple was always outside the city gates for this reason) he was identified with the Greek smith-god *Hephaestus*, who was fire in its constructive aspects.

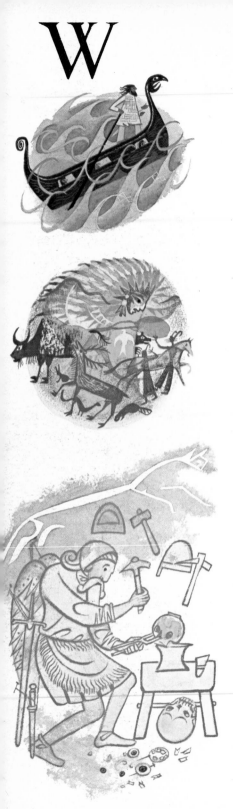

W

Wachabe: Wachabe, the black bear was regarded by the Osage Indians (a Sioux tribe from the Missouri River) as a guardian power and a symbol of long life, strength and courage. His actions are the subject of many of the 'wigies' or sacred songs of the Osage, and formed the basis for their ceremonies.

Wade: Son of the sea-giantess Wachilt in Norse myth. His name occurs in a number of place-names in northern England, where he was remembered as a legendary giant. He was also said to have had a boat made of two halves of a tree tightly fitted together which had glass windows and could go underwater.

Wakahiru-me: Younger sister of *Ama-terasu*, the Japanese sun-goddess; she was goddess of the rising sun.

Wakataka: The creator-god of the Sioux Indians of mid-western America, who made first, the earth, and then a man and a woman who were the parents of the Sioux. He also made all furred animals that swim, and all the animals that are hunted for food.

Wang: Guardian of *Yu Huang* the Jade Emperor's palace door in Chinese myth. He was called 'the Official above all officials', and he was specially called on to drive away evil spirits.

Wata-tsu-mi: God of the sea in Japanese myth, son of *Izanagi and Izanami*. See *Hoho-demi*.

Wayland, Weland: Son of the giant *Wade*; famous as a smith in the poetry of the Anglo-Saxons. King Alfred used his name to show how great and famous men were subject to death: 'Where are now the bones of that famous and wise goldsmith Weland? I say the wise, since from the skilful man his skill can never depart, and can no more be taken from him than the sun can be turned from his course. Where are the bones of Weland now, and who knows where they may be?'

Alfred was, of course, a Christian, but he knew the pagan tale of Weland well. Weland the smith was famous for his marvellous work, but a king who envied his talent captured him and made him lame so that he could not escape. In revenge, he lured the king's two sons into his workshop, killed them, and made two richly jewelled drinking cups from their skulls, and a brooch from their bones. These he presented to the king, and then escaped by magic, flying away as if he had wings. The story has also come down to us in Norse tales, but the most famous place associated with Weland is Wayland's Smithy, a prehistoric stone monument on the Berkshire Downs near the White Horse carved in the chalk at Uffington. Here, as late as the eighteenth century, people believed that if you left a horse and some money, it would be shod when you returned, Wayland having done the work.

Wên Ch'ang: The Chinese god of literature, who was originally a scholar who lived in the third or fourth century A.D. He was greatly respected by the Taoists, and widely worshipped. Before his statue a black horse with two servants was placed; the servants were deaf and dumb, to show that the examinations were fair, because they could not be persuaded. He was usually shown with *K'uei-Hsing* and Chu I, the gods of examinations.

Wen-Shu Yen-K'ung: Chinese name of *Manjushri*.

Wild Hunt: In northern European folklore, a procession of damned souls who ride furiously through the air during storms. Their leader is sometimes said to be *Woden* or *Odin*.

Winds: The names of the spirits of the winds in Greek myth were: *Boreas*, the north wind, *Zephyrus*, the west wind, *Notus*, the south wind, *Eurus*, the east wind. *Aeolus* was their ruler. The Romans called them Aquilo, Favonius, Auster and Eurus.

Wisagatcak, Wisakedjak, Whiskey Jack: The trickster-god who created the world, according to the Cree Indians of Canada. He once tried to trap one of the giant beavers who lived at the beginning of the world, and made a dam across the beaver's creek. But he failed to catch the beaver, and all the beavers made magic against him, so that when he took the dam away, the water that flowed out of the creek covered all the land. Wisagatcak made a raft, and all kinds of animals climbed aboard. After a fortnight, the musk-rat dived down to find land; but it was so far down that he drowned. Then the raven went to look for it, but could find no sign of land whichever way he flew. It was only when Wisagatcak made his own magic with the help of the wolf that the earth came back. He made a ball of moss, which turned into earth and spread out over the whole world, so that the land rested on water.

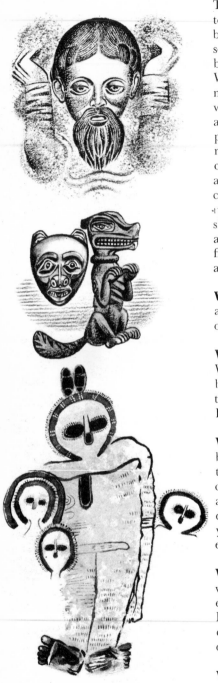

Wiyot: Wiyot appears as the first leader of men in the myths of the Juaneño Indians of California. There are different versions of his story. One tells how from the earth and sky (who were brother and sister and the first things to exist) soil and sand, stone and flint, and trees were born. After these came animals and finally Wiyot, from whom all men were descended. As men increased in numbers, the earth grew southward and men followed. Wiyot ruled men, but a plot was hatched against him and he was poisoned. The coyote, who had been assistant ruler under him, prevented him from being cured, and at his funeral tore off part of his body and swallowed it. A different version relates how a coyote stole his heart at the funeral, but Wiyot reappeared in the form of the moon. Some versions of the story go on to tell how *Chingichnich* appeared after Wiyot's death and turned the first humans into animals and plants, and created a new race of men.

Woden, Wodan, Wotan: The Anglo-Saxon and German names for *Odin*, from which we get our name for Wednesday, Woden's day.

Wolf: In some versions of the story of *Nanabozho*, Wolf takes the place of Chipiapoos, as Nanabozho's younger brother who is drowned and then revived. In the myths of western American Indian tribes, he appears as brother of *Coyote*.

Wondjina: In Australian aborigine myth, the beginning of the world was called the 'dreamtime', and according to one story, there were creatures called wondjina who lived then. They almost all became rock paintings when they died, and these paintings are retouched each year so that the wondjina will bring rain at the end of the dry season.

Wu Ti: The Five Rulers in Chinese myth. They were the four protectors of the regions of the empire, north, south, east and centre; the Yellow Emperor, *Huang Ti* was the protector of the centre. The worship of the fifth, the Black Ruler of the North, was instituted in the third century B C.

Wu Yo: The Five Sacred Mountains in Chinese myth, actual mountains which corresponded to the five areas protected by the *Wu Ti*. The most important was T'ai Shan, the eastern peak, in the province of Shantung, which was regarded as a very high-ranking god.

Xanthos and Balios: The two immortal steeds of the Greek hero *Achilles*, endowed with the power of speech. They were the children of Zephyrus, the west wind, and the *Harpy* Podarge.

Xilonen: Aztec goddess of the young corn.

Xipe Totec: The 'skinned god' in Aztec myth, god of spring. Each year he was stripped of his skin, just as a seed loses its husk, as a sacrifice to ensure that the new season would return again. He was regarded as a despised, diseased creature before his sacrifice, suffering from scabs and sores, but as a splendid god once he had lost his old skin, his decay and renewal corresponding to that of nature. He was said to be *Quetzalcoatl* in a different form.

Xiuhtecuhtli: Aztec god of fire, also called Huehueteotl, 'the Old God', because his rites were very ancient. Sacrifices to him were particularly cruel: human victims were thrown on red-hot coals, and their hearts were then torn out.

Xochipilli: Aztec god of youth and beauty and of pleasure and feasts; his consort was Xochiquetzal, beloved of *Tezcatlipoca*.

Xolotl: Twin brother of *Quetzalcoatl*, Aztec god of wisdom. He was the companion of the sun, in the shape of a cripple; but he was also the god who played the ritual ball-game called *tlachtli* in a magic court, which was the heavens itself; so he controlled the movements of the stars.

Yadavas: The people over whom the Hindu god-hero *Krishna* ruled.

Yakshas: The spirits who attended the Hindu god of wealth, *Kuvera*; they are sometimes regarded as wicked, sometimes as beneficial, granting fertility. Yakshas are the attendants of *Devi* in her aspect as *Durga*, and are definitely evil.

Yakushi Nyorai: The Japanese Buddha of healing, who overcame disease by his skill and knowledge; one of the four principal Buddhas in Japan.

Yama: The god of the dead in Hindu myth, who judges men according to their deeds and places them either in one of the twenty-eight hells or sends them to be reborn on earth. His dogs wander among men, selecting those who are due to die. Older myths speak of Yama's heaven as well, where the righteous are splendidly received and entertained.

Yamm: The god of the sea and of chaos in Canaanite myth, against whom *Baal* fights.

Yang and Ying: The male and female principles in Chinese thought: Yang was light, Ying darkness, and from these two the whole universe came. They are not really myths in themselves but part of the teaching of Chinese thinkers, and hence all Chinese myths tend to be organized on this pattern.

Yao: One of the great just emperors of Chinese myth, in whose reign phoenixes appeared at the imperial court. He resigned in favour of his minister Shun, who was also renowned for his righteousness.

Yao Wang: The Chinese god of medicine, who once rescued a snake from being killed by a shepherd. The snake proved to be the son of the dragon-king, *Lung Wang*, and the latter rewarded Yao Wang by teaching him the secrets of medicine. Yao Wang once removed a bone from a tiger's throat; it wagged its tail gratefully and became his watchdog.

Yazatas: The 'venerable ones' in Iranian myth, lesser gods such as the spirits of fire and water, though they included *Mithras*.

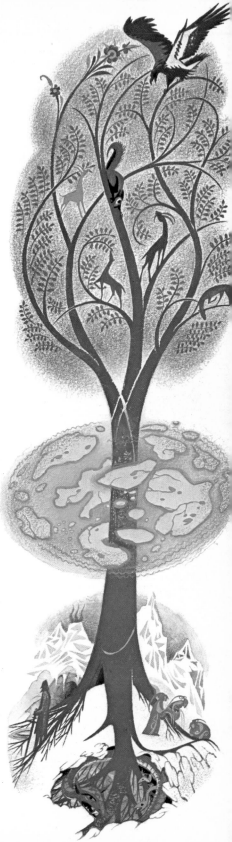

Yen-Lo Wang: Chinese name for *Yama*, god of the dead. He was, however, not the supreme lord of the dead, but only ruler of the fifth of the ten hells, having been dismissed as supreme lord because he was too lenient.

Yerah and Nikkal: The moon-god and goddess in Canaanite myth, whose marriage is described, in one of the few surviving texts from Canaan, as though it were an ordinary human wedding.

Yggdrasill: The 'world-tree' of Norse myth, which is a link between the separate worlds and which is the source of life. It is an ash tree, and it spreads out over the whole world of men, reaching up to the sky. It has three great roots, one in *Asgard,* one in the home of the giants, and one in *Niflheim.* It is always under attack: the serpent *Nidhogg* gnaws at the root which lies in Niflheim, along with a horde of other serpents. Four harts eat its shoots, led by the hart Eikthrynir. A great eagle, at war with Nidhogg, sits on top of it, and insults are exchanged between eagle and serpent by the squirrel *Ratatosk* which runs up and down the tree. Only the *Norns* care for it, watering it and whitening its roots with clay each day.

It is a source of knowledge, for *Odin* hung on it for nine nights and days to learn hidden knowledge; at its foot lies the spring guarded by *Mimir* from which Odin gains wisdom. Mimir also guards the tree.

It is the guardian tree of the world, just as a house or temple might have its own sacred guardian tree nearby.

At *Ragnarok,* it is shaken but not destroyed; and from its branches emerge *Lif* and *Lifthrasir* to repeople the world.

Yima: A great ruler of ancient times in Iranian myth, who had almost divine powers. He extended the earth three times because it became too small for the creatures living on it; and he saved mankind from being overwhelmed by the great flood and winter by building an enclosure. His only fault was to try to make men immortal by giving them sacrifices meant for the gods; for this he lost his throne and was overcome by the demon *Dahhak.*

Ymir: In Norse myth, a giant who was the first living creature, appearing from the melting ice on the edge of *Muspell.* From under his left arm the first man and woman grew, from his feet came the frost-giants. He was killed by *Odin,* Vili

287

and *Ve*, and all the frost-giants except *Bergelmir* were drowned in his blood, which became the sea. His skull was used to make the sky, his eyebrows became a wall round *Midgard*, the world of men. His brains became the clouds, his hair the trees, his bones the hills, and his flesh the earth.

Yo: A trickster in the myths of Dahomey in West Africa. He was distinguished by his great appetite, and most of the stories about him tell how his greed got him into trouble; but by using his magic powers he was usually able to escape punishment. He was neither a god nor a mortal: 'He is found everywhere. *Mawu* created him for no useful purpose. You cannot kill him, you cannot eat him. He is alone. One is enough for the world,' was how a storyteller described him.

Yo Fei: A Chinese commander who fought against the Tartars under the Sung dynasty in the twelfth century. From 1914, by official decree, he was worshipped as one of the two gods of war, the other being *Kuan Yu*.

Yomi-no-kuni: The Japanese underworld or 'land of gloom', home of the dead. It had two entrances, one a winding spiral road which began in the central province of Japan; the other was a great abyss on the sea-shore.

Yoskeha: In Iroquois Indian myth (from the north-eastern United States), Yoskeha was the grandson of *Ataensic*. He and his brother Tawiscara were twins; but they quarrelled before they were born, and Tawiscara killed their mother just after he was born. Yoskeha created everything good on the earth, while Tawiscara created all the unpleasant things when he tried to imitate Yoskeha. Ataensic disliked Yoskeha, because Tawiscara had persuaded her that he was responsible for their mother's death; but despite opposition from both of them, he managed to set the sun and moon in their places and to create man. In the end, he also succeeded in imprisoning Tawiscara in the underworld.

Yudhishthira: The eldest of the five *Pandava* princes, son of the god Dharma, heroes of the Hindu epic *Mahabharata*. Although it was he who was the leader of the family, Yudhishthira was also responsible for their misfortunes, particularly the loss of everything in the great gambling match against the Kauravas. See *Arjuna, Draupadi*.

Yu- Huang: The Jade Emperor in Chinese myth, identified with *Shiang Ti*, the heavenly ruler. He was born as heir to the imperial throne, but resigned after he had ruled for only a few days in order to become a hermit. He and *P'an Ku* were worshipped as the Great Creators.

Yu Shih: The Chinese rain-god, lord of the winds that blew from the ocean to the east of China and brought rain with them. He lived in the *K'un-Lun Mountain*, and had many magic powers: he could go through fire without being burnt, and through water and remain dry.

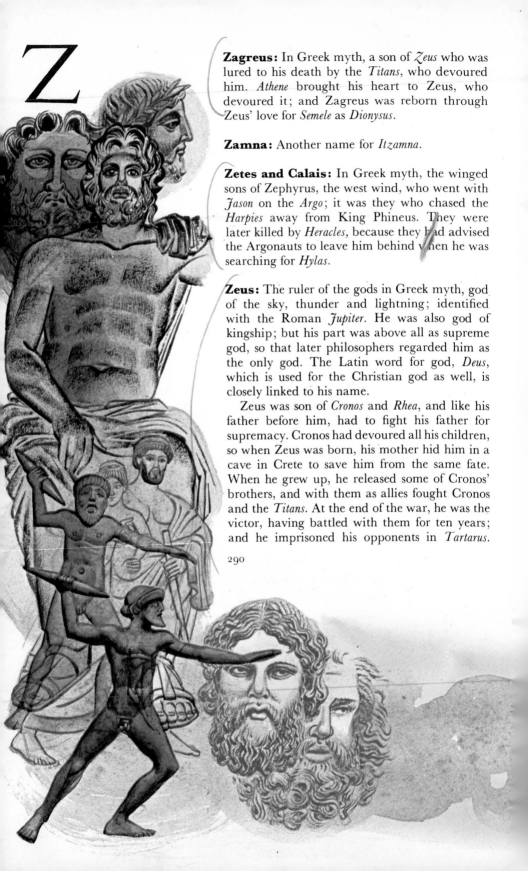

Zagreus: In Greek myth, a son of *Zeus* who was lured to his death by the *Titans*, who devoured him. *Athene* brought his heart to Zeus, who devoured it; and Zagreus was reborn through Zeus' love for *Semele* as *Dionysus*.

Zamna: Another name for *Itzamna*.

Zetes and Calais: In Greek myth, the winged sons of Zephyrus, the west wind, who went with *Jason* on the *Argo*; it was they who chased the *Harpies* away from King Phineus. They were later killed by *Heracles*, because they had advised the Argonauts to leave him behind when he was searching for *Hylas*.

Zeus: The ruler of the gods in Greek myth, god of the sky, thunder and lightning; identified with the Roman *Jupiter*. He was also god of kingship; but his part was above all as supreme god, so that later philosophers regarded him as the only god. The Latin word for god, *Deus*, which is used for the Christian god as well, is closely linked to his name.

Zeus was son of *Cronos* and *Rhea*, and like his father before him, had to fight his father for supremacy. Cronos had devoured all his children, so when Zeus was born, his mother hid him in a cave in Crete to save him from the same fate. When he grew up, he released some of Cronos' brothers, and with them as allies fought Cronos and the *Titans*. At the end of the war, he was the victor, having battled with them for ten years; and he imprisoned his opponents in *Tartarus*.

290

Zeus, *Poseidon* and *Hades* then cast lots for their father's domains, and Zeus held heaven, Poseidon the sea, and Hades the underworld.

Zeus married *Hera,* but he had numerous children by other goddesses and mortals, and it also seems that he married *Themis* before Hera. Hera was persistently jealous of his love-affairs, and persecuted any mortal who was loved by Zeus.

Zeus' authority was not always unchallenged; apart from his battle to gain power, he had also to fight the *giants* and *Typhon,* who nearly defeated him, and later the *Aloadai.* On another occasion he was rescued by *Thetis* when *Athene,* Hera and Poseidon plotted to overthrow him. But most Greek writers and poets portray him as securely established and even growing less fierce in his judgements as his rule continued, since such rebellions were things of the past. The last great defiance was that of *Prometheus,* who although severely punished, was eventually released.

291

Appendixes

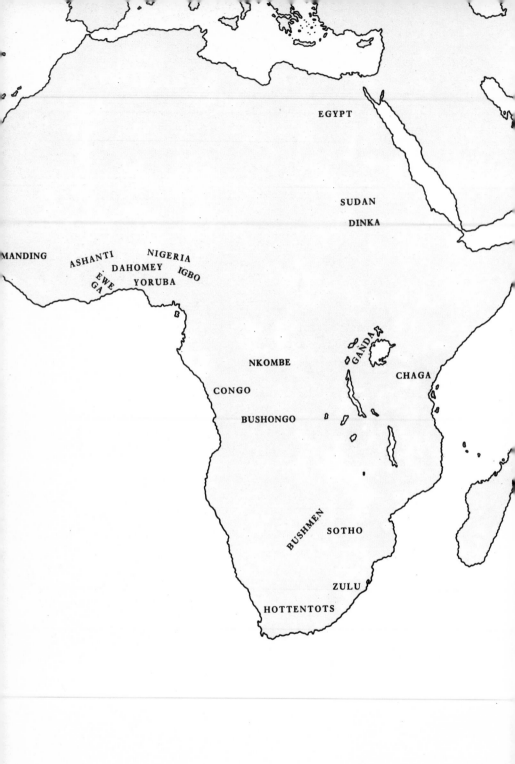

MANDING   ASHANTI   NIGERIA

DAHOMEY   IGBO

EWE   YORUBA

GA

EGYPT

SUDAN

DINKA

NKOMBE

CONGO

BUSHONGO

GANDA

CHAGA

BUSHMEN   SOTHO

ZULU

HOTTENTOTS

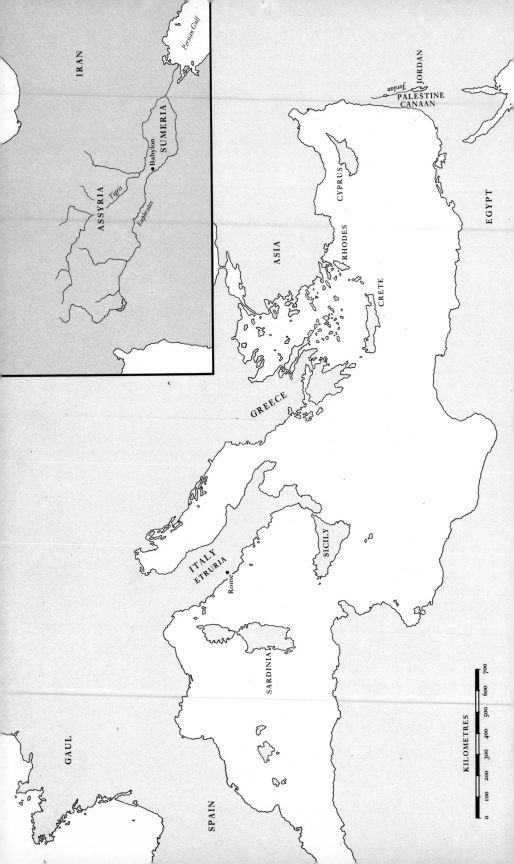

VERSIONS OF THE MYTHS

This is necessarily a very selective index; for a start, I have not attempted to deal with painting and sculpture, which illustrate single moments within the myths, and I have certainly overlooked a number of novels and shorter poems using mythical themes. So what follows is a kind of preliminary list for the reader who wishes to explore, rather than any kind of definitive catalogue.

Orpheus: Claudio Monteverdi, *Orpheus* (opera, 1607); C. W. Gluck, *Orpheus and Eurydice* (opera, 1762–74); Jean Cocteau, *Orphée* (play, 1927).

Ottar: Richard Wagner, *The Rheingold* (treasure theme) (opera, 1869).

Penelope: Gabriel Fauré, *Penelope* (opera, 1913).

Persephone: Igor Stravinsky, *Persephone* (melodrama, 1934–49).

Phaedra: Jean Racine, *Phèdre* (play, 1677); Robert Lowell, *Phaedra* (verse play, 1960).

Pohjola: Jean Sibelius, *Pohjola's Daughter* (tone poem, 1906).

Prometheus: Ludwig van Beethoven, *The Creatures of Prometheus* (ballet, c. 1800);

Robert Bridges, *Prometheus the Firegiver* (masque, 1884); P. B. Shelley, *Prometheus Unbound* (lyrical drama, 1820); Aeschylus, *Prometheus Bound* (play, c. 460 BC).

Savitri: Gustav Holst, *Savitri* (opera, 1916).

Semele: G. F. Handel, *Semele* (oratorio, 1744).

Seven against Thebes: Aeschylus, *Seven Against Thebes* (play, 469 BC).

Sigurd: Richard Wagner, *The Valkyries* (Siegmund and Sieglinde) (opera, 1870); Ernest Reyer, *Sigurd* (opera, 1884); William Morris, *Sigurd the Volsung* (poem, 1877).

Theseus: J. B. Lully, *Thesée* (opera, 1675); A. Gide, *Thesée* (dramatic poem.1946).

Troilus: William Walton, *Troilus and Cressida* (opera, 1954, 1976); Geoffrey Chaucer, *Troilus and Criseyde* (c. 1380); William Shakespeare, *Troilus and Cressida* (1609).

Trojan War: John Lydgate, *The history, siege and destruction of Troy* (poem, c. 1400); Jean Giraudoux, *La Guerre de Troïe n' aura pas lieu* (play, 1935). There are numerous translations of Homer's *Iliad*: e.g. in English, those by George Chapman (1611) and Samuel Butler (1898). *See also* Aeneas.

Tuonela: Jean Sibelius, *Four Legends* (tone poems, 1895).

Valkyries: Richard Wagner, *The Valkyries* (opera, 1870).

INDEX OF TOPICS

Pakrokitat, Qamaits,
Savitri, Taikomol, Tano,
To-Kabinana, Yama,
Yen-Lo Wang.

Demons, Devils: Bala
Rama, Chung Ku'ei,
Cyavana, Dahhak, Daityas,
Devi, Durga, Erlik,
Gualicho, Kaitabha,
Kappa, Krishna,
Kwannon, Lilith, Oni,
Rakshasas, Ravana, Shoki,
Tengu.

Dogs: Argos, Burkhan,
Cephalus, Cerberus,
Chiconamictlan, Garm,
Hecuba, Qiqirn, Sarama,
Tyr, Xolotl.

Door, Gates: Janus,
Mên-Shên, Sedu, Wang.

Dragon: Apsu, Azhi Dahaka,
Cadmus, Fafnir, Keresaspa,
Lludd, Lung Wang,
Menoeceus, Mushussu,
Nidhogg, Pa Hsien,
Python, Ryujin, Ryo-Wo,
Sigurd, Ssu Ling.

Drought: Devas (*Apaosha*),
Dn'il, Vritra.

Dwarfs: Alberich, Alviss,
Andvari, Curupira,
Dvergar, Gullinbursti,
Sukuna-Bikona, Suttung,
Vishnu (5).

Eagle: Llew Llaw Gyffes,
Ningirsu, Oshadagea,
Prometheus, Suttung,
Thunderbirds.

Earth: Akev, Ala, Apsu,
Asase Ya, Atira, Ciuacoatl,
Coatlicue, Dagon, Dione,
Eithinoha, Fulla, Gaia,
Geb, Hou T'u, Jord, Mah,
Nerthus, Ninhursag,
Nokomis, Odudua, Papa,
Prithivi, Prithu, Spenta
Armaiti, Tathene,
Tekkeitserktok, Tellumo,
Tlaltecuhtli, Tlazolteotl.

Earthquakes: Batara Guru,
Chibchachum, Poseidon,
Shesha, Taikomol,
Tepeyolhotli.

Eclipses: Avya, Rahu.

End of World: Einherjar,
Five Suns, Muspell;
Destroyed by fire: Brahma,
Caragabi, Ragnarok,
Taikomol, Taiowa.

Evening: Hastshehogan.

Evening Star: Astarte,
Ishtar, Savitri.

Evil: Angra Mainyu, Ama-
Tsu-Mikaboshi, Azazel,
Azhi Dahaka, Dahhak,
Daityas, Devas, Epunamun,

Mara, Pandora, Tlacolotl.
See also **Demons.**

Evil Eye: Balor.

Examinations: Chung
K'uei, K'uei-Hsing, Wên
Ch'ang.

Farming: Bachué, Gua,
Mars, Rongo, Shen Nung.

Fate, Fates: Atropos,
Carmenta, Clotho, Fates,
Norns, Ssu Ming, Urd,
Valkyries.

Feasts: Omacatl, Xochipilli.

Fertility: Adonis, Amen,
Astarte, Cabiroi, Demeter,
Dusares, Frey, Gefion,
Hathor, Inanna, Ishtar,
Min, Nehalennia, Osiris,
Pomona, Priapus,
Vertumnus, Xipe Totec.

Fever: Febris.

Fire: Agni, Amesha Spentas
(*Asha*), Atar, Aurva, Chu
Jung, Emakong, Five Sons,
Hephaestus, Keri, Mani,
Meri, Muspell, Nanabozho.
Pele, Pillan, Prometheus,
Rainbow Snake, Sui-Jen,
Surt, Tejeto, Tsao Chün,
Utgard-Loki, Vain-
amoinen, Vulcan,
Xuihtecutli.

First Man and/or Woman:
Ask, Ataensic, Atse
Hastin, Awonawilona,
Chingichnich, Coyote,
Garang, Gaya Maretan,
Hina, Kintu, Maiso,
Oxomoco, Tane,
Tucupacha, Unkulunkulu,
Wiyot, Ymir.

First Men: Finuweigh,
Huacas, Hunapu, Hurakan,
Inapertwa, L'ao T'ien Yeh,
Nareau, Nü Wa,
To-Kabinana.

Fishing: Hoho-demi, Hymir,
Mani.

Flood: Am, Anatiwa,
Arikute, Atonatiuh,
Chibchachum, Coyote,
Deucalion, Enlil, Five
Suns, Makonaima,
Ndengei, Taiowa,
Utnapishtim, Viracocha,
Vishnu (1), Yima.

Flowers: Clytie, Flora,
Hyacinth, Llew Llaw
Gyffes, Narcissus.

Flute-Playing: Euterpe,
Hunbatz, Marsyas, Pa
Hsien, Python, Terpsichore.

Food: Tonacatecuhtli,
Ukemochi.

Forest: Curupira, Miming,
Satyrs, Tapio.

Forgetfulness: Lethe, Lotus
Eaters, Meng P'o.

**Fortune, Fortune-Telling,
Luck:** Ekeko, Fortuna,
Hermes, Ifa, Kichijōten,
Kuan Yu, Lakshmi, Taurt.

Funerals: Ptah-Seker-Osiris,
Seker.

Gardens: Venus.

Giants: Aegir, Aloadai,
Atlas, Bergelmir, Bolthorn,
Child of the Water,
Cuchulainn, Cyclops,
Dharmapala, Five Sons,
Frost-Giants, Gefion,
Geirrod, Gerd, Giants,
Gilgamesh, Gymir,
Hecatoncheires, Hrimgerd,
Hrungnir, Hymir,
Jarnsaxa, Keresaspa,
Laestrygonians,
Nagenatzani, Odysseus,
P'an Ku, Suttung, Talus,
Tirawa-Atius, Utgard-Loki,
Vafthrudnir, Vainamoinen,
Viracocha, Wade, Ymir,
Zeus.

Goat: Heidrun, Utgard-Loki.

Gold: Midas.

Grain: Baal, Byggvir,
Chicomecoatl, Cinteotl,
Deohako, Hou Chi,
Mondamin, Nidaba,
Onatha, Peko, Tammuz,
Triptolemos, Veles,
Xilonen.

Hammer: Gullinbursti,
Hrungnir, Perkuno, Thor.

Hare: Ō-kuni-nishi.

Harvest: Disir. Ukko,
Veles.

Healing & Medicine:
Asclepius, Asgaya Gigagei,
Carancho, Chiron,
Cit-Bolon-Tum,
Dhanvantari, Dian Cecht,
Eir, Gahe, Imhetep, Nuadu
Argetlam, Ō-kuni-mishi,
Pa Hsien, Sakpata,
Sequana, Shamash, Shen
Nung, Trita, Yakushi
Nyorai, Yao Wang.

Hearth: Hestia, Tsao Chun,
Vesta.

Heaven, Paradise: Amida,
Amitabha, Apsarases,
Dilman, Etana, Hsi Wang
Mu, Huang Ti'en, Ixtab,
Kuma, K'un-lun
Mountain, Meru, Mugdala,
Olelbis, Olifat, Olympus,
O-Mi-T'o-Fo, Svarga,
Tagaro, Tennin, Tien,
Ti-Tsang Wang, Tlaloc,
Tonatiuh, Vaikuntha,
Valhalla.

Horses, Horse-Men:
Alfrodull, Arion, Ashvins,
Centaurs, Chiron,
Dadhyanc, Deianeira,
Diomedes, Enore, Epona,
Ganymede, Gullifaxi,
Heracles, Hrimfaxi,
Kinnaras, Laomedon,
Pegasus, Phaethon,
Poseidon, Rama, Sagara,
Skinfaxi, Sleipnir, Svadilfari,
Xanthos. Tishtrya,
Household: Hastshehogan,
Icheiri, Lares, Penates,
Tsao Chun.
Hunting: Artemis, Carancho,
Cephalus, Curupira,
Diarmaid, El-lal, Fu Hsi,
Grandfather, Maui,
Ningirsu, Ogun, Orion,
Pwyll, Skadi Sosondowah,
Tekkeitserktok.
Icebergs: Nootsikok.
Immortality: Eos, Hsien,
Hsi Wang Mu, Marpessa,
Maui, Pa Hsien, Peleus,
Sennin, Sibyls,
Utnapishtim, Yima.
Invulnerability: Achilles,
Caeneus.
Jackdaws: Pierides.
Jaguar: Balam, Kame, Keri,
Kuma, Tepeyolhotli,
Tezcatlipoca.
Justice, Law: Enlil, Forseti,
Ida-ten, Kuan Yu, Maat,
Rhadamanthus, Thor, Yao.
Lightning: Apocatequil,
Ccoa, Chac, Cyclops,
Ilyap'a, Lei Kung, Jupiter,
Vediovis, Zeus.
Lion: Heracles, Hiranya-
kashipu, Vishnu (4).
Literature: Wên Ch'ang.
Long Life: Shichi Fukujin,
Shou Hsing, Wachabe.
Love: Aphrodite, Astarte,
Cupid, Daphnis, Eros,
Freyja, Hathor, Kama,
Rati, Venus.
Luck *see* **Fortune.**
Lyre: Hermes, Melpomene,
Narada.
Magic Cauldron:
Bendigeidfran, Odrörir.
Marriage: Frigg, Fu Hsi,
Hera.
Medicine *see* **Healing.**
Memory: Huginn,
Mnemosyne.
Merchants: Ekchuah,
Mercury.
Mercy: Kuan Yin,
Kwannon.
Messenger: Hermes, Legba,
Nabu.

Metals: Khshathra Vairya.
Mirth: Uzume.
Monkey: Hanuman,
Hunapu, Hunbatz, Rama,
Sun Hou-Tzu.
Moon: Aah, Artemis, Avya
Changing Woman,
Ch'ang-O, Cupara, Juno,
Khensu, Kuma, Mah,
Mawu, Meri, Mundilfari,
Murungu, Nanamatzin,
Nyame, Phoebe, Selene,
Sin, Tecuciztecal, Thoth,
Tsuki-yo-mi, Viracocha,
Wiyot, Yerah.
Morning Star: Aurvandill,
Chuvalete, Morning Star,
Savitri, Sosondowah.
Mountains: O-yama, Esuni,
Qamaits, Skadi, Sumur,
Wu yo, Olympus.
Music: Apollo, Benten,
Dagda, Hermes,
Kinnaras, Linus,
Macuilzochitl, Orpheus,
Pan, Quetzalcoatl. *See*
Flute-Playing.
Necklace: Amphiaraus,
Brisingamen, Freyja,
Harmonia.
Net: Loki.
Night: Arikute, Evaki,
Hrimfaxi, Night,
Pulekukwerk, Qat, Ratri,
Tezcatlipoca, Tukma.
Nightingale: Philomela.
Numbers: Mixcoatl.
Old Age: Graeae.
Oldest Creature: Maponos.
Owl: Lulew Llaw Gyffes,
Tlacolotl.
Ox: Chih Nü, Gefion,
Mithras.
Pampas: Huasa Mallcu.
Paradise *see* **Heaven.**
Plants: Ameretat, Haumea,
Tagaro, Vainamoinen,
Venus.
Poetry: Bragi, Calliope,
Kvasir, Odin, Suttung,
Tenjin.
Prophecy: Apollo,
Cassandra, Cybele, Freyja
Nymphs, Sibyls, Suttung,
Tiresias.
Rain: Achinoin, Bacabs,
Chac, Chalchuihtlicne,
Chih Sung-Tzu, Darana,
Frey, Ilyap'a, Indra,
Itzamna, Leza, Parjanya,
Rainbow Snake, Sennin,
Shiwanna, Tlaloc,
Tsui'goab, Wondjina, Yu
Shih.
Rainbow: Anyiewo,
Chuchaviva, Hino, Iris,

Rainbow Snake.
Ram: Golden Fleece, Sc
Raven: Badb, Huginn,
Raven.
Rice: Inari.
Ring: Andvari, Draupnir,
Ottar.
River: Achelous, Acheron,
Galatea, Ganges, Hapi,
Kawa-no-kami, Lethe,
Naiads, Oya, Sarasvati,
Satet, Sequana, Styx,
Tano, Vaitarani, Varuna.
Sacrifice: Iphigeneia, Itzli,
Taranis, Xipe Totec,
Xiuhtecuhtli.
Salaries: Lu Hsing.
Sea: Aegir, Ea, Glaucus, Ino,
Jingo, Kompira, Mama
Cocha, Manannan mac
Lir, Morrigan, Neptune,
Nereids, Nereus, Njord,
Ocean, Olokun, Posiedon,
Proteus, Ran, Sedina,
Tethys, T'ien Fei, Varuna,
Wata-tsu-mi, Yamm.
Seafaring: Aluluei,
Nehalennia, Tiphys.
Seasons: Ssu Ta T'ien Wang.
Ship: Skidbladnir.
Serpent, Snake: Aapep,
Abyrga, Anyiewo, Bachué,
Batara Guru, Bes,
Cecrops, Cherruve,
Eurydice, Garuda,
Helenus, Kaliya, Kuma,
Laocoon, Loki, Lotan,
Medusa, Melempus,
Midgard Serpent,
Mixcoatl, Mo-Li, Nagas,
Nahusha, Ndengei,
Nehebkhau, Nidhogg, Nü
Wa, Quetzalcoatl, Ra,
Rainbow Snake, Shesha,
Sisiutl, Ssu-Ling,
Susa-no-wo, Tiresias,
Yao Wang.
Sirius (star): Sothis,
Tishtrya.
Skiing: Skadi, Ull.
Sky: Anhert, Anu, Apsu,
Batara Guru, Buku, Dyans,
Gandharvas, Ilmarinen,
Ilmarinen, Kumush, Leza,
Mehurt, Nesaru, Nut,
Nyame, Obatala, Olorun,
Pulekukwerk, Rangi,
Tawhaki, Tiwaz, Uranus,
Varuna, Ymir, Zeus.
Sleep: Evaki.
Smallpox: Kinharingan,
Sakpata.
Smith: Cuchulainn, Goibniu,
Gua, Hephaestus, Mimir,
Ogun, Svarog, Telyaveli,
Tvastri, Vulcan, Wayland.

Snakes *see* **Serpents.**
Spear: Gungnir, Odin.
Speech: Benten, Nabu, Ogma, Ogmios, Vac.
Spring: Coatlicue, Rainbow Snake, Xipe Totec.
Squirrel: Ratatosk.
Stag, Hind: Gwydion, Heracles.
Stars: Beetle, Callisto, Cherruve, Gandharvas, Mixcoatl, Orion, Pulekukwerk. *See also* **Evening Star, Morning Star, Sirius.**
Stones: Deucalion, Seides, Shango, Tukma, Tuirenn.
Storms: Enlil, Kukulcan, Maruts, Poseidon, Rudra, Seth, Susa-no-wo.
Sun: Adaheli, Alfrodull, Ama-terasu, Apollo, Aten, Atum, Auf, Avya, Awonawilona, Cupara, Dudugera, Evaki, Five Suns, Helios, Horus, Hyperion, Inti, Iruwa, Khepra, Mawu, Meri, Mitra, Mundilfari, Murunga, Nanauatzin, Nyame, Phaethon, Pushan, Ra, Senx, Shakuru, Shamash, Surya, Tonatiuh, Viracocha, Vishrakarman, Wakahiru-Me.
Swallow: Philomela.
Swan: Leda, Lemminkainen, Ler, Midir, Oengus mac Oc, Swan Maidens, Tuonela.
Tattooing: Mataora.
Thought: Huginn, Utgard-Loki.
Thunder, Thunderbolt: Baal, Cyclops, Diti, Donar, Gua, Hino, Hurakan, Ilyap'a, Indra, Kami-nari, Lei Kung, Leza, Perkuno, Perun, Raiden, Seth, Shango, So, Thor, Thunderbirds, Tiermes, Ukko, Vajra, Zeus.
Tides: Achinoin.
Tortoise: Hermes, Ssu Ling, Vishnu (2).
Tragedy: Melpomene.
Travellers: Ekchuah, Odin.

Treasure: Dragon, Draupnir, Fafnir, Gulliubursti, Krishna, Ottar, Sigurd, Tuireun.
Tree of Life: Gaokerena.
Tree of Paradise: Amrita (*Parijata*), Andhaka (*Parijata*).
Trees: Baucis, Dryads, Hamadryads, Oreads, Tane, Yggdrasil, Ymir.
Laurel: Daphne.
Oak: Donar, Zeus.
Trickster: Autolycus, Coyote, Eshu, Hermes, Legba, Loki, Mantis, Sisyphus, Wisagatcak, Yo.
Truth: Maat.
Twins: Ahayuta Achi, Alci, Alemena, Apollo, Artemis, Ashvins, Baidrama, Castor, Dioskouroi, Heracles, Romulus, Taiowa, Yoskeha.
Underworld, Otherworld: Acca Larentia, Adlivun, Aeneas, Annwn, Baal, Charon, Chiconamictlan, Ciuateoteo, Cliodna, Cormac, Elysian Plain, Emma-O, Ereshkigal, Fand, Glasisvellir, Guayarakunny, Gymir, Hades, Hanhau, Hawaiki, Hel, Heracles, Hermod, Hiku, Hunapu, Ishtar, Izanagi, Jigoku, Kuma, Manannan Mac Lir, Mataora, Meng P'o, Mictlantecuhtli, Montezuma, Mot, Nakali, Naraka, Nehebkhan, Nera, Nergal, Niflheim, Odysseus, Orpheus, Osiris, Patala, Persephone, Pluto, Pohjola, Ra, Rutu, Shih-Tien, Yen-Wang, Styx, Tartarus, Theseus, Tuat, Tuonela, Vaitarani, Yomi-no-kuni.
Vegetation: Ceres, Pan, Payatamu, Tammuz.
Victory: Andraste, Amen, Svantovit, Verethraghna.
Volcanoes: Pele.
War: Ahayuta Achi, Amen, Anta, Aphrodite, Ares,

Badb, Bellona, Camaxtli, Hachiman, Hathor, Huitzilopochtli, Kartikeya, Kibuka, Kuan Yu, Mars, Menthu, Morrigan, Ningirsu, Odin, Ogun, Quirinus, Reshpu, Saxnot, Sekhmet, Septu, Tezcatlipoca, Tiwaz, Tu, Tyr, Yo Fei.
Watchman: Gjallarhom, Heimdall, Sosondowah.
Water: Anahita, Apsu, Chalchiuhtlicue, Covetina, Haurvatat, Keri, Sisuitl, Sul.
Waterways: Nine Heroes.
Wealth: Bhaga, Kompira, Kuvera, Shichi Fukujin, Ts'ai Shen, Yakshas.
Weather: T'u-Ti.
Weaving: Arachne, Penelope.
Whirlpool: Charybdis.
Whirlwind: Hurakan, Mo-Li.
Winds: Achinoin, Aello, Aeolus, Amen, Bacabs, Boreas, Dajoji, Eurus, Feng Po, Five Suns, Fujin, Maruts, Mo-Li, Njord, Notus, Odysseus, Quetzalcoatl, Shina-Tsu-Hiko, Vata, Vayu, Winds, Yu Shih.
Wine: Dionysus, Dubares, Liber, Shojo, Silenus.
Winter: Lif, Persephone, Ragnarok.
Wisdom: Alviss, Athene, Ea, Ganesha, Hoenir, Kvasir, Mimir, Minerva, Thoth, Vafthrudnir, Xolotl.
Wolf: Fenrir, Freki, Gwydion, Sigmund, Wolf.
Woodpecker: Picus.
Writing: Fu Hsi, Nabu, Oannes, Odin, Sarasvati, Seshat, Tenjin, Ts'ang Chien.
Youth: Amrita, Ambrosia, Apples of Youth, Hebe, Maponos, Oengus mac Oc, Oisin, Sibyl, Tir na Nog, Xochipilli.

INDEX OF MINOR CHARACTERS

Hiranyaksha see Vishnu (3).
Hjordis see Sigmund.
Ho-deri see Hoho-demi.
Ho Hsien-Ku see Pa Hsien.
Ho Po see Nine Heroes.
Hotei see Shichi Fukujin.
Hother see Hoder.
Hreidmar see Fafnir, Ottar.
Hsiang Chun see Nine Heroes.
Hsiang Fu-Jen see Nine
  Heroes.
Huanacauri see
  Paccari-Tambo.
Huehuetcotl see Xiuhtecutli.
Hugi see Utgard-Loki.
Hu-Hunapu see Hunapu.
Humbaba see Gilgamesh.
Iasion see Demeter.
Iblis see Azazel.
Idas see Marpessa.
Ikkaku Sennin see Sennin.
Iobates see Bellerophon.
Iolaos see Heracles.
Iole see Heracles.
Iowahine see Tane.
Irra see Nergal.
Isdzana-Ne-He see Na Ye'
  Nez Nane.
Itciai see Kuma.
Itys see Philomela.
Iwa-naga-hime see
  Ō-yama-tsuni.
Ixbalanque see Hunapu.
Jaburu see Sibu.
Jamadagni see Vishnu (6).
Javasandha see Krishna.
Jayadratha see Draupadi.
Jocasta see Oedipus.
Joukahainen see
  Vainamoinen.
Jurōjin see Shichi Fukujin.
Kalmashapada see Vasishtha.
Kamaikore see Enore.
Kansa see Krishna.
Kari see Fornjöt.
Kato'ya see Taiowa.
Kauravas see Bhima,
  Bhishma.
Kaviki see Tawhaki.
Kawelu see Hiku.
Khnathaitu see Keresaspa.
Kholumolumo see
  Moshanyana.
Kiberoth see Kuma.
Kingu see Apsu.
Kokomat see Tuchaipa.
Kokyangwuti see Taiowa.
Ko-no-hana-sakuya-hive see
  Ninigi, Ō-yama-tsuni.
Kuang Mu see Ssu Ta T'ien
  Wang.
Kundrav see Keresaspa.
Kung Kung see Nü Wa.
Kuo Shang see Nine Heroes.
Kurma see Vishnu.
Kusanagi see Susa-no-wo.

Kusha see Rama.
Kwammang-a see Mantis.
Kylliki see Lemminkainen.
Laertes see Odysseus.
Lakhmu and Lakhamu see
  Apsu.
Lamassu see Sedu.
Lan Tsa'ai-Ho see Pa Hsien.
Latinus see Aeneas.
Lava see Rama.
Lavinia see Aeneas.
Leucippus see Daphne.
Liban see Fand.
Lieh Tzu see Lao Tzu.
Li Hun see Nine Heroes.
Ling P'ao Tien-Esun see
  San Ch'ing.
Li T'ieh-Kuai see Pa Hsien.
Loeg see Fand.
Loeghaire see Cuchulainn.
Logi see Utgard-Loki.
Lohiau see Pele.
Louhi see Lemminkainen,
  Pohjolu, Vainamoinen.
Luchtine see Goibniu.
Lud see Gwyn.
Lug see Tuirenn.
Lugaid see Conall Cernach,
  Cuchulainn.
Lü Tung-Pin see Pa Hsien.
Lykos see Creon.
Macha see Morrigan.
Madhu see Kaitabha.
Madumda see Coyote.
Magni see Gullfaxi.
Malsun see Glooscap.
Mama Huaco, Mama
  Ipacura, Mama Oello,
  Mama Rawa see
  Paccari-Tambo.
Manabozho see Nanabozho.
Marawa see Qat.
Marjatta see Vainamoinen.
Marttanda see Adityas.
Mashenomak see Nanabozho.
Mashu see Gilgamesh.
Math mab Mathonwy see
  Gwydion.
Matholwch see Bendigeidfran.
Megara see Heracles.
Mehu see Finuweigh.
Melanippos see Tydeus.
Memnon see Eos.
Metaneira see Demeter.
Miao-shan see Kuan Yin.
Michabo see Nanabozho.
Mikumwesa see Glooscap.
Mil, Sons of see Amhairghin.
Mimerkki see Tapio.
Minyas, daughters of see
  Dionysus.
Miodhchaoin see Tuirenn.
Mitnal see Hanhau.
Mjollnir see Gullinbursti.
Mochni see Taiowa.
Moytura see Dagda, Tuatha

De Danann.
Mu see Hsi Wang Mu.
Muninn see Huginn.
Mysing see Fenja.
Nambi see Kinfu.
Na-naki-me see Ama-terasu.
Nanda see Krishna.
Naoise see Deirdre.
Narasimha see Vishnu.
Ngurunderi see Darramulun.
Nimrod see Ningirsu.
Noah see Deucalion.
Noatun see Njord.
Nodens see Nuadu Argetlam.
Nornagest see Norns.
Nosjthej see El-lal.
Nuvarahu see Mataora.
Ocelotonatiuh see Five Suns.
Ocypete see Harpies.
Oenomaus see Pelops.
Oineus see Meleager.
Oka see Keri.
Olelpanti see Olelbis.
Omecuatl, Ometecutli see
  Ometeotl.
Otos see Aloadai.
Palongawhoya see Taiowa.
Panamam see Pakrokitat.
Pandu see Bhishma.
Pare and Hutu see Hiku.
Parijata see Amrita, Andhaka.
Parthenopeius see Seven
  Against Thebes.
Patol see Naum.
Patroclus see Trojan War.
Pasiphae see Minos.
Payait see Pakrokitat.
Phegeus see Alcmaeon.
Phineus see Jason, Zetes.
Phorkys see Scylla.
Phrixus see Golden Fleece.
Pleiades, Pleione see Orion.
Plutus see Demeter, Kuvera.
Poia see Morning Star.
Polybus see Oedipus.
Polydectes see Danae, Perseus.
Polydorus see Hecuba.
Polymestor see Hecuba.
Poqanghoya see Taiowa.
Pragjyotisha see Naraka.
Prahlada see Vishnu (4).
Procne see Philomele.
Procris see Cephalus.
Procrustes see Theseus.
Proteus see Helen.
Pterelaos see Amphitryon.
Puana see Kuma.
Puma see Coyote.
Puna see Rata.
Pyrrha see Deucalion.
Quiyanhtonatiuh see Five
  Suns.
Ragnhild see Hidding.
Regin see Sigurd.
Rhea Silvia see Romulus.
Riiki see Nareau.

INDEX OF REAL NAMES
(PERSONS AND PLACES)

INDEX OF PLACES

Cariri Indians: Grandfather.
Karaya Indians: Anatriva.
Paressí Indians: Enore,
  Maiso.
Tupi Indians: Arikute.
Tupinamba Indians: Meri.
Britain: Andraste, Brigit,
  Covetina, Rhiannon,
  Saxnot, Sul, Wayland,
  Woden.
Canaan: Anat, Astarte, Baal,
  Dn'il, El, Lotan, Mot,
  Yamm, Yerah.
Caroline Islands: Aluluei,
  Luk, Olifat.
China: Ch'ang-O, Ch'eng
  Huang, Chen Jen, Chih
  Nü, Chih Sung-Tzu,
  Chu Jung, Chung Ku'ei,
  Erh Lang, Feng Po, Fu
  Hsi, Fu Shen, Heng Ha
  Er Chiang, Hou Chi,
  Hou T'u, Hsien, Hsi
  Wang Mu, Huang Ti,
  Huang Ti'en, Kuan Yin,
  Kuan Yu, K'uei-Hsing,
  K'un-Lun Mountain,
  Lao T'ien Yeh, Lao Tzu,
  Lei Kung, Lu Hsing,
  Lung Wang, Meng P'o,
  Mên-Shên, Nine Heroes,
  Nü Wa, O-Mi-T'o Fo,
  Pa Hsien, P'an Ku,
  Pi-Hsia Yuan-Kun, San
  Ch'ing, Sheng Jen,
  Shên I, Shen Nung,
  Shiang Ti, Shih-Tien
  Yen-Wang, Shou Hsing,
  Ssu Ling, Ssu Ming,
  Ssu Ta T'ien Wang,
  Sui-Jen, Sun Hou-Tzu,
  T'ai-Yo Ta-Ti, T'ien,
  T'ien Fei, Ts'ai Shen,
  Ts'ang Chien, Tsao
  Chün, Tung Wang
  Kung, T'u-Ti, Wang,
  Wên Ch'ang, Wen-Shu,
  Yen-K'ung, Wu Ti,
  Wu Yo, Yang, Yao, Yao
  Wang, Yen-Lo Wang,
  Yo Fei, Yu-Huang,
  Yu Shih.
Colombia:
  Chibcha Indians: Bachue,
  Bochica, Chibchachum,
  Chiminagagua,
  Chuchaviva.
  Choco Indians: Caragabi.
  Cuboe Indians: Avya.
Congo:
  Nkombe: Akongo.
Egypt: Aah, Aapep, Aker,
  Amenhetep, Amen-Ra,
  Ammut, Anta, Anubis,
  Apis, Astarte, Aten,
  Atum, Auf, Ausaas,

Bastet, Bes, Buchis, Geb,
Great Ennead, Hapi,
Hapy, Harmachis,
Hathor, Heqet, Horus,
Hu, Imhetep, Isis,
Khensu, Khepra,
Khnemu, Maat, Mehturt,
Menthu, Meshkent,
Mesta, Min, Mut,
Nefertem, Nehebkhau,
Neith, Nekhebet,
Nephthys, Nun, Nut,
Osiris, Ptah,
Ptah-Seker-Osiris,
Qebehsenuf, Ra, Reshpu,
Renenutet, Saa, Satet,
Seker, Sekhmet, Septu,
Serapis, Seshet, Seth,
Shu, Sothis, Sphinx,
Tathenan, Taurt,
Tefnut, Toth, Tuamutef,
Tuat, Upuaut.
Esthonia: Peko.
Etruria: Cacus.
Europe, East:
  Slavs: Cernobog, Svarog.
Far East:
  Buddhism: Amitabha,
  Avalokiteshvara,
  Bodhidharma,
  Bodhisattva,
  Dharmapala,
  Dhyanibodhisattvas,
  Dhyanibuddhas,
  Gokuraku-Jōdo,
  Maitreya, Manjushri,
  Mara, Mo-Li, Myôô,
  Shakra, Ti-Tsang Wang,
  Yakushi Nyorai.
Fiji: Ndengei.
Finland: Ilmarinen, Jumala,
  Kalevala, Kullervo,
  Lemminkainen,
  Luonnotar, Pohjola,
  Sampo, Tapio, Tuonela,
  Ukko, Vainamoinen.
Gaul: Belenus, Brigit,
  Cernunnos, Epona,
  Esus, Maponos, Ogmios,
  Sequana, Taranis,
  Tarvos Trigoranos,
  Teutates.
Germany: Alci, Donar,
  Frigg, Irminsul, Nerthus,
  Tiwaz, Woden.
Gilbert & Ellice Islands:
  Nareau.
Greece: Absyrtus, Achelous,
  Acheron, Achilles,
  Actaeon, Adonis,
  Adrastus, Aeacus, Aeetes,
  Aegeus, Aegisthus, Aello,
  Aeolus, Aerope,
  Agamemnon, Agave,
  Agenor, Ajax, Alcathous,
  Alcestis, Alemaeon,

Alcmena, Alcyone,
Alecto, Aloadai, Alpheus,
Althaea, Amazons,
Ambrosia, Amphiaraus,
Amphion, Amphitrite,
Amphitryon,
Andromache,
Andromeda, Antaeus,
Antigone, Apollo,
Arachne, Ares, Argo,
Argos, Ariadne, Arion,
Asclepius, Atalanta,
Athene, Atlas, Atropos,
Augeas, Autolycus,
Baucis, Bellerophon,
Boreas, Briareus, Briseis,
Britomartis, Cabiroi,
Cadmus, Caeneus,
Calchas, Calliope,
Callisto, Calypso,
Capaneus, Cassandra,
Cassiopeia, Castor,
Cecrops, Centaurs,
Cephalus, Cepheus,
Cerberus, Ceyx, Charon,
Charybdis, Chimera,
Chiron, Chryseis,
Cimmerians, Circe, Clio,
Clotho, Clytemnestra,
Clytie, Coeus, Coronis,
Creon, Crius, Cronus,
Cyclops, Daedalus,
Danae, Danaids,
Daphne, Daphnis,
Deianeira, Deidameia,
Deino, Demeter,
Deucalion, Diomedes,
Dione, Dionysus,
Dioskouroi, Doris,
Dryads, Echidna, Echo,
Eileithyia, Electra,
Eleusinian Mysteries,
Elysian Plain, Endymion,
Eos, Epigoni, Erato,
Erebus, Erechtheus,
Ericthonius, Eros,
Eteocles, Eumaeus,
Eumenides, Europa,
Eurus, Euryale,
Eurydice, Eurynomus,
Eurystheus, Euterpe,
Evadne, Fates, Furies,
Gaia, Galatea,
Ganymede, Geryon,
Giants, Glauce, Glaucus,
Golden Age, Golden
Fleece, Gorgons, Graces,
Graeae, Hades, Haimon,
Hamadryads, Harmonia,
Harpies, Hebe, Hecate,
Hecatoncheires, Hector,
Hecuba, Helen, Helenus,
Helios, Hephaestus,
Hera, Heracles,
Hermaphroditus,
Hermes, Hesione,

Hesperides, Hestia,
Hippolyta, Hippolytus,
Horai, Hyacinth, Hylas,
Hyperboreans,
Hyperion, Iapetus,
Icarus, Idomeneus, Ilos,
Ino, Io, Iolaos, Iphicles,
Iphigeneia, Iris, Ismene,
Ixion, Jason, Laertes,
Laestrygonians, Laius,
Laocoon, Laomedon,
Lapiths, Leda, Lethe,
Leto, Linus, Lotus
Eaters, Lycomedes,
Lycurgus, Maenads,
Maia, Marpessa,
Marsyas, Medea,
Medusa, Melampus,
Meleager, Melpomene,
Menelaus, Menoeceus,
Metis, Midas, Minos,
Minotaur, Mnemosyne,
Muses, Myrrha,
Myrtilus, Naiads,
Narcissus, Nausicaa,
Nemesis, Neoptolemus,
Nephele, Nereids,
Nereus, Nestor, Night,
Niobe, Notus, Nymphs,
Ocean, Ocypete,
Odysseus, Oedipus,
Olympus, Omphale,
Oreads, Orestes, Orion,
Orpheus, Palladion,
Pallas, Pan, Pandora,
Paris, Pegasus, Peleus,
Pelias, Pelops, Penelope,
Pentheselea, Pentheus,
Persephone, Perseus,
Phaedra, Phaethon,
Philoctetes, Philomela,
Philyra, Phoebe,
Pierides, Pirithous,
Python, Rhadamanthus
Rhea, Satyrs, Scylla,
Selene, Semele, Seven
Against Thebes, Sibyls,
Sirens, Sisyphus, Sphinx,
Styx, Talus, Tantalus,
Tartarus, Telegonus,
Telemachus,
Terpsichore, Tethys,
Thalia, Thamyris,
Themis, Theseus, Thetis,
Tiresias, Titans, Tityas,
Triptolemos, Triton,
Troilus, Trojan War
Tyche, Tydeus,
Typhoeus, Urania,
Uranus, Winds,
Xanthos, Zagreus,
Zetes, Zeus.

Guyana:
Arawak Indians:
Kururumany.
Warrau Indians: Aboré.

Hawaii: Hiku, Pele.
Holland: Nehalennia.
India: (*Hinduism*) Aditi,
Adityas, Agastya, Agni,
Ahalya, Airavata,
Amrita, Andhaka,
Angiras, Apsarases,
Arjuna, Ashvins, Asura,
Aurva, Bala Rama,
Bhaga, Bhagiratha,
Bharata, Bhima, Bishma,
Bhrigu, Brahma,
Brhaspati, Cyavana,
Dadhyanc, Daityas,
Daksha, Devi,
Dhanvantari, Diti,
Draupadi, Drona,
Drupada, Durga,
Durvasas, Duryodhana,
Dvaraka, Dyaus,
Gandharvas, Ganesha,
Ganges, Garuda, Gopis,
Govardhana, Hanuman,
Hari, Hiranyagarbha,
Hiranyakashipu, Indra,
Jagannath, Kaitabha,
Kala, Kali, Kaliya,
Kama, Kartikeya,
Kasyapa, Kinnaras,
Krishna, Kuvera,
Lakshmana, Lakshmi,
Loka, Lokapala,
Mahadeva,
Mahapurisha,
Mahendra, Makara,
Manu, Maruts, Matsya,
Maya, Meru, Mitra,
Mugdala, Nagas,
Nahusha, Namuci,
Nandi, Narada, Naraka,
Pandavas, Parashurama,
Parjanya, Parvati,
Pashupati, Patala,
Prajapati, Prithivi,
Prithu, Pururavas,
Purusha, Pushan, Radha,
Rahu, Rakshasas, Rati,
Ratri, Ravana, Ribhus,
Rishi, Rudra, Rukmini,
Sadhyas, Sagara,
Sarama, Saranyu,
Sarasvati, Savitri,
Shesha, Shishupala,
Shiva, Shri, Sita, Skanda,
Soma, Surya, Svarga,
Tarksya, Tirthankaras,
Tvastri, Ushas, Vac,
Vaikuntha, Vaishravana,
Vaivasvata, Vajra,
Vajrapani, Vamana,
Varaha, Varuna,
Vasishtha, Vasuki,
Vasus, Vaya,
Vidyadhavas, Vishnu,
Vishvakarman, Vritra,
Yadavas, Yakshas,

Yama, Yudhishthira.
Iran: Ahura Mazda,
Ameretat, Amesha
Spentas, Anahita, Angra
Mainyu, Atar, Azhi
Dahaka, Dahhak, Devas,
Fravashis, Gaokerena,
Gaya Maretan,
Haurvatat, Jamshid,
Keresaspa, Khshathra
Vairya, Mah, Mithras,
Ormuzd, Spenta
Armaiti, Tishtrya, Trita,
Vata, Verethragna,
Vohu Manah, Yazatas,
Yima.
Ireland: Ailill, Amhairgin,
Badb, Balor, Bran, Bres,
Brigit, Coailte, Cliodna,
Conall Cernach,
Cormac, Cuailgne,
Cuchulainn, Curoi,
Dagda, Danann,
Deirdre, Dian Cecht,
Diarmaid, Fand, Feinn,
Fionn, Fir Bolg,
Fomorians, Fraoch,
Goibniu, Labraid, Ler,
Lugh, Manannan Mac
Lir, Medhbh, Midir,
Morrigan, Nera, Nuadu
Argetlam, Oengus Mac
Oc, Ogma, Oisin,
Segais, Tir Na Nog,
Tuatha De Danann,
Tuirenn.
Japan: Aizen-Myoo,
Ama-terasu,
Ama-tsu-Mikaboshi,
Amitabha, Benten,
Emma-O, Fujin, Gyoja,
Hachiman, Hoho-demi,
Ida-ten, Inari, Izanagi,
Jigoku, Jizo, Kami,
Kami-mi-masubi,
Kami-nari, Kappa,
Kawa-no-kami,
Kichijōten, Kishimojin,
Kōbō Daishi, Kompira,
Kuni-toko-tachi,
Kura-Okami, Kwannon,
Miroku, Ningyo, Ninigi,
Ō-kuni-nushi, Oni,
Ō-yama-tsuni, Raiden,
Ryujin, Ryo-Wo, Sennin,
Shichi Fukujin, Shikome,
Shina-tsu-hiko, Shojo,
Shoki, Sukuna-bikona,
Susa-no-wo,
Taka-mi-masubi,
Tatsuta-hime, Tengu,
Tenjin, Tennin,
Tsuki-yo-mi, Ukemochi,
Uzume, Wakahiru-me,
Wata-Esu-mi,
Yomi-no-kuni.

Jordan:
  Petra: Dusares.
Lappland: Horagalles, Rutu,
  Seides, Tiermes.
Lithuania: Telvaveli.
Marianas Islands: Puntan.
New Guinea: Dudugera.
  Emakong.
New Hebrides: Tagaro.
New Zealand: Tawhaki.
Nigeria:
  Igbo: Ala.
Palestine: Lilith.
Papua: Gainjin.
Peru: Huacas, Inti,
  Pachacamac.
  Coastal Indians: Con, Mama
  Cocha.
  Incas: Apocatequil, Ilyap'a,
  Mama Huaco, Manco
  Capac, Paccari-Tambo,
  Tonapa, Viracocha.
  Kauri Indians: Ccoa.
  Mochica Indians: Ai Apaec.
Philippines: Finuweigh.
Polynesia: Haumea,
  Hawaiki, Hina, Mataora,
  Maui, Papa, Qat, Rangi,
  Rata, Rongo, Tane,
  Tangaroas, Tiki,
  To-Kabinana, Tu.
Prussia: Perkuno, Svantovit.
Rome: Acca Larentia,
  Achates, Aeneas,
  Aristaeus, Bellona, Bona
  Dea, Cacus, Carmenta,
  Castor, Ceres, Cupid,
  Cybele, Dei Consentes,
  Dido, Evander, Faunus,
  Febris, Flora, Fortuna,
  Janus, Juno, Jupiter,
  Lares, Latinus, Liber,
  Lucina, Mars, Mercury,
  Minerva, Mithras,
  Neptune, Ops, Orcus,
  Penates, Picus, Pluto,
  Romona, Proserpina,
  Pyramus, Quirinus,

Romulus, Saturn,
Silenus, Tellumo,
Terminus, Ulysses,
Vediovis, Venus,
Vertumnus, Vesta,
Vulcan, Winds.
Russia: Perun, Veles.
Samoa: Tangaloa.
Scandinavia: Aegir, Aesir,
Alberich, Alfar,
Alfrodull, Alviss,
Andvari, Apples of
Youth, Asgard, Ask and
Embla, Audhumla,
Aurvandill, Balder,
Bergelmir, Berserks,
Bestla, Bifrost Bridge,
Bolthorn, Bolverk, Bor,
Bragi, Breidablik,
Brisingamen, Brynhild,
Buri, Byggvir, Disir,
Dragon, Draupnir,
Dvergar, Einherjar, Eir,
Fafnir, Fenja, Fenrir,
Fornjöt, Forseti, Freki,
Frey, Frigg, Frodi,
Frost-Giants, Fulla,
Fylgja, Garm, Gefion,
Geirrod, Gerd, Giants,
Gimle, Ginnungagap,
Gjallarhorn, Glasisvellir,
Gleipnir, Gollveig,
Gorm, Grimnir, Gullfaxi,
Gullinbursti, Gungnir,
Gunnlod, Gylfi, Gymir,
Hadding, Heidrun,
Heimdall, Hel, Hermod,
Hild, Hildisvin,
Hlidskjalf, Hoder,
Hoenir, Hraesvelg,
Hrimfaxi, Hrimgerd,
Hrungnir, Huginn,
Hymir, Idunn, Ing,
Jarnsaxa, Jörd,
Jötunheim, Kvasir,
Landvaettir, Lif, Lodur,

Loki, Magni, Menglod,
Midgard,
Midgard-serpent,
Miming, Mimir,
Modgud, Mundilfari,
Muspell, Naglfari,
Nidhogg, Niflheim,
Njord, Norns, Od, Odin,
Odrorir, Ottar,
Ragnarok, Sceaf, Scyld,
Sif, Sigmund, Sigurd,
Skadi, Skidbladnir,
Skinfaxi, Sleipnir,
Starkad, Surt, Suttung,
Svadilfari, Swan
Maidens, Thialfi, Thor,
Thorgerd Holgabrud,
Trolls, Tyr, Ull, Urd,
Utgard, Utgard-Loki,
Vafthrudnir, Valaskjalf,
Valhalla, Vali,
Valkyries, Vanir, Ve,
Vidar, Vigrid, Wade,
Yggdrasill, Ymir.
Sudan:
  Dinka: Garang.
Sumatra: Batara Guru.
Sumeria *see* **Babylon.**
Surinam: Adaheli.
Tahiti: Tangaroa.
Tasmania: Inapertwa.
Tibet: Drag-Gshhed, Nagas,
  Tara.
Turkey: Corybantes, Cybele.
Venezuela:
  Yaruro Indians: Kuma.
Wales: Annwn,
  Bendigeidfran,
  Gwydion, Gwyn, Llew
  Llaw Gyffes, Lludd,
  Llyr, Manawydan,
  Maponos, Nisien,
  Pryderi, Pwyll,
  Rhiannon.
West Indies:
  Carib Indians: Achinoin,
  Baidrama, Icheiri.